READING SPIRITUALITIES

The phenomenon of 'sacred text' has undergone radical deconstruction in recent times, reflecting how religion has broken out of its traditional definitions and practices, and how current literary theories have influenced texts inside the religious domain and beyond. *Reading Spiritualities* presents both commentary and vivid examples of this evolution, engaging with a variety of reading practices that work with traditional texts and those that extend the notion of 'text' itself. The contributors draw on a range of textual sites such as an interview, Caribbean literature, drama and jazz, women's writings, emerging church blogs, Neopagan websites, the reading practices of Buddhist nuns, empirical studies on the reading experiences of Gujarati, Christian and post-Christian women, Chicana short stories, the mosque, cinema, modern art and literature. These examples open up understandings of where and how 'sacred texts' are emerging and being reassessed within contemporary religious and spiritual contexts; and make room for readings where the spiritual resides not only in the textual, but in other unexpected places.

Reading Spiritualities includes contributions from Graham Holderness, Ursula King, Michael N. Jagessar, David Jasper, Anthony G. Reddie, Michèle Roberts, and Heather Walton to reflect and encourage the interdisciplinary study of sacred text in the broad arena of the arts and social sciences. It offers a unique and well-focused 'snapshot' of the textual constructions and representations of the sacred within the contemporary religious climate – accessible to the general reader, as well as more specialist interests of students and researchers working in the crossover fields of religious, theological, cultural and literary studies.

Reading Spiritualities
Constructing and Representing the Sacred

Edited by

DAWN LLEWELLYN
Lancaster University, UK

DEBORAH F. SAWYER
Lancaster University, UK

ASHGATE

Published by
Ashgate Publishing Limited
Gower House
Croft Road
Aldershot
Hampshire GU11 3HR
England

Ashgate Publishing Company
Suite 420
101 Cherry Street
Burlington, VT 05401-4405
USA

www.ashgate.com

British Library Cataloguing in Publication Data
Reading spiritualities: constructing and representing the sacred
  1. Sacred books – History and criticism
  I. Llewellyn, Dawn, 1977– II. Sawyer, Deborah F., 1956–
  200

Library of Congress Cataloging-in-Publication Data
Reading spiritualities : constructing and representing the sacred / [edited by] Dawn Llewellyn and Deborah Sawyer.
    p. cm.
  Includes bibliographical references and index.
  ISBN 978-0-7546-6329-4 (hardback : alk. paper) 1. Sacred books – History and criticism.
  I. Llewellyn, Dawn, 1977– II. Sawyer, Deborah F., 1956–
  BL71.R43 2008
  200–dc22

2008020259

ISBN 978-0-7546-6329-4

Mixed Sources
Product group from well-managed
forests and other controlled sources
www.fsc.org Cert no. SGS-COC-2482
© 1996 Forest Stewardship Council
FSC

Printed and bound in Great Britain by
TJ International Ltd, Padstow, Cornwall

Contents

List of Tables

Notes on Contributors

María Antonia Álvarez is a Senior Lecturer at the National Distance Learning University in Madrid, Spain. She has written widely, in English and in Spanish, on Chicana authors and she has recently contributed to *Approaching Cultures through English: Diversity in Context* (2007) and has also published in *Teatro y Memoria en las Segunda Mitad de Siglo* and *Religion y Cultura*.

Maria Beatrice Bittarello holds a PhD in Religious Studies from the University of Stirling. Her research focuses on the contemporary recreations of ancient classical myths and the relationship between religion and popular culture, particularly in Internet Paganism. Recent publications include articles on goddess pilgrimages in the *Journal of Tourism and Cultural Change* and on body, religion and technology in popular culture and Paganism in the *Journal of Contemporary Religion*. As well as authoring several book reviews she has written on the issue of ancient and contemporary virtual worlds. Her comparative and interdisciplinary approach draws on religious, cultural and feminist studies and methodologies.

Raana Bokhari is completing her PhD at the University of Cambridge. She studied Law at Manchester University, taught law at an FE college, and was a research associate at Lancaster University from 1995 to 1999, where she also completed her MA. She contributes to BA and MA teaching programmes in both Religious Studies and Education and Social Exclusion. She has published journal articles in adult education and regularly contributes to *Faith Initiative* and the *Muslim World Book Review*. Her forthcoming publications include 'Places and Perspectives: Gujarati Muslim Women in Leicester' in *Citizenship, Security and Democracy: Muslim Communities and Activism in the West*, (2008).

Graham Holderness is Professor of English at the University of Hertfordshire, and author or editor of numerous studies in early modern and modern literature, drama and theology. Recent books include *Cultural Shakespeare: Essays in the Shakespeare Myth* (2001), *Visual Shakespeare: Essays in Film and Television* (2002) and *Textual Shakespeare: Writing and the Word* (2004). He is also a creative writer whose novel *The Prince of Denmark* was published in 2002, and whose poetry collection *Craeft* (2002) was awarded a Poetry Book Society recommendation. Graham's current project is *Ecce Homo: Christ in Fiction*. Some of this work has been published in journals such as *Harvard Theological Review, Literature and Theology* and *Journal for the Study of the New Testament*. He is an elected Fellow of the English Association, the Royal Society of Arts and the Royal Society of Medicine, and Sub-deacon at the Church of St Michael and All Angels, Chiswick.

Michael N. Jagessar has previously taught at Queen's Foundation for Ecumenical Theological Education in Birmingham and is currently the Secretary for Racial Justice and Multifaith Ministry with the United Reform Church. He has published widely on Black and Caribbean theology and literature. His works include *Full Life For All: The Work and Theology of Philip A. Potter* (1997) and two recent publications with Anthony G. Reddie: *Postcolonial Black British Theology* (2007) and *Black Theology in Britain: A Reader* (2007). He is the reviews editor of *Black Theology: International Journal.*

David Jasper is Professor of Literature and Theology at The University of Glasgow and his work focuses on the interplay between literature, culture and theology. He has published extensively on these themes and co-founded and remains on the editorial board of the journal *Literature and Theology.* His most recent publications are *The Sacred Desert: Religion, Literature, Art and Culture* (2004), and *The Oxford Handbook of English Literature and Theology* (with Andrew Hass and Elisabeth Jay, 2007).

Ursula King is Professor Emerita of Theology and Religious Studies, Senior Research Fellow and Associate Member of the Institute of Advanced Studies, University of Bristol, and Professorial Research Associate, Centre for Gender and Religions Research, School of Oriental and African Studies. She has published widely on religion and gender, comparative studies of spirituality, and Pierre Teilhard de Chardin. Most recently, she has edited (with Tina Beattie) *Gender, Religion and Diversity: Cross-Cultural Perspectives* (2004) and acted as the Gender and Religion Consultant for the Second Edition of the *Encyclopaedia of Religion* (2005). Ursula King has a new book in press, *The Search for Spirituality,* which looks at personal, social and planetary dimensions of different spiritualities with reference to the possibilities of global flourishing.

Dawn Llewellyn is a doctoral candidate in the Department of Religious Studies, Lancaster University. Her current project examines the uses of literary texts in the development of women's and feminist spiritualities, signifying her research focus on feminist theology, gender theory, feminist literary criticism and empirical methods. She has most recently contributed to *Feminist Spiritualities: The Next Generation* (forthcoming) and was also the principle conference organiser of *Reading Spiritualities* (Lancaster, 2006).

Katharine Sarah Moody is a PhD candidate in the Department of Religious Studies, Lancaster University. Her research explores the emerging church and draws on postmodern theory and theology. Her primary research interest concerns Christianity and culture, drawing from multiple disciplines including philosophy, theology, and the sociology of religion. She has published on the relationship between technology and theology, and on participatory internet methodologies. Her research blog can be found at opensourceresearch.blogspot.com/.

Anthony G. Reddie is a Research Fellow and Consultant in Black Theological Studies for the Methodist Church and the Queen's Foundation for Ecumenical Theological Education in Birmingham. He is the author of a number of books, including *Acting in Solidarity* (2005), *Dramatizing Theologies* (2006), *Black Theology in Transatlantic Dialogue* (2006) and *Postcolonial Black British Theology* (co-edited with Michael N. Jagessar (2007)). He is also the editor of *Black Theology: An International Journal*.

Michèle Roberts is the author of many novels including *The Wild Girl* (1984), *Impossible Saints* (1998), and most recently *Reader, I Married Him* (2004). She was the winner of the 1992 WH Smith Literary Award and Booker Prize short-listed nominee for *Daughters of the House* (1992). She was elected a Fellow of the Royal Society of Literature in 1999 and recipient in 2000 of the Chevalier de l'Ordre des Arts et des Lettres. Michèle Roberts has been Professor of Creative Writing at the University of East Anglia and Visiting Professor in Writing at Nottingham Trent University. She is Chair of the British Council's literature advisory panel and is a regular book reviewer and broadcaster. Her latest work is her memoir *Paperhouses* (2007).

Deborah Sawyer is Reader in Religion and Gender in Religious Studies, Lancaster University. Her monographs include *Midrash Aleph Beth* (1993), *Women and Religion in the First Christian Centuries* (1996), *God, Gender and the Bible* (2002) and is co-editor (with Diane Collier) of *Is there a Future for Feminist Theology?* (1990) and (with Paul Morris) *A Walk in the Garden: Biblical, Iconographical and Literary Images of Eden* (1992). Deborah has also published widely on biblical studies, hermeneutics and the influence of religion on the construction of gender and contributed to *Encyclopaedia of Religion* (2005) and *The Blackwell Companion to the Bible and Popular Culture* (2006).

Ozayr Saloojee is an Assistant Professor in the School of Architecture at the University of Minnesota. His primary research interests include questions of tradition and modernity in Islamic Architecture, issues of identity and culture in contested sites as well as developing curiosities about the work of the great Ottoman architect, Sinan. He remains active as a designer and consultant in Islamic and related architectural projects. He is currently developing a book on Elial Saarinen's last built work Christ Church Lutheran, in Minneapolis – and co-organized an international symposium on Architecture, Ethics and Spiritual Geographies (April 2008).

Heather Walton is the Director of the Centre for the Study of Literature, Theology and the Arts at the University of Glasgow. She has written extensively on women, culture and spirituality and recent works include *Literature Theology and Feminism* (2007) and *Imagining Theology: Women Writing and God* (2007). She is co-editor of the *Journal of Theology and Sexuality*.

Acknowledgements

We would like to thank the contributors to this volume for their enthusiasm and patience during the editing process. We would also like to thank those who participated in the original conference; their input helped make it such an exciting and stimulating event. Thanks also to Ashgate Publishing and to those colleagues – the staff and postgraduates of the Department of Religious Studies, Lancaster University – who have supported this project throughout.

Dawn would like to thank her family – Dad, Mum, Claire and Bransby – for everything. This is for them, with love.

Deborah's thanks go to her family, friends and animals for their constant love, support and tolerance, and she dedicates her contribution to this volume to Dawn Llewellyn with special gratitude for all the long hours she has dedicated to ensuring its publication.

Introduction

Deborah F. Sawyer and Dawn Llewellyn

'Sacred' and 'text' are two concepts that have undergone radical deconstruction in recent times, and their myriad reconstructions reflect how religion has broken out of its traditional definitions and practices, and how current literary theories have influenced texts inside the religious domain as well as beyond it. *Reading Spiritualities* presents both commentaries on and examples from a variety of contemporary hermeneutics that work with traditional texts and those that extend the concept of 'text' itself. As literary theory has explored the implications of 'the death of the author'[1] likewise in the context of religious studies subjective, standpoint hermeneutics have been displacing traditional, post-Enlightenment searches for 'the' objective meaning, authorial or otherwise. We begin this volume by considering how ideas of sacred text have been conceived and received in these changing and new contexts, utilising the metaphor of journeying to convey the open-endedness of this project, and indeed this is a metaphor that is implicitly sustained throughout.

Postmodernity is the usual label attached to readings that display the trend to displace ontology with experience, or universalism with relativism, but this shift in western religious thinking did not emerge entirely from the rarefied theoretical circles of academia, in contrast, a very significant catalyst in the process occurred within the context of political revolution. The emergence of liberation theology in Latin America in the 1970s was a key marker in the fragmentation of meaning regarding biblical texts as they had been studied in the mindset of modernity. The idea of working *with* bias rather than denying it directly opposed the European schools that had developed the 'scientific' methods of historical criticism. Liberation theology heralded the acceptance and value of subjective meaning against the Enlightenment goal of objective meaning.

In the early 1970s, alongside the work of liberation theologians who saw their roles almost in amanuensis terms, writing up the theology of the people who were challenging the political status quo inspired by the biblical theme of liberation, feminist theologians were discovering their voices and articulating their agendas from the margins of mainstream traditions. In the context of western and colonial religion, ground was shifting radically in terms of race, power, and gender. Once experience becomes the standpoint for hermeneutics, not only does the concept of meaning become multiple, even infinite, but the boundaries of what might constitute sacred text itself become destabilized.

---

1 Roland Barthes, 'The Death of the Author,' in Seán Burke, (ed.), *Authorship: From Plato to the Postmodern* (Edinburgh, 1977), pp. 125-30 and Michel Foucault, 'What Is an Author?' in Donald. F. Bouchard (ed. and trans. Donald F. Bouchard and Sherry Simon) *Language, Counter-Memory Practice: Selected Essays and Interviews by Michel Foucault* (Ithaca, 1977), pp. 113-38.

Following in the footsteps of liberation theologians, feminist biblical scholars allowed preeminence to biblical texts that advocate inclusion of the marginalized and liberation for the oppressed in an era when western culture had at least partially embraced forms of 'political correctness' and aspects of a feminist agenda. Phyllis Trible and Elisabeth Schüssler Fiorenza, working on the Hebrew Scriptures and Christian scriptures respectively and employing diverse methodologies, are two notable figures who share the hermeneutical stance of feminism in their aim to uncover positive attitudes to women in the Bible.[2] Their scholarship is characteristic of second wave feminism that was inspired by political feminism of the 1960s and 1970s that focused on patriarchy as the essential characteristic of western society, culture and politics. Simone de Beauvoir's classic analysis *The Second Sex* divulged woman as the 'other' whose existence upholds the authenticity and supremacy of male ascendancy.[3] Feminist biblical scholars named the many biblical texts that collude with and enable patriarchal systems through the type of relationships depicted between God and human beings, and between men and women. In effect these feminist scholars were searching out a 'canon within the canon', a tendency evident down the centuries, but distinctly prevalent in a variety of contemporary contexts, as George Aichele comments in his re-appraisal of the notion of 'canon'.[4]

Experiences of marginality may share much common ground but to focus on such commonality means the loss of the unique and the exceptional. The context of feminist theology, stemming from the traditions of Christianity and Judaism, does offer a very useful illustration of this point. Christian and Jewish feminist theology of the second half of the twentieth century was born out the experience of exclusion experienced by women within traditional religion. The cause of this exclusion was identified as patriarchy, the same cause identified by contemporary political second wave feminists. However, this telescopic vision of women's experience naturally attracted critique through its lack of association with huge parts of the world, as well as whole sections of societies within the 'developed' world. This critique marked the beginning of what is commonly described as third wave feminism. As early as 1979 we can find a clear articulation of the critique of a 'universal feminism' in Audre Lorde's letter to Mary Daly, a key radical feminist in both political and theological arenas: 'The white women with hoods on in Ohio handing out KKK literature on the street may not like you, but they will shoot me on sight.'[5] Alice Walker named 'womanism' as an alternative to and critique of the concept of a universal feminism

---

2   For example, see Phyllis Trible, *God and the Rhetoric of Sexuality* (Philadelphia, 1978); *Texts of Terror: Literary-Feminist Readings of Biblical Narratives* (Philadelphia, 1984) and Elisabeth Schüssler Fiorenza, *Bread Not Stone: The Challenge of Feminist Biblical Interpretation* (Boston, 1995 [1984]); *But She Said: Feminist Practices of Biblical Interpretation* (Boston, 1992) and (ed.), *Searching the Scriptures: A Feminist Introduction,* vol. 1. (New York, 1993) and (ed.), *Searching the Scriptures: A Feminist Commentary*, vol. 2. (New York, 1994).

3   Simone de Beauvoir, *The Second Sex*, trans. H.M. Parshley, (New York, 1970).

4   George Aichele, *The Control of Biblical Meaning: Canon as Semiotic Mechanism* (Harrisburg, Pennsylvania, 2001.)

5   Audre Lorde, 'An Open Letter to Mary Daly', *Sister Outsider: Essays and Speeches by Audre Lorde* (Ithaca, 1984) pp. 66-71.

with the now famous definition: 'Womanist is to feminist as purple is to lavender.'[6] The impetus for the evolution of womanism grew not only from the great unease felt about the tendency to universalise women's experience, but also the obvious privileged position of the white, western women activists, whose ascendancy came via the labour of women who were poor and without privilege, that is to say, via, 'this bridge called my back.'[7] Ironically the original exclusion suffered by the women who had been at the vanguard of second wave feminism, was inadvertently being dealt out by them to women of difference. Second wave feminism in this light appears more as part of the Enlightenment project rather than a critique of it. The hermeneutical stance taken by womanism represents just one of the positions of difference featured in third wave feminisms alongside others such as *mujerista*, Asian, women of colour, and lesbian approaches. These positionings, whilst keenly aware of the issue of gender, also foreground matters of race and social status, and in doing so uncover new meanings of sacred texts through their particular biases.

Feminist and womanist hermeneutics and the wider issues they raise reflect the context of postmodernity, and one particular initiative in recent biblical scholarship widened the lens further, presenting critical observations of a number of contemporary postmodern engagements with the Bible. For instance, *The Postmodern Bible* was put together by a collective of scholars who had, amongst other specialisms, particular interests in the interface between current literary theory and biblical studies, including structuralism and poststructuralism, psychoanalytical theory, reader-response criticism, as well as womanist and feminist criticism.[8] However, these discussions were still fenced inside the academy and could therefore be open to the criticism voiced by Audre Lorde, 'What does it mean when the tools of a racist patriarchy are used to examine the fruits of that same patriarchy? It means that only the narrowest perimeters of change are possible and allowable.'[9] The insights from literary criticism are undoubtedly invaluable for understanding the construction and deconstruction of sacred literature, but just as invaluable are the insights gained from experiential hermeneutics spoken from postcolonial and other contexts previously drowned out by the weight and pervasive power of western imperialistic academia.

The example of the phenomena of feminist and womanist hermeneutics illustrates the creative fragmentation of interpretative stances and methodologies in relation to sacred texts. The Bible is just one collection of sacred texts, possibly uniquely influential through the history of western ascendancy and imperialism, but what has been happening to it is being mirrored in religious contexts that cherish their own sacred literature, often rediscovered in new ways with new meanings in the context of postcolonialism.

---

6   Alice Walker, *In Search of Our Mothers' Gardens: Womanist Prose* (London, 1984) p. xi.

7   Cherrie Moraga and Gloria Anzaldúa, (eds), *This Bridge Called my Back: Writings by Radical Women of Color* (New York, 1983).

8   The Bible and Culture Collective, *The Postmodern Bible* (New Haven and London, 1995).

9   Audre Lorde, 'The Master's Tools Will Never Dismantle the Master's House' in *Sister Outsider: Essays and Speeches by Audre Lorde* (Ithaca,1984) pp. 110-13.

Opening up sacred texts to encounter and be interpreted and applied in diverse contexts, meeting with experience rather than being used to control it, removes not only boundaries that had been erected by hierarchical institutions of authority, but also the academic boundaries demarcating where sacred texts may be studied. In the context of postmodernity, religion is recognized as a key construct, supporting beliefs and institutions that lie at the foundation of modernity. In studying its effects on the world today, religion and its accompanying sacred texts move outside the confines of specialist subject areas such as biblical studies, religious studies, oriental studies and so on, into the wider arena of the arts and social sciences. Sacred texts are now part of the curriculum for departments of literature, as well as loci where gender and cultural studies feature across a variety of disciplines within academia. This movement from conventional contexts to new and alternative ones not only opens up the texts to be read from new perspectives, but also pushes to the limits the very concept of what might constitute sacred text.

This volume has been constructed to reflect this complex interdisciplinary environment in which sacred text is being explored in contemporary scholarship. Furthermore, in *Reading Spiritualities* examples of the ways in which sacred texts themselves are being reinterpreted or even redefined are identified by the contributors. It explores how texts, other than those traditionally considered as sacred, are being read to access the spiritual, religious, divine. Sacred texts, as Robert Detweiler notably observes, share a number of key features. They are usually understood to claim divine inspiration, to reveal divinity, to contain hidden meanings, to need nominated interpreters, to be able to transform lives, to found ritual and are able to evoke a divine presence.[10] While informed by the legacy of the scriptural traditions associated with the religious, this volume seeks to read for the spiritual beyond this inheritance. The conversations taking place in this volume maintain the possibility of 'sacred texts' but beyond the traditionally closed margins of religious structures.

'Beyond' prepositions the 'text' past the materiality of texts such as the Qu'ran, the Hebrew scriptures or Buddhist writings (texts that are part of this collection), but recognises the thread connecting previous textual interactions with the sacred to present reconstructions and representations – without eschewing the very notion of 'sacred' or 'text'. We understand 'text' in this volume to be phenomena that can be 'read', that is, open to meaning either communal, individual, or both. Opening up the definition in this way, away from the straitjacket of bound covers, we can discover and engage with the sacred evident in art, architecture, film, music, the internet, as well as literature.

Sacred texts continue to linger but the contributions to this volume are not duologues between the writings of religious traditions and their interpretations. Rather, the authors of *Reading Spiritualities* offer inter-textual dialogues. The influences and echoes of sacred texts are woven through many of the chapters of this book, evolving constructions and representations that feed back into sacred texts, illustrating the concept of a hermeneutical cycle. In sum, 'beyond' still recalls a relationship with 'sacred text', from which the reading experiences presented in this volume move on to explore other textual destinations.

---

10 Robert Detweiler, 'What is a Sacred Text?' *Semiea* 31,1985, pp. 213-30.

This volume examines the ways in which the concept of sacred text remains significant, but its defining features are being housed in other textual homes, capturing examples of its changing contexts and applications. Therefore it turns to interactions between the sacred and textual with a cross-disciplinary lens. As King suggests, a mirror is a useful tool for comparison and contrast, presenting a close but never exact image.[11] It can reflect back the ways in which sacred texts continue to undergo reformation not only in religious studies, but in creative writing, literary studies, qualitative research, textual criticism, cultural theory, architectural studies, and the emerging discipline of internet studies, and through a rich selection of texts. These contexts are represented in this volume where we include an interview and chapters that explore Caribbean literature, drama and jazz, women's writings, websites, the reading practices and experiences of Buddhist nuns, Gujarati, Christian and post-Christian women, Chicana short stories, the mosque, modern art and literature. This range of examples aims to open up understandings of where and how 'sacred texts' are emerging, to break away from assumptions as to where and how sacred texts are being reassessed, and to make room for readings where the spiritual resides not only in the textual, but in some more unexpected places.

In effect the essays collected here explore and celebrate the possibilities of sacred texts. As notions of sacred text are loosened from canonical and authoritative anchors, they become mercurial; changing in their form, content and context. The chapters embrace this, and search for meanings of the sacred in text, as well as looking for means of creating the sacred locally. *Reading Spiritualities* does not make claims to subvert the western temper to the understandings of reading, text, spirituality, religions or the sacred, nor their association with a largely post-Christian framework, but it does gesture toward contextual experiences, aware of the vigilance needed to trouble the untenable nature of dominant structures. In this vein we hesitate to offer hard and fast definitions of key terms, such as, 'spiritual', 'religious', 'divine', 'sacred', and so on. In our context such definitions have to remain subjective, and their meanings to be relative to their particular contexts. For example, if we move towards defining the traditional as 'religion' and the post-traditional as 'spirituality' then we deny whole traditions of spirituality that have been part of belief systems from their inception. Likewise to refuse any application of the term 'religion' to contemporary non-traditional experience can appear more as a value judgment than a credible form of reference.

The author of each chapter in this volume has chosen their frame of reference that best communicates their work, and the sum total displays the richness of contemporary language within the infinite domain of the sacred. Together the chapters present a wide panoramic of the contemporary religious landscape. We have divided this volume into four parts, beginning with a prologue that introduces each section in more detail. These four parts give a useful structured range of expression to the interweaving of 'sacred' and 'text' and reflect the areas we have selected to present the changing textual scene of the sacred, while still allowing the chapters to speak to each other within and across the partitions and headings.

---

11 See King, Chapter 4.

We begin with *Spiritual Journeys* to note the textual movement of turning beyond the sacred to other textual imaginings and the effect this has had on the religious histories of the authors and their communities. The contributors look outward to other readings, and back to the Bible to explore the holistic transformative potential of readings that can facilitate an empowering repositioning of religious identity. As the writers of *Spiritual Journeys* open the notion of sacred texts by creating, or facilitating other creative voices to imagine the divine and to reflect theologically, authority comes into question, the theme of the following section and a key feature of sacred texts.

Part two, *Authority,* illustrates significant ways in which authority is being understood in contemporary religious climates both in relation and in contrast to the way it is presented in traditional religion, especially in relation to sacred texts. It explores the way authority, as a concept, in its association with sacred texts is being deconstructed and challenged. In particular, our authors in this section pay attention to the deliberate strategies that are utilized to open up the authority of sacred texts, and that of their interpreters, while they also discuss the potentially disquieting consequences when these strategies are uncritically employed.

The next part, *Readers and Texts*, ties the themes of spiritual journey and authority together by conveying the subjective experiences of readers as they discuss and reflect their own engagements with their sacred texts. This includes a textual exploration of how Chicana authors have named the mythical figure of the Virgin of Guadalupe a sacred text to articulate the multiple possibilities of womanhood. In one chapter, the voices of women from a Gujurati community consider the influence of an Urdu reformist text; while another chapter considers the reflections of post-Christian women upon their readings of literary texts as part of their evolving religious and spiritual lives.

The final section, *Accessing the Spiritual* offers readings of four different texts from the diverse worlds of architectural studies, film, internet studies and modern art and literature. These chapters recognise that as the concept of sacred text is shifting, text can take almost infinite forms. In this section, a building (the mosque), web sites, cinema and human and divine bodily spaces are offered as examples where the sacred is constructed and represented. Each author responds discretely to their chosen texts, and is sensitive to the alternative structures of their particular medium as they textually and theoretically explore a range of religious and cultural sites that belong to Islam, Neo-paganism and Christianity. *Accessing the Spiritual* recalls how the sacred can be experienced and the spiritual encountered textually.

This collection is set at a juncture in which religious structures remain in some locations, but are also breaking out of established meanings and practices in others. This is an interesting time for students of the sacred, a time when modern and postmodern activities converse with biblical hermeneutics, literary theories and genre specific textual criticisms. Within this busy milieu, the intention of this volume is to pause and frame – at least momentarily – a range of contemporary conversations with and about texts and their relationships to the sacred.

Bibliography

Aichele, George, *The Control of Biblical Meaning: Canon as Semiotic Mechanism* (Harrisburg, Pennsylvania: Trinity Press, 2001.)

Barthes, Roland, 'The Death of the Author,' in Seán Burke, (ed.), *Authorship: From Plato to the Postmodern* (Edinburgh: Edinburgh University Press, 1977): 125-30.

de Beauvoir, Simone, *The Second Sex*, trans. Parshley, H.M, (New York: Knopf, 1970).

Detweiler, Robert, 'What is a Sacred Text?' *Semiea* 31, 1985: 213-30.

Foucault, Michel, 'What Is an Author?' in Donald F. Bouchard (ed. and trans. Donald F. Bouchard and Sherry Simon) *Language, Counter-Memory Practice: Selected Essays and Interviews by Michel Foucault* (Ithaca: Cornell University Press, 1977):113-38.

Lorde, Audre, 'An Open Letter to Mary Daly', *Sister Outsider: Essays and Speeches by Audre Lorde* (Ithaca: Crossing Press, 1984): 66-71.

Lorde, Audre, 'The Master's Tools Will Never Dismantle the Master's House' in *Sister Outsider: Essays and Speeches by Audre Lorde* (Ithaca: Crossing Press): 110-13.

Lorde, Audre *Sister Outsider: Essays and Speeches by Audre Lorde* (Ithaca: Crossing Press, 1984).

Moraga, Cherrie and Gloria Anzaldúa, (eds), *This Bridge Called my Back: Writings by Radical Women of Color* (New York: Kitchen Table Press, 1983).

Schüssler, Fiorenza, Elisabeth, *Bread Not Stone: The Challenge of Feminist Biblical Interpretation* (Boston: Beacon Press, 1995 [1984]).

Schüssler, Fiorenza, Elisabeth, *But She Said: Feminist Practices of Biblical Interpretation* (Boston: Beacon Presss, 1992).

Schüssler, Fiorenza, Elisabeth, (ed.), *Searching the Scriptures: A Feminist Introduction,* Vol. 1. (New York: Crossroad, 1993).

Schüssler, Fiorenza, Elisabeth, (ed.), *Searching the Scriptures: A Feminist Commentary*, Vol. 2. (New York Crossroad, 1994).

The Bible and Culture Collective, *The Postmodern Bible* (New Haven and London: Yale University Press,1995).

Trible, Phyllis, *God and the Rhetoric of Sexuality* (Philadelphia: Fortress Press, 1978).

Trible, Phyllis, *Texts of Terror: Literary-Feminist Readings of Biblical Narratives* (Philadelphia: Fortress Press, 1984).

Walker, Alice, *In Search of Our Mothers' Gardens: Womanist Prose* (London: The Women's Press, 1984).

PART I
Spiritual Journeys

Part I

Spiritual Journeys

Dawn Llewellyn

Beginning this collection are the textual spiritual journeys of Michèle Roberts, Anthony G. Reddie and Michael Jagessar. 'Spiritual journeys' reflects the autobiographical temper within these chapters, as each author conjoins their readings of sacred text with self-reflexivity on their own spiritual, religious or theological positioning. As an interview, the form and content of Roberts's contribution is highly personal. Roberts's writing life has wrestled with the tensions between Catholicism and feminism and this interview, or conversation, discusses a number of themes: becoming woman through language, the supplementation of art for religion, her fascination with women mystics and heretics, the use of her novels by feminist theology and her experiences of contemporary feminism. Michael Jagessar's interdisciplinary approach brings Caribbean literature in dialogue with Caribbean theology, and argues for mutual permeability between them. Although less overt in drawing on his subjective experiences, he highlights the diversity and contradictions of the theological impulse in Caribbean writings alongside his own multilayered location. Reddie's piece is impassioned. It is eclectic in juxtaposing his personal history with a variety of inspiring texts: jazz music and the writing, performing, and acting of drama with the doing of theology. His experiences infuse his chapter, and as with Jagessar, such experiences are inflected with the movement of Black disaporian British culture.

The three contributions to this section give expression to the notion of textual spiritual journeys as the holistic transformative potential of texts. Each chapter explores how texts can enable personal and social movement beyond hegemonic religious structures, with each contributor employing a metaphor that encompasses the experiences of this journey. Michèle Roberts's interview, 'getting a/cross god' encapsulates her personal struggle to overcome God and the difficulties in the relationship between spirituality and being woman. Her autobiographical account of wrestling to 'get a/cross god', has been a journey she has written in order to become woman. There are at least two inferences from her intriguing title that suggest movement from religion to her ambivalent reconciliation with its traditions. First, it implies her gradual realization that through her Catholic inheritance she has received an angry and patriarchal concept of God, the rejection and loss of which leaves a chasm. However, rather than leaving it impassable, her writing is the way, as a second meaning of this metaphor might refer, to reach across and bridge the 'god-shaped hole.' Anthony Reddie and Michael Jagessar individually situate their work in the wider context of the journeys travelled through diasporic Black theology. Reddie opens up the possibility of transformation by using the motifs of 'acting in solidarity' and a 'jazz aesthetic' to blend drama and jazz improvisation to enable Black congregations and communities to actively and reciprocally participate in critical theological reflection. 'Acting in solidarity' evokes praxis through performance in community, using drama to actively communicate expressions of theology from the experiences of Black peoples. Reddie couples this with a 'jazz aesthetic.' Although jazz has a specific structure, extemporization and collaboration are crucial to its form. Inflecting 'acting in solidarity' with a 'jazz aesthetic' is a way of doing theology from 'below' to enliven Christian pedagogy and preaching, and to also subvert the dominant and exclusive – a spiritual journey that begins with the everyday experiences of Black communities towards a transforming emancipatory theology. Michael Jagessar imagines an interdisciplinary conversation between Caribbean literature and theology, arguing that without retrieving spiritual themes that are integral to Caribbean literatures, local God-talk will remain untouched by Caribbean identities and its capacity for liberating transformation will be hindered. The metaphor of dialogue touches upon the spiritual journey. The dialogue between Caribbean literature and theology has the potential to leave behind the essentialising tendencies of colonial western hermeneutics and travel to other imagined liberated places. Jagessar embraces imagination as a theological tool that can take the experiences of colonialism beyond the boundaries of the oppressed/oppressor binary. For Reddie and Jagessar the spiritual journey represents traversing the dominant whiteness of much Christianity, while Roberts's journey corresponds to leaving existing patriarchal narratives and arriving at an easy resignation toward Christianity.

For all three authors, the spiritual journey is textually undertaken by oscillating beyond, and between, existing sacred texts and re-creating other textual traditions. Roberts, Reddie and Jagessar travel between Biblical motifs and counter traditions to represent and image manifestations of the sacred. In Roberts's case, the rejection of the sacred book because of the invisibility of women led to her re-write biblical stories, placing women at the centre of them. This is a strategy reminiscent of feminist reforming hermeneutics and the gynocritical approaches that uncovered the writing history of women authors; Roberts commences with the scriptures but revises them, placing her work within and outside the canon. Michael Jagessar is also exploring theological stories told outside, but in conversations with biblical narratives. He notes that Caribbean literature is akin to midrash, for this genre pushes the Bible past boundaries and limits, and offers (to use Jagessar's suggestive term) alter*native* traditions that awaken an alter*native* consciousness of Caribbean God-experiences and God-talk. However, biblical myths are still woven into the writings of Caribbean writers such as Olive Senior, Derek Walcott and Earl Lovelace. These authors have captured the deep resonance that biblical images leave on the Caribbean psyche, but as Jagessar demonstrates, the literary imagination destablises this resonance. Reddie draws on the metaphor of jazz improvisation to unbalance the perceived fixity of the biblical text so it can be contextualised and applied to the changing contexts of congregations. As jazz relies but also goes beyond its form to reach the fullest expression of its content, so Reddie argues, preaching and pastoral theology should appropriate and improvise to suit the audience. For Reddie, a jazz hermeneutic remembers the scriptural traditions, but avoids being limited or constrained by them.

This section brings the re-creation of sacred texts alongside these spiritual journeys embarked upon by Roberts, Jagessar and Reddie. However, the notion of sacred texts is broad, widened by an emphasis on the process of the spiritual journey. The 'getting across' of Roberts, the 'improvising' of Reddie and Jagessar's 'conversing' move the defining edges of the reading and writing of sacred texts.

Chapter 1

'Getting a/cross god':
An Interview with Michèle Roberts

Michèle Roberts, Dawn Llewellyn and Deborah F. Sawyer

DL and DFS: The title of this interview is 'getting a/cross god.' Would you like to-say something about how you've managed to confront and then get a/cross 'him'?

MR: Well, it's odd because as a child, God was God, not gendered. The God I encountered and felt I experienced and had mystical raptures to do with – it wasn't until I left home as an adolescent and went to university that I began to be more critical of God. I suppose I'd entered the culture outside the family, so, I had a kind of purchase point from which to be critical, and I lost my faith very quickly. Standing on the steps outside Somerville Library with my arms full of books realizing that nuns – I thought I'd had a religious vocation – weren't allowed to sit up all night reading so I lost my vocation. I thought I can't possibly be a nun, I want to read all night. And God went away. And it's as though in that absence of God I realized I was having to excavate from the God-shaped hole, but my God-shaped hole was full of folklore, stories, prejudices, terrible guilt, and dreadful spiky feelings. But I also realized that it was a treasure, that Catholicism had given me enormous spiky pain, because if you were given all these images and metaphors and stories you could work with them. I did discover that through therapy and the Women's Movement. So I began, I think, to think I'd got a/cross god. I'd been given this cross, spiky God who seemed to be served by misogynist priests who disliked women very much and who feared women very much. Then I discovered that there was something there to wrestle with, that it wasn't enough to make an intellectual decision to lose God, to say, I don't believe in you anyway! One had to be like an archaeologist and excavate the God residue in the psyche. So 'getting a/cross god', I suppose was realizing that he went on existing in my life in the guise of male therapy and certain sorts of male intellectuals, and certain kinds of male academics I had encountered. And I had to go on fighting with God. So it was a very kind of intimate wrestling.

DL and DFS: If you were going to theorize that a little bit, would you see it as Freudian, phallus God?

MR: Yes, I think so. It's interesting that as a child I encountered God as a sort of maternal God, if I gendered God. There was something about a beautiful space in church, or a beautiful space in the convent, or a chapel, which is to do with darkness and sort of dazzlingness and mystery. It was completely not body and therefore not gender. And yet when I began to be critical of God at the age of eighteen, God seemed to be very gendered and phallic. And God seemed to be really lining up with some of the Marxists that I met who'd read Lacan, and who said 'man has a self because he has the phallus.' He can speak and woman is a kind of not man, she is a lack, she is a nothingness, she is a hole, and she can not speak. That nearly sent me mad! Because that's what you were as a woman, and then if you spoke you turned into a man, so woman had no speech. I suppose what saved me was the political practice of the Women's Movement, the love of women, going into therapy with a sympathetic woman, but also beginning to read, and to read Freud, and be critical, and to discover people like Kristeva and Cixous and Irigaray in translation. I cannot say I read them in the original French! I read digested versions, care of the feminists! I began to realize that there were women in the world feeling as tortured as I was. That was a kind of project to look at language, and investigate language, and remake language and I wasn't alone.

DL and DFS: That sounds very much like Irigaray's 'becoming woman.' We should keep 'woman' but make 'woman' ourselves instead of having it made for us. She talks about 'becoming woman' from within, rather than from without.[1] Does that resonate for you?

MR: Yes, yes it does. I think my theoretical practice is incredibly eclectic and incredibly contradictory because I'm not really an academic and I'm not really a theorist – perhaps all academics are incredibly eclectic! I'm a writer so I'm just picking and choosing metaphors and images that suit me at the moment. So on the one hand, I'd invoke the notion of sexual difference that women have to invent. I do think things like giving birth to children – that fact is a fact – and women do it. OK, in these days we'll soon have men giving birth to children I'm quite sure. But I suppose for my generation the body matters to that extent. Yet, on the other hand, I feel, having invoked difference therefore I'd want to invoke likeness. Men are my brothers, not just my lovers but my brothers, my comrades, and we're incredibly alike. So, sometimes I'm really into the Irigaraian notion and sometimes I'm not and I don't think I'm logical about how I use these theorists and their theoretical perceptions.

DL and DFS: It's that idea of developing a self that seems to come through in what you are saying. Although this sounds essentialist, for Irigaray not only are women being denied a sense of self but being denied a sense of God, because God has been traditionally represented through male language. Until women have the divine, then they can never be subjects as men are subjects. Until women can say 'I can represent the divine' or 'the divine can be represented through me', women will never be subject.

---

1   Luce Irigaray, 'Divine Women' in Morny Joy, Kathleen O'Grady and Judith L. Poxon, (eds), *French Feminists on Religion: A Reader* (London and New York, 2002), pp. 41-8 and 'The Redemption of Women' in Luce Irigaray, *Key Writings* (London and New York, 2004), pp. 150-64.

MR: I think that's fascinating. If I've arrived at that point it was through going away from Christianity and looking at other myths. Particularly Greek myths, because they are Mediterranean, I do live in a Western culture and I don't feel comfortable just borrowing myths from other cultures. It doesn't seem to reverberate enough. But the Greek myths seem to be enough in my sort of rooted past that they've meant a great deal to me. I don't believe in goddess worship, but I think those myths about the goddesses, by reading things like *The Odyssey*, gave me a sense of women being divine and also being kind of cruel and behaving badly. That was very important. That it wasn't about a perfected image of the divine.

DL and DFS: So more immanence than transcendence?

MR: I felt very uncomfortable with the word divine. I probably still do because it was so much about a Christian God who was up there, a male who was the Father. When I talk about the divine, I always point to my belly. The divine is in there. I mean I love that image in the Old Testament of the *Shekinah*, the indwelling God of the Old Testament. Judaism actually has a contact, I think, with the female divine through *Sophia* and the *Shekinah*. And that's amazing because we've had to cover that in Christianity. It's very hidden, it's been very denied.

DL and DFS: How has your own work been part of 'getting a/cross god'?

MR: Well I suppose I could start with the idea of the sacred book, that as a little Catholic girl I grew up knowing that the Bible was the founding sacred book. I think I loved the music of that book, because when you read it in good translations it's rapturous music and there's rapturously beautiful things in it. Then I suppose when I got into my twenties and thirties and found the political sense and language of feminism I became self-conscious about my past and what had made me. I just could see that the sacred book didn't have enough women in! They were just ignored, and I found that very inspiring. So I was trying to – I don't know what I was trying to do! I just felt enraged that we'd been suppressed, and sort of wiped out and denied and misunderstood and vilified. And actually, it felt like to save my own life I had to re-write these stories and put women at the centre of them. The Mary Magdalene story was the first and I wrote *The Wild Girl* because I had just made a transition from being a single woman who'd had lots of lovers – both gay and straight – into marrying. I was suddenly someone who was approved of by the church, who could be seen as holy because she was married and her sexuality was kind of fenced. From that vantage point, I began to think about who I'd been before and why I couldn't have been as holy if I'd had lovers and not married, but was sexual. And that's when the figure of Mary Magdalene swam up because of course she is that contradiction, she and the Virgin. They're like two faces of a woman, split with this axe of the church. I suppose at the same time we were thinking about the end of the Cold War, we'd been through Chernobyl and people were talking about the end of the world in panicky ways. Greenham Common, that was very important. So this image of a woman who kind of strode into the world and talked about sex and death and politics was very important to me and it was Mary Magdalene. It took ages to form and it had to be a fifth Gospel. I always believe form and content must integrate so how else could I tell Mary Magdalene's story except through a Gospel? It had to be Mary Magdalene who wrote it, it had to be an 'I' and what interested me is that it was the first time I'd used 'I' in a novel. And yet it was more truthful to be Mary Magdalene than to be writing in the third person, when I was stuck trying to escape from myself and not hem myself in. But of course, I was, in a kind of clumsy way, an awkward way. There was something marvellous about holding up this mask and saying, 'I am Mary Magdalene'. I did feel she spoke through me. I know that sounds arrogant.

DL and DFS: You felt her voice?

MR: Yeah, it was ... it was amazing. I did masses and masses of research. It wasn't just a kind of possession or an inspiration, it was very researched. I wanted to take on the sacred books of our culture because they left us out. Then I took on the Old Testament and took on Mrs Noah's version of history in *The Book of Mrs Noah*. That was doing something similar. If you've got that great moment when civilisation is almost lost, and then the Ark travels across the sea and there's new birth – if you can't make women central to that, then ...!

The Ark is an image of pregnancy, and because I couldn't have a baby, because I was feeling like a complete failure – I couldn't have a baby, my marriage was breaking down, I couldn't write a book, I couldn't do things – it was wonderful to write about Mrs Noah and sort of invoke failure and to write about the negative.

DL and DFS: So with The Wild Girl *and* The Book of Mrs Noah *did you feel that you'd dealt with scripture at that point?*

MR: I think so, yes. I think that made me see that you took off from the old books, but you had to re-write them. I was then interested in heretical books and I realized that was my position as a writer and as a woman *vis-à-vis* the church. I began to do an enormous amount of reading, I remember that wonderful book by Dronke[2] about medieval women writers and most of them were religious women. I found that totally inspiring and I began to see that the heretical women were the ones that I loved because they were somehow clashing with the authorities. They had visions; they felt they saw God and they had to give their version of that. They were going to get into trouble right up to the Reformation. I suppose that was my way of naming myself as someone who was still embroiled in the church – I'd got that far – so I was still embroiled, I hadn't just fled and left it. Intellectually, it was still there in my psyche. But I had a kind of position I could take up which was heretical. For example, I used Teresa of Avila in *Impossible Saints* to explore the whole idea of heresy, politics, visionary utterances and how dangerous they are.

DL and DFS: The female saints you've written about are often hysterics. They're so iconoclastic and anarchic and yet embodied. Their theology is their body but they're living theology.

---

2   Peter Dronke, *Women Writers of the Middle Ages* (Cambridge, 1984).

MR: I love the hysterics. They're the wonderful ones. They're so iconoclastic and anarchic and they're so in disguise, speaking different languages, they're such a site of such power. I see it as sort of acting out or uttering an unconscious of the theology somehow. They're kind of using the church's language in saying these are the things that matter, because it's a female dramatising it and acting it in her own body. In some respects they are feminists. Hysterics are feminists. They are the women saints I'm really, really intrigued by and I'm sure I'll write about them. I suppose I would take a psychoanalytical view that these figures are somehow dramatising the conflicts that women have. They're more interesting than the Virgin who's kind of smooth because she's been split off from Mary Magdalene, whereas these women are a kind of a mess and they're saying that's what life is for women. It's a contradictory mess! And yet it's about violence, it's about pain, it's about suffering, it's about rebellion, and yet it's all under the cloak of the church at the same time. So it's both safe and dangerous, that's why they're so wonderful. They embody these opposites.

DL and DFS: Mary lost that 'mess' and wasn't allowed to have that. Even childbirth was taken away from her so she became a nothing, a non-sexed being. So these women took on theology through their bodies, a kind of schizophrenia between bodies and religion. They actually put them together and that's what was so scary about them for the church.

MR: Yes, they're real loose cannons and the Church wants to control them and it can't always. I mean, when you think, Bernadette got picked, I think, because perhaps she was the most tameable or the most amenable. There were about 300 other little girls all round the Pyrenees all having visions at the same time! But they were a bit wilder, a bit naughtier, a bit nastier.

DL and DFS: The German scholar Elisabeth Gössmann talks of a 'women's-counter tradition' rather than heresy. She sees 'his-story' running alongside and parallel to 'her-story'. But 'her-story', women, always have to turn to direct revelation because they can't access the magisterium.[3]

MR: No, they can't, and that interested me a lot that some of the women I read about, some of the Beguins weren't educated, so if they'd wanted to read the Bible, or think about theology they couldn't. You've got to trust revelation then, and I like that. It wasn't just that women are somehow more close to the divine in some rapturous, bodily way to do with the essential, it's actually something as material as whether you can read or write.

DL and DFS: A strategy, as it were? Rather than this idea of women essentially being in touch with the divine?

---

3   Elisabeth Gössmann, 'The Image of God and the Human Being in Women's Counter-Tradition' in Deborah F. Sawyer and Diane Collier, (eds), *Is There a Future for Feminist Theology?* (Sheffield, 1999) pp.11-24.

MR: Yes, a strategy. Yes, I don't go for women essentially being in touch with the divine. At all. What interested me as well was someone like Teresa of Avila who was almost had up. She was in trouble with the Inquisition, she had to sort out her Jewish heritage and she invented this amazing theology that includes Jewish tropes. There's a lot of work being done on that now. She had men friends who revered her mind and spoke with her and so I'd go along with the idea of counter tradition. But the male and female traditions interweave through friendships, don't they? I think that's important to me, as a feminist, that women can listen to men's revelations and vice versa. Some one like Hilda and that double monastery at Whitby, where monks and nuns could be quite close. I love that idea. I mean I'm not a radical feminist in that sense that women must be on the mountain and men sort of somewhere else. I have at certain moments had a radical feminist strategy but politically I'm not.

DL and DFS: In terms of women's position in the tradition, you've commented on women's ordination. Do you still question the authenticity of women as members of the clergy?

MR: Hmm, it was discussions with Sara Maitland. She, I think, left the Anglican Church and became a Catholic because she felt the theology wasn't there to support women as priests in the Anglican church – which shocked me, actually. I think she felt that women were being put into drag a bit as Anglicans. I don't really know what I think about that because I'm not really interested in Christianity. But what I love in Italy is the way that Italian Catholics live out all these contradictions. So you get these really stroppy nuns or these really stroppy women academics all in congregations because there is a place for the feminine in culture. I think women have a place and can speak. OK, it might be a restricted place of 'la mama' stuff, but at least there's a place for women. Whereas in Protestant culture, because it's just the logos, it's as though women don't exist at all and it's harder, I think, sometimes. Women aren't visible, they're just words, like men are words. So I quite like Catholicism, on reflection, that it has this space.

DL and DFS: Those themes very much came through in Reader, I Married Him, *in the wonderful figure of Leonora, the smoking, drinking, feminist nun.*

MR: She's partly based on Patricia Duncker and she's partly based on my Italian friend Giuliana.

DL and DFS: But Leonora had the space within the cloisters, and within Catholicism there is that ambivalence about sexuality.

MR: I remember going to midnight mass in Florence and there's all these gorgeous, voluptuous Italian women in fur coats smoking away at the back of the church – and the colour! They have this feminine place, there's the Virgin and we know that at her back is the Goddess. I remember going to Naples and finding there a road shrine to Our Lady of the Pomegranate and of course that's Hera, the Goddess of Heaven with a pomegranate! So that tradition kind of speaks to me. Come to London and you might go to a Protestant Church and everyone's dowdy and dour and the women don't dare to be women. They are men in drag, some of them! Or else they speak a kind of, I don't know, a pompous and priggish feminism which I loathe, equally! I like loud-mouthed feminists, but not tidy Anglican women. I think that's awful, they've been squished.

DL and DFS: How would you describe yourself in terms of religion or spirituality?

MR: I don't like the word spirituality, because it invokes the split between body and spirit that I think I've spent my life fighting and trying to integrate through my writing and I've realized quite recently that, I think that's what I'm doing. So I can't say 'spirituality' anymore. Religion is problematic because it often means organized religion and it, you know, can be oppressive. I think I'm a great believer in rituals. That we really need them. But then I think we need to make them. I think we need to invoke something beyond worthy humanist sentiments at funerals! I suppose I still feel I'm drawing on a tradition, like I still read seventeenth-century mystical poets like George Herbert. I mean I read all those people over and over again and go on loving them and adoring what they're on about. So the tradition and the history of religious writing means a great deal to me, and therefore the history of rituals does. I would never ever go to church on a Sunday to worship, it just wouldn't occur to me as something that would be valid for me. I mean, if I'm saying my prayers it would be in the garden, it would be a spontaneous outpouring wherever I am. I hate church services. I really hate them! I just hate men telling us what to think, what to feel. I hate men preaching sermons! I can't bear it. I think I'd go to church more if there were beautiful women with long hair and long cloaks.

DL and DFS: When you're in France do you feel any differently?

MR: Well it's interesting. Where I live in France it was a religious stronghold under the revolution as much of Brittany was, it's still very religious. At every crossroads there is an old stone crucifix and very often with a niche in the middle where there is a Virgin. So you've got the spirit of the crossroads and she's female in some way. The churches are really interesting because they are really old and tatty and they haven't been smartened up post Vatican II, they're just old tatty churches filled with lots of nice stuff. There's something about the spirit of the countryside who is a woman, who is earthly. That really appeals to me because that connects to my robust lovely farmer female neighbour. It makes sense that Catholicism, Christianity, was an agricultural religion. It's harvest, and bareness and rebirth, it's a tradition that links back to farming people having to find a way to think about or symbolize their hopes and fears and terrors about being alive and fragile and vulnerable.

I go to church if my neighbours ask me. When someone dies in the village, the whole village goes to the funeral so I will go if it's someone I knew, I'll go to my friends' christening of their babies and I'll go to weddings. I think those moments are very important. I'd want to write a poem about that as well. I think it's very beautiful that the people I live amongst don't go to church every Sunday. They're busy peasants! Perhaps I'm sentimental, and perhaps a tourist outsider as well but there is a harshness too.

I think for me art has replaced religion. I used to know Marion Milner, an analytical writer who wrote a lot about artists and writing and painting. From her I felt very validated and supported in this kind of idea that there are great turning points in our lives and we have to make art about them, we've got to make sense about them through symbolizing them. Which might be cooking a lovely lunch, it might be making love, it might be a bunch of flowers. It doesn't have to be a poem. I think that's where religion reverberates for me, which is in ritual moments of daily life. About big mysteries like, what the hell is sex? What is birth? What is death? I mean, but I don't just want old clichés. I want things to be renewed. I would love it if you could go to a village funeral and someone could stand up and read a poem they'd written, if you could have both those things together I'd be amazed. You can't in France. And yet I don't want the humanist funeral full of awful, awful clichés and horrible, horrible language either.

DL and DFS: Do you have any thoughts about a female, non-priestly communion?

MR: Well that's a wonderfully optimistic view. I do think there's a real problem in that there are few priests because they won't have women priests, there are these doddering old male priests serving four parishes and they could have far more parishioners. More masses means women priests, but they haven't got there yet. I suppose, I don't believe in that central mystery of the Eucharist any more, that's just gone. I suppose that's just a lie because I think it's the woman who gives her blood and her body to nourish people. That's a sacrament of pregnancy and childbirth but that's denied that's given to a man. That so outrages me. I could never be a Catholic again. Maybe if a woman could do that I'd believe in it. Maybe. But to me it's an essentially female sacrament and yet women are the one lot who aren't allowed to appropriate it.

DL and DFS: Yes, it's been appropriated. For instance, John's depiction of the crucifixion in the Gospel, when the centurion pokes the sword in the side of Christ and out flows the water and blood of Christ. That represents the birth of the Church and it's such an explicit appropriation of female imagery assumed into the male body. It may not have been intended in the Gospel, but that's how it could be seen in early church tradition. That blood and water become male giving, rather than the ultimate act of female giving.

MR: I think we have to go forwards. I suppose in a very naïve mythical sense you could see a move from the Mother Goddess to the Father God, and now to 'no God' or 'gender free God', a kind of linguistic muddle. Something will happen out of it. I don't know what. I used to think they'd be a bi-sexual God, androgynous God but I don't think that's quite the right way of looking at it. Well, it doesn't seem to be happening anyway. Whereas God's just got buried. I think God's in the unconscious. That's where I think God is. In the darkness, as a mystery and it's not a gendered God, it's the unconscious, it's the not knowing, it could be in the writing of a poem.

God isn't anything more than a shorthand for, maybe, interconnectedness. I suppose, I just think more and more as we get older we're all moments in a bit of music, we're all bits of dust in a sunbeam, we're all these interconnected cells and that's what God is maybe. It's almost like Gaia theory perhaps.

DL and DFS: Do you have any concept of life after death?

MR: No, I don't objectively or scientifically. But on the other hand, I know that I've had intense relationships with people who are dead. Through dreams, so whether that's just a function of the extraordinary human imagination, which is alright by me actually. That's about love reaching toward the loved dead person and establishing a relationship or whether there is a sort of realm outside time, outside space, outside the body in which we encounter each other. I suppose, because life after death has been used as such a way of putting people down and consoling people I really, really want to believe in this life and I don't want to be on my death bed with regrets. That's like an experiment. I'll find out, won't I? When I'm dead. But now is what matters. I'm an existentialist in that sense. You've got to live now, and that's because I've seen several people on their death beds who've said, if only I'd done this, this and this.

DL and DFS: In terms of your writing, do you feel that you no longer need to wrestle with life after death, God, god and Catholicism?

MR: I think it's not a pressing subject anymore. I suppose I've worked out that I believe that the resurrection and life after death happen through language. I remember reading John Evelyn's diaries when I was about 14, for O-level, and knowing I'd stood in the presence of someone who was dead but his language was alive. That's what it is about for me, it's just a very basic materialist thought actually. But to me, that's the miracle. I mean that seventeenth-century language is what makes Evelyn alive. He is alive in that language. He wrote it. It's his language. I couldn't write that, and I think that's just the most beautiful and wonderful thing. That's how I feel about art. I stand in front of a painting that is really amazing and, ah! Caravaggio is speaking to me! So, the body dies, yes, but what you've made in your life goes on, and for some people that's children.

DL and DFS: You often write about ghost stories.

MR: Yes, I love ghost stories, I love hearing about them. More and more as I get older I think that ghost stories are just stories and that's essentially what they are. They're always retrospective looking back at someone, which is a story. Which is fantastic. I know weird things happen all the time. I've had very, very strange telepathic experiences; I've felt in very close touch with dead people, so I'm not kind of closing it off. I hope I'm not being arrogant, but I don't believe in a conventional religious life after death. But I somehow feel it's all around us!

DL and DFS: Is that the convent girl still lurking?

MR: I suppose I'll go on being fascinated by certain images and certain symbols, so the image of the convent goes on fascinating me. Because for me it's about this part time space where I can be in. I can be a part-time nun, or a part-time hermit, or a part-time writer, a part-time lover, a part-time aunt and that seems to be connected to femaleness somehow. That you don't have to be this one thing. You can be in a bit of a muddle, a chaos, a contradiction and that seems to be where I'm living now. I might even be a part-time believer. I mean, I do say my prayers sometimes. I do, praising, hurrah! Wonderful God! Oh the creation! Or I do, help, help! I'm in despair! And that's part-time believing, and there's a lot of part-time believing, and not believing.

I've had a lot of mystical experiences, what happens is you lose ego. So you're not self, you're not 'I', you're just really part of the field, part of the tree and that's the most joyful times I've ever had in my entire life. That's the most beautiful joy.

DL and DFS: Does that happen when you're writing?

MR: It isn't always the same joy. It's often turmoil and strife and trouble but the happiest moments seem to be when I lose myself from my own ego and writing can then just be becoming part of a flow. You're a flow of words and you're in the words and it's wonderful. Humanism seems to be very connected to notions of self, and at some moments, woman needs to have a self. She needs that. I like being a professor in some ways because it means I've got some authority, and at other times I don't want to be a professor at all. I hate it and loathe it and I just want to be a grubbing person in a field, you know. So I think I vary.

DL and DFS: Do you ever see that as divine inspiration when you're writing?

MR: Well, I think when I was writing *The Wild Girl* I felt in touch with something that wanted to get spoken. Maybe that was just personal desire. But I suppose it felt like something wider than that, beyond that. Sometimes I can use a kind of religious vocabulary to talk about writing, and sometimes I can't. Sometimes I'll talk about being haunted or possessed and sometimes I'll talk about being inspired which is more religious. Sometimes I'll just talk about playing with words, which is much more twentieth century. I've experienced great pleasure and delight when I've felt I've contacted something that's beyond certainly me and beyond my little twenty-first century life. But again whether we would just say that's the imagination, I mean, I'm newly thinking about it and I'm in a great intellectual muddle about it. What is the imagination? What does it mean to imagine? I've forgotten everything I've thought about, and my new novel will be an attempt to think that out.

So I don't know any answers to that!

DL and DFS: Your work is often used by religious feminists and theologians who draw upon women's writing as a source for feminist critiques and revisions of religion.

MR: Well, I'd just say that I'm extremely grateful to, and delighted if anyone thought my writing was any bloody use at all! So if theologians wanted to use it I'm honoured. I suppose I feel, when you're making a piece of art – I don't mean art with a capital 'A' – then it's got its own language and its own body and that's precisely what you're doing. So, if somebody's working in the theological and making a connection, that's lovely. But what I'm doing is not what she is doing, but if she wants to speak to me, I'm honoured. To me art is not theology, but I can see they overlap, they touch, they talk to each other.

DL and DFS: So you're quite happy for your work to take on a life of its own?

MR: Yes! I mean it is so fantastic to be read by other people who are thinking about stuff! We're all trying to come at something, we're all overlapping, so I'm very, very happy when people use what I've written.

DL and DFS: Are you ever tempted to say, 'that's not what I meant'?

MR: Well, I think I do in bad moods! There are bad moods where I want to control my work but most of the time, you've got to let it go and people will make of it what they want. You have to. Also, by the time it's out you're normally at work on the next thing.

I suppose, because I'm wrestling so much with people who read an enormous amount of literary theory and who think you can't make a piece of art until you've read the relevant theory, and then you can make the art. To me that's a bit like you can't pray until you've read the theology. I suppose I feel really angry with that attitude. I would read the theory and theology to nourish myself but then to make my piece. That's all I want to do. Just make my piece which has a body and thought – it is a kind of body that speaks. I've been so nourished by reading feminist theology and anthropology and sociology I think we're in a great web of speaking to each other but I think our products are slightly different with different languages.

I'm terribly grateful to the work of feminist scholars; I think that's really important to say. I know that I've been very, very nurtured by the research done by women. That's been really, really important to me, research about women's cultural history. I don't just come out of my essential self thinking I'm feeding myself all the time with intellectual stuff.

DL and DFS: The Wild Girl is still read as a very important feminist theological text.

MR: But at that point, that was over twenty years ago, I was still very, very embroiled with Catholicism and it was part of my exit to write my novel. So I felt I was writing a new theology, I was, you know, hey world! Look! Listen! Women, women, women! But that was twenty years ago so I don't think I feel quite like that now. But I'm drawn back and back to women, religion and female religious figures getting replaced by writers. I am fascinated by Charlotte Brontë, George Sand and Elizabeth Gaskell. They're my saints now I think. They're all people who wrestled with religion as well, but I still love the figures of the saints and will go on telling stories about them.

DL and DFS: How powerful, do you think, has the impact of feminist theology been on the church? It's been over twenty-five years since Mary Daly wrote Beyond God the Father *and yet the Church is still dominated by a male presence.[4] What do you think has happened to feminist theology?*

MR: Well, I think we're living in a moment of reaction. Feminism is being fought back all the time. There's fundamentalist Christianity on the up rise, we've got [Tony] Blair having quite narrow-minded views of what religion is. It's not a good time. Which is why we've got to be stronger and more rebellious than ever.

Bibliography

Daly, Mary, *Beyond God the Father: Towards a Philosophy of Women's Liberation* (Boston: Beacon Press, 1973).

Dronke, Peter, *Women Writers of the Middle Ages* (Cambridge: Cambridge University Press 1984).

Gössmann, Elisabeth, 'The Image of God and the Human Being in Women's Counter-Tradition' in Deborah F. Sawyer and Diane Collier, (eds), *Is There a Future for Feminist Theology?* (Sheffield: Sheffield Academic Press, 1999): 11-24.

Irigaray, Luce 'Divine Women' in Morny Joy, Kathleen O'Grady and Judith L. Poxon, (eds), *French Feminists on Religion: A Reader* (London and New York: Routledge, 2002): 41-8.

Irigaray, Luce, 'The Redemption of Women', in Luce Irigaray, *Key Writings* (London and New York: Continuum, 2004): 150-64.

Irigaray, Luce, *Key Writings* (London and New York: Continuum, 2004).

Joy, Morny, Kathleen O'Grady and and Judith L. Poxon, (eds), *French Feminists on Religion: A Reader* (London and New York: Routledge, 2002).

Roberts, Michèle, *The Wild Girl* (London: Methuen, 1985).

Roberts, Michèle, *The Book of Mrs Noah* (London: Virago, 1987).

Roberts, Michèle, *Impossible Saints* (London: Virago, 1997).

Roberts, Michèle, *Reader, I Married Him* (London: Virago, 2006).

Sawyer, Deborah, F. and Diane Collier, (eds), *Is There a Future for Feminist Theology?* (Sheffield: Sheffield Academic Press, 1999).

---

4   Mary Daly, *Beyond God the Father: Towards a Philosophy of Women's Liberation* (Boston, 1973).

Chapter 2

The Sacred in Caribbean Literature: A *Theo*logical Conversation

Michael N. Jagessar

The presenting issue

A cursory perusal of the works of Caribbean novelists, poets, and artists will underscore the importance of faith, religiosity, religion(s) and belief(s). Artists, poets and composers are often exposing the holy in the ordinary, providing a way for human beings to experience, question and praise it. Caribbean prose and poetry, as Gordon Collier has noted, always had 'a spiritual and spirited edge to it' and 'a relaxed insistence on divine immanence within the tangible, natural world is never far away.'[1] Was this in the mind of Antonio Benítez-Rojo when he wrote: 'I study the Caribbean as a turbulent system, beneath whose disorder (the impossibility of Caribbeanness) there are regularities that are repeated (the possibility of Caribbeanness)?'[2] Is it possible to consider Caribbean religiosity, practice of faith and spirituality as a 'repeated regularity' that runs throughout all aspects of Caribbean life? I suggest it is. Silvio Torres-Saillant[3] notes that the 'omnipresence of religion' as a theme of 'repeated regularity' running through Caribbean literature is so evident that

> A list of all the literary works from the archipelago that touch on religious matters, including those that do so in a negative way by denying or challenging the validity of the sacred, would include the bulk of Caribbean literary works.[4]

To neglect religiosity as 'repeated regularity' would impoverish our discourse. There is the need to come to grips with 'the profound religious sensibility' of Caribbean writers and 'the relationship between subversion and the sacred'.[5]

---

1 Gordon Collier, '"At the Gate of Cultures" of the New World: Religion, Mythology, and Folk-Belief in West Indian Poetry' in Jamie S. Scott, (ed.), *And the Birds Began to Sing: Religion and Literatures in Post-Colonial Contexts* (Amsterdam, 1996), pp. 227-49:277.

2 Antonio Benítez-Rojo, *The Repeating Island*, trans. James Maraniss (Durham NC, 1992), p. 17.

3 Silvio Torres-Saillant, 'The Cross-Cultural Unity of Caribbean Literature' in A. James Arnold, (ed.), *A History of Literature in the Caribbean: Volume 3 Cross-Cultural Studies* (Amsterdam and Philadelphia,1997), pp. 57-78.

4 Ibid., pp. 70-71.

5 Ibid., p. 85.

Presently, there is much interest in the variety of Caribbean (popular) religions, how these have grown and the accommodation/syncretism that resulted from the meeting of the established religion and that of former slaves and indentured labourers.[6] There is a need to articulate the connection between Caribbean literature, these discourses, an evolving Caribbean theology and recent articulations of Black God-talk (theology). As a theologian, what strikes me, is that in theorizing Caribbean themes and/or studies there is a tendency to gloss over the fundamental reality and importance of faith/spirituality and its impact on Caribbean peoples and their psyches. Is it impossible to theorize about Caribbean experiences and themes without understanding and analyzing this? As Robert Beckford puts it in the Black-British context:

> Spirituality is a major force in contemporary Black British life ... One cannot do comprehensive cultural or political work on Black existence and ignore the importance of Black religion and spirituality.[7]

A similar point is made by Althea Prince who observes that

> the sociology of the Caribbean clearly needs to include knowledge of the religious body of the Caribbean. For religion is part of the whole of the people - a part of what comes out of their belly. In essence, it is a large part of a Caribbean topology of B-E-I-N-G, a part of the universe in which Caribbean people abide.[8]

When, however, the fact of Caribbean religious influence and spirituality has been recognized, the theorizing is usually done within historical, sociological

---

6   Basdeo Mangru, 'Tadjah in British Guiana: Manipulation or Protest?' in Basdeo Mangru, *Indenture and Abolition* (Toronto, 1993), pp. 43-58; Miguel Barnet, *Afro-Cuban Religions*, trans. Christine Renata Ayorinde, (Kingston & Princeton 2001); Roger Bastide, *African Civilizations in the New World*, trans. Peter Green (London1971); Barry Chevannes, *Rastafari: Roots and Ideology* (Syracuse, 1998); Leslie Desmangles, *The Faces of the Gods: Vodou and Roman Catholicism in Haiti* (Chapel Hill, 1992); Margarite Fernández Olmos & Lizabeth Paravisini-Gebert, *Sacred Possessions: Vodou, Santeria, Obeah, and the Caribbean* (New Brunswick, 1997); Margarite Fernández Olmos & Lizabeth Paravisini-Gebert, *Healing Cultures: Art and Religion as Curative Practices in the Caribbean and Its Diaspora* (New York, 2001); Margarite Fernández Olmos & Lizabeth Paravisini-Gebert, *Creole Religions of the Caribbean: An Introduction from Vodou and Santeria to Obeah and Espiritismo* (New York, 2003); Frances Henry, *Reclaiming African Religions in Trinidad: The Socio-Political Legitimation of the Orisha and Spiritual Baptist Faiths* (Mona, Jamaica, 2003); Aisha Khan, *Callaloo Nation: Metaphors of Race and Religious Identity Among South Asians in Trinidad* (Durham NC, 2004); Frank J. Korom, *Hosay Trinidad: Muharram Performances in an Indo-Caribbean Diaspora* (Philadelphia, 2003); Dianne M. Stewart, *Three Eyes for the Journey: African Dimensions of the Jamaican Religious Experience* (New York 2005).

7   Robert Beckford, *God of the Rahtid: Redeeming Rage* (London, 2001) p. 52.

8   Althea Prince, 'How Shall We Sing the Lord's Song in a Strange Land? Constructing the Divine in Caribbean Contexts,' in Patrick Taylor, (ed.), *Nation Dance: Religion, Identity, and Cultural Difference in the Caribbean* (Bloomington, Indianapolis, 2001), pp. 25-31:25-6.

and anthropological frameworks[9] and more than likely through the optic of a mid- nineteenth century neo-European Christianity. At the same time, Caribbean theologians at 'home' (Caribbean) and in the Diaspora are yet to engage with Caribbean literature. Voices from Caribbean 'God-talkers' such as Mulrain[10], Bodhoo[11], Taylor[12], Sankeralli[13], Erskine[14], Williams[15] and Murrell, Spencer and McFarlane[16] who have engaged (to an extent) with Caribbean religions from a theological (and religious) perspective are yet to engage theologically with Caribbean literature.[17]

If Caribbean theologians seem to fall into the habit of designed unawareness when it comes to theological themes in Caribbean literature, one can also posit that there seems to be a degree of reservation in Caribbean literary discourse in wanting to engage with the significance of Caribbean religiosity (faith and spirituality) as important dimensions of Caribbean literature.[18] Melvin B. Rahming highlights this point in his plea for literary critics to engage with 'the spiritual terrain of creative texts'[19] especially from Caribbean and African writers. What Rahming misses, however, are the literary voices that stand out. In the Caribbean, for instance, there are exceptions evident in the significant contributions of Gordon Rohlehr, Jennifer Rahim and Gordon Collier. In terms of the early discussion on articulating a Caribbean theology during the 1970s, Rohlehr's name comes up as a voice crying in the wilderness for theologians to note the role of the 'spiritual' in the Caribbean

---

9   See, Khan, *Callaloo Nation,* p. 252.

10 George Mulrain, *Theology in Folk Culture: The Theological Significance of Haitian Folk Religion* (Frankfurt am Main, 1984).

11 Gerald Boodoo, 'The Faith of the People: The *Divina Pastora* Devotions in Trinidad,' in Hemchand Gossai and Nathaniel Samuel Murrell, (eds), *Religion, Culture and Tradition in the Caribbean* (Basingstoke, 2000), pp. 65-72.

12 Patrick Taylor, *The Narrative of Liberation: Perspectives on Afro-Caribbean Literature, Popular Culture, and Politics* (Ithaca, 1999) and Taylor, *Nation Dance.*

13 Burton Sankeralli, *At the Crossroads: African Caribbean Religion and Christianity* (Trinidad & Tobago, 1995).

14 Noel Erskine, *Decolonizing Theology: A Caribbean Perspective* (New York, 1981).

15 Lewin Williams, *Caribbean Theology* (New York, 1994).

16 Nathaniel Samuel Murrell, William Spencer, Adrian McFarlane, (eds), *Chanting Down Babylon: The Rastafari Reader* (Philadelphia, 1988).

17 There are two notable exceptions to this. First, Patrick Taylor suggests that Caribbean writers 'draw from a popular tradition of resistance that still lives in religion and language, tales, music, song, poetry, and drama.' (see Taylor, *The Narrative of Liberation,* p. 228.) Second, Darren J.N. Middleton's 'Riddim Wise and Scripture Smart: Interview and Interpretation with Ras Benjamin Zephaniah,' in Gossai and Murrell, *Religion, Culture, and Tradition,* pp. 257-70.

18 With regard to Caribbean literature, one can reasonably argue that much of the literary discourse and criticism focuses on language and cultures regarding Caribbean identity, history and cultural production. But, just as language and culture(s) have shaped Caribbean identity and history, so too one can convincingly contend have religions, faith and spirituality (as a repeated regularity).

19 Melvin B. Rahming, 'Theorizing Spirit: The Critical Challenge of Elizabeth Nunez's *When Rocks Dance* and *Beyond the Limbo Silence,*' *Studies in the Literary Imagination* (2004), pp. 1-21:2.

psyche as this is reflected in Caribbean literature.[20] Rahim's essay, 'Patterns of Psalmology in Lovelace's *The Wine of Astonishment*'[21] is one of those rare pieces in which the kind of interdisciplinary conversation I am interested in happens. Here she engages with Walter Brueggemann, a contemporary Biblical scholar from North America in the context of her reading of *The Wine of Astonishment*. Gordon Collier's essay 'At the Gate of cultures of the New World'[22] and the volume *Mapping the Sacred*,[23] are two other key contributions to the much-needed conversation between theology and Caribbean literature. It is also important to note the input of Paula Burnett, in particular her chapter on Walcott's employment of myth in *Derek Walcott: Politics and Poetics*.[24] The fact that these are all reflections from the perspective of literary critics underscores the necessity of the kind of conversation I am calling for. I wish to challenge Caribbean theologians to reach out and receive the offerings of Caribbean literature – to glue their ears onto the spaces of the Caribbean literary canvas in order to discern raw materials for Caribbean theological articulation. At the same time, I want to impress on my colleagues in Caribbean studies (literary and others), the importance of such an ongoing dialogue, which will be true to the 'whole' Caribbean psyche.

The undertaking: fragments of a conversation

In making a case for theological conversation with Caribbean literature, this essay offers fragments of such a conversation. Conversation is the operative metaphor here. My fundamental point is that religious references (subtle and overt) in Caribbean literature are not incidental. They find a deep place in the Caribbean psyche and soul. It ought to take a central place in any theorizing on the Caribbean. In engaging with Caribbean fiction from a theological entry point, I am interested in asking questions such as: What is the role of faith and the sacred in Caribbean literature? Does theology shape cultural identity or does cultural identity shape our God-talk? What is the role of the Bible, or any religious texts, in the works and imaginations of Caribbean writers? In what ways do authors and their fiction contribute to the theological debates regarding Caribbean identity and community? What insights can Caribbean literature provide to help theologians counter totalising proclivities, over-dependence in exactitudes and dead/deadly dogmas? How does Caribbean literature challenge the way in which Caribbean Christian theology has been written, read, understood and articulated? How can Caribbean writers, poets and artists stir the theological imagination towards releasing some of the biblical texts and theological

---

20 Gordon Rohlehr, 'Man's [sic] Spiritual Search in the Caribbean Through Literature,' in Idris Hamid (ed.) *Troubling of the Waters* (Trinidad, 1973). See also, *The Shape that Hurts and Other Essays* (Port-of-Spain, 1992), pp. 187-204.

21 Jennifer Rahim, 'Patterns of Psalmology in Lovelace's *The Wine of Astonishment*', *Caribbean Journal of Religious Studies* 16/2 (1995): 3-17.

22 Collier, '"At the Gate of Cultures."'

23 Jamie S. Scott and Paul Simpson-Housley, *Mapping the Sacred: Religion, Geography and Postcolonial Literatures* (Amsterdam, 2001).

24 Paula Burnett, *Derek Walcott: Politics and Poetics* (Gainsville, Florida, 2000).

notions from the shackles of ideological and cultural captivity in order to become relevant in the Caribbean context(s)?

Clarifying terms and locating myself

Given my approach, it is important that I define some of the terms I am using or at least explain how I am employing these. I am using Caribbean religiosity to embrace Caribbean people's faith and faithfulness that includes their spirituality. Hence, religiosity, faith, spirituality, and sacred are used interchangeably. It is not *only* Christian. By spirituality I mean the totality of one's interrelated existence as embodied in ways of life, modes of thinking and the diverse expressions of behaviour and attitudes toward the mystery that surrounds one's immediate context and world.[25] The term 'Black' is used as a political term or construct to describe the collective racial identity of Caribbean peoples. This is used specifically in the case of articulating a theological perspective different from that of the Western theology. By Caribbean theology I mean Caribbean 'God-talk'. The departure point here is God-talk that is expressed in and through the reality of Black experiences and struggles.[26] Theology or God-talk is a work of faith inseparable from the lived experiences of everyday life and ought to point towards liberating transformation.[27]

My entry point into this conversation is that of a Christian theologian whose heritage constitutes both Muslim and Hindu influences.[28] Also, as one whose life has been shaped in the Caribbean, my theology, theologizing and hermeneutics reflect this Caribbean heritage – especially its rainbow nature embracing a diversity of peoples, religions, cultures and the ongoing dialogue and interaction in this context. God-talk (theology) for me is done within the rich world of Caribbean diversity, contradictions, ambivalence and the exciting possibilities and gateways this offers.

---

25 See Choan S. Song, *Third-Eye Theology: Theology in Formation in Asian Settings* (Guildford & London, 1980), p. 10.

26 See, Michael Jagessar, *Life in All Its Fullness* (Zoetermeer, 1997), p. 127. See also, Anthony G. Reddie, *Faith, Stories and the Experience of Black Elders: Singing the Lord's Song in a Strange Land* (London, 2001), p. 40.

27 The notion of 'God-talk' within this framework is laced with multiple meanings. It can mean that *God talks* or that we can *dare to talk about* God, even *discern the tongue of God* or that God-talk is inseparable from *human-talk*. The most humbling implication of this is the provisional and tentative nature of *theology*, lest one misrepresents the Divine.

28 A caveat in terms of my interest in this conversation is both necessary and appropriate. I am a Caribbean theologian by training with a keen interest in Caribbean culture, identity, religions and literature. My MA research is in the area of theology and Caribbean literature (specifically the works of Wilson Harris) and my PhD work on the life and work of the Caribbean theologian Philip Potter, the first Black leader of the World Council of Churches. I teach Interfaith Studies, Black and Asian Theologies and Post-Colonial Biblical Hermeneutics.

Caribbean literature, the imagination and theology

The Divine, whatever form, shape and name, is always immanent in the whole of Caribbean life with all the numerous contradictions of life. Caribbean religiosity and religious expressions/ideas are readily manifested as a collective experience of Caribbean peoples. Contrary to what experts and Christian theologians would have us believe, boundaries are amorphous and Caribbean people's religiosity is characterized by a natural and healthy dialogue and fusion of cultures and religions. The Divine pops up with a nagging regularity and in various forms, shapes and images. God, at least in the Caribbean, does not suffer from a chronic housing problem. Yet, God in much of Christian theology in the Caribbean is still to be 'de-enveloped' (released) and embodied in Caribbean flavour and tempo. Austin Clarke problematizes the issue very graphically by having the narrator in *Easter Carol* reflect on her mother's experience in two different churches.

> There she could testify how God helped her when she didn't know where the hell she could get six cents from to buy flour and lard and oil to make bakes for her children. There she could clap her hands and stamp her feet till the floor boards creaked with emotion, and jump up in the air and praise God and for all that feel God was listening. But in the Church of England she was regimented to sit-and-stand exercise of dull, religious drilling. And she always complained to Lavignia that she did not understand one word of what the parson was talking about. He used words that simple, common people could not understand. And, never, never 'have I seen anybody stand up in the Church of England and say Amen, Halleluiah to God'. It was such a strange Church to her.[29]

In the Caribbean context, one could hardly disagree that in the religious imagination of many Christians it is not only the established Churches and their theologies that seem strange. God is also strange, 'a foreigner, a kind of white expatriate who is not God of our own history, but an outsider, standing over and against' Caribbean people.[30]

Using the insights of liberation theologies, I wish to firstly contend that theology is dead when divorced from real life, practices and people's stories, myths and histories.[31] Authentic theology plumbs the depths of a people's life and living. God-talk is integral to the narratives that shape our lives. Our problem is that much of the inherited biblical theology and hermeneutics bought into the western Bultmanian emphasis on 'de-mythologizing' the Scriptures. A product of his European culture, Rudolph Bultmann argued that because the cosmology of the New Testament is largely mythical there is the need for it to be translated for the purpose of *kerygma* (teaching). Theology's task is to peel off the *kerygma* from its mythical embodiment – to demythologize it. What resulted was the re-clothing with European garments

---

29 Austin Clarke, 'Easter Carol,' in *When He was Free and Young and He Used to Wear Silk: Stories* (Toronto, 1971), pp. 1-12:5.

30 Michael Jagessar, 'Wilson Harris, the Imagination and the "Infinite Rehearsal": A Theological Perspective' in Hena Maes-Jelinek, (ed.), *Wilson Harris: The Uncompromising Imagination* (Australia, 1991), pp. 221-29:224. Here I was drawing on an insight of the late Dr. Idris Hamid, *In Search of New Perspectives*, p. 8.

31 Sallie McFague, *Metaphorical Theology* (Philadelphia, 1982), p. 17.

– modern myths. This is the legacy that much of Caribbean theology inherited and has largely internalized.[32] That must now give way to Caribbean myth-making and the phenomenon of story becomes the culturally viable mode of communication and viable theological method or form. We should also consider and accept the category of story as a counter-point for theologizing and exploring the sacred with a Caribbean flavour and tempo. It is here the works of Caribbean writers and poets are of theological importance.

My second contention is that the encounter between *theos* and *logos* also involves the attempt to analyse, criticise, deconstruct/reconstruct and de-code/re-code our inherited theological notions. In the 1980s, the Taiwanese theologian Choan S. Song called for a 'third-eye theology' to see beyond the dead theology of 'two-dimensionality'.[33] This challenge of doing of theology with a 'third eye' involves the continuing activity of the human imagination.[34] Caribbean writers, poets and artists have been most perceptive in unearthing and accounting our people's agony and anguish, history, anger, joy, pain, laughter and the contradictions of life and living. They are the ones who perceive the world with the profound working of the imagination and who are ideally placed to enable us to see beyond the façade and the facile in order to catch glimpses of the deep religious meaning of the interior of life and the world.[35]

The hiatus between the Caribbean people's spirituality, their perception of the Divine and that of Caribbean Christian theology may be located in the language used to represent the Divine. Metaphors of God 'as King, Ruler, Lord, Master and Governor, and the concepts that accompany them of God as absolute, complete, transcendent and omnipotent',[36] allow no room for reciprocity not to mention the association they have with notions of empire and colonial power. For one of the key features of the colonial agenda is control over language.[37] Hence, biblical scholars like Musa Dube and R.S. Sugirthrajah[38] are closely scrutinizing the various forms

---

32 Rudolph Bultmann, *Jesus Christ and Mythology* (London, 1960). Bultmann's agenda was based on his diagnosis that the 'modern' European person could neither take, nor had time for myth. The problem is that Bultmann and others saw fit to speak on behalf of the rest of humankind.

33 Song, *Third-Eye Theology,* p. 11.

34 See Gordon Kaufman, *Theology for a Nuclear Age* (Manchester, 1985).

35 See John Bowker, *Hallowed Ground: Religions and the Poetry of Place* (London, 1993).

36 Sallie McFague, *Models of God: Theology for an Ecological, Nuclear Age* (Philadelphia, 1987), p. 19.

37 See, Bill Ashcroft, Gareth Griffiths, Helen Tiffin, (eds), *The Empire Writes Back: Theory and Practice in Post-Colonial Literatures* (New York, 1995), p. 283.

38 Musa Dube, *Postcolonial Feminist Interpretation of the Bible* (St. Louis, Missouri, 2000); Musa Dube and Jeffrey Staley, *John and Postcolonialism: Travel, Space and Power* (London, 2002); Fernando Segovia, *Interpreting Beyond Borders* (London, 2000); Kwok Pui-lan, (ed.), *Postcolonial Imagination and Feminist Theology* (London, 2005); R.S. Sugirtharajah, ed., *The Postcolonial Bible* (London, 1998); R.S. Sugirtharajah, *Postcolonial Criticism and Biblical Interpretation* (Oxford, 2002); R.S. Sugirtharajah, *Postcolonial Reconfigurations: An Alternative Way of Reading the Bible and Doing Theology* (London, 2003).

of representations in the texts and the different ways that these are implicated in the imperial agenda and consequent oppression of the 'subaltern'. For representations are never exact or value free. As Edward Said has demonstrated in *Orientalism*, representations as constructed images are not harmless likeness. They convey messages that influence the ways the Orient and its natives are perceived and need to be interrogated for their ideological content.[39]

The crucial question for Caribbean God-Talk relates to finding new metaphors and symbols through which the Divine can be conceived. As I noted in 1991:

> It is imperative that the language used to express the relationship between God and the created order, especially in the Caribbean, be radically revised, a revision which must begin at the level of the imagination.[40]

One of the Caribbean writers who emphasize the importance of the imagination and the need for imaginative daring is Wilson Harris. Harris's concern is the state of neglect to which the imagination has been relegated. Hence, he speaks of the 'illiteracy of the imagination'.[41] Harris, as Michael Gilkes has observed, is interested 'with the way in which the creative imagination is able to re-discover the deep, cross-cultural roots of all established traditions'.[42] Writing in *The Womb of Space* (1983), Harris gives us an insight into the significance of the role of the imagination for Caribbean writers.

> The paradox of cultural heterogeneity, or cross-cultural capacity, lies in the evolutionary thrust it restores to orders of the imagination, the ceaseless dialogue it inserts between hardened conventions and eclipsed or half-eclipsed otherness, within an intuitive self that moves endlessly into flexible patterns, arcs or bridges of community.[43]

Likewise, Derek Walcott sees art and poetics 'as helping the world to *imagine* not only its heterogeneity but its *potential* difference'.[44] To dismantle 'the obsessional codes which threaten society' calls for the engagement of 'the creative imagination', otherwise history becomes a repeated spiral of exploiter/exploited and oppressor/oppressed.[45]

The lack of imagination or imaginative daring that Harris speaks of is also endemic among theologians. Brueggemann, for instance, notes 'in our time we can notice the absence of poetic imagination in some of the religious hucksters who

---

39 Edward Said, *Orientalism: Western Representations of the Orient* (London, 1978).

40 Jagessar, 'Wilson Harris, the Imagination and the "Infinite Rehearsal"', p. 224.

41 Wilson Harris, 'A Talk on the Subjective Imagination,' in Hena Maes-Jelinek, (ed.), *Explorations: A Selection of Talks and Articles* (Aarhus, 1981), pp. 57-67:57. See also, 'Literacy and the Imagination' in Michael Gilkes, (ed.), *The Literate Imagination: Essays on the Novels of Wilson Harris* (London: Macmillan, 1989), pp. 13-30.

42 Gilkes, *The Literate Imagination*, p. ix.

43 Wilson Harris, *The Womb of Space: The Cross-Cultural Imagination* (Westport, 1983), p. xviii.

44 Burnett, *Derek Walcott*, p. 100. [The first emphasis is mine.].

45 Harris, 'Literacy and the Imagination'.

promise certitude by flattening out all the rich metaphors.'[46] While resources for doing theology are not lacking, our dilemma is located in our suspicion of the imagination. Having inherited Christianity with all its Euro-centric baggage, we have become neatly locked into a largely Protestant theological mindset that has relegated the act of the imagination to the realm of 'hocus-pocus' which is viewed with much suspicion. We have lost the sense of magic, mystery and awe. These have had to go underground and through *limbo gateways* are embodied in much of popular Caribbean religiosity. Further, while Black theological discourses emphasise experience, there is still much work to be done in the area of 'imagination'. We need to radically revise and find new stories to break this hold. I, therefore, see a joint venture with our writers, poets, dramatists and artists. To decode and re-read the number of resources available, to find new metaphors to represent the Divine and the world that would counter a 'uniform kind of narrative, a uniform kind of frame',[47] it is imperative that the imagination be deepened and the power of theological imaging be strengthened.[48]

The imagination helps us to plumb deep into existence and open gateways into reality that are usually closed to us.[49] And having pushed us as far out as we are meant to extend, the imagination is where reality begins.[50] The narratives of the Creation in Genesis underscore how God images the human person out of God's own self. By this act God imparts to humankind the ability to image all creation in relation to God. Thus, with this gift of imaging the poet, writer, painter and theologian (among others) perceive the Divine, the universe, human beings and their relationships and all the ambiguities and contradictions that we live with. As Aritha van Herk writes: 'I suspect that if there is any way for us to measure the boundless possibilities of spirituality and faith, the reach of the imagination is perhaps the closest we can come.'[51]

Caribbean literature offers a ripe *space* for nurturing a counter-imagination in a context of what Wilson Harris calls 'the illiteracy of the imagination'. Imagining differently anchors Caribbean folks' struggle to be self-defining – to own their heritage and experiences as they dream a present and a future that is grounded on hope. No wonder our writers make good use of memory or the act of recalling in their effort in creating a new possibility or reality. In providing memories, narratives, visions, images and metaphors that are not easily domesticated, Caribbean literature can enable us to imagine worlds where ideas and stories are re-staged/rehearsed and dialogue can cross-fertilise across cultural boundaries. Hence, they do offer Caribbean theologians more useful, dynamic and cathartic metaphors than those we are accustomed to. These linger in the hearing and the talking and offer possibilities

---

46 Walter Brueggemann, *Hopeful Imagination: Prophetic Voices in Exile* (Philadelphia, 1986), pp. 25-6.

47 Harris, 'Literacy and the Imagination,' p. 15

48 See, Choan S. Song, *Theology from the Womb of Asia* (London, 1988), pp. 8-16.

49 See Harvey Cox, *The Feast of Fools: A Theological Essay on Festivity and Fantasy* (Cambridge, Massachusetts, 1969), p. 62ff.

50 Alexander Dru, (ed. and trans.), *The Journal of Kierkegaard* (London, 1958), p. 243.

51 Aritha van Herk, *A Frozen Tongue* (Sydney, 1992), p. 107.

for imagining a 'new heaven and a new earth', in other words, the 'more' of a world transformed.

One scholar, who gives theological/biblical content to the imagination, is Walter Brueggemann.[52] He contends that the inability to discern the imaginative power of the biblical texts to transform and evoke new possibilities may be located in our proclivity for 'the firm' and 'settled truth' in the 'technical certitude of this age'. Thus, we miss the envisioned alternative 'of the daring of poetic speech to move beyond settled reality' and 'walk to the edges of alternatives'[53] as manifested in the prophetic imagination.

The process of imagining and tapping into the imagination of God is analogous to the hermeneutic process of *midrash*.[54] Here the biblical text is pushed beyond limits and outside the boundaries, extended or elaborated, turned upside down and inside out as 'truth' gets broken, perverted and re-arranged. What is not said in the text becomes just as significant as what is said. In the process, meanings and insights never imagined and perceived before become evident. I contend much of Caribbean literature to be already *midrashic,* enabling us to liberate and release the imagination and give God and the Spirit more space to move freely within the texts at the edges/ boundaries[55], and between the text and the context, and the reading community and its context. My view is that Caribbean theology and literature can unearth the experiences of the peoples of the Caribbean, giving them structure and clarity, and letting the power of the imagination find new metaphors to make them accessible to people and keep them alive.

A related and important issue is the relationship between Caribbean stories and theology. I contend that Caribbean stories are theological. God created human beings because God loves stories. God exists because humans are story/mythmakers. What can be more theological than people's life stories? A cursory glance through the pages of religious texts will reinforce this point. The biblical narratives, for instance, used images and metaphors common to the people, subjectively telling stories of how people perceived God to be acting in their lives and events related to them. The Bible is the storybook *par excellence* for Christians. Narrative is not a choice we make when it comes time to explore 'truth'. It is the way we encounter truth(s): 'not in crisp propositions, but in messy tales of encounters between people and people, between people and creation, between people and God[s]'.[56]

It is in this context that I am suggesting that theology needs to be imaged and not merely conceptualized. It would be unfair, however, to expect Caribbean/Black

---

52 See Walter Brueggemann, *Hopeful Imagination*; *The Prophetic Imagination* (Philadelphia, 1978) and *Finally Comes the Poet: Daring Speech for Proclamation* (Minneapolis, 1989).

53 Brueggemann, *Finally Comes the Poet*, pp. 4-5.

54 *Midrash* means to 'seek out' or 'to inquire'. It is used in a dual way to describe a method and a genre of literature in which the imagination is used extensively in the interpretation and re-interpretation of biblical texts to release and extend the texts to existential experiences.

55 I understand boundary as more than the perception of where things separate. I perceive boundary as the edge or margin where things join and assume new shapes.

56 Barbara Brown Taylor, 'Never-Ending Story' in *Christian Century* 120/5 (March 8, 2003), p. 37.

literature to preach the gospel since that is not its function. Caribbean literature ought not to be evaluated on the basis of any religious texts. Insofar as human beings are confident of God's love for them, they do not need the sermon. But insofar as we humans are inclined to make a name for ourselves and build homogenous towers of Babel at the expense of the 'Other', as we become locked into uniformed narratives and functions and bow down to the dominant culture, then we need something like a sermon to proclaim the counter-cultural way of the Divine and we can be grateful for any help that writers provide in understanding ourselves, the world, human values and ultimately, the Divine. Caribbean theologians, like our writers, poets and artists are called not to preach and give advice; our vocation is to stir, to evoke and offer an alter*native* consciousness, to surprise and to imagine a different world through 'porous'[57] (not fixed) language. For people and communities are transformed not by preaching about the moral/ethical high ground but by a *con-version* of the imagination.[58] In this regard, I am very sympathetic to the insight of van Herk who observes:

> Perhaps we have to be willing to radically alter our imagining of what or who the Deity or Deities is. Perhaps we have to alter our definition of faith and spirituality. Perhaps we have to re-incorporate the natural world that has been so truncated, so removed from contact with the spiritual world. Perhaps we have to look at and think carefully about what the early goddesses meant. There is no room for dogma or inflexible structure, if we are to encourage people to have faith. We must give them the one arm, the one reach they have, the reach of the imagination.[59]

God-talk and Caribbean literature

In the 1970s Gordon Rohlehr[60] observed that Caribbean literature is 'one of the places the theologian will need to explore' to 'ask the age-old ultimate questions in a Caribbean accent'.[61] While not too critical of his narrow understanding of the role of a theologian, Rohlehr's insight on the need for theology to dialogue with Caribbean literature is important. He went on to ask: 'Does an artist have to conform to a system of belief in order to be able to make artistic use of the symbols or rituals of that belief?' If European writers have made use of the religious imagination of their time what should 'stop the Caribbean artist from making effective use of such systems or fragments of systems' as they may find in their context.[62] Much later in 1992, Rohlehr is able to locate the significance of the 'religious paradigm' as a 'shape or trope accessible for aesthetic extension into form'.[63] Referring to the

---

57 Brueggemann, *Hopeful Imagination*, p. 24.

58 Paul Ricoeur, *The Philosophy of Paul Ricoeur,* C. Reagan and D. Stewart, (eds), (Boston, 1979).

59 van Herk, *A Frozen Tongue*, p. 119.

60 Rohlehr, 'Man's [sic] Spiritual Search in the Caribbean through Literature', pp. 187-204.

61 Ibid., p. 190.

62 Ibid., pp. 199-200.

63 Rohlehr, *The Shape that Hurts and Other Essays*, p. 5.

works of Roger Mais and Edward Kamau Brathwaithe, he notes how the sermon, testimony, the Bible, Anglican liturgical tones and Shouter rhythms have served as influential forces to the styles and content of the two Caribbean writers and much of Caribbean music.[64] Of Brathwaithe's collection of *Barbajan Poems* (1994) Rohlehr notes that Brathwaithe 'illustrates the widespread view of the inseparability of the earthly and sacred in Caribbean life'.[65]

Derek Walcott in his famous essay 'The Muse of History' observed:

> the subject African had come to the New World ... with a profounder terror of blasphemy than the exhausted, hypocritical Christian. He understood too quickly the Christian rituals of a whipped, tortured, and murdered redeemer.[66]

Walcott goes on to suggest that in addressing Christianity, 'the captured warrior and the tribal poet had chosen the very battleground which the captor proposed' not as a sign of 'defeat' but rather, through 'conversion' to reconstitute the cosmology of a European world. He notes: '[w]hat was captured from the captor was his God'.[67] Thus, the Rastafarians, as one example, hijacked 'the oppressor's God in a move that sought to discommode the oppressor ... [w]resting the Christian message from the Messenger.'[68] While Walcott himself has no use for the institutional church and its high priests, he locates his faith (a non-conformist) in God as significant to his creative imagination.[69] His poetics 'constantly uses language as rite: for invocation, praise, awe, all kinds of prayer ...'[70]

Indeed, Caribbeans deploy religious imageries, stories and texts – especially the Bible – to effectively construct a landscape of experience and to re-interpret the New World historical experience through the biblical texts and accounts of Genesis, the Psalms of lament, the Prophets, apocalyptic writings and redemption/salvation.[71] This reconstruction and revision is related to the Caribbean peoples' struggles for justice, to become subjects of their history created in the *imago Dei* as any other person. Consequently, '[t]his struggle has made the Bible a valid text and a rich source of metaphors, images, and symbols for interpreting Caribbean history and articulating the vision of an alternative Caribbean.'[72]

---

64 Ibid., pp. 21-4.

65 Ibid., p. 70.

66 O. Coombs, (ed.), *Is Massa Day Dead?* (New York, 1974), pp. 1-12.

67 Ibid., p. 11.

68 Rex Nettleford, 'Discourse on Rastafarian Reality,' in Nathaniel Samuel Murrell, William David Spencer, and Adrian Anthony McFarlane, (eds), *Chanting Down Babylon*, (Philadelphia, 1998), pp. 311-25:315.

69 Walcott speaking at the University of Milan (May 22nd, 1996) and as quoted in Burnett, *Derek Walcott,* p. 101.

70 Walcott speaking at the University of Milan (May 22nd, 1996), p. 101.

71 See, Diane J. Austin-Broos, 'Pentecostal Community and Jamaican Hierarchy' in John W. Pulis, (ed.), *Religion, Diaspora and Cultural Identity: A Reader in the Anglophone Caribbean* (Netherlands: 1999), pp. 215-45:227.

72 Leslie R. James, 'Text and the Rhetoric of Change: Bible and Decolonization in Post-World War II Caribbean Political Discourse,' in Gossai and Murrell, *Religion, Culture and Tradition in the Caribbean*, pp. 143-66:162.

The importance and influence of the Bible and biblical narratives in the writings of Caribbean authors have been noted by a number of authors. Whether as a conscious or unconscious undertaking, biblical narratives with their archetypal stories are engraved on Caribbean minds and imaginations. Caribbean literature is laced with biblical/religious names, imagery, allusions, epigraphs, parallelisms etc. No wonder Olive Senior notes that she 'grew up on the bible'[73] and Ramabai Espinet contends that the biblical narratives comprise of such 'a potent source of myth and symbol within the English language' that it is only natural that this is integrated in her writings, deliberately or not.[74]

God-talk and the sacred in Caribbean literature

If it is not surprising that Caribbean writers/poets 'wrestle with the spiritual imperative that pervades their historical perspective,'[75] what then are some of the themes running through Caribbean literature that have theological implications?

A quick glance at some of the works of Caribbean writers does suggest themes and insights of theological significance. For instance, Roger Mais's *Brother Man* (1954) highlights a Rastafarian Christ-Saviour figure, while *The Hills Were Joyful Together* (1953) reveals how Christian beliefs shape the actions and attitudes of several characters. Earl Lovelace's *The Wine of Astonishment* (1982) focuses on a small congregation of Spiritual Baptists and underscores the integral relationship between Caribbean literature and the religious imagination. Jamaica Kincaid's *At The Bottom of the River* (1978) and *A Small Place* (1988), Edwidge Danticat's *Krik? Krak!* (1995) and *The Farming of Bones* (1998), Michelle Cliff's *Abeng* (1984), and *No Telephone to Heaven* (1987) and Olive Senior's *Arrival of Snake Woman and Other Stories* (1989) do more than reclaim the mythic and more importantly, they counter the notion of women as representing sin/evil à la the biblical Garden of Eden and their work represents the potential for female agency, including a deep spirituality. Gérard Etienne's *Crucified in Haiti* (1979), René Depestre's *The Festival of the Greasy Pole* (1974) and Ismith Khan's *The Crucifixion* (1961) are interesting located counter-discourses to the traditional Christian understanding of the Cross and redemption and are laced with multiple meanings. Jan Carew's *The Wild Coast* (1958), Andrew Salkey's *A Quality of Violence* (1958), Samuel Selvon's 'Turning Christian' in *Foreday Morning: Selected Prose 1946-1986* (1989) and the works of Edward Kamau Brathwaithe, Wilson Harris and Derek Walcott all draw from and point to the sacred and offer insights into revising Caribbean God-talk.[76] What follows are two themes and their theological connections, which I will explore.

---

73 Kwame Dawes, *Talk Yuh Talk: Interviews with Anglophone Caribbean Poets* (Charlottesville and London, 2001), p. 85.

74 Ibid., p. 123.

75 Silvio Torres-Saillant, *Caribbean Poetics: Toward An Aesthetic of West Indian Literature* (Cambridge, 1997), p. 88.

76 See Torres-Saillant, *Caribbean Poetics,* where a similar point is made.

Spinning/re-visioning biblical texts and theological notions

The use of the biblical allusions, imagery and narratives in Caribbean literature is significant to a re-reading of biblical narratives. Of interest are the ways these are played with, revised and extended by writers and poets. Wilson Harris's re-visioning of texts and theological notions are especially pertinent to my undertaking. I sense that he, among others, symbolizes best the *midrash* tradition of pushing the boundaries that tend to be so quickly drawn around biblical texts, beyond the proclivity locked in by dogma and exactitudes.

Harris's works refer extensively to the sacred. Throughout *The Guyana Quartet* (1985) the notion of redemption, with much 'spiritual' overtones, is evident. I agree with Hena Maes-Jelinek that there is an evident 'reticence among critics to comment on the religious strain in his fiction'.[77] While Harris's works are free from 'any institutional religious affiliation', it is clear that 'the self-sacrificial outcome of his characters' quest' and their salvific overtones as embodied in Donne and his crew (*Palace of the Peacock*, 1960), Cristo (*The Whole Armour*, 1962), Christ and the virgins (*Jonestown*, 1996), Anselm (*The Four Banks of the River Space*, 1990) and Dreamer (*The Dark Jester*, 2001) all point to the Christian tradition.[78] His imagination, however, moves beyond the Christian tradition to include a dialogue of and interplay with all religions and their gods and goddesses. The motive is intentional: 'subverting humanity's tendency to absolutize its necessarily partial views and of acknowledging that these are rooted in an immanent creative Spirit beyond them.'[79]

The Guyana Quartet is also filled with a number of biblical references including the biblical overtones associated with *The Whole Armour* and *The Secret Ladder* (1963). Harris's use of these passages is very interesting. For instance, the Lukan reference 'through the tender mercy of our God when the day shall dawn upon us from on high'[80] is a reference to Zechariah's prophecy of the role of John the Baptist. The point of comparison, however, is that the child in the womb of the insignificant Beti (*The Whole Armour*) is to be the hope of the future community. The verse taken from the parable of 'the wicked husbandmen'[81] is located in the context of the rejected stone becoming the cornerstone. The rejected and marginalized Oudin becomes the agent of change and hope. Yet, there is a bigger picture if this is read from a postcolonial biblical perspective – the relationship of the husbandmen to colonial history and how this is repeated today. The foregoing are insights that Caribbean hermeneutics can employ in re-reading such texts through postcolonial optics. Then there are the notions of journeying (*Palace of the Peacock*) and covenant (*The Far Journey of Oudin*, 1961) and the inversion of the seven days of creation as employed both in *The Palace of the Peacock* and *The Secret Ladder*. Harris does not strictly

---

77 Hena Maes-Jelinek, 'Introduction: Approaching Wilson Harris's Creativity,' in Hena Maes-Jelinek and Bénédicte Ledent, (eds), *Theatre of the Arts: Wilson Harris and the Caribbean* (Amsterdam and New York, 2002), pp. ix–xxi:.xiv.

78 Ibid., p. xiv.

79 Ibid.

80 Luke 1:78.

81 Luke 20:9.

follow the Judeo-Christian pattern, but revises it to puncture any notion of a fixed and consecrated origin. No wonder an organizing metaphor for Harris is 'infinite rehearsal' with its simultaneous possibilities.

Derek Walcott also has some interesting things to say about the need to re-interpret the Hebrew paradigms that theologians use in their discourse, especially in the articulation of a liberation theology. Reflecting on the narratives related to the Hebrew tribes, their suffering, migration and hope of deliverance from bondage and Caribbean history, Walcott correctly notes that while 'the Old Testament epics of bondage and deliverance provided the slave with a political parallel' there was a contradiction in terms of 'the ethics of Christianity', which 'tempered his vengeance and appeared to deepen his passivity'.[82] The question is: How do we account for 'the zeal with which the slave accepted both the Christian and the Hebraic, resigned his gaze to the death of his pantheon and yet deliberately began to invest a decaying faith with a political belief?'[83] According to Walcott, one should not read this as defeat but 'the willing of spiritual victory, for the captured warrior and the tribal poet had chosen the very battle ground which the captor proposed, the soul'. The God of the dominant was hijacked by the dominated, as the slave immediately grasped the meaning of a humiliated, whipped, crushed body hanging on the cross to their own situation.[84]

With this insight Walcott himself questions and revises the notion of the Divine in the way he uses Genesis to retell the 'origin' or 'discovery' of the Antilles. This is located in 'the lantern of a caravel and that was Genesis'.[85] The consequences as a result of this encounter are evident in the following lines: 'Then there were the packed cries,/the shit, the moaning/ Exodus',[86] which is also a clear reference to the biblical story of Exodus. He also employs the biblical narrative of the Ten Commandments and Ark of the Covenant, 'mantled by the benediction of the shark's shadow',[87] to question the presence of the Divine (theodicy). Interestingly, Walcott's poem 'God Rest Ye Merry Gentlemen' is a very poignant re-working of theological notions using the title of a traditional Christmas Carol. Appropriating the rhetoric of repetition[88], as is evident is such terms as 'Black', 'white', 'broken' as well as description of the streets etc., Walcott offers a different lens or hermeneutic in an oppositional/subversive reading of the traditional carol.

---

82 Derek Walcott, *What the Twilight Says: Essays* (London, 1998), pp. 44-5.

83 Ibid., p. 45.

84 Ibid., pp. 46-7.

85 Walcott, 'The Sea is History' in *Collected Poems 1948-1984* (London and Boston, 1992), p. 364.

86 Walcott, *What the Twilight Says*, p. 364.

87 Ibid.

88 José Luis Martínez-Dueñas Espejo and José María-Fernández, *Approaches to the Poetics of Derek Walcott* (Lewiston, Queenston, Lampeter, 2000), pp. 139-147.

Caribbean suffering and the good God (theodicy)

Western Christian theological discourse has articulated the notion of a good God, Creator of first things and all. The sticking point has been the world of evil especially when most of it has been committed by agents and servants and in the name of the Christian God. In defence of the goodness of God, theories ranging from the freedom of will to the argument that God allows evil to happen to make God's justice and goodness manifest have evolved.[89] Suffering and evil are seen as moral necessity for God knows best. God, of course, works in all creatures but does not participate in their sins as God is above all of that. God's goodness, while impartial, is not necessarily for everyone. There is no place for the pagans of Africa, the Americas, and Asia who continue to pray to unknown gods and 'breathe through the heats of their desire'. The 'chosen ones' (Europe/West) have been divinely commissioned to enter these 'dark' corners of the earth to bring them the true divine light. Such theological positioning of theodicy articulated by western theologians is being countered by the multiplicity of theologies from Black, Asian, Latino/a, Rastafarian, Hispanic, Feminist, Womanist, and postcolonial perspectives.

The problem of suffering, evil and the role of a good God need re-working in Caribbean theology. Caribbean writers have wrestled with and continue to wrestle with the problem of suffering/evil and in their own way call the above notions of theodicy into question. How can one defend a theodicy that on the one hand presents a God who is vulnerable in Christ (nailed to a Cross) and, on the other hand, one that removes God from any contact with evil on the premise that evil and suffering is a moral necessity? That surely falls flat in the face of the Caribbean history of extermination of native Indians and the enslavement of Africans and Indians through slavery and indentureship.

Roger Mais's two novels can serve as good starters for a conversation. *The Hills Were Joyful Together* drawing its title from the Psalms, is set in a Kingston slum and gives us a profound insight into life among very poor people and the attempts to transcend the excruciating cycle of miseries in that context. How do we make sense, Mais is asking us, of the cruel and fatalistic world of Surjue, Rema, Flitters, Shag, Euphemia and BajunMan in the light of the notion of a good God, creator of all? What is the relationship between the notion of fatalism which sees the whole community as victims of blind chance locked into structures and powers outside of their control and the view of a God who loves all, is in control and cares for all? In Mais's perception, Christian theology as articulated in the Caribbean is unable to offer an answer as it (especially the notion of theodicy) seems to be in contradiction to the reality experienced here. Hope, in Mais's view, lies in the community's ability to assume responsibility. Failure to do so spells death no matter what the understanding of theodicy. In wrestling with the question of theodicy, Mais in *Brother Man* turns to a Rastafarian (John Power) who bears much resemblance to the Christ figure. Mais, grappling with the meaning of human lives in such contexts as abject poverty and violence within the Divine plan for the good of all creation, opens up the possibility

---

89 See G.W. Leibniz, *Theodicy: Essays on the Goodness of God, the Freedom of Man and the Origin of Evil* (Chicago, 1998).

for us to take more seriously the tragic nature of human vulnerability (specifically Caribbean) while not losing sight of systemic evil, the need to take moral and collective responsibility to counter it, and at the same time challenging our notions of a transcendent God.

Another Caribbean writer who addresses the question of suffering and evil is Earl Lovelace whose writings recognize the importance of religion and spirituality in Caribbean life. In addressing the problem of theodicy in the contemporary Caribbean, Earl Lovelace allows one of his characters in *While Gods are Falling* (1965) to put the issue this way:

> I look for a God of this world, I look for God to come into Webber Street and down George Street and up Laventille. I look for God, or for the power of God ... to do something about the poverty and oppression and the crime in the world. When I do not see an end to these things, when I see them continuing and getting worse, I ask, where is God? ... Look at the amount of masses that are sung, and the amount of gospels read! But look at this city and ask really ask yourself, if there is anything or anyone like God in it and you must answer no, there is no God here. If he was here, he has left. And I hear it is so all over the world.[90]

His later novel, *The Wine of Astonishment* (1982) traces the survival of a small congregation of Spiritual Baptists but is also about celebrating the ability to transcend oppression. The text actually opens with the narrator Eva trying to get her head around the 'donkey years' of suffering her people had to endure. Hence her question: 'But what sin we commit? What deed our fathers or we do that so vex God that He rain tribulation on us for generations?'[91] It seems to me that Lovelace is exploring human vulnerability from a Caribbean perspective. While his major thrust is to locate redemption through suffering in the context of faith, he is not working with a notion that sees suffering and evil as a moral necessity to make God's goodness manifest. He is questioning what kind of a God would allow this to happen and what to do about it. Lovelace is actually directing our gaze on both the oppressed and the oppressor, on the enemy within and without, on the afflicted persons as well as those who inflict the suffering/pain in a systemic manner.

Related to the notion of theodicy is that of the matter of the *Imago Dei* in the Caribbean person. Merle Collins states the issue quite powerfully. She writes: 'God, they told me then/made me/in his own image and likeness/almost.'[92] A fundamental premise for Caribbean theologizing is that of the image of the Divine in the Caribbean person – male and female. This is important given that the violence meted out on Caribbean peoples is related to the perception of their 'humanness'. For Christian Europe to enslave whole nations and peoples from the remotest corners of the earth, it had to find a way to rationalize that the people(s) were less than human beings and thus lacking of the *Imago Dei*. This is the context in which one needs to understand and locate the very radical claim of the Rastafarians that 'God is [hu]man', that is, their humanizing of God. In re-making God in the image of the Caribbean human,

---

90 Earl Lovelace, *While Gods are Falling* (London, 1965), p. 151.
91 Earl Lovelace, *The Wine of Astonishment* (London, 1982), p. 1.
92 Merle Collins, 'A Journey' in *Rotten Pomerack* (London, 1992).

'the tribe in bondage learned to fortify itself by cunning assimilation of the religion of the Old World. What seemed to be surrender was redemption. What seemed the death of faith was its rebirth.'[93] Moreover, Collins's challenge throws back the question to us Caribbean males about our oppression of women and re-inscribing of the very thing we are critiquing.

A luta continua ...

The foregoing discourse is merely an attempt to give shape to fragments of my thinking on theological themes in Caribbean literature. In this discourse, *conversation* is an operative metaphor for me. It is a conversation to be continued. I perceive the nature of this undertaking as an opportunity 'to *fund*' the imagination by 'voicing of a lot of little pieces out of which [we] can put life together in *fresh configurations.*'[94] I am hopeful of the ripe possibilities of such fresh configurations and re-configurations. Caribbean God-talk needs to be authentic to its calling – to plug into reality and ask the hard and difficult questions. It can learn from Caribbean literature to risk re-thinking, re-visioning and re-imagining in order to open up *spaces* where play, difference, transformation and paradoxes can live together.[95] It is these spaces that authentic God-talk is birthed, lives and breathes – not in our neat, sanitized dogmas and our penchant for quick answers to complex questions driven by an obsession for stricture and certainty.

Bibliography

Arnold, A. James, (ed.), *A History of Literature in the Caribbean: Volume 3 Cross Cultural Studies* (Amsterdam and Philadelphia: John Benjamins Publishing Company, 1997).

Ashcroft B., Griffiths G., Tiffin H., (eds), *The Empire Writes Back: Theory and Practice in Post-Colonial Literatures* (New York: Routledge, 1995).

Austin-Broos, Diane J., 'Pentecostal Community and Jamaican Hierarchy' in John W. Pulis, (ed.), *Religion, Diaspora and Cultural Identity: A Reader in the Anglophone Caribbean* (Netherlands: Gordon and Breach Publishers, 1999):215-45.

Barnet, Miguel, *Afro-Cuban Religions*, trans. Christine Renata Ayorinde (Kingston: Ian Randle Publishers & Princeton: Markus Wiener Publishers, 2001).

Bastide, Roger, *African Civilizations in the New World*, trans. Peter Green (London: C. Hurst and Company, 1971).

Beckford, Robert, *God of the Rahtid: Redeeming Rage* (London: DLT, 2001).

Benítez-Rojo, Antonio, *The Repeating Island*, trans. James Maraniss (Durham NC: Duke University Press, 1992).

---

93 Walcott, *What the Twilight Says,* p. 43.

94 Brueggemann, *Texts Under Negotiation*, pp. 19-20. The latter emphasis is mine.

95 See, Marion Grau, *Of Divine Economy: Refinancing Redemption* (New York and London, 2004).

Boodoo, Gerald, 'The Faith of the People: The *Divina Pastora* Devotions in Trinidad,' in Hemchand Gossai and Nathaniel Samuel Murrell, (eds), *Religion, Culture and Tradition in the Caribbean* (Basingstoke: MacMillan, 2000):65-72.

Bowker, John, *Hallowed Ground: Religions and the Poetry of Place* (London: SPCK, 1993).

Brathwaithe, Edward Kamau, *Barbajan Poems 1492-1992* (Kingston & New York: Savacou North, 1994).

Brown Taylor, Barbara, 'Never-Ending Story' in *Christian Century* 120/5 (March 8, 2003):37.

Brueggemann, Walter, *Hopeful Imagination: Prophetic Voices in Exile* (Philadelphia: Fortress Press, 1986).

Brueggemann, Walter, *The Prophetic Imagination* (Philadelphia: Fortress Press, 1978).

Brueggemann, Walter, *Finally Comes the Poet: Daring Speech for Proclamation* (Minneapolis: Fortress Press, 1989).

Brueggeman, Walter, *Texts Under Negotiation: The Bible and Postmodern Imagination* (Augsburg Fortress: Minneapolis, 1993).

Bultmann, Rudolph, *Jesus Christ and Mythology* (London: SCM, 1960).

Burnett, Paula, *Derek Walcott: Politics and Poetics* (Gainsville, Florida: University of Florida Press, 2000).

Carew, Jan, *The Wild Coast* (London: Secker & Warburg, 1958).

Chevannes, Barry, *Rastafari: Roots and Ideology* (Syracuse: Syracuse University Press, 1998).

Clarke, Austin, *When He was Free and Young and He Used to Wear Silk: Stories* (Toronto: House of Anansi Press, Ltd., 1971).

Clarke, Austin, 'Easter Carol,' in *When He was Free and Young and He Used to Wear Silk: Stories* (Toronto: House of Anansi Press, Ltd., 1971):1-12.

Cliff, Michelle, *Abeng* (New York: Plume-Penguin, 1984).

Cliff, Michelle, *No Telephone to Heaven* (New York: Plume-Penguin, 1987).

Collier, Gordon, '"At the Gate of Cultures" of the New World: Religion, Mythology, and Folk-Belief in West Indian Poetry' in Jamie S. Scott, (ed.), *And the Birds Began to Sing: Religion and Literatures in Post-Colonial Contexts* (Amsterdam: Rodopi, 1996): 227-49.

Collins, Merle, *Rotten Pomerack* (London: Virago, 1992).

Collins, Merle, 'A Journey' in *Rotten Pomerack* (London: Virago, 1992).

Coombs, O., (ed.), *Is Massa Day Dead?* (New York: Anchor Press, Doubleday, 1974).

Cox, Harvey, *The Feast of Fools: A Theological Essay on Festivity and Fantasy* (Cambridge, Massachusetts: Harvard University Press, 1969).

Danticat, Edwidge, *Krik? Krak!* (New York: Soho, 1995).

Danticat, Edwidge, *The Farming of Bones* (New York: Soho, 1998).

Dawes, Kwame, *Talk Yuh Talk: Interviews with Anglophone Caribbean Poets* (Charlottesville and London: University Press of Virginia, 2001).

Depestre, René, *The Festival of the Greasy Pole*, trans. Claudia Harry. (Montreal, Editions du Marais, 2006).

Desmangles, Leslie, *The Faces of the Gods: Vodou and Roman Catholicism in Haiti* (Chapel Hill: University of North Carolina Press, 1992).

Dru, Alexander, (ed. and trans.), *The Journal of Kierkegaard* (London: Collins Fontana Books, 1958).

Dube, Musa, *Postcolonial Feminist Interpretation of the Bible* (St. Louis, Missouri: Chalice Press, 2000).

Dube, Musa and Jeffrey Staley, *John and Postcolonialism: Travel, Space and Power* (London: Sheffield Academic Press, 2002).

Erskine, Noel, *Decolonizing Theology: A Caribbean Perspective* (Maryknoll New York: Orbis Books, 1981).

Etienne, Gérard, *Crucified in Haiti*, trans. Carrol F. Coates, (Charlottesville, University Press of Virginia, 1990).

Fernández Olmos, Margarite and Lizabeth Paravisini-Gebert, *Sacred Possessions: Vodou, Santeria, Obeah, and the Caribbean* (New Brunswick: Rutgers University Press, 1997).

Fernández Olmos, Margarite and Lizabeth Paravisini-Gebert, *Healing Cultures: Art and Religion as Curative Practices in the Caribbean and Its Diaspora* (New York: Palgrave-St. Martin's Press, 2001).

Fernández Olmos, Margarite and Lizabeth Paravisini-Gebert, *Creole Religions of the Caribbean: An Introduction from Vodou and Santeria to Obeah and Espiritismo* (New York: New York University Press, 2003).

Gilkes Michael, (ed.), *The Literate Imagination: Essays on the Novels of Wilson Harris* (London: Macmillan, 1989).

Gossai Hemchand and Nathaniel Samuel Murrell, (eds), *Religion, Culture and Tradition in the Caribbean* (Basingstoke, London: MacMillan, 2000).

Grau, Marion, *Of Divine Economy: Refinancing Redemption* (New York, London: T&T Clark International, A Continuum Imprint, 2004).

Hamid, Idris, *In Search of New Perspectives* (Trinidad: CCC, 1972).

Hamid, Idris, *Troubling of the Waters* (Trinidad: Rahaman Printery Ltd., 1973).

Harris, Wilson, *Palace of the Peacock* (London: Faber & Faber, 1960).

Harris, Wilson, *The Far Journey of Oudin* (London: Faber & Faber, 1961).

Harris, Wilson, *The Whole Armour* (London: Faber & Faber, 1962).

Harris, Wilson, *The Secret Ladder* (London: Faber & Faber, 1963).

Harris, Wilson, 'A Talk on the Subjective Imagination,' in Hena Maes-Jelinek, (ed.), *Explorations: A Selection of Talks and Articles* (Aarhus: Dangaroo Press, 1981): 57-67.

Harris, Wilson, *The Womb of Space: The Cross-Cultural Imagination* (Westport, Connecticut: Greenwood Press, 1983).

Harris, Wilson, *The Guyana Quartet* (London: Faber & Faber, 1985).

Harris, Wilson, 'Literacy and the Imagination', in Michael Gilkes, (ed.), *The Literate Imagination: Essays on the Novels of Wilson Harris* (London: Macmillan, 1989).

Harris, Wilson, *The Four Banks of the River Space* (London: Faber & Faber, 1990).

Harris, Wilson, *Jonestown* (London: Faber & Faber, 1996).

Harris, Wilson, *The Dark Jester* (London: Faber & Faber, 2001).

Henry, Frances, *Reclaiming African Religions in Trinidad: The Socio-Political Legitimation of the Orisha and Spiritual Baptist Faiths* (Mona, Jamaica: University of the West Indies Press, 2003).

Jagessar, Michael, *Life in All Its Fullness* (Zoetermeer: Boekencentrum, 1997).

Jagessar, Michael, 'Wilson Harris, the Imagination and the "Infinite Rehearsal": A Theological Perspective' in Hena Maes-Jelinek, (ed.), *Wilson Harris: The Uncompromising Imagination* (Australia: Dangaroo Press, 1991): 221-229.

James, Leslie R. 'Text and the Rhetoric of Change: Bible and Decolonization in Post-World War II Caribbean Political Discourse,' in Hemchand Gossai and Nathaniel Samuel Murrell, (eds), *Religion, Culture and Tradition in the Caribbean* (Basingstoke, London: MacMillan, 2000).

Kaufman, Gordon, *Theology for a Nuclear Age* (Manchester: Manchester University Press, 1985).

Khan, Aisha, *Callaloo Nation: Metaphors of Race and Religious Identity Among South Asians in Trinidad* (Durham NC: Duke University Press: 2004).

Khan, Ismith, *The Crucifixion* (London: MacGibbon & Kee, 1961).

Kincaid, Jamaica, *At the Bottom of the River* (New York: Vintage, 1978).

Kincaid, Jamaica, *A Small Place* (New York: Farrar, Straus, Giroux, 1988).

Korom, Frank J., *Hosay Trinidad: Muharram Performances in an Indo-Caribbean Diaspora* (Philadelphia: University of Pennsylvania Press, 2003).

Leibniz, G. W., *Theodicy: Essays on the Goodness of God, the Freedom of Man and the Origin of Evil* (Chicago: Open Court, 1998).

Lovelace, Earl, *While Gods are Falling* (London: Collins, 1965).

Lovelace, Earl, *The Wine of Astonishment* (London: Heinemann Educational Books, 1982).

Maes-Jelinek, Hena, (ed.), *Explorations* (Aarhus: Dangaroo Press, 1981).

Maes-Jelinek, Hena, (ed.), *Wilson Harris: The Uncompromising Imagination* (Australia, 1991).

Maes-Jelinek, Hena, 'Introduction: Approaching Wilson Harris's Creativity,' in Hena Maes-Jelinek and Bénédicte Ledent, (eds), *Theatre of the Arts: Wilson Harris and the Caribbean* (Amsterdam and New York, NY,: Rodopi, 2002):ix-xxi.

Maes-Jelinek, Hena and Bénédicte Ledent, (eds), *Theatre of the Arts: Wilson Harris and the Caribbean* (Amsterdam and New York, NY: Rodopi, 2002).

Mais, Roger, *Brother Man* (Portsmouth, NH: Heinemann, 1954).

Mais, Roger, *The Hills were Joyful Together* (Portsmouth, NH: Heinemann, 1953).

Mangru, Basdeo, 'Tadjah in British Guiana: Manipulation or Protest?' in Basedo Mangru, *Indenture and Abolition* (Toronto: TSAR Publications, 1993): 43-88.

Mangru, Basdeo, *Indenture and Abolition* (Toronto: TSAR Publications, 1993).

Martínez-Dueñas, Espejo, José Luis and José María-Fernández, *Approaches to the Poetics of Derek Walcott* (Lewiston, Queenston, Lampeter: The Edwin Mellen Press, 2000).

McFague, Sallie, *Metaphorical Theology* (Philadelphia: Fortress Press, 1982).

McFague, Sallie, *Models of God: Theology for an Ecological, Nuclear Age* (Philadelphia: Fortress Press, 1987).

Middleton, Darren J.N.,'Riddim Wise and Scripture Smart: Interview and Interpretation with Ras Benjamin Zephaniah,' in Hemchand Gossai and Nathaniel

Samuel Murrell, (eds), *Religion, Culture, and Tradition in the Caribbean* (Basingstoke, London: MacMillan Press Ltd., 2000): 257-70.

Mulrain, George, *Theology in Folk Culture: The Theological Significance of Haitian Folk Religion* (Frankfurt am Main: Verlag Peter Lang, 1984).

Murrell, Nathaniel Samuel, William Spencer, Adrian McFarlane, (eds), *Chanting Down Babylon: The Rastafari Reader* (Philadelphia: Temple University Press, 1988).

Nettleford, Rex, 'Discourse on Rastafarian Reality,' in Nathaniel Samuel Murrell, William David Spencer, and Adrian Anthony McFarlane, (eds), *Chanting Down Babylon: The Rastafari Reader* (Philadelphia: Temple University Press, 1998): 311-325.

Prince, Althea, 'How Shall We Sing the Lord's Song in a Strange Land? Constructing the Divine in Caribbean Contexts,' in Patrick Taylor, (ed.), *Nation Dance: Religion, Identity, and Cultural Difference in the Caribbean* (Bloomington, Indianapolis: Indiana University Press, 2001):25-31.

Pui-lan, Kwok, *Postcolonial Imagination and Feminist Theology* (London: SCM Press, 2005).

Pulis, John W., (ed.), *Religion, Diaspora and Cultural Identity: A Reader in the Anglophone Caribbean* (Netherlands: Gordon and Breach Publishers, 1999).

Rahim, Jennifer, 'Patterns of Psalmology in Lovelace's *The Wine of Astonishment*', *Caribbean Journal of Religious Studies* 16/2 (1995):3-17.

Rahming, Melvin B., 'Theorizing Spirit: The Critical Challenge of Elizabeth Nunez's *When Rocks Dance* and *Beyond the Limbo Silence*,' *Studies in the Literary Imagination* (Fall, 2004): 1-21.

Ramchand, Kenneth and Sushiela Nasta, (eds), *Foreday Morning: Selected Prose 1946-1986* (Harlow, Essex: Longman, 1989).

Reddie, Anthony G., *Faith, Stories and the Experience of Black Elders: Singing the Lord's Song in a Strange Land* (London: Jessica Kingsley Publishers, 2001).

Ricoeur, Paul, *The Philosophy of Paul Ricoeur*, in C. Reagan and D. Stewart, (eds), (Boston: Beacon Press, 1979).

Rohlehr, Gordon, 'Man's [sic] Spiritual Search in the Caribbean Through Literature,' in Idris Hamid, (ed.), *Troubling of the Waters* (Trinidad: Rahaman Printery Ltd., 1973): 187-204.

Rohlehr, Gordon, *The Shape that Hurts and Other Essays* (Port-of-Spain: Longman Trinidad, 1992).

Said, Edward, *Orientalism: Western Representations of the Orient* (London: Routledge and Kegan Paul, 1978).

Salkey, Andrew, *A Quality of Violence* (London: Hutchinson, 1958).

Sankeralli, Burton, *At the Crossroads: African Caribbean Religion and Christianity* (Trinidad & Tobago: Caribbean Conference of Churches, 1995).

Scott, Jamie S., (ed.), *And the Birds Began to Sing: Religion and Literatures in Post-Colonial Contexts* (Amsterdam: Rodopi, 1996).

Scott, Jamie S., and Paul Simpson-Housley, *Mapping the Sacred: Religion, Geography and Postcolonial Literatures* (Amsterdam: Rodopi, 2001).

Segovia, Fernando, *Interpreting Beyond Borders* (London: Sheffield Academic Press, 2000).

Selvon Samuel, 'Turning Christian' in Kenneth Ramchand and Sushiela Nasta, (eds), *Foreday Morning: Selected Prose 1946-1986* (Harlow, Essex: Longman, 1989): 202-10.

Senior, Olive, *Arrival of Snake Woman and Other Stories* (Harlow, Essex: Longman, 1989.

Song, Choan, S., *Third-Eye Theology: Theology in Formation in Asian Settings* (Guildford and London: Lutterworth Press, 1980).

Song, Choan, S., *Theology from the Womb of Asia* (London: SCM Press Ltd., 1988).

Stewart, Dianne M., *Three Eyes for the Journey: African Dimensions of the Jamaican Religious Experience* (New York: Oxford University Press, 2005).

Sugirtharajah, R.S., (ed.), *The Postcolonial Bible* (London: Sheffield Academic Press, 1998).

Sugirtharajah, R.S., *Postcolonial Criticism and Biblical Interpretation* (Oxford: OUP, 2002).

Sugirtharajah, R.S., *Postcolonial Reconfigurations: An Alternative Way of Reading the Bible and Doing Theology* (London: SCM Press, 2003).

Taylor, Patrick, *The Narrative of Liberation: Perspectives on Afro-Caribbean Literature, Popular Culture, and Politics* (Ithaca: Cornell University Press 1999).

Taylor, Patrick, (ed.), *Nation Dance: Religion, Identity, and Cultural Difference in the Caribbean* (Bloomington, Indianapolis: Indiana University Press, 2001).

Torres-Saillant, Silvio, 'The Cross-Cultural Unity of Caribbean Literature' in A. James Arnold (ed.), *A History of Literature in the Caribbean: Volume 3 Cross Cultural Studies* (Amsterdam and Philadelphia: John Benjamins Publishing Company, 1997): 57-78.

Torres-Saillant, Silvio *Caribbean Poetics: Toward An Aesthetic of West Indian Literature* (Cambridge: Cambridge University Press, 1997).

van Herk, Aritha, *A Frozen Tongue* (Sydney: Dangaroo Press, 1992).

Walcott, Derek, *Collected Poems 1948-1984* (London and Boston: Faber & Faber, 1992).

Walcott, Derek, 'The Sea is History' in Derek Walcott, *Collected Poems 1948-1984* (London and Boston: Faber & Faber, 1992).

Walcott, Derek, *What the Twilight Says: Essays* (London: Faber & Faber, 1998).

Williams, Lewin, *Caribbean Theology* (New York: Peter Lang Publishing Inc., 1994).

Chapter 3

Dramatic Improvisation:
A Jazz Inspired Approach to Undertaking
Theology with the Marginalized

Anthony G. Reddie

My introduction to jazz music did not come through the traditional route of being exposed to African American culture – that was to come later. No, one of the seminal moments in my life emerged when raking through my father's old record collection. My parents are from the Caribbean island of Jamaica and came to Britain in the 1950s, returning to Jamaica in 1991, where they presently reside. What first sparked my interest in the wonder that is jazz music was listening to a record by the premier instrumental group in Jamaica during the 1960s, The Skatalites. The Skatalites perfected a style of music that was a fusion of North American Jazz and Caribbean Calypso. My odyssey into the magical world that is jazz came via The Skatalites and their rendition of *Eastern Standard Time*.[1]

This central thesis of this essay is that by aligning jazz aesthetics, which include the thematic practice and trope of improvisation, alongside the notion of the embodied creativity of Christian inspired drama, one can conceive of a framework in which ordinary marginalized and oppressed Black people can be enlivened and empowered so as to challenge White hegemony. This essay seeks to highlight the juxtaposition of Christian inspired drama and jazz music as a means of highlighting the dramatic and improvisatory impulse of Black people within a religio-cultural framework.

In the first section of this essay, I want to provide some historic background on the development of drama as a medium for communicating ideas of God and the values and the underlying message of the Christian faith. I want to argue that one of the ways in which we can help marginalized and oppressed peoples, those who often do not have a voice in our post-modern globalized world, is by means of their active participation in the process of theological reflection. By means of Christian drama, marginalized and oppressed peoples can be enabled to take an active and committed role in the development of new ways of thinking about and acting in solidarity with God, as revealed in the life, death and resurrection of Jesus, by the power of the Holy

---

1 Don Drummond and The Skatalites, 'Eastern Standard Time', *Foundations of Ska*, Disc One, (Heartbeat, 1997).

Spirit.[2] So what is Christian drama and how can Christian drama be influenced by the spirit of improvisation which resides within the practice of jazz music?

The development of my own writing

As a frustrated non-musician, I have approached the task of writing drama (which incorporates many of the central themes to be found within Black and liberation theologies) in order to empower marginalized and oppressed peoples, by way of jazz music. In effect, I have sought to write drama as if I were a jazz musician. I have tried to capture the rhythms and cadences of jazz by means of creatively putting words and dialogues together on the page. In *Acting in Solidarity* I have created many dramatic pieces that invite marginalized and oppressed peoples to improvise and play with reality in order that they might be inspired by the Spirit of God to imagine a new future – a future that exists beyond the constricted and limited world in which they presently live.

Acting In Solidarity represents the edited collected works of this process of theological exploration by means of drama over a period of several years. This book is not a detailed analysis of the utility of drama as a means of theological exploration.[3] Rather, this is a collection of work that seeks to address a range of concerns within Christian life and experience through a dramatic format. The framework of this text and the concept that accompanies it is one that seeks to use drama as a means of enabling ordinary people to reflect critically on the Christian faith, and to be active agents within that dramatic and dialectical process of truth searching and truth telling. This work has been developed in order to provide ordinary people outside of the academy with an agency (so often denied them within the conventional bounds of orthodox or traditional theological reflection) that can assist in the development and the building of theology from the 'bottom-up'.[4]

My intention in this essay is to outline an approach to the doing of theology (in terms of articulation and pedagogy) by means of drama and dialogue, with a view to developing a more accessible method for engaging in God-talk that is reflective of the experiences especially of, but not limited to, those of Black people and their accompanying expressions of faith. This essay builds on *Acting in Solidarity* in which drama was used as a means of undertaking theological reflection. However, it takes that work one stage further and begins to supplement that initial thinking with my theorizing of jazz aesthetics as a means of creating a more dialogical and improvisatory framework for undertaking theological reflection with often marginalized and oppressed peoples in Britain.

I began writing drama whilst at the University of Birmingham where I did a degree in History, specializing in Church history. As I was beginning to develop

---

2   An extended account of the ideas presented in this chapter can be found in Anthony G. Reddie, *Acting In Solidarity: Reflections in Critical Christianity* (London, 2005).

3   That detailed work is contained in the 'sequel' to this book. See Anthony G. Reddie, *Dramatizing Theologies: A Participative Approach to Black God-Talk* (London, 2006).

4   The notion of building theology from the bottom up is a theme that is addressed in *Dramatizing Theologies*, pp.128-61.

my writing skills, I was very much influenced by the work of Paul Burbridge and Murray Watts. Burbridge and Watts's highly influential texts on Christian drama spurred me and many of my peers into our first youthful forays into creative dramatic writing. *Time To Act*,[5] *Lightning Sketches*,[6] and *Red Letter Days*[7] became required reading for myself and my writing and performing peers within Birmingham University Meth.Soc.[8] Aside from offering a wealth of scripted material for public performances, Burbridge and Watts's books provided a much needed justification for such apparent reckless nonsense that was seen to be done in the name of Christ and Christian expression. Coming from a conservative Methodist evangelical background, I had imbibed a great deal of the implicit suspicion towards the dubious enterprise of 'play acting'. I had been socialized within a non-conformist tradition of dutiful piety which ensured that only those expressions of human activity which were perceived as being unequivocally efficacious and praiseworthy were given any kind of legitimacy. Burbridge and Watts provided a robust and stout defence for Christian drama:

> A lot of people who have been brought up in a strict church tradition regard drama as wrong. You notice that we say "Christian tradition" for the simple reason that we not believe that genuine Christian tradition, least of all the Bible, condemns the performance of plays or sketches. But nonetheless church traditions of various kinds have opposed the theatre (justifiably in many cases, bearing in mind the corruption in theatres and acting troupes since time immemorial). This, however, is a separate issue. The nature of drama cannot be blamed for the abuses of actors, just as commerce cannot be held responsible for corrupt practices in the business world.[9]

These authors gave me and my peers much needed justification to transcend the restrictive church backgrounds from which we had emerged. If drama was not in itself inherently bad, then was there a positive rationale for engaging in this form of creative enterprise, save for the youthful desire to 'show off' in front of our peers? Burbridge and Watts continue their case by stating: 'Drama is a gift from God to help us explore the world, enjoy it, to be moved by suffering, to laugh at the funny side of life, to provoke ourselves and others to thought.'[10] Drama, as the authors remind us, has been an important element within the Christian tradition in Britain since the early medieval period:[11]

---

5   Paul Burbridge and Murray Watts, *Time To Act* (London, 1979).

6   Paul Burbridge and Murray Watts, *Lightning Sketches* (London, 1981).

7   Paul Burbridge and Murray Watts, *Red Letter Days* (London, 1986).

8   For the majority of my time whilst a member of Birmingham University Methodist Society (Meth.Soc.), I was a part of a Christian drama group called *Rise 'n' Shine*. *Rise 'n' Shine* existed from 1987 to 1991 and performed at the annual Greenbelt Christian Arts Festival for a number of years, winning a prize in the Fringe in 1991. The core members of the group were Charles (Chas) Bayfield, Rupert Kaye and Anthony G. Reddie.

9   Burbridge and Watts, *Time to Act,* p.112.

10   Ibid.

11   Ibid.

The earliest English drama derives from the Latin mass of the middle ages. The simple refrains of the liturgy were elaborated first into dramatic dialogues between the officiating priests and then into playlets on the events in the life of Christ. Latin soon gave way to the vernacular and the result of this development was the many different cycles of Mystery Plays, some of which have been revived and are regularly performed today.

Jazz music as a heuristic for a process of improvised critical Christian reflection

I want to outline a practical approach to Christian ministry which, drawing on the aesthetics of jazz music, attempts to put into practice some of the theoretical conceptions of 'acting in solidarity – a process of improvised critical Christian reflection'. I realize that this method for reflecting and doing theology assumes a level of dramatic expertise and an accompanying level of confidence on behalf of the theologian or educator. In order to amplify the utility and accessibility of this approach to doing theology with, and uncovering the theological voice of those who are often made voiceless, I want to use jazz music as a framework in which to house some of my reflections.

By using jazz music as a model for 'acting in solidarity – a process of improvised critical Christian reflection' I hope to 'bring to life' many of the salient features of this emerging theory for articulating and undertaking theology with marginalized and oppressed peoples. Jazz music, particularly when allied to the practice of ministry, especially those elements that fall within the wider purview of practical theology, can become a helpful illustration for demonstrating the dramatic possibilities of such disciplines as preaching, Bible study or Christian education, for example.

I have termed this approach a 'jazz hermeneutic' for ministry. I believe this approach to thinking about and discussing God in the context of jazz ideals and practice can enliven some of the worst moribund conceptions of Christian praxis in the early twenty-first century.

And all that jazz!

So before I begin on the odyssey of imaginative leaps and post-modern game playing, I must say something about my notion of a jazz hermeneutic. One of my extra-curricular activities is listening to jazz. My favourite musician is the great John Coltrane. Coltrane was born in the small town of Hamlet in North Carolina in 1926 and was the master of the tenor and soprano saxophone. His seminal album, entitled *A Love Supreme*[12], recorded in 1964, is cited along with Miles Davis' *Kind of Blue*[13] as being one of the most influential jazz LPs of all time. Coltrane's journey from jobbing pro to almost literal God-like status (there is a church in San Francisco

---

12   John Coltrane, *A Love Supreme* [Deluxe edition)] (Impulse Records, 2002).
13   Miles Davis, *Kind of Blue* (Columbia, 1959).

named after John Coltrane, which plays his music as a part of their liturgy and have styled him a latter day Saint)[14] began with a mystical experience in the early 1960s.

Prior to his spiritual awakening, Coltrane's biography reads like the stereotypical tortured genius of a particularly bad black and white 1940s' Hollywood film noir. In jazz history there is a distinctly sad litany of depressed broken people whose mock tragic lives stain the collective memory of this inventive and creative art form. These are predominantly African American men and women who were geniuses on the stage and pathetic wrecks off it. People who could create sublime art in the moment, in the time it takes to blink, and yet were often deemed subhuman creatures the moment they stopped playing or singing.[15]

In an attempt to traverse the huge chasm between the incandescently sublime and the absurdly and sinfully ridiculous, many of these luminaries turned to drugs and other forms of stimulants to help them make sense of the painful contradictions of being human. Billie Holiday, Charlie Parker, Art Tatum, Lester Young, Ma Rainey and my personal hero, John Coltrane, all succumbed to the pernicious threat stalking them, namely humiliation and absurd nothingness – the plight of being Black people in a world of pernicious racism.

But Coltrane was different. In the early 1960s, Coltrane underwent a period of distinct personal change. He described this as a spiritual awakening. He emerged from this period of change a profoundly different man. He renounced drugs and alcohol and dedicated his music to discovering the spiritual realm that flourishes within human experience and is evident across the whole cosmos.

Coltrane, like all the great jazz musicians, is able to straddle that delicate balance between that which is given and the newness of each performance or individual encounter with the tradition, which in turn, yields new insights and knowledge. In metaphorical terms, this delicate process of living with the tensions of creating 'the new' from the 'already established' has been likened to the art of standing on a high-backed chair and pushing that object onto two legs and seeing how far one can push and retain balance before you lose control and fall onto the floor.

Jazz musicians are constantly re-working an established melody in order to create something new and spontaneous for that split moment in time in mid- performance. Duke Ellington once remarked that there has never existed a jazz musician who did not have some inclination of what he or she was going to play before they walked onto the stage.[16] One's improvisation is never totally created or made up on the spot. One does not create new art in a vacuum. All jazz improvisation is a negotiation between what has been conceived previously and what emerges in that specific moment, either on stage or in the recording studio.

Jazz music is a potentially rich paradigm for all people involved in the task of doing, reflecting upon and writing theology. I make this claim with one principal thought in mind, namely, that jazz music represents both the best and worst in human

---

14 See www.saintjohncoltrane.org

15 See Geoffrey C. Ward and Ken Burns, *Jazz: A History of America's Music* (London, 2001).

16 Ward and Burns, *Jazz*, pp.290-91

nature. It straddles the contradictions between a group of intensely fierce individuals who come together to join forces to make music.

Jazz music is a voluntary engagement, for jazz is a form that eschews rigid conventions or categorizations. It insists on mutuality and community, and yet it has, since the early 1920s, been built around the searing geniuses and contradictions of brilliant soloists. It is free form and yet demands certain rules and conventions, working alongside and with others, those with whom one might not possess any sense of empathy or love, save for the act of making music in that split moment of time.

Jazz represents the tension between time and eternity; between immanence and transcendence; between the sense that art is created within and through context, and yet it appears to carry within it the traces of inspiration and magic that comes from another space and time. When theologians investigate the contradictions of individuality and community, between being bound by conventions and yet being compelled to go beyond all that is known and accepted as given, one is dealing with the most fundamental of existential concerns. The questions jazz poses are concerns for Christian faith and for all humanity. What does it mean to improvise on a given melody? How far can one go before what you are creating is no longer faithful to the melody and sources that inspired the artist in the first instance? How inclusive can we be? Can anyone join, or do we have or need certain limits or boundaries to help define who or what the band or the community is meant to be and become?

Using jazz as a metaphor for doing theology with the marginalized is to be engaged in the serious task of creating a framework in which all people are enabled to become participants in a process of critical thinking, reflection and then action. What I like about jazz music is the sense, that at its best, everyone gets their chance to shine. In extensive improvisation, everyone gets their moment in the sun – even the drummer! Drummers, especially thinking of Ringo Starr, for example, often get a bad press. And yet in jazz, not only are drummers the bedrock of the rhythm section, but in the case of the late great Art Blakey and before him Chic Web, drummers have even been known to become band leaders.

Jazz music at its best gives everyone their turn. In linking the aesthetics of jazz music to the practical discipline of Christian drama, in which participants are enabled to improvise upon a written text and then explore it for new meanings and theological connections, I have attempted to create a model of theological exploration in which all persons are active participants. It is a process of acting in solidarity – a process of critical Christian reflection.

Jesus was a jazz musician

In *Nobodies to Somebodies*[17] I devised some reflections based upon Jesus' encounter with the woman who had the issue of blood, as recorded in Luke, Chapter 8. I want to draw upon this passage again, but locate my reflections within the context of a

---

17 Anthony G. Reddie, *Nobodies to Somebodies: A Practical Theology for Education and Liberation* (Peterborough, 2003).

jazz hermeneutic. I want to concentrate my thoughts on the actions of Jesus in this narrative. Identifying Jesus as a jazz musician will help us to look at this familiar story with new eyes.

I believe that Jesus shows us how to improvise within the context of his ministry. The numerous encounters Jesus has with others as they are detailed in the Gospels (I have always found Luke's accounts of particular help in this regard) are reminders of the power of improvisation. It is the power of responding to circumstances in such a way that the 'giveness' of the context is radically re-altered and something startling and new emerges. Whether it is Jesus' encounter with the Canaanite women (Matthew 15: 21-28) or the rich young man (Mark 10: 17-22), the engagement with others inspires Jesus to bring about new insights and learning. This engagement is one that straddles the tension between that which exists (the tradition of Judaism) and that which is becoming (the reinterpretation of that tradition).

Just as the jazz musician must engage with the context in which he or she is located, so too must the Christian theologian. Whilst John Coltrane might play one of his celebrated compositions, such as *Chasin' the Trane*[18] hundreds of times in any one year, every individual performance of that piece would be unique. The context in which it might be performed, even if within the same club for an audience that might have heard this composition before, perhaps only some few hours previously, still remains unique. No two performances are ever the same, because people and how they respond to the time and space in which they are housed at that precise moment in time are never the same. The motivation, the concerns and themes that exist outside of that time and space from which they have emerged, are never identical.

Just as Jesus' sometimes obscure use of parables and stories was an invitation to his first listeners to become active participants in a process of critical thinking and renewed action, for the sake of Kingdom, so too are the dramatic sketches at the heart of this approach to theological reflection. Using a jazz framework for doing theology in groups who are often marginalized and oppressed, demands that all participants are willing to enter into the 'internal logic' of the dramatic sketch. By internal logic, I am referring to a process in which the participant takes seriously the perspective of the character they are playing, and imbues the role with a sense of seriousness. This mode of behaviour is not unlike that demanded of participants in Thomas Groome's[19] or Jerome Berryman's[20] respective approaches to practical theology. In using the term practical theology, I am referring to a mode of theological exploration that is concerned with exploring the intersections between the theory and practice of theological reflection. In Groome's and Berryman's respective schemas for undertaking theological reflection within the context of educational ministries, the authors approach the task of 'doing theology' by means of engaging with ordinary

---

18 John Coltrane, 'Chasin' the Trane', *Live At The Village Vanguard: The Master Takes* (GRP Records, 1961).

19 See Thomas H. Groome, *Sharing Faith: A Comprehensive Approach to Religious Education and Pastoral Ministries* (San Francisco, 1991) and *Christian Religious Education: Sharing Our Story and Vision* (San Francisco, 1999).

20 Jerome W. Berryman, *Godly Play: An Imaginative Approach to Religious Education* (Minneapolis, 1995).

people. In the context of Groome's work, he outlines an approach he describes as 'Shared Praxis', in which communities of faith are enabled to reflect critically on their collective and individual agency within a specific context, with a view to re-making and re-framing the essential meaning of the Gospel for their specific time and space. Berryman's work differs slightly in emphasis, in that he is concerned with enabling predominantly young children to find ways of experiencing and expressing the numinous within the context of a community of faith and contemporary ecclesial practice. My notion of 'acting in solidarity – a process of critical Christian reflection' operates on the similar logic of both of these respective approaches to practical theology. The similarities lie in the use of participation and contextual engagement as the means by which one begins to interrogate the relationship between the theory and practice of religious observance. In the context of this dramatic enactment of theological reflection, the 'internal logic' of the drama is the sense that the world as defined by sketch, no matter how improbably or absurd, is in some sense real and to be taken seriously. This is a sense of asking participants to suspend their critical, realist judgements, in order to enter into the internal logic and dynamic of a piece of drama.

Jazz music requires that all the players engage with one another and in some sense trust each other during the improvisation process. Jazz cannot work without there being a sense of trust and mutuality in the process of improvisation. In this respect, perhaps the greatest responsibility of all leaders/facilitators who want to use this particular approach and method to doing theology with the marginalized is the need to provide an environment in which participants can be enabled to ask critical questions of Christianity and some of the underlying theology that underpins many of the accepted norms of the faith.

Whilst I am not pretending to be neutral in terms of my own personal interpretation of the faith and the resulting practice of the Church, my interest in creating this work is not to impose my particular perspectives on others. Rather, my intention in writing and creating this work is to challenge people to reflect critically on the Christian faith and the working out of that within their lives.

Creating 'a jazz hermeneutic' for empowering the voiceless

In order to highlight the connections between a 'jazz music hermeneutic' for theology and ministry and the overarching concept of 'acting in solidarity - a process of critical Christian reflection', I want to use the practical discipline of preaching as a means of showing how using jazz music can reshape aspects of traditional Christian practice in order to empower those who are marginalized and oppressed. In particular, I want to draw upon many of the traditions inherent within Black preaching styles as a means of demonstrating, that at its best, many of the historic traditions found in Diasporan African patterns of worship and preaching exemplify a number of the salient features of jazz improvisation inherent within jazz music.

The art, discipline and practice of preaching in light of the Black experience in Black majority church settings has always carried with it a distinct ideological and theological stance. The subjugated selfhood of Black people, distorted and abused by the ravages of racism and White hegemony, have responded to and taken their cue from the preacher, for a positive vision of what it means to be a Black human being.[21] Grant Shockley has outlined the educational role played by the pastor in many Black churches, whether in an explicit dialogical form in the sermon, or more implicitly, in the realms of pastoral care.[22] This context, the worship and the role of the preacher within this milieu represents a prime exemplar for incarnating many of the salient features of 'acting in solidarity – a process of critical Christian reflection'.

In order to highlight the connections between a 'jazz music hermeneutic' of theology and ministry and the overarching concept of 'acting in solidarity – a process of critical Christian reflection' I want to juxtapose these two themes through the filter of Christian drama.

Re-interpreting Black worship in light of a 'jazz hermeneutic'.

This dialectical relationship between the text and the performer finds echoes in the world of biblical interpretation.[23] The similarities, however, extend way beyond biblical studies. This dialectical exchange is also reflective of the relationship between the jazz musician and the inherited melody, and the preacher in his or her relationship with the Biblical text and Christian tradition in the sermon. Within the context of worship, the preacher is negotiating with the text and the congregation. The ongoing dynamic that is worship within many Black majority churches, is to my mind, reminiscent of many of the features evident in a dramatic sketch.

Remaking the moment every time

Just as the jazz musician has to respond to the unique context of every performance, bringing new knowledge to life in a split second, so too must the preacher. The preacher has to respond to the promptings of the spirit and the expectations and needs of the congregation. The preacher cannot rely upon what was said the previous week or in a past service – the past in this respect is a foreign country to which there is no return. Even replaying the old sermon, repeating the existing words of the text, is never the same, even second time around. The uniqueness of each occasion demands the freshness of approach and ingenuity of the occasion. The new performance remains connected to past versions of the melody. Whilst the two performances are similar, they are never the same. Similarly, with the preacher, past

21 Andrew White, 'The Role of the Black Church in the Liberation Struggle' *Spectrum* (No.47, Jul/Aug 1971), pp.10-12.

22 Grant S. Shockley, 'Black Pastoral Leadership in Religious Education' in Robert L. Browning, (ed.), *The Pastor as Religious Educator* (Birmingham, Ala., 1987), pp.179-206.

23 See Justin S. Ukpong, Musa W. Dube, and Gerald O. West, et.al., *Reading the Bible in the Global Village: Global Perspectives on Biblical Scholarship* (Atlanta, 2002). See also Gerald O. West, 'Contextual Bible Study in South Africa: A Resource for Reclaiming and Regaining Land, Dignity and Identity' in McGlory T. Speckman and Larry T. Kaufmann, (eds), *Towards an Agenda for Contextual Theology: Essays in Honour of Albert Nolan* (Pietermaritzburg, South Africa: 2001), pp.169-84.

dramatic performances of the sermon in worship may influence the present, but each new enacted sermon is unique in its own right.

The performative integrity of the preacher in bringing new knowledge to life within the context of worship is reflected in the ongoing dynamic of action and reflection in the dramatic performance of the sketch. In writing the dramatic sketches in *Acting in Solidarity* I attempted to enable ordinary marginalized lay people, using the spirit of jazz improvisation to play around with my dramatic sketches in order to re-imagine a new way of understanding and living out the Christian faith. What emerged from the various performances were a number of reflections, which highlighted the differing perspectives and perceptions of the various participants. Each new performance gave rise to new insights and knowledge and as Romney Moseley argues, critical reflection is aided by a process of repeated performance and the ongoing analysis of reality and subjective selfhood. [24]

Just as the participant in the drama constantly re-engages and re-negotiates with the text, this is equally the case with the preacher and the jazz musician. The improvisation of the jazz musician is built around the process of engaging with the inherited melody and then having the confidence to go beyond that fixed nature of the text. The improvisation is the link between the fixity of the text and the openness of the context.

The improvisation of the preacher exists in the interchange between fixity of the text (scripture) and the fluidity of the context (the congregation and the overall worship service). The best preachers are able to apply the text to the context and use the former to give new life and fresh insight to the latter. In effect, the best preachers are constantly in the business of exemplifying many of the salient features of a dramatic theology.

In the many performances I have witnessed of the sketches in *Acting in Solidarity* it has been interesting to observe the ways in which the various participants are enabled by means of repeated performance to go beyond the limits of the text. Whilst the improvisatory process often lacks the sheer verve and loose-limbed creativity often found in jazz or in preaching, there is, nonetheless, a genuine development of new ideas and thinking, which takes the participant beyond the conventional limits of the drama.

The dramatic possibilities in Black preaching and the wider context of worship offer comparative points of analysis with jazz music (a 'jazz hermeneutic') and the wider framework of 'acting in solidarity – a process of critical Christian reflection.' The role of the preacher in Black worship is that of the dramatic focus for the performative qualities of all the accompanying players. Black preachers represent the dramatic focus for the dramatic potential of all the participants in the worshipping congregation.

In 'acting in solidarity – a process of critical Christian reflection', the process of theological reflection is facilitated by a collaborative process of interaction and engagement, within a participative 'call and response' dynamic between the various

---

24 Romney Moseley, *Becoming A Self Before God: Critical Transformations* (Nashville, Tenn, 1991), pp.88-100.

players in the drama. In jazz, this interaction takes place between the musicians and the audience; in Black worship it exists between the preacher and the congregation.

In both contexts, the dramatic possibilities echo many of the salient features I have described in my concept of 'acting in solidarity – a process of critical Christian reflection'. In terms of this overarching framework of both the articulation and the doing of theology, the active involvement of marginalized and oppressed peoples is not only necessary – it is indeed normative to the whole process. And yet, in the midst of this nascent theory, I hope, by making recourse to the accompanying framework of jazz, to demonstrate that aspects of this approach to liberative, Black theological reflection has always been in evidence within Black religio-cultural contexts.

Improvisation as a helpful middle-way

The beauty of improvisation, as I have hopefully demonstrated, is the facility it possesses to get us beyond the traditional and, dare one say, the sterility of perennial arguments around evangelical and liberal approaches to Christian theology. Improvisation within jazz music is neither stuck with the seeming rigidity of the past, represented by tradition, or with the perceived relativism of late and post modernity. At the heart of the debates surrounding evangelical and liberal approaches to the interpretation of Christianity, lay the often thorny problem of Biblical authority. Yet, as Vincent Wimbush has illustrated, until quite recently, Black people have not been consumed by such arguments surrounding the literal or more allegorical interpretations of the Bible.[25]

Prior to the 1940s and 50s, Black peoples' engagement with the Bible was not characterized by, the sometimes, arcane arguments around doctrine and metaphysical postulations. Rather, the critical question was, what was going to alleviate our suffering and how did the Bible attest to God's solidarity with poor Black people in the past, in order that the future could be redeemed?[26] This point is amplified by Wimbush when he writes:

> African Americans interpreted the Bible in light of their experiences … As the people of God in the Hebrew Bible were once delivered from enslavement, so in the future, the Africans sang and shouted, would they. As Jesus suffered unjustly but was raised from the dead to new life, so they sang, would they be 'raised' from their 'social death' to new life. So went the songs, sermons and testimonies.[27]

The creative improvisation of Coltrane can be seen in the dramatic iconoclastic work of James Cone, the founding father of Black theology. James Cone argues that the central motif within the meta-narrative of the Bible is that of God's revelation in human history, exemplified in Christ, in order to liberate from oppression all those

---

25 Vincent L. Wimbush, *The Bible and African Americans: A Brief History* (Minneapolis, 2003), pp.63-70.
26 Ibid., pp.19-46.
27 Ibid., p.24.

who have been *denied a voice*.[28] Many marginalized and oppressed peoples have read and interpreted the Bible in light of their own context and experience. They have done so in order to locate the overarching truth of God's revelation in history. This process has involved them looking within and behind the text in order to locate themes that attest to the reality of their existential condition. Writing with reference to the Exodus motif within the Bible, which remains an emblematic theme for Black people in South Africa during the epoch of Apartheid, Robert Beckford writes

> For Blacks it was paradigm (Exodus) of how God was going to set them free from the political bondage ... Given the dangers of bias, ideological approaches to the text require a high degree of self awareness and also sensitivity to the bias within the biblical text and the context of the reader. Greater awareness forms part of the checks and balances of reading a passage of Scripture ideologically.[29]

Within the context of jazz music, the musician, as I have outlined previously, is not limited by the notation or the exactitude of the melody as he or she has received it. The art of improvisation is the challenge to find new meaning and phrases to transform an existing melody, without departing from the original to such an extent that the previous incarnation is obliterated. In effect, it is the delicate synthesis of bringing the new from the old - bearing witness to what has gone before, but not being limited or constrained by it.

The need to bring new meaning and fresh insights from the Bible, whilst remaining connected to the traditions that have informed the collective whole that is 'Holy Scripture' has always been the high challenge presented to Black preachers. It is the challenge to 'bring afresh' for the immediate context without doing violence to the text from which one's inspiration is drawn.[30] Essentially, I am arguing that Black preachers within the ongoing dynamic that is Black worship are improvisers and that improvisation provides a helpful framework for helping us to move beyond the limited binary of evangelical and liberal arguments around Biblical authority. Improvisation allows us to play with the dichotomy of being faithful to the spirit inherent within the Word of God, without locking ourselves into rigid positions that assert that the WORD has to be taken literally and is inerrant.

So utilizing a jazz hermeneutic can enliven our contemporary approaches to preaching and interpretation of the Gospel. Perhaps, of greater import, when allied to Christian drama it can enable ordinary lay people, many of whom are Black people living in a racist context that is postcolonial Britain. It can empower them to become improvisers themselves and to find the courage to play an inherited melody with new vigour, imagination and panache; and most importantly, to own that playing as their own creation. In the words of Jesus, they will find the courage to be so inspired that their improvisation will harness the pre-eminent Spirit of God in order that they might discover life, and that life might be in all its fullness. After all the

---

28 James H. Cone, *God Of the Oppressed* (San Francisco, 1975), pp. 62-83.

29 Robert Beckford, *God and the Gangs* (London: Darton, Longman and Todd, 2004), pp. 102-3.

30 Ermal Kirby 'Black Preaching'. *The Journal of The College of Preachers* (July 2001), pp. 47-50:48.

verbiage and rhetoric, what we are left with, in terms of articulating a dramatic improvised approach to doing theology with marginalized peoples, is the essence of jazz improvisation itself.

Bibliography

Beckford, Robert, *God and the Gangs* (London: Darton, Longman and Todd, 2004).

Berryman, Jerome W., *Godly Play: An Imaginative Approach to Religious Education* (Minneapolis:Augsburg 1995).

Browning, Robert L., (ed.), *The Pastor as Religious Educator* (Birmingham, Ala.: Religious Education press, 1987).

Burbridge, Paul and Murray Watts, *Time To Act* (London: Hodder and Stoughton, 1979)

Burbridge, Paul and Murray Watts, *Lightning Sketches* (London: Hodder and Stoughton, 1981).

Burbridge, Paul and Murray Watts, *Red Letter Days* (London: Hodder and Stoughton, 1986).

Cone, James H., *God of the Oppressed* (San Francisco: Harper-San-Francisco, 1975).

Groome, Thomas H., *Sharing Faith: A Comprehensive Approach to Religious Education and Pastoral Ministries* (San Francisco: Harper-San Francisco, 1991).

Groome, Thomas H., *Christian Religious Education: Sharing Our Story and Vision* (San Francisco: Jossey-Bass 1999 [1980]).

Kahn, Ashley, *A Love Supreme: The Creation of John Coltrane's Classic Album* (London: Granta Books, 2002).

Kirby, Ermal, 'Black Preaching', *The Journal of The College of Preachers* (July 2001): 47-50.

Moseley, Romney, *Becoming A Self Before God: Critical Transformations* (Nashville, Tenn.: Abingdon, 1991).

Reddie, Anthony G., *Nobodies to Somebodies: A Practical Theology for Education and Liberation* (Peterborough: Epworth Press, 2003).

Reddie, Anthony G., *Acting In Solidarity: Reflections in Critical Christianity* (London: DLT, 2005).

Reddie, Anthony G., *Dramatizing Theologies: A Participative Approach to Black God-Talk* (London: Equinox, 2006).

Shockley, Grant S., 'Black Pastoral Leadership in Religious Education' in Robert L. Browning, (ed.), *The Pastor as Religious Educator* (Birmingham, Ala.: Religious Education press, 1987):179-206.

Speckman, McGlory T., and Larry T. Kaufmann, *Towards an Agenda for Contextual Theology: Essays in Honour of Albert Nolan* (Pietermaritzburg, South Africa: Cluster publications, 2001).

Ukpong, Justin S., Musa W. Dube, Gerald O. West, et al., *Reading the Bible In the Global Village: Global Perspectives on Biblical Scholarship* (Atlanta: The Society for Biblical Literature, 2002).

Ward, Geoffrey C., and Ken Burns, *Jazz: A History of America's Music* (London: Pimlico, 2001).

West, Gerald O., 'Contextual Bible Study in South Africa: A Resource for Reclaiming and Regaining Land, Dignity and Identity' in McGlory T. Speckman and Larry T. Kaufmann, *Towards an Agenda for Contextual Theology: Essays in Honour of Albert Nolan* (Pietermaritzburg, South Africa: Cluster publications, 2001): 169-84.

Wimbush, Vincent L., *The Bible and African Americans: A Brief History* (Minneapolis: Fortress Press, 2003).

White, Andrew 'The Role of the Black Church in the Liberation Struggle'. *Spectrum* (No.47, July/August 1971): 10-11.

Discography

Coltrane, John 'Chasin' the Trane', *Live at the Village Vanguard: The Master Takes* (Impulse Records, 1961).

Coltrane, John, *A Love Supreme* [Deluxe edition] (Impulse Records, 2002).

Davis, Miles, *Kind of Blue* (Columbia/Legacy Records, 1959).

Drummond, Don and The Skatalites, 'Eastern Standard Time', *Foundation of Ska*, Disc One (Heartbeat, 1997).

PART II
Authority

Part II

Authority

Dawn Llewellyn

Authority is a crucial concern in considering the processes of constructing and representing ideas of the sacred. Set against fundamental social changes which posit a need to deconstruct, interrogate and approach traditional sources of authority with suspicion, new conceptions of textual authority are emerging. Ursula King, Heather Walton and Katharine Moody explore the ways that authority, as it circles round the textual, is opening and closing in these contexts by and for certain communities. Ursula King's work has always challenged western religious feminists to look beyond our own religious frameworks. By using the spiritual and religious transformations that have been occurring in global Buddhist women's movements, she alerts us to the way in which women outside of western religions are 'gendering the spirit', achieving spiritual and religious transformation and innovation by creating new meanings with 'readings' of their traditions and practices in light of their, and their community's, experiences. Heather Walton's work suggests the need for a renewed relationship between feminist theology and literature. While Walton shows the various ways in which women's writing has fruitfully charged feminist theology by subverting authoritative images and narratives in traditional sacred texts, she argues it is perhaps time to challenge previous reading strategies and the circumscribed set of texts that can overshadow and restrict this partnership. Katharine Moody sets her exploration of authority and its context in the development of the 'emerging church'. She highlights how the onset of postmodernity has encouraged new textual values, which are also associated with cyber-based practices such as blogging. However, Moody draws attention to the way such practices can inadvertently re-inscribe authority to a select few.

The communities at the centre of these essays, Buddhist women activists, Christian feminist theology, and the emerging church are claiming the authority to create new meanings from and out of 'sacred text' as a critical reaction to authority *over* community. One location in which authority is being realigned by women is within women's Asian spiritualities. King illustrates how Buddhist women are appropriating sacred textual practices from which they have been previously excluded. This is integral to their spiritual growth and has been facilitated by women arming themselves through education with the 'spiritual literacy' that enables them to re-read and redefine traditional sacred texts, spiritualities and religious communities in innovative ways. The term 'spiritual literacy' is politically eloquent. Literacy is taken for granted by those that have it, but is a competence that too many (for instance, women) have not been afforded. Spiritual literacy acknowledges that securing spiritual flourishing is dependent upon admission to textual authority and recognizes the gains that can be made when traditional seats of authority (textual and others) are agitated when women become equipped with knowledge of their sacred scripts. King argues that the West needs to view the attainments of women's redefinitions of spirit and spirituality through a 'comparative mirror' to ascertain the new perspectives that Asian traditions mirror back. Staring through the comparative mirror reflects how women, collectively rather than individually, from outside the Judeo-Christian world are reinterpreting their religious legacy, working for greater participation in religious practices, encountering autonomy and claiming spiritual authority.

While King surveys the advantages when authority is reclaimed, Walton and Moody offer a note of caution. Without reflexivity, authority can be re-inscribed onto patterns of text-reader interactions, a gesture that mirrors the closure of sacred text to those who do not fit traditional paradigms. For Moody, this is occurring within the emerging church blogosphere. As emerging church members participate in the textual culture of blogging, web technologies at first appear to democratize the creation of sacred texts.[1] Readers of emerging church blogs are able to link and comment on sites hosted by emerging church members and communities, contributing actively to form and content. The blogosphere seems to lend itself to the emerging church's aspiration to question the boundary between writers (the agents of authority) and readers (the recipients) and fulfil the reader's 'desire for interactivity'. However, by analysing the statistical methods for measuring blogging activity, and the editing privileges held by the blogger, Moody demonstrates that the very mechanisms that enable blogging are responsible for curtailing the reader's position as the centre of meaning-making. In the emerging church blogosphere the author is 'resurrected' and reinstated as an authoritative function.

Heather Walton also advises vigilance against uncritical reflection on reading strategies that aim to destabilize authority. Walton questions the way religious feminism has naturalized women's writing as the obvious partner to feminist theology. Furthermore, she warns, this dependence has led to a textual closure and a curtailing of an open right to response as these literary products are being read as 'sacred texts.' Women's literature has had an invaluable impact upon women's concepts of the spiritual and religious and feminist theology has adopted a diverse range of strategies for utilizing this inspiring resource. However, as Walton argues, while literature has been used to reform, reject, re-write authoritative structures and to revision Biblical narratives, the divergent hermeneutical uses of literature share a common dependence upon realist literature written by women. The biographical eclipses the literary content of the literature as the authority of the author is wrapped in her identity as a woman, and thus she is 'read' as having unique access to imagining the spiritual and religious experiences of women. Rather than embracing 'death of the author' discourses, religious feminists have wanted to leave the authority for their alternative textual traditions in the creative hands of women writers. To counter this narrowing of literature, Walton suggests a re-focus on language as the means through which readers can engage more radically and creatively with their sacred

---

1   See Bittarello, Chapter 11.

texts. Walton wants to retain 'our sacred texts' but wants to encourage a less inhibited list of what that might include.

In this section, King, Walton and Moody examine authority in terms of how it is understood in contemporary religious climates, both in relation to and in contrast to the way it is presented in the sacred texts of traditional religions.

Chapter 4

'Gendering the Spirit': Reading Women's Spiritualities with a Comparative Mirror

Ursula King

'Gendering the Spirit' refers to the brilliant title of a collection of essays edited by the Pakistani woman scholar Durre S. Ahmed who works in psychology, communications and cultural studies.[1] This unusual expression points to the globally emerging narratives of women and spirituality which have to be read with the help of a 'comparative mirror', to cite the American feminist historian of religions, Rita M. Gross, who has long argued that western scholars need to look at religions other than their own since these provide a 'mirror' with which to examine their religious traditions and see them in a new light.[2] Jeannine Hill Fletcher, who has also reflected on this expression, speaks appreciatively of 'the gift of the comparative mirror' for recognizing the value of difference.[3] I want to argue that we need to examine women's spiritualities in a wide comparative context in order to discover what new perspectives women's spiritualities in other, especially Asian, traditions mirror back to us.

Durre S. Ahmed's book discusses different women's spiritualities in Hinduism, Buddhism, Islam and Christianity in South and South East Asia. Ahmed convincingly argues that in a globally postmodern world the subject of women and religion 'remains postcoloniality's last frontier'[4] that has to be contested and transcended. In the past, women and religion have often both been colonized and exploited whereas now we are challenged by the question of how women's situation of unfreedom and dependency, experienced in so many religions, can be overcome and replaced by a newly gained autonomy and freedom.

The decolonizing of women and religion involves a decolonizing of the imagination, mind and heart. A radical critique of the profound imbalance in the

---

1 Durre S. Ahmed, (ed.), *Gendering the Spirit. Women, Religion and the Post-Colonial Response* (London and New York, 2002).

2 Rita M. Gross, 'Feminist Theology as Theology of Religions' in Susan Frank Parsons, (ed.), *The Cambridge Companion to Feminist Theology* (Cambridge, 2002), pp. 60-78.

3 Jeannine Hill Fletcher, 'Shifting Identity. The Contribution of Feminist Thought to Theologies of Religious Pluralism', *Journal of Feminist Studies in Religion* 19/2 (2003), pp. 5-24:23.

4 Ahmed, *Gendering the Spirit,* p. 27.

gendered knowledge and experience of spirit, transcendence and the Divine is called for, since these realities have been largely constructed in an exclusionary manner to the detriment of women. Differently expressed, in the past women have been *defined* and largely *confined* by religion whereas now, by contrast, women are actively *redefining* religion and spirituality for themselves. Women are moving from a primarily passive mode to a more active mode by exploring and expressing in new creative ways the realms of spirit in culture, community and personal life. An integral part of these contemporary cultural developments are women's efforts across different religions to reinterpret their religious heritage, seek greater participation and visibility, gain access to the highest spiritual attainments, and experience spiritual autonomy and freedom which bestow greater spiritual authority to them than has been customarily granted in the past.

The literature on women's spiritualities, whether feminist, ecofeminist, Wicca, pagan, Goddess-oriented or grounded in traditional religious sources has grown to almost unmanageable proportions, but on the whole its overall focus remains predominantly western since the re-reading and re-construction of religious traditions has been primarily undertaken by women from Christian or Jewish backgrounds. The term 'feminist theology' is often exclusively associated with these two traditions and the main texts that are re-read from a critical hermeneutical perspective of suspicion are often drawn from biblical sources. Rita M. Gross[5] insists that it is important to move away from this one-sided, exclusive stance and take religious diversity seriously by using the 'comparative mirror' when looking at feminist theologies and spiritualities. When examining texts in search of religious and spiritual meaning for constructing spiritualities, most of the examples given remain usually firmly grounded in western/Christian/Jewish categories.

The need for more plurality is also emphasized in Diane M. Collier's and Deborah F. Sawyer's introduction to their volume *Is There a Future for Feminist Theology?* published in 1999. While diversity is addressed in theoretical and methodological terms in western works, dialogue with non-western contexts is often missing. As the editors clearly state:

> This on-going lack of engagement by feminist theology, and gender theory itself, with experience outside Western culture artificially limits the issues of gender and religion. From our perspective, this is the major task for the next millennium. The traditional dichotomy between East and West, a meta-narrative of a past age, needs to be dissolved to allow the vast plurality of global experiences to take centre stage.[6]

The need for a widening of focus to take into account the rich variety of women's spiritualities at a global level thus invites a wide use of the comparative mirror.

---

5   Gross understands 'feminist theology' in an inclusive sense, taking wider religious diversity into account. See her entry on 'Feminist Theology: An Overview' in Lindsay Jones, (ed.), *Encyclopaedia of Religion. Second Edition* vol. 5: 3031-34 (New York, 2005). Further references will be to EOR.

6   Diane M. Collier and Deborah F. Sawyer, 'From Isolation to Integration? New Directions in Gender and Religion' in Deborah F. Sawyer and Diane M. Collier, (eds), *Is There a Future for Feminist Theology?* (Sheffield, 1999), pp.11-24: 24.

Space constraints oblige me to restrict my discussion to Buddhist women, but for the purpose of clarification, I begin with some general reflections.

Gender, spirit and spirituality

Spirituality is often discussed in such general terms that no attention is given to either women or gender. If spiritual practice and understanding are related to all parts of life, then one of the most significant markers of human life is gender, and the difference it makes to spirituality. Other markers are race, ethnicity, different sexual orientation, colonial and postcolonial cultures, to name the currently most discussed categories of difference. All these have an impact on spirituality and deserve separate discussion, but this would go beyond the limits of the present paper. I have chosen instead to focus on the category of gender in relation to spirituality.

It is not my primary task here to sharpen the rather fluid concept of spirituality. To provide some clarification, though, it is important that spirituality is not understood in an essentialist manner but is perceived as rooted within a thoroughly historicized and contextualized framework. This means that it makes more sense to speak of *spiritualities* in the plural rather than of spirituality in the singular. I propose an open-ended, general definition whereby spiritualities quite simply connote those ideas, practices and commitments that nurture, sustain and shape the fabric of human lives, whether as individual persons or communities. Spirituality can also be seen in terms of relating to oneself, to others, and to the world. Differently expressed, spirituality is a living process of going inward and outward, relating to other people, to the whole of life, to nature and the cosmos. In traditional philosophy and theology this has been understood as the dialectic of immanence and transcendence, the encounter between the human spirit and a greater reality beyond the merely human, often perceived as Divine Spirit, or as an ultimate source of transcendent liberation and freedom.

Many traditional stereotypes subtly influence people's attitudes and expectations when thinking about spirituality. Most fundamental and pervasive of these are the customary associations with masculinity and femininity in western culture. Masculinity is often perceived as directly linked to reason, transcendence, and divinity, whereas femininity is associated with body, immanence and humanity. Such stereotypical links, established through essentialist categories, help to provide some, though not all, explanations why women were often deemed not to have direct and easy access to the exalted, transcendent heights of the spirit.

For women's equal participation in spiritual life, especially for spiritual teaching and direction, it is essential that women are fully trained and equally qualified in their intellectual and spiritual attainments in a comparable manner to men. This was already recognized at the 1893 Chicago World's Parliament of Religions when one of the women speakers mentioned the new opportunities for women in religion, stating that 'Women are becoming masters of the languages in which the great sacred literatures of the world are written. They are winning the highest honours that the universities have to bestow ...'[7] This comment was part of one of the opening speeches at the 1893 Parliament, just as another woman speaker interpreted the then new women's movement as due to divine providence, and spoke of 'the hard-earned release of the feminine in human nature from bondage to the masculine'. She acknowledged that 'We are still measurably ignorant of the nature of woman in women, of her real capacities, inclinations, and powers, nor shall we know these *until women are free to express them in accordance with their own ideas*, and not as hitherto, *in accordance with man's ideas of them'* (emphasis added).

These words of 1893 were then mainly addressed to western women from a predominantly Christian and Jewish background. Today such reflections can be applied to women from all religions. It is fascinating to see how many Jewish and Christian women have become trained in the languages and interpretation of their sacred scriptures, and are qualified to teach about them up to the highest academic level. The same development can now be observed among women in Hinduism, Buddhism, Islam, and many other religious traditions. Not many western people are aware of the '*silent revolution*'[8] that is occurring among women in religions. Few scholars study the way in which women in non-western traditions are now acquiring both scholarly and spiritual competences and authority. Sometimes this is only acknowledged with reluctance by their own communities, or it is even sharply resisted. Contemporary Hindu, Buddhist, Muslim women and those from other religions who possess a critical feminist awareness and an activist inclination to work for change in their culture and religious tradition, all show that for women to gain equal access to the realm of the spirit and exercise authority in spiritual matters, traditionally divisive gender patterns have to be transcended. This requires a huge effort, for it is vital that women gain full access to literacy and education at all levels. That does not only mean the ability to read and write, but also to understand and authoritatively interpret religious texts and ideas, and to offer spiritual advice. Education is the indispensable key for these developments, for without education women are like 'a bird without wings', as one Tibetan Buddhist nun put it.[9] For the decolonization of our imagination and knowledge, for the affirmation of subjectivity and identity, women require not only full literacy, but what I call *spiritual literacy*. They need to claim full access to the experience of spirit in terms of mind, intellect,

---

7   For full details of this and the following quotation see Ursula King, 'Rediscovering Women's Voices at the World's Parliament of Religions' in Eric J. Ziolkowski, (ed.), *A Museum of Faiths. Histories and Legacies of the 1893 World's Parliament of Religions* (Atlanta, Georgia, 1993), pp. 325-43.

8   This expression has been applied to women in Islam and Buddhism. Pieternella van Doorn-Harder uses it with regard to Muslim women in Indonesia whose new awareness about gender issues she describes as an irreversible process, 'part of a silent revolution'; see her book *Women Shaping Islam: Reading the Qu'ran in Indonesia* (Urbana and Chicago, 2006), p. 195. See also Hema Goonatilake's paper 'A Silent Revolution: The Restoration of the *Bhikkhuni* Order in Sri Lanka' (IAHR Regional Conference on the Study of Religions in India, Dec. 11-14, 2003, New Delhi, India).

9   Yolande van Ede, 'Of Birds and Wings. Tibetan Nuns and their Encounters with Knowledge' in Karma Lekshe Tsomo, (ed.), *Innovative Buddhist Women. Swimming Against the Stream* (Richmond, Surrey, 2000), pp. 201-11: 202.

wisdom, and transcendence, whether expressed in cultural creativity in general or specifically in terms of a spiritual quest.

The creative tensions that exist in the field of spirituality and gender, and the new spiritual ideas, rituals, and practices that are emerging out of the women's and also men's movements in religion and spirituality bear witness to much zest, energy, and fresh creativity. They can be read as signs of the spirit in contemporary culture, pointing toward radical spiritual transformations and perhaps new beginnings.

Spiritual literacy and transcendence

Writers on spirituality in the west are often neither unaware of women's lively debates and radical reform movements in other parts of the world nor are they acquainted with *the newly emerging spiritualities* among women of the South, previously often referred to as the so-called Third World.[10] Anyone meeting women from different cultures and faith traditions soon realizes that many intellectual and practical changes are happening all over the world in response to the development of women's, feminist, and gender thinking over the last few decades.

For the first time in human history a growing number of women from different religious and secular backgrounds are articulating their own spiritual experiences, reflections and quests not simply as particular *individuals*, but women as a *group* are doing this around the globe. A social rather than a merely individual phenomenon spreading over the entire planet, this is a radically new development that will have a profound impact on the future of religion and spirituality, and on that of the human species as a whole. Women from all religions and cultures are actively engaged in the transformation of their own religious and cultural traditions.

Although there exists considerable cross-cultural diversity, there can be little doubt that women from different faiths, deeply involved with transformative spiritual practice, are increasingly in dialogue with each other. They are developing a global network of contacts that is steadily growing in spite of many criticisms, backlashes, personal difficulties and disappointments.[11] Durre S. Ahmed rightly asks what difference religious and spiritual writings by and about women will make. This question can be extended to what difference new ideas and practices, organizational and institutional changes in the area of religion will make to women as a group and to different societies. Ahmed responds to her own question with the following comment:

> ... there is a difference between the past as it has been steadily punctuated by radical forms of women's spirituality and as it is being manifested today. The difference has to do with

---

10 For an earlier discussion see Ursula King, 'A Newly Emerging Spirituality' in Ursula King, (ed.), *Feminist Theology from the Third World. A Reader* (London and Maryknoll, NY, 1994), pp. 299-394.

11 From a Christian interfaith dialogue perspective, the diversity and wide geographical spread of women's contacts is well documented in the large, pioneering study by Helene Egnell, *Other Voices. A Study of Christian Feminist Approaches to Religious Plurality East and West* (Uppsala, 2006).

literacy, with reading and writing, and the inevitable transformation of consciousness – in analysis, comprehension, knowledge, cognition and communication – that is engendered through literacy. Never before in history have so many women been empowered through 'the word', enabling them to articulate their ideas and share these with vast numbers of other women and men. Literacy and language is crucial to consciousness and communication. Given the explosion in technology today, vast numbers of females have at their disposal a variety of media through which they can express, analyse and above all communicate and share with each other the most radical of conceptions. Granted, there are also many who still do not have access to either literacy or the new information technologies. But neither did the West become literate overnight once Gutenberg invented the printing press.[12]

Ahmed's book *Gendering the Spirit* provides examples of spiritual ideals of the past and of the newly emerging spiritualities shaped by the subjectivities and experiences of Asian women facing wide political and social injustice. The 'reading' of their texts, contexts and life situations makes these women both activists in a practical sense and explorers of the spiritual possibilities and dimensions of human life, enabling them to develop a new spiritual literacy and new spiritual aspirations.

With the rise of literacy among women, another surprising development worldwide is the ongoing discovery of the spiritual heritage of women across different religions and cultures. So many spiritual 'foremothers', female saints, mystics and female religious communities are being discovered and rediscovered today. Yet a comparative historical enquiry provides much evidence that most religions have validated women's lives more in terms of domestic observances and family duties than they have encouraged women's search for religious enlightenment, spiritual adventure and perfection. Imprisoned by the daily tasks of *immanence*, by the recurrent demands of immediacy that the maintenance and nurture of personal and community life required, women have been so much equated with immanence that the realms of *transcendence* remained largely out of their reach, forbidden to their desire.

There are many exceptions to this statement, but in spite of the existence of what Elisabeth Gössmann calls women's 'counter-tradition',[13] one must ask how far women have really had access to a spiritual space of their own? How far were they really encouraged to pursue, or were ever admitted to the pursuit of, similar spiritual ideals and disciplines as men? How far could women provide spiritual advice and leadership for both women and men? It is only in our postmodern era that women *as a group* can respond in greater numbers to the lure, invitation, challenge and gift of *transcendence*.

'Transcendence' is a much critiqued and problematized concept in contemporary feminist and theological writing, but it is still a very useful category that needs to be revalued and re-appropriated. Not in an essentialist or dictionary sense as 'existing apart from, not subject to the limitations of, the material universe',[14] but with the meaning given to it by the physicist Henry A. Garon. Writing on the mystique of

---

12 Ahmed, *Gendering the Spirit*, p. 27.

13 Elisabeth Gössmann, 'The Image of God and the Human Being in Women's Counter-Tradition' in Sawyer and Collier, *Is There a Future for Feminist Theology*, pp. 26-56.

14 *The Concise Oxford Dictionary* (Oxford: 1990), p. 1296.

things in the cosmos, he describes transcendence simply as 'the movement toward levels of awareness beyond what is immediate. Transcendence comes into play when we cease picturing our world as "plain old matter" and begin to recognize ourselves as privileged to be a part of it. It involves the use of our imagination and a willingness to navigate deeper in spirit.' Garon also quotes Thomas Merton saying: 'As humans, we look within ourselves and discover an unspeakably deep dimension. Then we look outside and find depth without end there, too. And in time it grows apparent that the two worlds are one and the same.'[15]

Without deciding on sharply bounded philosophical definitions, transcendence can thus be understood as a category of depth and outreach, of going further and beyond, taking part in the process of an ongoing exploration of how to become and be more human.[16] The whole area of cultural creativity, whether in the arts, sports, politics or science, is part of this human search for transcending the immediate here and now, a transcendent outreach that becomes further focused in the spiritual quest and realms of religion. Whereas women have gained access through literacy to all areas of culture, *spiritual literacy* – whenever and wherever they have acquired it – enables women today to re-read and redefine traditional texts, practices, spiritualities and religious communities in new ways, seeking the life of the spirit through reaching out for transcendence, not as an essentialist reality but as a process of moving beyond the circles of immediacy of confining immanence. This allows for greater freedom, spiritual growth and transformation. It enables women to create new spiritualities and redefine old ones, or even to appropriate traditional spiritual forms and practices from which women had hitherto been excluded.

Women's new opportunities in the field of religion and spirituality include their taking up traditional paths of renunciation in Hinduism, becoming gurus in their own right, or the reclaiming of full ordination for Buddhist nuns in Sri Lanka and other Theravada countries. Throughout history, individual women have struggled to pursue a spiritual path, often against great odds and obstacles. The histories of Jain, Buddhist, and Christian nuns provide ample examples of great spiritual devotion and attainment. Yet through centuries women had to struggle to create their own religious communities, since their gender always provoked male resistance to their claim to autonomy, independent power, and spiritual authority. Women's religious activities often remained constrained and controlled by male religious hierarchies, and this is often still the case today. Although the word 'nun' carries a specific, historically circumscribed meaning, especially in Catholic Christianity, it is now widely used to refer to women ascetics and renunciates across different religious traditions.

---

15 Henry A. Garon, *The Cosmic Mystique* (Maryknoll, NY, 2006), p. 52.

16 A brief investigation shows that philosophers seem to use more often the words 'transcendent', 'transcendental' and 'transcendentalism' than the noun 'transcendence' which figures far more among Christian theologians who apply it mainly to God. For a more unusual approach see Charles Hartshorne's article on 'Transcendence and Immanence' in EOR, vol. 13: pp. 9281-6. The concept 'transcendent' is also used in a comparative context, as for example in Anne Vallely's study of Jain women ascetics in Rajasthan. Anne Vallely, *Guardians of the Transcendent. An Ethnography of Jain Ascetic Community* (Toronto, 2002).

In spite of a number of monographs that have been published, the comparative phenomenological study of nuns remains so far still relatively undeveloped.[17]

Throughout history women, like men, have experienced a strong calling to follow single-mindedly a dedicated religious path in search of liberation or *moksha*, holiness and perfection, or that of selfless service to others, through pursuing a life of renunciation, meditation, prayer, fasting and other ascetic practices. Because of the widely accepted division of gender roles and the assumed equation of mind and spirit with the male sphere, and that of body and sexuality with the female sphere, women often had a great struggle to free themselves from traditional gender assumptions in order to pursue such a path. The comparative history of female asceticism and women's religious communities, most of which still has to be written, provides fascinating evidence of women's quest for spirit and transcendence as do contemporary women's movements and their spiritualities.

The Global Buddhist Women's Movement

One of the most striking examples of the innovative process of 'gendering the spirit' is *Sakyadhita,* the global Buddhist women's movement inaugurated in 1987 in Bodhgaya in the presence of the Dalai Lama. Founded for Buddhist nuns and lay women in East and West, the fourfold aims of this movement are

1. to create a global network of communication among Buddhist women;
2. to educate women as teachers of Buddhism;
3. to conduct research on women in Buddhism;
4. to work for the establishment of the Bhikkhuni Sangha.

So far, *Sakyadhita* has organized eight international conferences in different Asian countries. Much effort goes into education and the reinterpretation of texts, but also on reforming unjust, non-egalitarian practices, and on the development of socially engaged Buddhism, where the issues for Buddhist women in Asia are different from those of Buddhist women in the West.

The president of *Sakyadhita,* the Venerable Karma Lekshe Tsomo, is an American Buddhist nun ordained in the Tibetan tradition who spent many years in India but teaches now at the University of San Diego, California. She has edited the papers given at different Sakyadhita conferences in a series of volumes[18] that provide an inspiring documentation of the transformative processes taking place

---

17 A more detailed discussion of these issues is found in Ursula King, 'Nuns: An Overview', EOR, vol. 10: pp. 6756-9.

18 Karma Lekshe Tsomo, (ed.), *Sakyadhita: Daughters of the Buddha* (Ithaca, NY, 1988); *Buddhist Women Across Cultures: Realizations* (Albany, NY, 1999); *Innovative Buddhist Women: Swimming Against the Stream*; *Buddhist Women and Social Justice. Ideals, Challenges, and Achievements* (Albany, NY, 2004) and *Out of the Shadows: Socially Engaged Buddhist Women* (Delhi, 2006).

among Buddhist women.[19] Karma Lekshe Tsomo has provided some illuminating reflections on women's spiritualities in the light of the encounter between Buddhism and feminism, arguing that women's traditional roles in Buddhist cultures have been changed without any direct link to the women's movement in the West and that these changes are virtually unknown to outsiders. She sees the Buddhist women's movement as 'Mahaprajapati's Legacy',[20] that is the legacy of the Buddha's aunt who, as the first nun in Buddhism, began the Bhikkhuni Sangha. Now that gender equality has become part of the demand for a new global ethic, the question is how can the Buddhist tradition be re-envisioned along egalitarian lines?

In most, although not all, Asian countries the number of Buddhist nuns is less than that of monks. In Taiwan, however, there are two thirds more nuns than monks; Korea also has a large number of nuns whose experiences, like those of other nuns, have rarely been recorded in Buddhist texts nor have they been much investigated by scholars. This is changing now that Buddhist women have organized themselves to study their own history and activities. More and more Buddhist women are researching Buddhist women's history, as is evident from recent publications, especially from Tsomo's volume *Innovative Buddhist Women. Swimming Against the Stream* wherein several writers underline the need for equal opportunities for education, ordination and leadership for women in Buddhist cultures. A pivotal role in the development of Buddhist women's spirituality is played by Buddhist nuns as celibate female practitioners fully dedicated to Buddhist Dhamma teaching. The contemporary controversy over the higher ordination of Buddhist nuns in Theravada countries well illustrates how women from one major non-western religious tradition are pressing for spiritual and practical equality.

Central to this controversy is the situation in Sri Lanka. The order of Sri Lankan nuns originally came from India in the third century BCE and it was Sri Lankan nuns in turn who took the Bhikkhuni Sangha to China in the fifth century CE. The lineage of fully ordained nuns now no longer exists in any Theravada country, but only in Mahayana countries, where the very legitimacy of the Chinese Bhikkhuni lineage, so important for reviving full ordination in Theravada countries, rests on their fifth century foundation by Sri Lankan Bhikkhunis. The Chinese nuns established their own *Vinaya* tradition, the *Dharmagupta Vinaya*, and transmitted full ordination to nuns in Korea and Vietnam.

In Sri Lanka, the full ordination was lost after the eleventh century for reasons that are unclear. The Bhikkhuni Sangha was never re-established until a Buddhist reawakening occurred in the colonial context of the nineteenth century. Women ascetics, called *dasasilmatas* ('mothers of ten precepts'), were reintroduced into the island without being given full ordination or full recognition as Bhikkhunis. There are currently over 4000 *dasasilmatas* in Sri Lanka. The dominant interpretation of the Theravada tradition remains still in the hands of the monks who are mostly unwilling to share their wealth, power and prestige with the nuns. However, in the 1980s a

---

19 For further research on Buddhist nuns see Ellison Banks Findly, (ed.), *Women's Buddhism, Buddhism's Women. Tradition, Revision, Renewal* (Boston, 2000).

20 See Karma Lekshe Tsomo, 'Mahaprajapati's Legacy: The Buddhist Women's Movement: An Introduction' in Tsomo, *Buddhist Women Across Cultures,* pp.1-44.

movement developed for the re-establishment of Bhikkhunis which received the support of some monks. The full ordination controversy has raged in Sri Lanka and other Buddhist countries of the Theravada tradition for some time now. Several full ordination ceremonies have been held since 1988, first in a Chinese convent in Los Angeles, followed by other ceremonies in India (Sarnath, 1996; Bodhgaya, 1998) and in Sri Lanka. The first Sri Lankan Bhikkhuni to receive higher ordination in 1996 was Kusuma Devendra, a well-known woman scholar with a doctorate in Buddhist philosophy who had taken renunciation after bringing up a family and had worked for the revival of the female Sangha for many years. In her detailed account on the ordination controversy Ranjani de Silva writes about Kusuma Devendra: 'Because Buddhists in Sri Lanka had been listening to her Dhamma talks on television and radio for over fifteen years, they were greatly inspired by her ordination and received the news with great joy.'[21]

Between 1998 and 2001, seven Bhikkuni ordinations were held in Sri Lanka and more than 350 Bhikkhunis were ordained. According to a recent note by Hema Goonatilake who has written and lectured extensively on the restoration of the Bhikkhuni Order in Sri Lanka, there were nearly 500 Bhikkhunis in Sri Lanka in 2006.[22] This is in stark contrast to an earlier situation in 1993 when the Sri Lankan government still forbade the very use of the term 'Bhikkhuni', whereas the presence and public recognition of Bhikkhunis has now become part of public discourse. Progressive, learned monks have started to train more *dasasilmatas* for higher ordination, and many also receive higher education. Currently there are more than a thousand fully functioning nuns' communities (known as *aramayas,* for nuns without full ordination), largely located in remote villages where the nuns are recognized as leaders. According to Goonatilake, several nuns from India, Vietnam, Malaysia, Thailand, Myanmar, and even the USA and Czech Republic have now received higher ordination in Sri Lanka. The full restoration of the Sri Lankan Bhikkhuni Order in 1998 has a significant impact on other Theravada countries. The issue of full ordination is crucial for the gaining of institutional equality for Buddhist women, but it is also of great importance for the development of women's spirituality in Buddhism.

In Mahayana countries, the strongest resurgence of Buddhism is found in Taiwan where over 60% of all ordained Buddhists are women. No other Bhikkhuni Sangha is as strong as that of Taiwan. One nun has founded an academic Buddhist studies program and a university, whereas another is professor of Buddhist Studies at the nations' premier university. In China, where Buddhism was repressed between 1949 and 1980 by the communist regime, some Buddhist monasteries have been reopened since 1980. So far, Buddhist training and ordination have attracted more women than men, in fact more than the government regulated nunneries can accommodate.

A new ground-breaking study comparing the lives and thoughts of Buddhist nuns in Sri Lanka and Taiwan has been undertaken by the Taiwanese scholar Wei-

---

21 See Ranjani de Silva, 'Reclaiming the Robe: Reviving the Bhikkhuni Order in Sri Lanka' in Tsomo, *Buddhist Women and Social Justice*, pp. 119-35:127.

22 Mentioned in a postscript to Goonatilake's paper, 'A Silent Revolution'.

Yi Cheng.[23] Motivated by the perceived gap between western feminist discourse on Buddhism and the actual lives of Asian Buddhist women, her detailed fieldwork reveals the quite different social, political and historical contexts of Buddhist nuns in Taiwan and Sri Lanka, and the different role that Buddhism plays in these two countries. The rich data gathered reveal a complex picture and document the profound processes of transformation among Buddhist women in hitherto unknown detail. The author thereby seeks to achieve the demarginalization of Asian Buddhist nuns within scholarship, but also points to the regrettable lack of cross-tradition communication. The relatively recent foundation of *Sakyadhita* as a global Buddhist women's movement with many cross-tradition connections between the different branches of Theravada and Mahayana will no doubt help to change this situation. Its president, Karma Lekshe Tsomo, speaks of 300 million Buddhist women in the world (of which only 1% are western women) who must work for their social and spiritual liberation. She writes:

> A major revaluing of women in the tradition is crucial - both a renewed affirmation of women's spiritual worth and an increased appreciation of women's spiritual practice. In the Buddhist worldview, spiritual practice and helping living beings are accorded the highest value ... while literacy is not essential to human happiness, for many women literacy is a major step toward empowerment, allowing women access to improved livelihood, to information on health and hygiene, to upward social mobility, to personal development and greater self-confidence, to greater educational options for their children, and to the texts that encode their spiritual heritage.[24]

According to Karma Lekshe Tsomo, the meeting of Buddhist and feminist perspectives is fertile ground for innovation and mutual enrichment on many levels. In her view, 'Buddhist women around the world have initiated intercultural dialogue on a deeply personal, deeply spiritual level. Women are proving the immense value of listening to different voices and learning from the wisdom of each. They are ready to explore a new mode of spirituality that is openhearted, inclusive, wise and genuinely kind, what His Holiness the Dalai Lama calls 'a true spirituality that is beyond religion'.[25]

This statement remains too general to tell us anything specific about Buddhist women's spirituality, whether that of nuns or lay women. More detailed research such as that of Wei-Yi Cheng is needed to investigate women's different religious practices in different countries. We need to know much more about women's own way of reading particular Buddhist texts, traditions and spiritual ideals, and how such reading differs between women in Buddhist cultures and Buddhist women in the West.

---

23 Wei-Yi Cheng, *Buddhist Nuns in Taiwan and Sri Lanka. A Critique of the Feminist Perspective* (London and New York, 2007).

24 Tsomo, *Buddhist Women Across Cultures,* p. 31ff.

25 Ibid., p. 296.

Conclusion

What is mirrored in all these women's activities and readings of religious texts and contexts? First, education and literacy open up new, hitherto unknown pathways to the spirit for women. They produce an empowering spiritual literacy through which, in a movement of critical self-reflexivity, emerges a new dynamic that leads to active transformation and innovation. This is evident from the upsurge of activities associated with the global *Sakyadhita* network which provides just one example of the vast plurality of global experiences and experiments among women in the field of spirituality. They are complemented by many others still awaiting further investigation. A remarkable parallel is provided by a movement among European Christian women of different denominations who came together in 1986 – one year before the foundation of *Sakyadhita* – to form the European Society for Women in Theological Research to achieve similar educational aims. It would be worthwhile to undertake a comparative study of these two women's organizations, one Buddhist and predominantly Asian, the other Christian and mainly European, by mapping their respective activities over the last twenty years.

Secondly, through an active engagement with their faith tradition, and the reading of their sacred literature in the light of contemporary experience, women have become cultural critics, activists and reformers shaping their own lives and that of their communities. This is as true of Buddhist women as it is of Christian, Jewish, Hindu or Muslim women or those of any other faith.

Thirdly, the social activism and engagement of many Asian women is nourished by their faith tradition and rooted in a spirituality of engagement for life. Speaking about the oral interpretation and re-telling of biblical stories among Asian Christian women, Kwok Pui-lan has commented that 'In many Asian cultures, the scriptures have been chanted, recited, memorized and performed for millennia because the spoken words are considered more sacred than written words'.[26] But women in Hinduism and Budddhism were for millennia even excluded from the spoken word – the chanting, reciting, memorizing and teaching of religious texts was forbidden to them. It is only during the twentieth century that they gained access to chanting the Vedas or the Buddhist Sutras or the teaching of the Dhamma, and this is by no means permitted or accepted everywhere. Widening the access to foundational religious texts for women in Buddhism, Hinduism and Islam is as radical an act as when the Christian Bible was first translated into vernacular languages in Europe – a radical act that was widely protested and resisted, and over which some people lost their lives. Women's open access to the scriptures of Hinduism, Buddhism and Islam represents a similar revolution which has only just started and whose outcome is by no means certain. The rich diversity of women's redefinition of spirit and spirituality represents a global movement of 'gendering the spirit' pregnant with promise and hope, not only for women in Asia and the West, but for the entire planet.[27]

---

26 Kwok Pui-lan, *Introducing Asian Feminist Theology* (Sheffield, 2000), p. 53.

27 A longer version of this article can be found in Ursula King, *Religion och Existens. Årskrift för Teologiska föreningen i Uppsala* (2006), pp. 37-54.

Bibliography

Ahmed, Durre S. (ed.), *Gendering the Spirit. Women, Religion and the Post-Colonial Response* (London and New York: Zed Books, 2002).

Cheng, Wei-Yi, *Buddhist Nuns in Taiwan and Sri Lanka. A Critique of the Feminist Perspective* (London and New York: Routledge, 2007).

Collier, Diane M., and Deborah F. Sawyer, 'From Isolation to Integration? New Directions in Gender and Religion' in Deborah F. Sawyer and Diane M. Collier, (eds), *Is There a Future for Feminist Theology?* (Sheffield: Sheffield Academic Press, 1999): 11-24.

De Silva, Ranjani, 'Reclaiming the Robe: Reviving the Bhikkhuni Order in Sri Lanka' in Karma Lekshe Tsomo, (ed.), *Buddhist Women and Social Justice. Ideals, Challenges, and Achievements* (Albany, NY: State University of New York Press, 2004): 119-35.

Egnell, Helene, *Other Voices. A Study of Christian Feminist Approaches to Religious Plurality East and West* (Uppsala: Studia Missionalia Svecana C., 2006).

Findly, Ellison Banks, (ed.), *Women's Buddhism, Buddhism's Women. Tradition, Revision, Renewal* (Boston: Wisdom Publications, 2000).

Fletcher, Jeannine Hill, 'Shifting Identity. The Contribution of Feminist Thought to Theologies of Religious Pluralism', *Journal of Feminist Studies in Religion* 19/2 (2003): 5-24.

Garon, Henry A., *The Cosmic Mystique* (Maryknoll, NY: Orbis Books, 2006).

Goonatilake, Hema, 'A Silent Revolution: The Restoration of the *Bhikkhuni* Order in Sri Lanka' (IAHR Regional Conference on the Study of Religions in India, Dec. 11-14, 2003: New Delhi, India).

Gössmann, Elisabeth, 'The Image of God and the Human Being in Women's Counter-Tradition' in Deborah F. Sawyer and Diane M. Collier, (eds), *Is There a Future for Feminist Theology?* (Sheffield: Sheffield Academic Press, 1999): 26-56.

Gross, Rita M., 'Feminist Theology as Theology of Religions' in Susan Frank Parsons, (ed.), *The Cambridge Companion to Feminist Theology* (Cambridge: Cambridge University Press, 2002): 60-78.

Gross, Rita M., 'Feminist Theology: An Overview' in Lindsay Jones, (ed.), *Encyclopaedia of Religion, Second Edition* (New York: Macmillan Reference USA, Thomson & Gale, 2005), vol. 5: 3031-34.

Hartshorne, Charles, 'Transcendence and Immanence', in Lindsay Jones, (ed.), *Encyclopaedia of Religion, Second Edition* (New York: Macmillan Reference USA, Thomson & Gale, 2005), Vol.13: 9281-6.

Jones, Lindsay, (ed.), *Encyclopaedia of Religion. Second Edition* (New York: Macmillan Reference USA, Thomson & Gale, 2005).

King, Ursula, 'Rediscovering Women's Voices at the World's Parliament of Religions' in Eric J. Ziolkowski, (ed.), *A Museum of Faiths. Histories and Legacies of the 1893 World's Parliament of Religions* (Atlanta, Georgia: Scholars Press, 1993): 325-43.

King, Ursula, 'A Newly Emerging Spirituality' in Ursula King, (ed.), *Feminist Theology from the Third World. A Reader* (London and Maryknoll, NY, 1994): 299-394.

King, Ursula, (ed.), *Feminist Theology from the Third World. A Reader.* (London: SPCK and Maryknoll, NY: Orbis Books, 1994).

King, Ursula, 'Nuns: An Overview', in Lindsay Jones, (ed.), *Encyclopaedia of Religion, Second Edition* (New York: Macmillan Reference USA, Thomson & Gale, 2005), vol. 10: 6756-9.

King, Ursula, *Religion och Existens. Årskrift för Teologiska föreningen i Uppsala* (2006): 37-54.

Parsons, Susan Frank, (ed.), *The Cambridge Companion to Feminist Theology* (Cambridge: Cambridge University Press, 2002).

Pui-lan, Kwok, *Introducing Asian Feminist Theology* (Sheffield: Sheffield Academic Press, 2000).

The Concise Oxford Dictionary of Current English (Oxford: Clarendon Press, 1990).

Sawyer, Deborah F., and Diane M. Collier, (eds), *Is There a Future for Feminist Theology?* (Sheffield: Sheffield Academic Press, 1999).

Tsomo, Karma Lekshe, (ed.), *Sakyadhita: Daughters of the Buddha* (Ithaca, NY: Snow Lion Publications, 1988).

Tsomo, Karma Lekshe, (ed.), *Buddhist Women Across Cultures: Realizations* (Albany, NY: State University of New York Press, 1999).

Tsomo, Karma Lekshe, (ed.), *Innovative Buddhist Women: Swimming Against the Stream* (Richmond, Surrey: Curzon Press, 2000).

Tsomo, Karma Lekshe, (ed.), *Buddhist Women and Social Justice. Ideals, Challenges, and Achievements* (Albany, NY: State University of New York Press, 2004).

Tsomo, Karma Lekshe, (ed.), *Out of the Shadows: Socially Engaged Buddhist Women* (Delhi: Sri Satguru Publications, 2006).

Tsomo, Karma Lekshe, 'Mahaprajapati's Legacy: The Buddhist Women's Movement: An Introduction' in Karma Lekshe Tsomo, (ed.), *Buddhist Women Across Cultures: Realizations* (Albany, NY: State University Press of New York): 1-44.

Vallely, Anne, *Guardians of the Transcendent. An Ethnography of a Jain Ascetic Community* (Toronto: Toronto University Press, 2002).

Van Doorn-Harder, Pieternella, *Women Shaping Islam: Reading the Qu'ran in Indonesia* (Urbana and Chicago: University of Illinois Press, 2006).

Van Ede, Yolande, 'Of Birds and Wings. Tibetan Nuns and their Encounters with Knowledge' in Karma Lekshe Tsomo, *Innovative Buddhist Women. Swimming Against the Stream* (Richmond, Surrey: Curzon Press, 2000): 201-11

Ziolkowski, Eric J., (ed.), *A Museum of Faiths. Histories and Legacies of the 1893 World's Parliament of Religions* (Atlanta, Georgia, 1993): 325-43.

Chapter 5

Our Sacred Texts:
Literature, Theology and Feminism

Heather Walton

Lost in the library

For more than a decade now I have been researching and writing about the ways in which religious feminists have used literature written by women in their theological work.[1] The impetus to do so has come from my own love of both literature and theology. However, a keen interest in both fields was given sharp form and focus as I prepared to teach a course on feminist theology for undergraduate students back in 1995. Reading again the hugely influential collection of essays *Womanspirit Rising*[2] I was struck by the pivotal role women's literature had played in inspiring women to find new ways of describing their apprehension of the sacred and their understanding of the divine.

To understand the significance of this reading encounter it is necessary to travel back in time to an almost unimaginable space before the widespread availability of feminist scholarship.[3] It was extremely difficult to access 'academic' writing about women in relation to their lived experience – as opposed to the peculiar categories into which patriarchal culture had assigned them. Virginia Woolf commented hilariously on the frustrations women faced in searching for their identity amongst the index cards of the library catalogue. She found them to be both invisible in the fullness of their personhood and endlessly dissected into the very peculiar and particular categories constructed by male scholars. She was also famously denied admission to the prestigious resources of the academy in a way that initially caused her grief and anger but later encouraged her to muse that it might be better to be locked out of the library than locked in.[4]

---

1   See, for example Heather Walton, *Literature, Theology and Feminism* (Manchester, 2007) and *Imagining Theology: Women, Writing and God* (London, 2007).

2   Carol Christ and Judith Plaskow, (eds), *Womanspirit Rising: A Feminist Reader in Religion* (San Francisco, 1979). This text brought together, as a resource for discussion and teaching, the work of the first generation of women whose work in theological studies was to decisively influence the discipline. Many of the essays in this collection are now widely regarded as generative texts.

3   This is not of course to imply that women's scholarship did not exist prior to this point but rather that it was neither highly regarded nor widely available.

4   Virginia Woolf, *A Room of One's Own* (London, 1977), p. 29.

In the immediate post war years women scholars began to address this situation but found it extremely difficult to gain acceptance for their work. Partly due to their singular characters and prominent public personas two women did achieve a degree of acceptance and respect within the academy. The works of Margaret Mead[5] and Simone de Beauvoir[6] were listed in the library catalogues. These were eagerly read by students keen to counter the invisibility of women in their curriculum and find solutions to the dilemmas they faced within their own lives. But there was little else. Indeed, when I arrived at university myself some thirty years later the women's studies section of the library consisted of one shelf located in a mysterious space between mythology and folklore. You had to pull a piece of string to turn on the light in the obscure corner where it was hidden. The exciting new books on feminist theology that were being published were also difficult to find. They were tucked away amongst the heavy, hard-backed tomes catalogued under 'doctrine of man'.

In a context where women's scholarship was not available as a resource it was difficult to mount an effective challenge to male-centred thinking. What is commonly regarded as the first work of feminist theology, Valerie Saiving's essay 'The Human Situation: A Feminine View,'[7] drew upon the work of Margaret Mead to justify the contention that there were fundamental differences between male and female experience.[8] However, feminist attempts at reconstructing the traditional academic disciplines could not be sustained as an extended midrash upon the work of those very few women who were judged credible within the university. For feminist scholarship generally, and feminist theology in particular, a huge step forward occurred when women's literature began to be claimed as an authentic source of insight into the truth of women's lives. *Womanspirit Rising* contains a dramatic description of how its editors, Carol Christ and Judith Plaskow, 'discovered' in literature women's experience made manifest in print in a manner that was, for them, far more productive than the philosophical, historical and anthropological reflections of Mead and de Beauvoir. The theological trajectories taken by both women were decisively influenced by their readings of fiction and their debates about its content with other women.

The great leap forward

In her first major work, *Sex, Sin and Grace,*[9] Plaskow follows Saiving's lead and pays the customary homage to Mead and de Beauvoir. But, she defiantly states,

---

5   For example, Margaret Mead, *Male and Female: A Study of the Sexes in a Changing World* (Westport, 1977 [1949]).

6   Simone de Beauvoir, *The Second Sex*, trans. H.M. Parshley (London, 1972 [1949]).

7   Valerie Saiving, 'The Human Situation: A Feminine View' in Christ and Plaskow, *Womanspirit Rising,* pp. 25-42.

8   Her argument was that the grammar of theology was predicated upon 'the basis of masculine experience and thus views the human condition from a male standpoint. Consequently these doctrines do not provide an adequate interpretation of the situation of women.' Saiving, 'The Human Situation,' p.27.

9   Judith Plaskow, *Sex, Sin and Grace: Women's Experience and the Theologies of Reinhold Niebuhr and Paul Tillich* (Washington,1980).

'their accounts of womanhood must be confirmed and deepened by recent literature by and about women ... it is only through literature that the dynamic of women's experience can begin to emerge in all its complexity.'[10] Plaskow goes on to argue that women's literature was a resource that must be brought into a vital dialogue with male-centred theological thinking. Christ took the implications of her reading further. Women were starving, she declared, desperate for a sustenance that could not be found in Western culture's sacred texts. Instead of reading themselves 'sideways ... into stories in which the daughters do not exist ... [women] must devour literature which reflects our experience'.[11] She quickly came to believe that literature was not a supplement to theology but that women's writing contained, *within itself*, pointers towards the ways in which women have apprehended and approached the divine.[12]

Christ and Plaskow were making a daring move in using literature in this way. This was an epoch in which the Protestant theologian Karl Barth was enjoying a renaissance and both had been students at Yale where a sharp divergence between sacred narratives and cultural fictions was beginning to be asserted.[13] However, they must not be viewed in isolation, as free creative spirits; they were also tuning in to powerful signals being transmitted elsewhere in religious thinking and literary theory. Stephen Crites' curious but evocative essay 'The Narrative Quality of Experience'[14] had already made a link between the deep sacred narratives of a culture and its profane narratives expressed predominantly through literature.[15] Crites' work inspired a whole generation of theologians whose identities had not been affirmed within Western theological institutions to use literature as a theological resource.[16]

---

10 Ibid., p. 34.

11 Carol Christ, 'Spiritual Quest and Women's Experience' in Christ and Plaskow, *Womanspirit Rising,* pp.228-45: 230.

12 Her most celebrated work, *Diving Deep and Surfacing: Women Writers on the Spiritual Quest* (Boston, 1980), explores archetypal stages of women's spiritual journeys as these are presented in the work of five women authors.

13 See Hans Frei, *The Eclipse of Biblical Narrative: A Study in Eighteenth and Nineteenth Century Hermeneutics* (Yale, 1974).

14 Stephen Crites, 'The Narrative Quality of Experience' in S. Hauerwas and L. Gregory Jones, (eds), *Why Narrative? Readings in Narrative Theology* (Eugene, Or, 1989 [1971]), pp. 65-88.

15 Crites distinguishes three forms of narrative. First there are sacred stories which orient the life of people through time and lie 'deep in the consciousness of a people,' forming a mythopoetic inheritance which is anonymous and communal. These stories are 'not like monuments ... but like dwelling places. People live in them,' Crites, 'The Narrative Quality of Experiences,' p.69. Secondly, there are mundane stories which consist both of the literary resources of culture and the everyday narrative communications that facilitate daily living. 'Here we find stories composed as works of art as well as the much more modest narrative communications that pass between people,' (Crites, 'The Narrative Quality of Experiences', p. 71.). Between sacred and mundane stories there is distinction without separation. New conjunctions are always possible in response to changing circumstances and mediating between these narrative forms is a third type – that of experience as consciously grasped *always* in narrative form.

16 For a discussion of the impact of Crites's essay see Michael Goldberg, *Theology and Narrative: A Critical Introduction* (Philadelphia, 1991), pp. 12-16.

Within literary studies the emerging school of gynocriticism[17] was also making claims that extended far beyond the modest assertion that you could learn about women's lives from reading their writing. It was now also being argued that literature written by women was the vehicle for a submerged female tradition which ran like a golden thread through history and connected us to the sacred wisdom of our foremothers. This idea, which both Christ and Plaskow have both explored in their later work, finds perhaps its clearest expression in the writings of the poet, critic and theologian, Alicia Ostriker.[18] She claimed that in the sacred narratives of our culture, *as well as in the work of contemporary women artists and writers*, is to be discovered the repressed traces of women's awareness of the female divine, 'shimmering and struggling at the liminal threshold of consciousness'.[19]

A tremendous impetus is given to the development of feminist theology through the turn to literature. But these were fast moving times and political debates within feminism resulted in the rapid reassessment of many early positions. In the 1980s the characterization of women's literature as the authentic expression of 'every woman's' lived reality and deepest convictions was increasingly challenged. Black and lesbian feminists asserted the *difference* of their own experience and traditions and, after some painful and acrimonious debates, the force of this position came to be widely acknowledged. Two aspects of the controversy are important in the context of this essay. First, prominent white religious feminists, such as Mary Daly and Christ herself, were amongst those who were most severely criticized for their appropriation of black women's writing.[20] It is my belief that the strong commitment already made to reading literature as a theological resource was the principle reason why these thinkers felt able to disregard the cultural specificity of the works they drew upon. Second, black and lesbian theologians themselves, found literature to be their own most powerful ally in asserting the particularity of their identity and thus destabilizing the universal. Katie Cannon's *Black Womanist Ethics* exemplifies the way some womanist theologians turned to literature in order to explore the '"living space" carved out of the intricate web of racism, sexism and poverty'[21] in which black women were able to celebrate black life and 'make a reaffirmation of their spiritual roots'.[22]

---

17 The term employed by English speaking feminist theorists in the 1970s and 1980s to indicate that their literary and critical concerns were related to female culture and women's traditions. For an indication of the creativity and breadth of gynocritical thinking see Elaine Showalter, (ed.), *The New Feminist Criticism: Essays on Women, Literature and Theory* (London, 1986).

18 For example, Alicia Ostriker, *Stealing the Language: The Emergence of Women's Poetry in America* (London, 1987) and Alicia Ostriker, *Feminist Revision and the Bible* (Oxford. 1993).

19 Ostriker, *Feminist Revision and the Bible,* p. 50.

20 These criticisms were made on the basis of their inappropriate use of the work of black writers including Alice Walker and Notzake Shange. For a discussion of the controversies that resulted see Susan Thistlethwaite, *Sex, Race and God: Christian Feminism in Black and White* (London,1989).

21 Katie G. Cannon, *Black Womanist Ethics* (Atlanta, 1988), p. 7.

22 Ibid., p. 174.

The 90s saw the growing influence of postmodernism upon feminism. The recognition of difference became but one aspect of an enlarged focus upon alterity, desire, the obligation to the 'other'.[23] Once again literature was turned to as a resource. This time not because it affirmed specific identities but rather because it was understood to embody the particularity, contingency and heterogeneity of women's lives. As such it stood in clear contradiction to the logocentric, universalizing discourses of philosophy and theology. Kathleen Sands, for example, employs women's literature to construct a theology that is restless, provisional, accountable and able to address the 'radical plurality of goods and powers that has become the truth at the end of modernity'.[24]

In the space of a very few years we see women's literature employed in differing, and even contradictory ways, by feminist theologians. Such is the continuing diversity within the movement that all of the hermeneutical strategies outlined above can still be encountered in contemporary work – one approach has not overcome all the others despite the important distinctions between them! This is an interesting phenomenon in itself but one that becomes easier to comprehend when we recognize that in all these divergent uses literature is characterized in a similar way. In each one 'she' is represented as a female voice speaking out against the monolithic discourses of the male centred tradition. In her care are the spiritual insights of women that have passed unrecognized and unacknowledged within mainstream scholarship. As Sands argues, the moves made by women like Christ and Plaskow in the early 1970s have succeeded in firmly establishing 'women's literature as a theological source that while still largely ignored by andocentric religious studies has become vital to most religious feminists'.[25]

Two steps back

And feminist scholarship in theology is undoubtedly richer and deeper and more creative because this is the case. However, it is also true that, as well as opening up many new avenues of thought, the way literature has been read by religious feminists has also closed off and restricted others. This process began early on. The specific works of literature that initially so inspired Christ and Plaskow were the novels of Doris Lessing. These were widely read within the emerging feminist movement.[26] Elaine Showalter wrote of Lessing:

---

23 This raises two important questions for feminists. The first is, 'How far is the move to the high grounds of poststructuralist theory a means of escaping the concrete responsibilities towards the specific 'others' we encounter in everyday social relations?' The second is, 'What are the links between feminist discourses of the other (from de Beauvoir onwards) and the development of postructualism?' For a discussion of both these topics see Walton, *Literature, Theology and Feminism*, pp.77-93.

24 Kathleen Sands, *Escape from Paradise: Evil and Tragedy in Feminist Theology* (Minneapolis, 1994), p.38.

25 Ibid., p. 124.

26 For a discussion of Lessing's significance see Gayle Greene *Changing the Story: Feminist Fiction and the Tradition* (Chicago, 1991), p.106.

> She has an extraordinary, barometric sensitivity to the social climate … she anticipates trends … the encyclopaedic study of intellectual and political women in *The Golden Notebook* preceded and in a sense introduced the Women's Liberation Movement.[27]

Lessing's oeuvre is remarkable not only for its social challenge but also for the spiritual themes it articulates. Although Christ, in particular, was initially deeply interested in the mystical aspects of Lessing's writings[28] she later came to place more value upon a spirituality generated out of women's solidarity and material connections to the world than on the forms of psychic mediation which are represented in Lessing's more speculative texts. She began to distrust literature that distracted attention away from the everyday problems women face or failed to offer positive accounts of women engaged in emancipatory processes of self-discovery. She felt no compunction at all about advising women authors that their feminist readers required they

> write stories in which the spiritual and social quest can be combined *in the life of a realistic woman*. And also one task facing readers is not to be fully satisfied with women's literature until it does so.[29]

The decided preference for realist literature, texts that appear to represent genuine women in clear and unambiguous ways, is one which has been sustained by religious feminists, following Christ. Even when deeply symbolic novels, such as Marilynne Robinson's *Housekeeping*,[30] or haunted and mysterious texts, like Toni Morrison's *Beloved*,[31] are the subject for reflection the discussion generally omits their literary peculiarities and reads them as if they were describing 'real life'.

The requirement that feminists are provided with trustworthy and inspiring accounts to read extends itself into a concern for the authors of texts. Clearly the works of men are not to be relied upon but neither are those books written by women whose credentials are suspect. These include bourgeois women, literary women who appear to place more significance upon writing than action, and avant-garde women authors whose work is esoteric or inaccessible. An awful lot of literature falls through the net and what remains is often stripped of its literary form and read for content alone. In other words it is not read as literature – it is read for what it contributes to developing the theological projects of religious feminists. I would go further and argue it is read as sacred text.

Reading sacred texts

I have argued so far that most religious feminists draw upon a circumscribed range of literary texts in their theological work. These tend to be realist in genre (although

---

27 Elaine Showalter, *A Literature of Their Own: British Women Novelists from Charlotte Brontë to Doris Lessing* (London, 1977), p. 307.

28 As found, for example in, Doris Lessing, *The Four Gated City* (London, 1990).

29 Carol Christ, *Diving Deep and Surfacing,* p. 40.

30 Marilynne Robinson, *Housekeeping* (London, 1981).

31 Toni Morrison, *Beloved* (London, 1987).

magical realism is permitted if the author is Latin American, Asian or Black) and to have been produced by a woman writer whose personal identity reassures readers that her writing can be treated as a valid source. The texts thus selected are read in a particular way – and this is not between the lines! The feminist theologian seeks to distil a (generally positive) message from their content that is of use to her in her own project. Whilst literature has undoubtedly served religious feminists extremely well, they are in now in danger of subordinating 'her' creative resources to the imperious demands of theology. As Annelies van Heijst,[32] argues feminist theologians are too often reading for recognition, 'because they wish to see their meanings (theological or feminist themes) endorsed in the literary text'.[33] In so doing they obliterate, 'the *literary* character of the text' and, I would add, this restricts the power literature has to challenge and change our thinking.

But of course, nobody is out there directing religious feminists what to talk about in their book groups or what to read in bed. I think the restricted reading practices that are now becoming problematic for us can best be understood as an unwelcome outcome of the otherwise very productive turn to literature in feminist theology. The fact that certain texts are read in certain ways is integral to the processes through which all communities of readers engage with what, for them, functions as sacred text. An important essay by Robert Detweiler is relevant to the discussion here. In 'What is a Sacred Text?'[34] Detweiler argues that when a body of people start to privilege certain texts as sacred, forms of canonical regulation inevitably occur. The favoured works begin to be read differently, criticism is constrained and interpretations restricted; the text is accorded a special status and the 'free play of response,'[35] curtailed.

Detweiler goes on to argue that the believer approaches a sacred text with the expectation that it will mediate for her 'some divine reality and hence connect her to that reality'.[36] Religious feminists have sought in literature spiritual encounters that are deeply connected to their embodied experience, that are identity affirming, politically empowering and personally nurturing.[37] Women's literature is well equipped to serve as a channel for such epiphanies. However, it is also able to testify to the more terrifying forms in which divinity can appear and, indeed, the apparent absence of God in a world of intense suffering. Courageous theological reflection

---

32 Annelies van Heijst, *Longing for the Fall* (Kampen, 1995).

33 Ibid., p.256.

34 Robert Detweiler, 'What is a Sacred Text?' *Semeia*, 31, 1985, pp. 213-30.

35 Ibid., p. 214.

36 Ibid., p. 221.

37 In the early days of feminist theology, Rosemary Radford Ruether made an affirmation of the full humanity of women the touchstone against which to test the validity of all theological truth claims. She wrote, 'Theologically speaking, whatever diminishes or denies the full humanity of women must be presumed not to reflect the divine, or an authentic relation to the divine, or to reflect the authentic nature of things.' This critical principle remains foundational to feminist theological understanding. Whilst it has functioned as an important standard through which to critique misogynist theological systems, the assumption that God is good and nice and a girl is certainly a domestication of the divine. Rosemary Radford Ruether, *Sexism and God Talk* (London, 1983), p.19.

requires the challenge of these darker encounters and the meeting with forms of alterity that do not so much support our theological constructions as grind them into fragments. If feminist theology is to advance from the impasse that many believe it is now experiencing, then literature could once again prove to be a vital resource. However, we would need to approach literary texts in a different spirit. This would entail calling into question our own reading practices, becoming aware of the ways in which others have viewed the relationship between literature and theology and communicating the critical insights feminism can bring to interdisciplinary conversations.

Losing innocence

A lot is at stake in making this move.

As director of a centre resourcing interdisciplinary research in theology and the arts, I am dismayed and frustrated by the fact that few of my colleagues or students currently working in this area display any awareness of the ways in which feminist theologians have been reflecting upon literary texts for more than thirty years. The fact that scholarship produced by groups that lack status in the academy is easily marginalized and ignored is widely documented (see for example Moi[38] and Krondorfer[39]). I do, however, acknowledge that there are reasons other than the politics of academic life why this work has been overlooked. Our seclusion has been maintained because the tone and content of our writing differs markedly from that of other scholars in the field, because our concerns have been practical rather than theoretical and most of all because we have not been reading literature 'as literature'.[40] If we now seek to engage with wider conversations we would need to abandon the notion that literature straightforwardly communicates sacred truths to us in forms that do not require critical interrogation. We would be required to consider genre, form, symbolism and other significant literary categories. Worse than this we would soon find ourselves risking the fall into theory.

Whilst a cautious engagement with poststructuralism has been evident in the work of feminist theologians for a number of years there has been a marked reluctance to bring the insights of theory to bear upon our readings of women's literature. We have preserved a strong sense of reverence when approaching those literary texts which we have identified as revealing women's spiritual insights. Quite understandably we have been worried that deconstructive readings would obscure the clear challenges communicated in these works. We have also feared that moves

---

38 Toril Moi, 'Feminist Theory After Theory,' in M. Payne and J. Schad, (eds), *life.after. theory* (London, 2003), pp. 133-67.

39 Bjorn Krondorfer, 'Who's Afraid of Gay Theology,' *Theology and Sexuality,* 13/3, pp. 257-74.

40 Indeed our preferred term 'women's writing' effectively 'un-disciplines' literary works which can then more easily be put to a variety of uses (for a discussion of all these issues see Walton, *Imagining Theology,* pp. 18-34).

to proclaim the 'death of the author'[41] would mean that we could no longer claim that women's writing functioned as a special source of insight into our identity and experience. Furthermore, as the fundamental impulse in feminist theology has been to range 'female' literary texts against the 'male' texts of the tradition, it has been strategically necessary to maintain a strong connection between the author and her text. This assures that the difference we claim for women's writing can be sustained. As Chris Weedon argues, it is 'the author who guarantees the presence of this difference by her womanhood'.[42]

For all of these reasons the epistemological assumptions and critical methods of poststructuralism have appeared as more of a threat than an opportunity for religious feminists reading literature. To an existing deep suspicion that *all* theory represents a masculine form of rationality that is damaging and disempowering for women we have brought additional concerns that poststructuralism is particularly obscure, elitist and apolitical. As Lidia Curti argues a 'general hostility to theory,' has been intensified in the case of poststructuralism because of its apparent undue 'stress on language and its neglect of the social'.[43]

Ironically what we have most feared, a focus upon language – within which topics such as literary form, textuality, the nature of 'writing' become issues of concern – is precisely what enables communities of readers to engage with their sacred texts in radical, innovative and creative ways. We lose our innocence when we realize that language does not represent but forms (and re-forms) our world. A space then opens up between readers and texts, between authors and texts, between sacred words and human words which is the space of our freedom to interpret, interject and imagine. I believe feminist theology needs to enter this space in order to encounter the strangeness and the disturbing power of literature once again. I admit it may seem incongruous that in a period in which it is widely pronounced that high theory has had its day and chastened forms of materialist criticism are re-emerging,[44] I appear to be advocating a turn to the text rather than a return to the world. I could respond, with conviction, that in order to achieve the second naiveté one has to outgrow the first. However, I am not principally concerned that feminist theology becomes more sophisticated, less gauche, easier to take to parties and more entertaining to sit with at high table. What preoccupies me is the need for feminist theology to discover in their engagement with literature new forms of political energy in a period when some prominent women theologians are calling for a repudiation of emancipatory visions and a return to orthodoxy.[45]

---

41 See Roland Barthes, 'The Death of the Author,' in Roland Barthes, *Image, Music, Text* (London, 1977), pp. 142-49 and Michel Foucault, 'What is an Author?' in J. Harari, (ed.), *Textual Strategies: Perspectives in Post-Structuralist Criticism* (Ithaca, 1979).

42 Chris Weedon, *Feminist Practice and Poststructuralist Theory* (Oxford, 1987), p. 154.

43 Lidia Curti, *Female Stories, Female Bodies: Narrative, Identity and Representation* (Basingstoke, 1998), p. 13.

44 See, for example, Judith Butler, John Guillory, Kendall Thomas, (eds), *What's Left of Theory? New Work on the Politics of Literary Theory* (London, 2000).

45 In an important essay, Susan Parsons critiques the whole developmental arc of feminist theology as it originated in the affirmation of experience and has been sustained through a

Does this mean turning our back on the work of the past and all the readings of women's literature that have been so important in the emergence of feminist theology? I think not. My argument rather has been that unreflective adherence to certain ways of reading has resulted in us unwittingly engaging in processes of sacralization that are now confining us instead of leading us into a wider space. There is no requirement that we declare former hermeneutical strategies invalid because of this. Indeed it would be ridiculous to do so when, as I have already pointed out, feminist theology has cherished a variety of ways of reading for many years now without finding it necessary to choose between them. What is necessary, however, is that we recognize our readings as precisely that – hermeneutical strategies. We have never simply taken books down off the shelf and read them. There has always been a great deal more going on than that. In our new encounters with literature we should take pride in the ingenious solutions feminist theologians found to many epistemological problems through their literary work but also look to extend the potential of reading into areas of crucial importance which we have yet to engage with, although beginnings are already being made, an example of which, that sets out potential new directions in reading practices, I now consider below.

Poesis and trauma

In a groundbreaking essay entitled 'Theology and the Poetics of Testimony' Rebecca Chopp[46] engages with the work of Shoshona Felman[47] concerning the ways in which the silence of trauma can best be overcome.[48] Chopp concurs with Felman that straightforward factual accounts are often simply inadequate to bear the burden of unspeakable sufferings. They misrepresent them whilst attempting to contain them, therefore those that seek to bear testimony must turn to other forms of language. Chopp is concerned that theology (which in its philosophical and systematic modes at least, has privileged rational forms of discourse) can be opened up to receive the challenges of testimony and argues that this will entail recognizing the special role that poetics, that is innovative (literary) forms of language, can play:

---

shared discourse of social transformation. She sees the feminist 'turn into the world' (p. 129) as evidence of a practical atheism that has now reached an inevitable dead end. For Parsons, it is time for religious feminists to return home and go back to church on Sundays instead of seeking secular reforms 'as if divine providence could be taken into human hands' (p. xv). See Susan Parsons, 'Feminist Theology as Dogmatic Theology,' in Susan Parsons, (ed.), *The Cambridge Companion to Feminist Theology* (Cambridge, 2002), pp.114-32.

46 Rebecca Chopp, 'Theology and the Poetics of Testimony,' in Delwin Brown, Sheila Greeve Davaney and Kathryn Tanner, (eds), *Converging on Culture: Theologians in Dialogue with Cultural Analysis and Criticism* (Oxford, 2001), pp. 56-70.

47 Shoshona Felman and Dauri Laub, *Testimony: Crises of Witnessing in Literature, Psychoanalysis and History* (London, 1992).

48 I have also found Felman's work very important in the development of my own thinking. For my rather different response to issues raised in her writing see Walton, *Literature, Theology and Feminism*, pp. 30-6.

[Poetics] is an invention, for it must create language, forms, images to speak in what in some way has been ruled unspeakable or at least not valid or credible to modern reason. Compared to rhetoric poetics does not seek so much to argue as to refigure, to reimagine and refashion the world. Poetics is a discourse that reshapes, fashions in new ways, enlarges and calls into question the ordering of discourse[49]

Although inspired by Felman, Chopp's thinking on this issue draws deeply on the hermeneutical theories of Paul Ricoeur. Ricoeur's argument is that semantic innovation is not only a means of breaking silence concerning issues of vital concern, it is also a cultural intervention that destabilizes the existing order. Taking metaphor as the representative of language in militant action, Ricoeur writes that new linguistic conjunctions tear down the fragile shelters we have built to stabilize our lives and changes 'our way of dwelling in the world ... metaphor shatters not only the previous structures of our language but also the previous structures of what we call reality'.[50]

In Ricoeur's thinking, this image of the metaphor as the place where impossible elements combine to generate creative energy comes to represent what can be achieved through literature. As extended metaphoric utterance, literature can probe our darkness to its deepest core and brand our eyes with new revelations: 'The more imagination deviates from that which is called reality in ordinary vision the more it approaches the heart of reality ... Under the shock of fiction reality becomes problematic for us.'[51]

This is a very different approach to literature from those we have encountered within feminist theology up till now. It values the generative power of language to make the existing order of things 'unhomely' for us and propel us into processes of imaginative transformation. Literature is celebrated precisely for its literary qualities; because it speaks strangely to us, finds words for things that do not exist or have been previously unspoken, is not true or realistic and is not caught in the many nets of commonplace assumptions that tie us to the ground. These conventional webs of meaning Chopp refers to as the 'social imaginary' – a term widely used to describe the cultural representations that sustain, 'common understanding that makes possible common practices and a widely shared sense of legitimacy'.[52] Literature is one of the most powerful means that we have of contesting with the common sense forces of the social imaginary and communicating faith in what we have not seen but hope for.

Chopp is a deeply political theologian and her thinking is important because it offers a justification for an engagement with literature (indeed art in all forms – including avant garde art, complicated, difficult art *and art produced by men*) that does not require a repudiation of political responsibility. Her primary motivation, following Felman, was to find a means of attending to unspeakable suffering. However, this trajectory led her to affirm that creative forms of expression have a

---

49 Chopp, 'Theology and the Poetics of Testimony, p. 61.

50 Paul Ricoeur, *A Ricoeur Reader: Reflection and Imagination,* (ed.), Mario Valdes, (Hemel Hempstead, 1991), p.55.

51 Ibid., p. 33.

52 Charles Taylor, *Modern Social Imaginaries* (Durham and London,2004), p. 25.

destabilizing potential in the social sphere and that theologians should consider the import of this in their own writing. The final part of Chopp's essay offers a brief speculative consideration of what a theology that affirms 'poesis' might resemble and what new insights might emerge if we lost our fear of unreason and learned to appreciate the art in our theological craft.

These are exciting challenges and promise much. For my own part I think that even more radical and daring gestures are possible if we are prepared to imagine an aesthetics of feminist theological thinking – a move long overdue.[53] But perhaps a step at a time is best. The first step might be to learn to love literature without requiring that she promises to be 'true' – to seek a more open relationship with our sacred texts.

Bibliography

Barthes, Roland, 'The Death of the Author,' in Roland Barthes, *Image, Music, Text* (London: Fontana, 1977): 142-49.

Brown, Delwin, Sheila Greeve Davaney and Kathryn Tanner, (eds), *Converging on Culture: Theologians in Dialogue with Cultural Analysis and Criticism* (Oxford: Oxford University Press, 2001).

Butler, Judith, John Guillory and Kendall Thomas, (eds), *What's Left After Theory: New Work on the Politics of Literary Theory* (London: Routledge, 2000).

Cannon, Katie, *Black Womanist Ethics* (Atlanta: Scholars Press, 1988).

Christ, Carol, and Judith Plaskow, (eds), *Womanspirit Rising: A Feminist Reader in Religion* (San Francisco: Harper and Row, 1979).

Christ, Carol, 'Spiritual Quest and Women's Experience' in Carol Christ and Judith Plaskow, (eds), *Womanspirit Rising: A Feminist Reader in Religion* (San Francisco: Harper and Row, 1979): 228-45.

Christ, Carol, *Diving Deep and Surfacing: Women Writers on the Spiritual Quest* (Boston: Beacon Press, 1980).

Chopp, Rebecca, 'Theology and the Poetics of Testimony,' in Delwin Brown, Sheila Greeve Davaney and Kathryn Tanner, (eds), *Converging on Culture: Theologians in Dialogue with Cultural Analysis and Criticism* (Oxford: Oxford University Press, 2001): 56-70.

Crites, Stephen, 'The Narrative Quality of Experience' in Stanley Hauerwas and L. Gregory Jones, (eds), *Why Narrative? Readings in Narrative Theology* (Eugene, Or: Wipf and Stock Publishers, 1989 [1971]): 65-88.

Curti, Lidia, *Female Stories, Female Bodies: Narrative, Identity and Representation* (Basingstoke: Macmillan, 1998).

de Beauvoir, Simone, *The Second Sex*, trans. H.M. Parshley (London: Pan Books, 1972 [1949]).

Detweiler, Robert, 'What is a Sacred Text?', *Semeia 31* (1985): 13-230

---

53 For the beginnings of this process see Walton, *Literature, Theology and Feminism*, p. 167-93.

Felman, Shoshona and Dauri Laub, *Testimony: Crises of Witnessing in Literature, Psychoanalysis and History* (London: Routledge, 1992).

Frei, Hans, *The Eclipse of Biblical Narrative: A Study in Eighteenth and Nineteenth Century Hermeneutics* (Yale: Yale University Press, 1974).

Foucault, Michel, 'What is an Author?' in Josue Harari, (ed.), *Textual Strategies: Perspectives in Post-Structuralist Criticism* (London: Methuen): 141-60.

Greene, Gayle, *Changing the Story: Feminist Fiction and the Tradition* (Chicago: University of Chicago Press 1991).

Goldberg, Michael, *Theology and Narrative: A Critical Introduction* (Philadelphia: Trinity Press, 1991).

Harari, Josue, (ed.), *Textual Strategies: Perspectives in Post-Structuralist Criticism* (London: Methuen): 141-60.

Hauerwas, Stanley and L. Gregory Jones, (eds), *Why Narrative? Readings in Narrative Theology* (Eugene, Or: Wipf and Stock Publishers, 1989 [1971]).

Krondorfer, Bjorn, 'Who's Afraid of Gay Theology,' *Theology and Sexuality,* 13/3: 257-74.

Lessing, Doris, *The Four Gated City* (London: Paladin, 1990).

Mead, Margaret, *Male and Female: A Study of the Sexes in a Changing World* (Westport, Ct: Greenwood Press, 1977 [1949]).

Moi, Toril, 'Feminist Theory After Theory,' in M. Payne and J. Schad, (eds), *life. after.theory* (London: Continuum, 2003): 133-167.

Morrison, Toni, *Beloved* (London: Chatto and Windus, 1987).

Ostriker, Alicia, *Stealing the Language: The Emergence of Women's Poetry in America* (London: The Womens' Press, 1987).

Ostriker, Alicia, *Feminist Revision and the Bible* (Oxford: Oxford University Press, 1993).

Parsons, Susan, 'Feminist Theology as Dogmatic Theology' in Susan Parsons, (ed.), *The Cambridge Companion to Feminist Theology* (Cambridge: Cambridge University Press): 114-32.

Parsons, Susan, (ed.), *The Cambridge Companion to Feminist Theology* (Cambridge: Cambridge University Press).

Payne, Michael and John Schad, (eds), *life.after.theory: Interviews with Jacques Derrida, Sir Frank Kermode, Toril Moi, Christopher Norris* (London: Continuum, 2003).

Plaskow, Judith, *Sex, Sin and Grace: Women's Experience and the Theologies of Reinhold Niebuhr and Paul Tillich* (Washington: University Press of America, 1980).

Robinson, Marilynne, *Housekeeping* (London: Faber and Faber, 1981).

Ruether, Rosemary Radford, *Sexism and God Talk* (London: SCM Press).

Saiving, Valerie, 'The Human Situation: A Feminine View' in Carol Christ and Judith Plaskow, (eds), *Womanspirit Rising: A Feminist Reader in Religion* (San Francisco: Harper and Row, 1979): 25-42.

Sands, Kathleen, *Escape from Paradise: Evil and Tragedy in Feminist Theology* (Minneapolis: Fortress Press, 1994)

Showalter, Elaine, *A Literature of Their Own: British Women Writers from Charlotte Brontë to Doris Lessing* (London: Virago, 1977).

Showalter, Elaine, (ed.), *The New Feminist Criticism: Essays on Women, Literature and Theory* (London: Virago, 1986).

Taylor, Charles, *Modern Social Imaginaries* (Durham and London: Duke University Press, 2004).

Thistlethwaite, Susan, *Sex, Race and God: Christian Feminism in Black and White* (London: Geoffrey Chapman, 1989).

Valdes, Mario, (ed.), *A Ricoeur Reader: Reflection and Imagination* (Hemel Hempstead: Harvester Wheatsheaf, 1991).

van Heijst, Annelies, *Longing for the Fall* (Kampen: Kok Pharos Publishing House, 1995).

Walton, Heather, *Literature, Theology and Feminism* (Manchester: Manchester University Press, 2007).

Walton, Heather, *Imagining Theology: Women, Writing and God* (London: T and T Clark, 2007).

Weedon, Chris, *Feminist Practice and Poststructuralist Theory* (Oxford: Blackwell, 1987).

Woolf, Virginia, *A Room of One's Own* (London: Grafton Books, 1977).

Chapter 6

The Desire for Interactivity and the Emerging Texts of the Blogosphere[1]

Katharine Sarah Moody

Introduction

On our right, projected on a large screen, a pair of hands rips up the Bible, a Stanley knife slices at the pages, and a black marker pen blots out words and sentences. On our left, the hands unfold scrunched-up pages and smooth down inked-out scraps. The pieces are pasted into a blank book, the snippets stuck in unsystematically, with no attempt to recreate the original whole out of the fragments. These video loops are part of a 'theodrama' performed by Ikon, an 'iconic, apocalyptic, heretical, emerging, and failing' 'transformance art' collective from Belfast, Northern Ireland.[2] Ikon's multi-media performance poses multiple questions for the gathering, rather than providing singular answers from a fixed interpretive authority. There is not only a hint of the new interactive relationships possible between individuals and the biblical text, but between individuals and all forms of text.

This theme is being echoed by an increasing number of contemporary Christian communities across North America, the UK, Australia, New Zealand, and Western Europe; communities who articulate their religious identities in the language of emergence, and specifically through the use of the marker 'emergent' or 'emerging church'. But this term remains difficult to define and the communities themselves remain resistant to any form of classification which might be exclusive of difference.[3] These communities are concerned to be incarnate in contemporary culture, as it begins a gradual but significant postmodern turn. Within these communities, there is a critique of Christianity's damaging capitulations to modernism and an exploration of Christian identity, theology and community in shifting cultural contexts.

1   I would like to thank the Arts and Humanities Research Council for enabling me to undertake my doctoral studies.

2   wiki.ikon.org.uk This performance, entitled 'Fundamentalism,' was staged at the Greenbelt Festival, Cheltenham, UK, on Sunday 27 August 2006.

3   I prefer the language of 'emerging Christian communities' to reflect some unease with the institutional connotations of the word 'church', to indicate an emphasis on community and relationship, and to reflect an understanding of Christian identity as something which one is continually becoming, 'emerging' into, rather than ever fully being, having, or inhabiting. This language remains problematic, however, as several communities are not exclusively Christian. Where I use the phrase 'emerging church' to either indicate the parameters used in an Internet search or the language used by others, it shall be presented in quotation marks.

The emergence of these forms of Christian community is aided by the advent of Web 2.0 interactive technologies.[4] The recent phenomenon of blogging is particularly significant for their existence and development. It is assumed that the interactivity of these technologies facilitates the desired move from Christians as passive consumers towards Christians as active creators, participants in the creative agency of a creative God, and their suggested participatory, collaborative, and egalitarian nature is held to reflect emerging concerns about outdated social structures among Christian communities.

This chapter explores blogging in the context of emerging Christian communities, reflecting on this form of computer-mediated communication in order to establish the nature of blogs as texts. Firstly, I identify several new values associated with text in postmodernity which are highlighted by an exploration of the blogosphere. In particular, the cyber location of these texts serves to underline the cognitive and affective desire for interactivity which feminist literary theorist Lynn Pearce identifies in conventional reading practices and processes. Secondly, therefore, I present two mechanisms by which creative textual interaction is achieved – commenting and linking – and through which new text values are made visible. However, I argue thirdly that linking patterns are conversely creating authorities.[5] Finally, I suggest that blogging potentially reinstates the position of the author in the reader-text relationship – a major disparity between new text values and text in the blogosphere.

New text values: the desire for interactivity

The use of texts by emerging Christian communities reflects a shift in reading and writing practices, one among many aspects of contemporary Western life which intersect with coexisting concerns among these communities. Tallskinnykiwi, aka Andrew Jones, an 'emerging church' blogger who has been blogging since 2001, writes that, 'It is obvious that there is a cross-over of values – new media values

---

4   The term 'Web 2.0' generally refers to a second generation of web-based communities and the technologies developed to facilitate the desired interactive networking of such Internet users. These developments from information provision to interactive engagement represent a shift from a readerly to a writerly relationship with online texts.

5   Recently, Heidi Campbell has noted the indeterminacy of the term 'authority' in studies of religion online. She concludes that distinctions need to be made by researchers with regard to different layers of religious authority, highlighting four differentiated forms or types of authority: hierarchies or roles, structures or systems, ideologies or beliefs, and texts or sources. See Heidi Campbell, 'Who's Got the Power? Religious Authority and the Internet', *Journal of Computer-Mediated Communication* 12(3), article 14 (2007). [accessed 05/11/07] http://jcmc.indiana.edu/vol12/issue3/campbell.html. In this current chapter, the term 'authority' is positioned in relation to two context specific usages; namely, 'authority' as equated with popularity, influence, and (thereby assumed) expertise by blog aggregators such as Technorati (see below), and 'authority,' on the one hand, as critiqued by emerging Christian communities and, on the other, as constructed as communally acknowledged voices of insight, dynamism, honesty, and humour.

and new church values'.[6] Blogging is thus a site where several interconnecting value systems can meet and find their expression. He draws attention to 'new media values,' alluding to new paradigms of software production and development such as Open Source Programming (OSP), which suitably connect with 'new church values' treasuring inclusivity and participation.[7] However, blogs can also be understood as a site where possible 'new text values' are more clearly seen and practiced than among conventional print-reading and -writing processes.

In the conclusion to *Feminism and the Politics of Reading*, Lynn Pearce reflects on the possible implications of what she refers to as 'interactive textual engagement' or ITE. Her work explores what happens to us when we read texts, 'verbal, visual or otherwise,' but her conclusion goes further to consider the increasing 'otherwise-ness' of texts in the 'cybernetic' twenty-first century.[8] She concludes that,

> ... these visions of our ITE-future appear simply to make visible things about reading that have always appertained, not least, as in my thesis here, that it is predicated upon a *desire*, at least, for interactivity ... [9]

The reader exercises their 'will-to-relationship',[10] but Pearce describes the frustrations of the reader when the textual other refuses to allow the interaction which we desire. We have done our part in the reader-text romance through various reader-strategies, including character-identification and extra-textual imaginings, but the text may not reciprocate and the reader is left feeling frustrated at the lack of 'intertextual attention' and 'recognition'.[11] These feelings of unrequited desire fuel the yearning for more interactive methods of encountering texts.

> ... I am craving a more interactive textual experience. And where once I (we) were prepared to put in the readerly labour to get this interaction from textual products, now we are more attracted to *textual processes* (such as electronic mail, MUDs [multi-user domains] and other interactive art forms) where our textual others are more readily responsive. [12]

For Pearce, the reader's desire for interaction seeks to affectively, as well as hermeneutically, engage with a variety of textual others. The reader desires

---

6   tallskinnykiwi, 'blogging and emerging church,' January 22, 2004.

7   OSP is a mode of software production and development that allows open access to the product's source materials, so that progress is made by any number of people working in community (for example, Linux and MediaWiki). See further, Eric Raymond, 'The Cathedral and the Bazaar,' 1997. Several websites related to emerging Christian communities utilize the OSP model, including Ikon's wiki, wiki.ikon.org.uk, and the collaborative theological project Open Source Theology, www.opensourcetheology.net. This model is being extended beyond software to become a paradigm for political and social organization and religious community. See, for example, Douglas Rushkoff, *Open Source Democracy: How Online Communication is Changing Offline Politics* (Demos, 2003).

8   Lynn Pearce, *Feminism and the Politics of Reading* (London, 1997), p.253.

9   Ibid., p.253, *her emphasis*.

10   Ibid., p.20.

11   Ibid., p.158.

12   Ibid., p.254, *her emphasis*.

interactivity beyond understanding the author and/or making his/her own cognitive meaning from the text. An emotional event occurs, the intensity of which creates a desire in the reader for the textual other(s) to know this, and respond in turn. There is a resultant frustration when this proves impossible.

Recognition of this desire for interactivity can be seen at the root of many developments in post-structuralist literary theory. In order to highlight where blogs as texts 'make visible things about reading that have always appertained', I draw attention to three interconnecting new text values: the readerly/writerly distinction, the death of the author, and the situatedness of meaning. Barthes's *lisible/scriptible* distinction between the readerly and writerly qualities of texts highlights the processes and practices of reading, rather than privileging the product – the text and its structure, closed by the author.[13] The connections made by readers of writerly texts enable readers to become writers themselves in the very reading of such texts. This new text value of the *scriptible* favours meaning-making as an interactive process, over the passive consumption of an already produced meaning limited by the author.[14] Similarly, Barthes's death of the author thesis highlights that the reader is the site where meaning is made, rather than the author,

> We know now that a text is not a line of words releasing a single "theological" meaning (the "message" of the Author-God) but a multidimensional space in which a variety of writings, none of them original, blend and clash ... there is one place where this multiplicity is focused and that place is the reader, not, as was hitherto said, the author. [15]

New text values stress plurality and intertextuality, Derridean '*différence*' and the Barthian 'already written' as a means of emphasizing the importance of both the reader and the reader's situatedness, his/her 'interpretive communities',[16] as the sites where meanings are made.

Blogs can be understood as cultural products which utilize new textual processes to increase the levels of interaction possible between text and reader. Blogs are interactive websites containing regularly updated entries or 'posts', modifying the format of a diary or log ('blog' is short for 'weblog') so that the most recent posts are displayed at the top of the page, with previous entries below in reverse chronological order. Authors ('bloggers') can blog about their lives, uploading photographs, video and sound files from daily or special events, or blog regarding more specialized topics of interest.[17] However, blogs differ from both private,

---

13 Roland Barthes, *S/Z: An Essay*, trans. Richard Miller. (Hill & Wang, [1970]1991).

14 Ann Jefferson, 'Structuralism and Post-Structuralism', in Ann Jefferson and Robey, David, (eds), *Modern Literary Theory: A Comparative Introduction* (London, [1982]1995), pp. 92-121.

15 Roland Barthes, 'The Death of the Author', in, Seán Burke, (ed.), *Authorship: From Plato to the Postmodern – A Reader* (Edinburgh, [1995]2003), pp. 128-29.

16 Fish, Stanley, *Is There a Text in This Class? The Authority of Interpretive Communities* (Cambridge, Massachusetts, [1980]2003), pp. 303-21.

17 The politics of definition have been acknowledged by Foucault. The cyber location of blogs means that the attribution of the term 'text' to these cultural products and 'author' to their producers necessitates an exploration of the ways in which such use might reveal not only

personal diaries, and logs written for a small, specialist audience such as a ship's log, in that they are 'published' on the Internet for anyone with web-access to read, the 'blogosphere' being the name given to the Internet-based spaces in which these blog-related activities occur, a part of that more general realm signified by the term cyberspace. Blogs allow individuals to store, organize, process, and distribute information, whether personal or more purposive. There are several technological features inherent in blogging which facilitate the textual interaction, attention, and recognition Pearce desires of 'interactive textual engagement', and which reflect the new text values mentioned above.

Mechanisms of textual interaction in the blogosphere

The cyber location of text in the blogosphere problematizes conventional notions of 'text' in several ways. Texts within the blogosphere cannot be easily categorised as written, verbal, or visual, since blogs combine these types of text.[18] There is not only the text of the individual blog posting, but also the variety of other texts surrounding that post; banners, taglines, side-bars, footers, blogrolls, links, and a host of other blog elements are significant for textual analysis. Two particular features of blogging –comments and links – further complicate ways in which authorship is assigned and text is circumscribed. Both these features reflect the new text value of interaction.

While blog posts are generally written by an individual (even where the blog is that of a community or collective, individual posts tend to be written by one member at a time), the mechanisms through which others can contribute to the page quickly make answering the question, 'who is this text's author?' more difficult. Below each individual post is space for comments from readers, who can respond and further the conversation between themselves, the blogger, and any number of online others. Comments, and the ease with which a user can launch their own blog, mean that the list of contributing authors to text in the blogosphere is never static, unlike printed texts where authorship is clearer and fixed. Readers can very easily enter the discussion, encouraging new patterns of thinking, and enabling new ideas to emerge. These interactions can take the dialogue beyond the original writer's blog entry so

---

the complexities of circumscribing text and assigning authorship in the blogosphere, but also the politics behind such language usage. The latter is particularly evident in definitions of the term 'blog' and its assignment to only certain cyber-spacial texts. See further Michel Foucault 'What Is an Author?' in Bouchard, Donald F., (ed.), *Language, Counter-Memory, Practice: Selected Essays and Interviews by Michel Foucault* (Ithaca, New York, [1977]1980), pp.113-38; Susan C. Herring *et al*, 'Bridging the Gap: Genre Analysis of Weblogs' (2004a) www.ics. uci.edu/~jpd/classes/ics234cw04/herring.pdf; Susan C. Herring *et al*, 'Women and Children Last: The Discursive Construction of Weblogs' (2004b) http://blog.lib.umn.edu/blogosphere/ women_and_children.html; and Matthieu O'Neil, 'Weblogs and Authority' (2005) incsub. org/blogtalk/images/O'Neil.Blogtalk.revised

18   There are written words, sound files, illustrations, videos, and photographs. There are also paralinguistic and non-linguistic texts, such as acronyms (like 'lol' for 'laugh out loud' and 'IMHO' for 'in my humble opinion') and emoticons (for example typing :-) or inserting ☺).

that the originating voice is more a facilitator of meaning-making than a dictator of meaning.

Commenting on 'emerging church' blogs particularly facilitates cognitive and affective conversations about the nature and experience of Christianity in theological, geographical, social, and political contextual localities, and are regularly used by the diverse collective of emerging Christian communities in their theological reflections about any number of contemporary and historical phenomena.[19] The previously perceived boundaries of theology, constructed as the systematic study of Christian revelation found in the Bible, Christian history, and church authority, are being extended through the creation of cybertexts which reflect theologically upon a much broader collection of cultural phenomena.[20] The interactivity denied by the closed texts of printed theological treatises is encouraged in the blogosphere, serving to create 'ordinary' theologians and theological communities, and to provide a platform for their textual interactions together.[21]

The cognitive and affective interactive engagements between readers and textual others that occur during the process of reading are made more visible in the blogosphere than with conventional texts by the provision of a space for such interactions to be articulated publicly in the comments section or in a reader's own blog. Here readers interact directly with a host of diverse textual others in the blogosphere, highlighting literally – through tangible written responses – the writerly qualities of these texts. Open reading, with readers free to make intertextual connections, moves very quickly into open writing, with readers free to then express those connections. The boundaries between writing and reading processes become

---

19 Topics include: technologically-supported human creations (such as blogs, music, film, art, Godcasts, vjing); other cultural artefacts (football, beer, tv, fashion, food); social networks (family, friends, work, Ireland, Manchester, Greenbelt); and political issues (environment, justice, Middle East, democracy, economics, gender equality, poverty) as well as more narrowly defined theological and ecclesiological concerns (mission, monasticism, labyrinth, Kingdom of God, truth, Bible, liturgy, youth ministry), and fluid markers of religious identity (emerging church, alternative worship, emergent).

20 Here I am using the term 'theological' in a Milbankian sense, acknowledging that all positions are at root fundamentally religious commitments. Reflections, then, have to be *Christianly* theological in nature. See further John Milbank, *Theology and Social Theory: Beyond Secular Reason* (Oxford, [1990] 2006) and James K.A. Smith, *Introducing Radical Orthodoxy: Mapping a Post-Secular Theology* (Grand Rapids, Michigan, 2004). For the impact of blogging on new understandings of what 'theology' is and who can be a 'theologian', see further Katharine Moody, 'Theo(b)logy: The Technological Transformation of Theology', in John La Grou and Len Hjalmarson, (eds), *Voices of the Virtual World: Participative Technology and the Ecclesial Revolution* (Wikiklesia Press, 2007), pp. 213-19.

21 The language of ordinariness has been borrowed and modified from the work of Jeff Astley. Whilst Astley seems to still hold a conventional notion of 'theology' as a systematic and bounded discipline, and simply replaces one set of privileged voices (the professional theologian, the ordained minister) with another (the untrained theologian, the unordained minister), extending an understanding of ordinariness to include *all*, regardless of education, usefully emphasises not only the priesthood of all believers but the theologian-hood of all believers. Jeff Astley, *Ordinary Theology: Looking, Listening and Learning in Theology* (Aldershot, 2002).

blurred into one process of participatory and collaborative production; a commenter, by definition, is both reader and writer.[22] While 'emerging church' bloggers state their intentions to discuss issues of Christianity and culture in their taglines or blog descriptions,[23] emphasis is placed upon this process of production, or 'conversation,' rather than the product or conclusion. This is an emphasis in line with the 'new church values' of emerging Christian communities, reluctant to predetermine the position towards which they are emerging.

In the process of networking and communicating, commenters frequently post hyperlinks to other blogs and sites. Commenters can help take the original text not only into new conceptual directions through their textual interactions, but also into new virtual directions, by posting hyperlinks in their comments which readers follow through cyberspace as they follow the conversation. The existence of links in comments underscores that texts within the blogosphere are not confined to one particular, nor easily delineated, location in cyberspace. A commenter might provide a link to a post or webpage which is related to the discussion but which was not authored by them, or to a blog post they themselves have written in response to the dialogue going on at the original blog site. Links allow the conversation to 'jump' from one cyber location to another, but the text continues in this new location, whether that is another blog, some other website, a still or video graphic, or a podcast. In important cognitive and affective senses, these other textual artefacts are all a part of the text of the original blog post, serving to highlight that text in the blogosphere extends beyond one cyber-spacial location.

Efimova, Hendrick, and Anjewierden utilize the sociology of public spaces, and particularly the observations of city life in Gehl's *Life Between Buildings*, to frame their investigation of blog communities, which can be seen to exist in the 'life between blogs', in the interactions between blogs as well as in the blogs themselves.[24] The metaphor can be extended further, however, and the language modified, in order to begin to see text in the blogosphere as a complex and mobile 'text between texts', text as a shifting network of textual artefacts. Here, text emerges from the connections and interactions between bloggers, commenters, and other linked-to authors, rather than around a single space. Just as links, quotations, summaries, and trackback can be understood as 'conversational glue',[25] these mechanisms act as 'textual glue'. They are the technological apparatus through which the 'text between texts' is dialogically connected across the blogosphere and the other territories of cyberspace. This text emerges through the reconfiguration of fragments from originating bloggers into

---

22 This fusion of reading and writing roles is also apparent in neologisms such as 'wreader'.

23 See for example, blogs such as JesusCreed, www.jesuscreed.org ('devoted to Jesus, historic orthodoxy, and their relationship to our world'); Lo-Fi Tribe, www.lofitribe.com ('regular commentary on religion and culture'); and Next Reformation, nextreformation.com ('conversations around spirituality, leadership, and the emerging church').

24 Lilia Efimova *et al*, 'Finding "the life between buildings": An Approach for Defining a Weblog Community.' (2005) https://doc.telin.nl/dsweb/Get/Document-55092/.

25 Lilia Efimova and Aldo de Moor, 'Beyond Personal Webpublishing: An Exploratory Study of Conversational Blogging Practices' (2005) https://doc.telin.nl/dscgi/ds.py/Get/File-44480, p.8.

cognitive and affective cultural products. Consumers recombine the raw elements of the text provided by bloggers into a 'text between texts' – the makings of blog communities.

The mechanisms of interactivity within the blogosphere, particularly commenting and linking, blur distinctions between writers and readers and accentuate the writerly nature of blogs as texts. New text values are made visible through the very technologies being used to undertake textual interactions in the blogosphere, where the text moves organically through cyberspace along discursive lines drawn by a plurality of commenters and linked-to authors. Authorship is recognized as communal, meaning as plural, and text as dispersed and mobile. However, while hyperlinks ostensibly serve to assist conversation through making virtual connections between dispersed fragments to create a 'text between texts', there are reasons for and consequences of linking which must be considered, beyond the immediate benefit of contextualizing the conversation and 'glueing' the text together. As links to and from blogs are used by search engines and aggregators such as Technorati to statistically measure blogs, there are costs to interactivity for a blogging community that wishes to hold to certain 'new church values' in their online reading and writing practices.

Interactivity and authority

Technorati (www.technorati.com) uses the linking patterns generated by interaction in the blogosphere to determine the 'authority' levels of individual blogs.[26] For example, in June 2007 tallskinnykiwi's blog had 2,489 blogs linking to it in the last 6 months, and so tallskinnykiwi.typepad.com's authority ranking was calculated as 937. Technorati then categorizes blogs into authority groupings (see table below).[27] That Technorati does not have an official 'Very Low' authority grouping for blogs who have less than 3 blogs linking to them is perhaps an estimation of those bloggers' status. These authority rankings are reliant on the linking patterns between bloggers, and, while they are primarily instruments and indicators of interaction, links therefore have significant wider implications.

---

26 The particular links used by Technorati to determine linking patterns, and therefore 'authority,' are permalinks, which function as permanent links to a particular post even after the post in question has been archived. Whilst links in BlogRolls are useful in determining the *popularity* of a blog (how often a link to a blog occurs in the blogrolls of other bloggers), they are not accurate indications of how often that blog is visited and/or read. Instead, levels of blog *influence* are measured according to the frequency of permalinks made to the blogs by other sites. Permalinks within the text of Blog B to specific posts of Blog A reveals that Blog A has been read and that the author of Blog B has engaged with it, thus suggesting that Blog A has been influential in some way – positively and/or negatively.

Responding to a blog post questioning Technorati's choice of language, Peter Hirshberg, CMO Technorati Inc., comments that 'authority' is 'something of a term of art' which 'shouldn't imply a value judgement.' Steve Rubel, 'What is Authority?' February 13, 2006, http://www.micropersuasion.com/2006/02/what_is_authori.html. However, if the language does not suggest value, a numerical ranking system certainly does.

27 Dave Sifry, 'State of the Blogosphere, October, 2006' (2006) technorati.com/weblog/2006/11/161.

A Technorati search for 'emerging church' blogs conducted in June 2007 returned 603 results, and analysis of this data suggests that there is a steep drop-off in authority after the highest ranking blogs.[28] At the top, there is a select group of bloggers whose blogs are read and linked to by a large number of other bloggers; they are followed by a greater number of bloggers whose link frequency, and therefore authority, correspondingly decreases as we move down the ranking; and finally there is the largest group of bloggers whose influence over the blogosphere is nonetheless minimal. The large number of blogs with less than 10 linking blogs (322) contrasts greatly with the select few blogs (7) receiving links from over 500 blogs. There are 112 'emerging church' blogs with only 1 or 2 other blogs linking to them in the last 6 months, and 56 without any linking blogs at all. The authoritative 'A-listers' and the 'long tail' are illustrated in the table and graph below.[29]

Table 6.1 Technorati 'emerging church' blogs search conducted 18 June 2007

Authority Grouping	Number of Blogs	Names of Blogs	Authority Rankings
Very High Authority (500 or more blogs linking in the last 6 months)	7	Jesus Creed	1,198
		tallskinnykiwi	937
		Pyromaniacs *	775
		Pomomusings	726
		The Cartoon Blog **	592
		The Ooze	541
		Emergent Village	514
High Authority (100 – 499 / 6 months)	42	* Pyromaniacs can be described as an 'anti-emerging church' blogging collective.	
Medium Authority (10 – 99 / 6 months)	232	** The Cartoon Blog is the blog of *Church Times* cartoonist Dave Walker.	
Low Authority (3 – 9 / 6 months)	154	The inclusion of these blogs in the list highlights difficulties with the Technorati ranking system, which	
Very Low Authority (0 – 2 / 6 months)	168	includes blogs with the tag 'emerging church', regardless of the 'emerging church'-ness of the blogs linking to them. Qualitative data is therefore a necessary supplement to link statistics.	

---

28 These findings were also shown in an analysis of hyperlink data collected by the aggregator Blogdex. See further Cameron Marlow, 'Audience, Structure and Authority in the Weblog Community' (2004) alumni.media.mit.edu/~cameron/cv/pubs/04-01.pdf, p.5.

29 The identification of the top 7 bloggers in my recent Technorati search findings with an actual A-list is, of course, arbitrary, as that division has been chosen by Technorati to distinguish between so-called 'High' and 'Very High Authority' blogs.

Table 6.2 Technorati 'authority ratings' for 'emerging church' blogs

These findings suggest a power law distribution which has been observed by researchers across many human systems.[30] Affected, even unconsciously, by the cumulative preferences of previous users, those new to the blogosphere reinforce the reading and linking choices made by others before them, 'with a small number of blogs becoming increasingly likely to be chosen in the future because they were chosen in the past'.[31] The system favours, therefore, the early birds who began blogging several years ago, such as tallskinnykiwi. Thus the already authoritative become even more so.

Herring *et al* find evidence of a three-fold blog typology, and an interrelationship between blog genre and authority can be demonstrated.[32] Filter blogs act as a sieve for readers, presenting summaries of and links to events and happenings external to the blogger – on- or off-line; journals contain the personal thoughts and experiences of the blogger; and k-logs (short for knowledge blogs) are 'repositories of information and observations with a coherent (typically technological) focus', with often longer essay-like posts.[33] Among 'emerging church' blogs, while many also contain elements of a journal, the majority are filters or k-logs, or a combination involving both links out to other sites (creating what social network analysts refer to as hubs) and essay-like posts which generate links in to them (creating authorities to which many other bloggers may link). Linking patterns act as conservative forces which maintain and augment the authoritative status of the already authoritative.

However, Shirky goes on to predict that the top bloggers will be forced to become less interactive as time goes on, unable to keep up with the demands for interaction as his/her blog readership increases. As a result, these blogs will become a form of 'broadcast outlet, distributing material without participating in conversations about it'.[34] While there are very few, if any, *purely* filter blogs among emerging Christian communities, the high ranking combinations of filter and k-log may soon become forced to operate as pure filters, with decreasing annotations in blog postings and decreasing interaction with commenters. Meanwhile, however, Shirky envisages that 'the long tail of weblogs with few readers will become conversational'.[35] In the future, therefore, it may become easier for 'low' authority bloggers and their readers to be interactive than for those at the other end of the spectrum. The number of links in and out of blogs in the Very High and High Authority Groups may continue to rise, but the number of *reciprocal* (i.e. clearly *inter*active) links may be found to be

---

30 A power law distribution curve can be roughly described thus: whatever is being ranked (here, inbound links from other blogs) the value for the Nth position will be 1/N, so that the value for the second ranked item will be 1/2 the value of the first ranked item; the value for the tenth ranked item will be 1/10 the value of the first ranked item; the value for the one hundredth ranked item will be 1/100 of the first ranked item; and so on.

31 Clay Shirky, 'Power Laws, Weblogs, and Inequality' (2003), www.shirky.com/writings/powerlaw_weblog.

32 Herring *et al*, 'Bridging the Gap: Genre Analysis of Weblogs,' and Herring *et al*, 'Women and Children Last: The Discursive Construction of Weblogs.'

33 Herring et al, 'Women and Children Last: The Discursive Construction of Weblogs,' p.4.

34 Shirky, 'Power Laws, Weblogs, and Inequality.'

35 Shirky, 'Power Laws, Weblogs, and Inequality.'

greater among the Medium and Low Authority Groups. While linking patterns might result in the creation and preservation of authorities within the blogosphere, these pressures may conversely result in the increased attraction of 'low' authority blogs as reading material for those seeking 'interactive textual engagement'.

Concluding thoughts: the blogger as resurrected author?

The mechanisms of interaction in the blogosphere – notably linking – are creating textual authorities. In turn, these authorities may become less able to deal with the demands of textual interaction from their readers, resulting in more filter-like blogs with less conversation occurring in the comments section, in other words, more readerly texts. The consequential decline in interactive writerly texts is a perverse result of the desire for interactivity in the reading of blog texts. The desire for interaction requires mechanisms of interactivity, and these mechanisms create authorities, the demands upon whom reduce the kinds of interactive texts desired to begin with. This pattern serves to reinstate the role of the originating author, the blogger, in a way inconsistent with the 'new text values' of the death of the author thesis and the 'new church values' of egalitarian participation; the blogger becomes a resurrected author of readerly texts.

While readers can engage with textual others through the ease with which they can become part of the authorship of the text themselves, this collaboration is asymmetrical and thereby open to domination by the author of the originating blog post, who has greater controlling powers over the comments and links left on his/her blog by others. Bloggers create 'protected spaces' through not only controlling the content of their blog posts to avoid flame wars and deter trolls, as Gumbrecht observes,[36] but also through the control exercised over comments. How he/she then chooses to exercise these powers reveals that, in some cases, the author is being resurrected in the guise of the blogger, and the text is being closed down as a result.

The textual interactivity desired by readers can be limited by the blogger, who, through sole access to the blog's HTML, is able to determine who is able to join the conversation by leaving comments and whose comments remain unedited. Bloggers can choose to disallow comments entirely, determine whether readers have to identify themselves in order to comment, and close comments on particular posts. They can edit or censor elements of a comment, or erase it completely. Bloggers can erase links as well as create them, thus severing the 'textual glue' made by themselves and others. Thus the blogger can return the text to that of a more readerly nature, if he/she wishes. They can even erase their blog in its entirety, though others may choose to simply leave the blog in cyberspace without contributing new posts.

Most 'emerging church' bloggers, and even 'anti-emerging church' bloggers, usually only exercise powers of edit, censorship, and erasure over matters of profanity rather than disagreement.[37] Where the (readerly) role of author as dictator

---

36 Michelle Gumbrecht, 'Blogs as "Protected Space,"' (2004), http://www.blogpulse.com/papers/www2004gumbrecht.pdf.

37 One particular 'anti-emerging church' blog, EmergentNo, frequently deleted comments and banned commenters, citing profanity and antagonistic or personally insulting comments

of meaning is consciously being resisted, bloggers endeavour to be transparent about any decisions that are made concerning the content of either their blog posts or the accompanying comments.[38] However, the mechanisms are there for bloggers to act as authors producing readerly texts, rather than as facilitators of interactive engagements with writerly texts. The possibilities for emphasizing singular meaning over plurality, product over production, agreement over conversation, indicate that the author is never entirely absent from readers' intertextual relationships in the blogosphere. While readers of conventional texts can engage with these texts without the author's knowledge, readers of blogs who become commenters (or even readers who become bloggers themselves and post links to the originating blog) cannot interact without the possible intervention of the original author.[39]

The possible resultant closure of the text mirrors the past story of text within the Christian tradition. Whilst plurality is at the heart of the New Testament, where the gospel narrative is told from multiple perspectives, fixed canons emerged through debate and dispute in the varying geographical regions of the religion. The desire to protect these texts from corruption generated an elevation of the orthodox text, and a censure and erasure of other written and spoken forms. The formation of church structures thus removed active textual creation from believers, making them instead the passive consumers of a text determined by the new authoritative hierarchies. Therefore, simultaneously, the development of the Christian canon was a closure of the text.

It may be that the dual desire of emerging Christian communities for textual interactivity *and* for resistance to exclusivist canonization processes means that 'low' authority blogs become the site of increased textual interaction, whilst 'high' and 'very high' authority blogs become more closed in nature. This possible future also echoes text in the Christian tradition, where in some quarters the meaning of the Biblical text has shut down (and shut out), whilst in others alternative textual histories of Christianity have been welcomed – from non-canonical and heretical texts such as *The Gospels of Thomas* and *Mary Magdalene*, to the more recent textual re-imaginings of Christian history, such as *The Da Vinci Code*.

---

as justification. This site, however, seems to have been intended as a readerly text, restricting dialogue between commenters and bloggers. Carla, a contributor, informs a commenter who is frustrated by the lack of interaction possible at EmergentNo that, 'you've made the mistake of assuming I'm attempting to "dialogue with emergent". I'm not making any attempt at all, and never have.' The purpose of EmergentNo was stated as 'to inform, to educate and equip.' The blog was completely deleted on June 25 2007, with the bloggers claiming 'mission accomplished.'

38 For example, while the text of a blog post can be edited, the altered elements thereby render commenters' responses groundless, and so many 'emerging church' bloggers make changes apparent by crossing through previous ~~text~~ or [parenthesizing] or *italicizing* updates, and explaining the reasons for any editing of comments.

39 'Lurkers', readers of blogs who do not leave comments, can engage in writerly textual interactions without expressing these engagements in public. They thereby do not open their engagements to the (possible) scrutiny of the blogger and other commenters. There may be, however, additional interlinking reasons why lurkers do not become commenters.

The generation of authoritative bloggers among emerging Christian communities may spearhead their self-understandings,[40] as well as enable the development of an interpretive community,[41] however, this move may also be a step in the direction of closing the conversation down to a select few, those deemed the interpreters *for* and drivers *of* this community. As a critique of the modernist exclusion of difference from the Christian tradition, emerging Christian communities may well find the move towards the resurrection of the author, and the resultant closure of text, to be troubling.

Bibliography

Astley, Jeff, *Ordinary Theology: Looking, Listening and Learning in Theology* (Aldershot: Ashgate Publishing Limited, 2002).

Barthes, Roland, *S/Z: An Essay,* trans. Richard Miller (Hill & Wang, [1970] 1991).

Barthes, Roland, 'The Death of the Author', in Seán Burke, *Authorship: From Plato to the Postmodern – A Reader* (Edinburgh: Edinburgh University Press, [1995] 2003): 125-30.

Brady, Mark, 'Blogging: Personal Participation in Public Knowledge-Building on the Web', (Colchester: University of Essex, 2005). www.essex.ac.uk/chimera/content/pubs/wps/CWP-2005-02-Blogging-in-the-Knowledge-Society-MB.pdf.

Brown, Dan, *The Da Vinci Code* (London: Corgi Adult, 2004).

Burke, Seán, *Authorship: From Plato to the Postmodern – A Reader* (Edinburgh: Edinburgh University Press, [1995] 2003): 125-30.

Campbell, Heidi, 'Who's Got the Power? Religious Authority and the Internet', *Journal of Computer-Mediated Communication* 12(3), article 14 (2007). [accessed 05/11/07] http://jcmc.indiana.edu/vol12/issue3/campbell.html.

Efimova, Lilia, Stephanie, Hendrick, and Anjo, Anjewierden, 'Finding 'the life between buildings':An Approach for Defining a Weblog community' (2005). https://doc.telin.nl/dsweb/Get/Document-55092/.

Efimova, Lilia, and Aldo de Moor, 'Beyond Personal Webpublishing: An Exploratory Study of Conversational Blogging Practices' (2005). https://doc.telin.nl/dscgi/ds.py/Get/File-44480.

Fish, Stanley, *Is There a Text in This Class? The Authority of Interpretive Communities* (Cambridge, Massachusetts: Harvard University Press, [1980] 2003): 303-21.

Foucault, Michel, 'What Is an Author?' in Donald F. Bouchard, (ed. and trans.), *Language, Counter-Memory, Practice: Selected Essays and Interviews by Michel Foucault* (Ithaca, New York: Cornell University Press, [1977] 1980): 113-38.

Gumbrecht, Michelle, 'Blogs as "Protected Space,"' (2004). http://www.blogpulse.com/papers/www2004gumbrecht.pdf.

Herring, Susan C., Lois Ann Scheidt, Sabrina Bonus, & Elijah L. Wright, 'Bridging the Gap: Genre Analysis of Weblogs' (2004a). www.ics.uci.edu/~jpd/classes/ics234cw04/herring.pdf.

---

40 See the contemporary work of Paul Teusner, http://teusner.org/phd/.
41 See Bryan Murley, http://emergingchurch.bryanmurley.com/.

Herring, Susan C., Inna Kouper, Lois Ann Scheidt, and Elijah L. Wright, 'Women and Children Last: The Discursive Construction of Weblogs' (2004b). http://blog.lib.umn.edu/blogosphere/women_and_children.html.

Jefferson, Ann and David Robey, (eds), *Modern Literary Theory: A Comparative Introduction* (London: B.T. Batsford Ltd., [1982], 1995).

Jefferson, Ann, 'Structuralism and Post-Structuralism', in Ann Jefferson, and David Robey, (eds), *Modern Literary Theory: A Comparative Introduction* (London: B.T. Batsford Ltd., [1982] 1995): 92-121.

La Grou, John and Len Hjalmarson, (eds), *Voices of the Virtual World: Participative Technology and the Ecclesial Revolution* (Wikiklesia Press, 2007).

Marlow, Cameron, 'Audience, Structure and Authority in the Weblog Community' (2004). alumni.media.mit.edu/~cameron/cv/pubs/04-01.pdf.

Milbank, John, *Theology and Social Theory: Beyond Secular Reason* (Oxford: Blackwell, [1990] 2006).

Moody, Katharine, 'Theo(b)logy: The Technological Transformation of Theology', in John La Grou and Len Hjalmarson, (eds), *Voices of the Virtual World: Participative Technology and the Ecclesial Revolution* (Wikiklesia Press, 2007): 213-19.

O'Neil, Matthieu, 'Weblogs and Authority' (2005). incsub.org/blogtalk/images/O'Neil.Blogtalk.revised.

Pearce, Lynn, *Feminism and the Politics of Reading* (London: Arnold, 1997).

Raymond, Eric, 'The Cathedral and the Bazaar' (1997). http://www.catb.org/~esr/writings/cathedral-bazaar/.

Rubel, Steve, 'What is Authority?' February 13, 2006. http://www.micropersuasion.com/2006/02/what_is_authori.html.

Rushkoff, Douglas, *Open Source Democracy: How Online Communication is Changing Offline Politics* (Demos, 2003).

Shirky, Clay, 'Power Laws, Weblogs, and Inequality' (2003). www.shirky.com/writings/powerlaw_weblog.

Sifry, Dave, 'State of the Blogosphere, October, 2006' (2006). technorati.com/weblog/2006/11/161.

Smith, James K.A., *Introducing Radical Orthodoxy: Mapping a Post-Secular Theology* (Grand Rapids, Michigan: Baker Academic., 2004).

tallskinnykiwi, aka Andrew Jones, 'blogging and emerging church', January 22, 2004 tallskinnykiwi.typepad.com/tallskinnykiwi/2004/01/blogging_and_em.html.

PART III
Readers and Texts

Part III

Readers and Texts

Deborah F. Sawyer

This part of the volume continues along the natural trajectory formed by the previous two, tying together the themes of 'spiritual journey' and 'authority' by conveying the subjective experiences of readers as they discuss and reflect on their own engagements with their sacred texts. The chapters that make up this part underline the importance of engaging with not only textual, but empirical methodologies in the contemporary study of the sacred. Many important developments in terms of beliefs and values are being made manifest outside the traditional sites of religion, that is, outside of theological debate in the academy or traditional places of worship. Alternative methodologies are required to try and make sense of how people are understanding and 'living out' the sacred. As we have seen in the chapters that make up our sections on spiritual journeys and authority, the sacred has been subjectivized, made relative to individual agency. This is not to claim this shift is only apparent in our contemporary contexts: Paul of Tarsus, for example, in the first century embraced embryonic Christianity on the basis of subjective experience. Indeed the context of postmodernity arguably has more in common with pre-modernity than the major monolithic trends of modernity itself. However, an important characteristic of postmodern contexts is their tendency to react against many of the presumptions of the Enlightenment project and modernity that actualized it. Consequently the spiritual journeys we are focusing on in this volume develop understandings of authority that make sense to the individuals undertaking them; they do not produce canons of scripture that claim authority or create magisterium to formulate doctrine. They may well be nurtured and sustained by elements of these, but they are obligatory neither in part or whole. Commentators need the appropriate methodological tools to contextualize and untangle the intricacies of the contemporary religious landscape, and theological discourses need to be grounded by the experiences of those who are their practitioners.

In this third part of the volume, we see examples of the agency of readers as they utilize particular texts to support and negotiate their faith and personal development. María Antonia Álvarez chronicles the role of the Virgin of Guadalupe in contemporary Mexican literature, exploring how Chicana authors have made the mythical figure of the Virgin a sacred text to express the diverse possibilities of being woman. Chicana feminist writers have identified the negative ways in which this figure historically has been instrumental in endorsing the low status of women in families and society through focusing on her role as nurturer and one who endures pain and suffering, encouraging women to emulate this in their lives. Rather than rejecting the figure of the Virgin entirely, feminist writers transform her into images that are affirmative powerful female icons. Álvarez explores how the writer Sandra Cisneros both transforms and adds nuances to the legends that reflect her own subjectivity as a writer. Here the sacred text – in this instance the figure of the Virgin – is reclaimed, rewritten and re-sacralized.

In Raana Bokhari's chapter, we are presented with a window into the lives of women from a Gujurati community. Bokhari focuses on how these women engage with a particular text, *Bihishti Zewar*, and how they estimate the influence of this late eighteenth century/early nineteenth century Urdu reformist work, composed by the Indian scholar Maulana Ashraf Ali Thanwi. This text was written with the intention of equipping women with a good knowledge of Islam, something which had normally been a male preserve, and, as the post-Raj period developed, to give them pride in their religious identity and provide a guide on how to be a 'respectable woman'. Through interviews with these women Bokhari assesses how relevant *Bihishti Zewar* is to women today who are part of a traditional Islamic community in the UK. Through the interviews, using this text as a focus, Bokhari is able to draw a fuller picture of the factors that inform and enrich the religious lives of these women. This work displays how texts that conveyed the sacred for one context are translated to another and negotiated for new diasporic situations.

Finally, Dawn Llewellyn draws on current literary theory and empirical research to demonstrate how the experiences of reading texts can illustrate both how sacred text can be redefined and how, through this process, alternative forms of communities can be identified. Perhaps more significantly, Llewellyn displays how studying women's spiritual experiences can uncover where the fragmented, individualized female self, identified through postmodern third wave feminist theory, is re-connecting and identifying commonality. She is critical of third wave feminism's 'religious-blindness' that misses key elements that are not only crucial to many women's lives but neglects instances where women's individual experiences in religious and spiritual settings are coinciding and becoming community outside usual religious settings.

Each of these contemporary 'snapshots' provides unique and valuable insights into how we might 'read spiritualities' and discover the reality of the sacred in postmodern and postcolonial contexts.

Chapter 7

Spiritual Themes and Identities in Chicana Texts: The Virgin of Guadalupe as a Role Model for Womanhood

María Antonia Álvarez

Introduction

The Virgin of Guadalupe is the patron saint of Mexico, and is its most powerful religious icon and a symbol of significant importance to the Mexican identity. She is considered by Mexican Catholics to be a manifestation of the Virgin Mary in the New World, recognized as 'The Empress of the Americas' and, according to Gloria Anzaldúa, her figure can serve as a Chicano emblem because she is 'the symbol of ethnic identity and of the tolerance for ambiguity that Chicano-mexicanos, people of mixed race, people who have Indian blood, people who cross cultures by necessity'.[1] Thus, the Virgin transcends the issues and categories of class, ethnicity, gender, age, ideology, religion, and demands scholarly treatment, because of the intercultural relationships represented by her and the interactive, diverse means and practices of individuals devoted to her. For this reason, this chapter will try to contrast the Virgin of Guadalupe and three female figures from Mexican culture: Tonantzin, Malinche and Llorona, alongside different Chicana texts.

The Virgin of Guadalupe – Tonantzin

The figure of the Virgin of Guadalupe appeared in 1531 to an Indian, on the site of a former shrine dedicated to Tonantzin,[2] the Aztec goddess who most resembled the Christian concept of the Mother of God. It is generally believed that the Virgin of Guadalupe was meant to represent both the Virgin Mary and Tonantzin, the indigenous Mexican goddess, or that the Virgin was a simplified and sanctified version of Coatlicue, the Aztec mother goddess. This syncretism may have provided a way for sixteenth-century Spaniards to gain converts among the indigenous population of early Mexico, and it may also have provided a method for sixteenth-century

---

1   Gloria Anzaldúa, *Borderlands/La Frontera: The New Mestiza* (San Franciso, 1987), p. 30.

2   The cult of the Virgin of Guadalupe has been denounced as disguised worship of the Aztec goddess Tonantzin. For instance, in 1611 by the Dominican, Martin de Leon, 4th Viceroy of Mexico.

indigenous Mexicans to covertly practise their native religion, since the Virgin of Guadalupe continues to be worshipped as a manifestation of Tonantzin to this day. Nevertheless, Guadalupe-Tonantzin gave the native Americans a hidden method to continue worshipping their own goddess in a Christianized form and 'became an important symbol of *criollo* and *mestizo* identity, as she appeared both to an Indian and as an Indian herself'.[3]

The Virgin of Guadalupe has always symbolized the Mexican nation since Mexico's War of Independence (1810-1821). Both Miguel Hidalgo[4] and Emiliano Zapata's armies travelled underneath the Virgin's flags, which were generally recognized as a symbol of all Mexicans. She is often considered a mixture of the cultures which blend to form Mexico, both racially and religiously, and is a common denominator uniting Mexicans. Mexico is composed of a vast patchwork of differences, linguistic, ethnic and class-based, and the Virgin is the tie that binds the nation into a whole.

The Virgin of Guadalupe is even called the first *mestiza* or the first Mexican, and a borderland reading of the Virgin presents her as a border-crossing goddess in her own right. The Virgin is a *mestiza* deity who displaces Jesus and God for believers on both sides of the border, and brings together people of distinct cultural heritages, while at the same time affirming their distinctness.[5]

In *Borderlands/La Frontera*, Gloria Anzaldúa proposes a *mestiza* consciousness that accepts without assimilating, that draws strength from both sides of the border, that has a female conscience, is more than just a hybrid of races and allows for a complicated understanding of gender. Rather than rejecting either white or Mexican culture, Anzaldúa says, 'we will have to leave the opposite bank, the split between the two mortal combatants somehow healed so that we are on both shores at once, see through serpent and eagle eyes'. The *mestiza* 'communicates that rupture, documents the struggle. She reinterprets history, and using new symbols, she shapes new myths.'[6] Based on the *mestiza* holy mother, Chicana visual artists have made important contributions to feminist re-significations of the Virgin of Guadalupe. Ester Hernandez's 1975 print, *La Virgen de Guadalupe Defendiendo los Derechos de los Xicanos*, depicts the Virgin as a black belt in the martial arts, and far from the gentle mother figure imagined in the traditional icon. This Virgin is physical, active, and strong, as Alicia Gaspar de Alba explains:

---

3   Alexandra Fitts, 'Sandra Cisneros's Modern Malinche: A Reconsideration of Feminine Archetypes in *Woman Hollering Creek*', *International Fiction Review* (Jan. 2002), pp. 11–23: 11.

4   When Hidalgo died, the new leader Jose Maria Morelos included in the Constitution the Virgin of Guadalupe's feast day – December 12th – and declared that the Virgin had been a great help in his victories.

5   Pope Benedict XIV declared Our Lady of Guadalupe the patron of New Spain, and approved liturgical texts in her honour. Pope Leo XIII granted new texts in 1891 and authorized the coronation of her image in 1895. Pope Saint Pius X proclaimed her the patron of Latin America in 1910. In 1935 Pope Pius XI proclaimed her patron of the Philippines and erected a monument in her honour in the Vatican Gardens. In 1966 Pope Paul VI sent a golden rose to her shrine.

6   Anzaldúa, *Borderlands/La Frontera*, pp. 22-3.

Chicana artists, like their male counterparts, were resisting class and race oppression, and affirming their differences as colonized subjects with their own cultural, historical and linguistic identity. But some of the Chicanas were also resisting [gender] oppression, internal to the Movement, and for this resistance they were labelled by the patriarchs and their female allies traitors to the Chicano Movement.[7]

Similarly, Yolanda M. Lopez's *Guadalupe Triptych* represents the Virgin as a grandmother which foregrounds women's strength. This means that Chicana feminist artists have reclaimed the Virgin as a Chicana feminist icon: 'Both Hernandez and Lopez's portrayals of the *Guadalupana* alter the passive femininity of the traditional image to communicate feminist empowerment through change and physical action.'[8]

For Chicana feminists, the Virgin's omnipresence incites feelings of ambivalence. Some, regardless of religiosity, accept her as a guardian presence, as a Mother; others consider her to be the virgin who appears in the binary of virgin/whore. For example, the novelist Sandra Cisneros writes: 'That was why I was angry every time I saw *la Virgen de Guadalupe*, my culture's role model for brown women like me. She was damn dangerous, an ideal so lofty and unrealistic that was laughable. Did boys have to aspire to be Jesus?'[9]

In their effort to re-signify the Virgin of Guadalupe, Chicana feminists have used a variety of strategies. Many have sought to reclaim the indigenous aspects of her identity, seeing her as the embodiment of pre-conquest goddesses such as Tonantzin, Coatlique, Coatlalopeuh or Tlazolteotl. The contributors to Ana Castillo's edited collection, *Goddess of the Americas: Writings on the Virgin of Guadalupe*,[10] follow this strategy, identifying the Virgin of Guadalupe as a symbol in which Spanish Catholicism combines with indigenous belief systems of female deities. Ivonne Yarbro-Bejarano explains this syncretism:

> It is important to remember the semiotic richness of the Virgin of Guadalupe in Mexican/ Catholic culture, productive of both religious and nationalist meanings. In her fusion of the Catholic Virgin Mother and the pre-conquest fertility deity Tonantzin, Guadalupe signifies the racial construction of Mexican national identity as the *mestizo* or hybrid product of the sexual union of Indian woman and male Spaniard.[11]

In Sandra Cisneros' story 'Little Miracles, Kept Promises', Rosario, the heroine, considers the Virgin of Guadalupe from the standpoint of indigenous Indian culture.

---

7   Alicia Gaspar de Alba, *Chicano Art Inside/Outside the Master's House: Cultural Politics and the CARA Exhibition* (Austin, 1998), p. 125.

8   Ibid.

9   Sandra Cisneros, *Woman Hollering Creek and Other Stories* (New York, 1991), p. 48.

10   Ana Castillo, (ed.), *Goddess of the Americas: Writings on the Virgin of Guadalupe* (New York, 1996).

11   Yvonne Yarbro-Bejarano, 'The Lesbian Body in Latina Cultural Production' in Emilie L. Bergmann and Paul Julian Smith, (eds), *¿Entiendes?: Queer Readings, Hispanic Writings* (Durham, North Carolina, 1995), pp. 181-97.

Rosario acknowledges the Virgin's other face, the face of Tonantzin, the powerful Aztec fertility goddess who gives life to the crops and protects her Indian people:

> I don't know how it all fell in place. How I finally understood who you are. No longer Mary the mild, but our mother Tonantzin. Your church at Tepeyace built on the site of her temple. Sacred ground no matter whose goddess claims it.[12]

Rosario has to reconstruct the Virgin of Guadalupe, has to retrieve her face of power – the face of Tonantzin – from her own Indian ancestry in order to go forward with her life. She describes the stages of her negotiation with the Virgin as a process that stretches over years. She rejects her, re-examines her, embraces her, and finally reconstructs her as a figure that she can understand, live with, and use as a model. To revise the traditional icons is to empower oneself, as Rosario implies in her address to the Virgin of Guadalupe:

> When I could see you in all your facets all at once the Buddha, the Tao, the true Messiah, Yahweh, Allah, the Heart of the Sky, the Heart of the Earth, the Lord of the Near and Far, the Spirit, the Light, the Universe, I could love you, and, finally, learn to love you.[13]

Thus, the Virgin of Guadalupe is a fusion of Spanish (the Catholic Virgin Mary) and indigenous (Tonantzin) cultures, in the same way as Mexican national identity is defined by a racial and sexual mixture in the sexual union of Indian woman and male Spaniard. That is what Victor Burgin calls the 'popular pre-conscious'.[14]

The Virgin of Guadalupe - Malinche

The conquest of the Americas also included a woman, Malinche, and for Chicana theoreticians she is an important figure. Aida Hurtado suggests in her essay '"Sitios y Lenguas": Chicanas Theorize Feminisms' that Chicana feminists did not choose this woman, Malinche, as the defining figure in their feminism yet, because of the role she represented in the history of Mexico, 'many male writers have saddled all women with Mexico's initial betrayal'.[15]

In his famous work *The Labyrinth of Solitude*, Octavio Paz reflects on Malinche's role in the formation of the Mexican consciousness. To him, she is *la chigada*, the violated Mother, but Malinche 'gave herself voluntarily to the conquistador'.[16] Historically, Malinche[17] is the ultimate traitor of Mexico. She facilitated Hernan Cortes's conquest of the Aztec empire by acting as translator between the Spanish

---

12 Cisneros, 'Little Miracles, Kept Promises', *Women Hollering Creek*, p. 128.

13 Ibid.

14 Victor Burgin, *The End of Art Theory: Criticism and Postmodernity* (Atlantic Highlands, NJ, 1986), p. 60.

15 Aida Hurtado, '"Sitios y Lenguas": Chicanas Theorize Feminisms', *Hypatia* 13/2 (Spring 1988), pp. 134-62:134.

16 Octavio Paz, *The Labyrinth of Solitude* (New York, 1961), p. 86.

17 According to Paz, Malinche's 'passivity is abject: she does not resist violence, but is an inert heap of bones, blood and dust. Her taint is constitutional and resides … in her sex'.

and the different Mexican tribes. But, in fact, the proof of her victimization lies in Cortes's abandonment once she had served his purposes. So, she is not only a traitor but also a woman who could not hold on to her man and realize that he was abusing her. This is why feminists have tried either to redeem her, to commiserate with her or to appropriate her as a feminist hero. Cherrie Moraga describes the impact that Malinche's story has had on Hispanic women's sexuality. She sees Chicanas' negative perceptions of themselves as 'sexual persons', and their 'consequential betrayal' of each other is rooted in 'a four-hundred year long Mexican history and mythology'.[18] The weight of guilt imposed on women for Malinche's betrayal of her people and for her sexual transgressions has led to a deeply conflicted self-image. In order to be true to her people, a Mexican or Chicana woman must deny her sexuality, for 'the woman who defies her role as subservient to her husband, father, brother, or son by taking control of her own sexual destiny is purported to be a "traitor to her race" by contributing to the "genocide" of her people'.[19]

For literary critic Tzvetan Todorov, Malinche is 'the first example, and thereby the symbol, of the cross-breeding of cultures':

> She thereby heralds the modern state of Mexico and beyond that, the present state of us all, since if we are not invariably bilingual, we are inevitably bi- or tri-cultural. Malinche glorifies mixture to the detriment of purity ... and the role of the intermediary. She does not submit to the other ...; she adopts the other's ideology and serves it in order to understand her own culture better, as is evidenced by the effectiveness of her conduct – even if *understanding* here means *destroying*.[20]

A number of Chicana writers have seen her as a victim not only of the conquistadors, but also of the sexism of Latin culture. In *La Malinche in Mexican Literature*, Sandra Messinger Cypess discusses Chicana writers' reconsideration of the legacy of Malinche, saying that 'they incorporated the figure into their creative works as another way to make her their own, to transform her into their own image, instead of accepting the image of Malinche constructed by patriarchal cultural forces'.[21]

Malinche is the figurative mother of all post-conquest Mexicans, and thus, of all Chicanos (Paz, *The Labyrinth of Solitude*, p. 85).

18 Cherrie Moraga, *Loving in the War Years* (Boston, 1983), p. 99. Many Chicanas physically inhabit the borderlands between Mexico and the U.S. (that place that is neither entirely one country nor the other, but a mixture of the two). However, the Mexican-American woman is not marginalized by her physical location as much as she is by both her sex and her ethnicity. According to Gloria Anzaldúa, 'this is her home / this thin edge of / barbwire' (Anzaldúa, *Borderlands/La Frontera*, 1987, p. 20). She must live on the fence because she can never occupy a full place in any of the cultures to which she nominally belongs: in the U.S. she is separated by her colour, her language and her history, and in Mexico she is defined and limited by the traditions of 'machismo' and the teachings of the Catholic Church.

19 Moraga, *Loving in the War Years,* p. 113.

20 Tzvetan Todorov, *The Conquest of American: The Conquest of the Other*, trans. Richard Howard (New York), p. 101.

21 Sandra Messinger Cypess, *La Malinche in Mexican Literature: From History to Myth* (Austin, 1991), p. 142.

Gloria Anzaldúa 'traces the figure of Malinche back to the powerful goddesses of the Aztecs', states Alexandra Fitts, explaining how she claims that the male-dominated culture, even before the time of the Conquest, 'sought to weaken the power of the primary creator goddess, Coatlicue, and divided her in two – the good mother, Tonantzin, and the sexual being, Thatzoteotl'.[22]

According to Ana Maria Carbonell, Malinche is like a mythic ghost who crosses through the pages of Chicana writers

> ... wailing at the loss of her child while she continues to combat the external forces disrupting her familial life. A victim of patriarchal abuse, this *Llorona* refuses to be silenced and let her son's *disappearance* vanish from the official record. Her presence registers the active transformation of familial separation and destruction into familial preservation and reconstruction. Instead of accepting defeat, she reconnects familial ties broken by government policies that sanction war, terrorize people, and create conditions of poverty. This behavior marks the endurance of the Coatlicue state – the incarnation of struggle prompted by acknowledging destructive forces and refusing to fall victim to them. [23]

The other side of *Malinchismo* is *Marianismo* or the veneration of the Virgin Mary especially in her Mexican version of Guadalupe: she is the Mother to imitate, the role model which Chicana womanhood should emulate and apply these same values to serving their husbands and children. Fitts thinks that with the incorporation of the ancient pantheon into the Catholic religion, 'the two opposing female figures metamorphosed into the Virgin of Guadalupe (the pure mother) and Malinche (the sexualized, evil temptress) though, ironically, it is Malinche who is the figurative mother of the *mestizo* race'.[24]

Gloria Anzaldúa sees both of these figures as 'working to oppress Mexican and Chicana women':[25] the Virgin of Guadalupe, by robbing them of their sexuality, and Malinche[26] by making them ashamed of both their gender and their Indian heritage. Anzaldúa calls 'not for a disavowal of these *mothers*', but rather 'a reconsideration of their legacy'. To cast them aside 'would further deny the Indian and Mexican past'; to embrace them unchanged 'would be an acceptance of gender roles that do not allow for sexual independence and self-expression'.[27]

According to Harryette Mullen, the church functions similarly 'as a cultural as well as a religious site: specifically as a site of origin for insider discourses'[28] of Mexican-American and other Latino cultures, through the exchange of prayers and

---

22 Fitts, 'Sandra Cisneros' Modern Malinche', p. 17.

23 Ana María Carbonell, 'From Llorona to Gritona: Coatlicue in Feminist Tales by Viramontes and Cisneros', *MELUS* 24/2 (Summer 1999), pp. 53-74:59

24 Fitts, 'Sandra Cisneros' Modern Malinche', p. 17.

25 Anzaldúa, *Borderlands/La Frontera*, p. 18.

26 In fact, it is not clear whether the historical Malinche was a willing accomplice of Cortes. She was probably given to Cortes as a slave, and was about fourteen years old at the time of the Conquest.

27 Anzaldúa, *Borderlands/La Frontera*, p. 18.

28 Harryette Mullen, 'A Silence Between Us Like a Language: The Untranslatability of Experience in Sandra Cisneros' *Women Hollering Creek*', *MELUS* 21/2 (Summer 1996), pp. 3-20:3.

religious services, for offerings made, and thanks given by devout Catholics whose religion syncretically embraces folk beliefs. As Ana Castillo writes in the introduction to *Goddess of the Americas*, 'we make no claim to represent the Catholic Church here, thank goodness. The only claim we make is our right to love her [the Virgin]'.[29] And Cisneros, in 'One Holy Night' tells us that the 'Boy Baby':

> ... was born in a street with no name, in a town called *Miseria*. His father, *Eusebio*, is a knife sharpener. His mother, *Refugia*, stacks apricots into pyramids and sells them on a cloth in the market. There are brothers. Sisters too, of which I knows little. The youngest, a *Carmelite*, writes me all this and prays for my soul, which is why I know it's all true.[30]

Also in Cisneros's interview with Pilar Rodríguez Aranda,[31] Cisneros speaks of her own difficulties in growing up with a negative and a positive role model, always held up before Malinche and the Virgin of Guadalupe:[32]

> *Virgencita de Guadalupe.* For a long time I wouldn't let you in my house. I couldn't see you without seeing my ma, each time my father came home drunk and yelling, blaming everything that ever went wrong in his life, on her. I couldn't look at your folding hands without seeing my *abuela* mumbling[33]: 'My son, my son, my son ...' Couldn't look at you without blaming you for all the pain my mother and her mother and all our mothers' mothers have put up with in the name of God.[34]

These *ghosts* still haunt her; thus, she writes not to exorcise, but to 'make peace' with them.

The Virgin of Guadalupe – Llorona

The Chicana, who stands astride Anglo and Mexican cultures, is not captive to the myths of either culture.[35] Cisneros tells us in 'Woman Hollering Creek' that the

---

29 Ana Castillo, 'Introduction' in Castillo, *Goddess of the Americas* (New York, 1996), pp. v-xxiv:.xxiii.

30 Cisneros, 'One Holy Night' in *Woman Hollering Creek,* p. 33.

31 Pilar Aranda Rodriguez, 'On the Solitary Fate of Being Mexican, Female, Wicked and Thirty-Three: An Interview With Sandra Cisneros', *The Americas Review,* 18/1 (1990), pp. 65-6.

32 Fitts explains how Sandra Cisneros's collection of stories *Woman Hollering Creek* depicts the situation of the Mexican-American women. Fitts, 'Sandra Cisneros' Modern Malinche', p. 11.

33 Malinche's complex, modern figure is Cisneros's reaction to the Virgin's passivity: she is at once victim and victimiser, as she turns her anger on others. In 'Never Marry a Mexican', the issues of race and gender are at odds for the main character, Clemencia, as her father is Mexican and her mother Chicana. The title of the story is her mother's often repeated advice, because she felt discrimination from both cultures: as a lower-class Chicana she was looked down on by her husband's upper-middle-class Mexican family, but she also suffered discrimination by mainstream U.S. society because of her dark skin.

34 Cisneros, 'Little Miracles, Kept Promises', p. 127.

35 Cisneros's feminine characters struggle to reconcile their Mexican past with their American present. Part of this negotiation is the incorporation of feminine archetypes from

liberated Chicana, Felice, can hear in the creek's voice either Llorona's lament or Tarzán's cry. Llorona is an Aztec female goddess transformed into a guilty reminder of a woman's sin. She betrays all of the traditional notions of motherhood, because when her children became a burden to her, she simply murdered them. Like Malinche, Llorona is a symbol of motherhood gone wrong. Malinche's betrayal of her children was in her sinful collaboration with their oppressive father, but Llorona's betrayal of motherhood is even more perverse. For this sin, she is doomed to an eternity of repentance with her continual wailing, as a reminder to all of her crime and of the repercussions of transgression. The creek is a 'hollering woman' but, unlike the landmarks named after the Virgin this name does not impose a single definition of femininity nor is it confined to a single culture – the creek has both a Mexican and an English name, 'a yell as loud as any *mariachi*', a cry of freedom.

Woman Hollering Creek is a real place in Texas near San Antonio, and Cleofilas, the protagonist of the story 'Woman Hollering Creek', wonders about the origin of this name and why the 'woman was hollering':

> *La Gritona*. Such a funny name for such a lovely arroyo. But that's what they call the creek that ran behind the house. Though no one could say whether the woman had hollered from anger or pain. The natives only knew the *arroyo* – once crossed on the way to San Antonio, and then once again on the way back – was called *Woman Hollering*, a name no one from these parts questioned, little less understood. [36]

The only answer that she can find is that 'hollering' is an inaccurate translation of *Llorona*, who could be said 'to wail' or 'to sob', but not exactly 'to holler'. Cleofilas's desire to understand the hollering woman derives more from personal circumstances than from her interest in geography. She has come to Texas from Mexico as a new bride, with the hope to live a fairy tale or a romance novel. Bored with life in her village, she longs for passion, excitement, new clothes, and a pretty house. However, not long after her arrival in Seguin, Texas, Cleofilas begins to realize that in some ways her life is like a 'soap opera ... only now the episodes got sadder and sadder'.[37]

As she grows more and more desperate in her marriage, Cleofilas, like Llorona, is drawn to the water. She sits by the creek that she had originally thought 'so pretty and full of happily ever after',[38] and begins to understand the despair that could drive

---

the Mexican tradition and the re-consideration of these figures in a way that will reflect the realities of the modern Chicana experience. Cisneros recognizes she had a responsibility to her community, since she was 'the first woman in my family to pick up a pen and record what I see around me, a woman who has the power to speak and is privileged enough to be heard'. (Sandra Cisneros, 'Notes to a Young(er) Writer', *The American Review* 15/1 (Spring 1997), pp. 75-87:76). That responsibility included recording what was and what could be, and how people around her lived and should live. Straddling two cultures actually enriched her life in many ways. However, as a child she felt mostly like an outsider who did not really fit in anywhere. It was not until her school years, when she began reading and writing, that she found ways to bridge the distance between Mexico and America herself.

36 Cisneros, 'Woman Hollering Creek', p. 46

37 Ibid., p. 52.

38 Ibid., p. 47

a woman to destruction. As she plays with her child, she thinks that she hears Llorona calling to her, and wonders about the quiet desperation that might have led her to such a violent action towards her children. She has a family in Mexico to whom she can turn, but it is her father rather than her mother who is the source of protection.[39] Cleofilas's father nurtured his daughter and sensed that her marriage would fail. That is why when she left home he assured her: 'I am your father. I will never abandon you.'[40] By giving the father this role, Cisneros complicates stereotypes of mothers and motherhood. Her father has always provided the strength and support she needs; when Cleofilas is concerned about the shame of returning to Mexico, she realizes the price she will pay if she stays is much higher. Pregnant with her second child, she tricks her husband into driving her to town for a doctor's visit, and once she is left alone in the office, she begs the nurse to help her escape. The nurse, Graciela, and her friend, Felice, become Cleofilas's most important allies. In this case, as opposed to Clemencia's situation in 'Never Marry a Mexican',[41] there is a bond of sisterhood, as two unknown women with whom she has little in common conspire to help her.

Felice agrees to drive Cleofilas and her son to the bus station in San Antonio, and when she is fleeing to safety, the stranger does something that shocks her: 'when they drove across the arroyo, the driver opened her mouth and let out a yell as loud as any *mariachi*'[42] while she explains:

> Every time I cross that bridge I do that. Because of the name, you know. Woman Hollering. *Pues*, I holler. She said this in a Spanish pocked with English and laughed. Did you ever notice, Felice continued, how nothing around here is named for a woman? Really. Unless she's the Virgin. I guess you're only famous if you're a virgin. She laughed again.

For the first time, Cleofilas is able to imagine a woman hollering for some reason other than pain or rage. Felice's yell is one of independence – 'a true *grito*'.[43] Also for the first time, Cleofilas is able to see her own strength and independence and laughs, rejoicing in her freedom.

Felice is presented as a modern, American woman, in contrast to Cleofilas the naïve immigrant, and her more assimilated position in United States culture enables her to envision a scream of joy rather than despair. She does not need to ask a husband to drive her anywhere: first, because she is not married, and second, because she has her own truck. Cleofilas marvels at this level of independence, and when she asked if

---

39 Cleofilas' mother is not present in her life, though it is not explained if she has died or has merely left.

40 Ibid., p. 43

41 The opposition is that in 'Never Marry a Mexican' Clemencia admits: 'I've been accomplice, committed premeditated crimes. I'm guilty of having caused deliberate pain to other women. I'm vindictive and cruel, and I'm capable of anything' (Cisneros, 'Never Marry a Mexican', p. 68). She also says that, though a painter, she must support herself in other ways: sometimes she acts as a translator (like Malinche) and also relies on the generosity of her lovers, which, she says, 'is a form of prostitution' (Ibid., p. 71).

42 Ibid., p. 55

43 Ibid., p. 21

it was 'her husband's', Felice said she 'didn't have a husband. The pickup was hers. She herself had chosen it. She herself was paying for it.'[44]

Ironically, it may also be Felice's distance from the Spanish language that leads to her interpretation of the creek's name. Though she speaks Spanish to Cleofilas, she frequently reverts to English, and her conversation with her friend Graciela is the reverse – English sprinkled with a few Spanish phrases. Like the other natives of the area, Felice seems to be unaware of the Spanish origins of the 'hollering woman' and does not translate the name back to Llorona, as does Cleofilas. She is happily ignorant of the hollering woman's association with pain and betrayal.

The story 'Woman Hollering Creek' acknowledges women's suffering, as Cleofilas sees her dreams break and her marriage decay. However, she does not succumb to despair; the only sobbing in the story is that of her husband, each time he beats her and begs forgiveness. Cleofilas neither drowns her sorrows nor abandons her children, but she saves them and herself by drawing on resources that come from both sides of the border; from Mexico she has her protective father and extended family, and from the U.S. she has women like Graciela and Felice, who are able to imagine a woman whose power does not have to come from either her virginity or the support of a man. Thus, this short story represents the re-consideration of the female archetypes that Cisneros, and also Anzaldúa, call for. According to Alexandra Fitts, Cleofilas learns from her time in the United States, that 'life is not a *telenovela* [soap opera] and that being a wife and a mother may not be the only possibilities open for women. While remaining true to her beliefs, she rejects the passive abnegation of the Virgin'.[45]

In one of the last stories in Sandra Cisneros's same collection, 'Little Miracles, Kept Promises', we also learn of the main character's (Rosario) struggles with her race, her gender, and her religious beliefs. Cisneros claims, in an interview with Reed Dasenbrock and Feroza Jussawalla, that the letter which the main character, Rosario, addresses to the Virgin models a border negotiation with a cultural icon. The Virgin of Guadalupe goes back and forth between Indian-Mexican cultural constructions of the ideal woman and, rather than settling on one side of the border or the other, she brings the two visions of sacred womanhood together in a single sentence. Rosario has been raging, apparently for years, at the Virgin of Guadalupe for 'all that self-sacrifice, all that silent suffering'[46] for modelling the passive endurance of misery and oppression that she sees reflected in her mother and grandmother. This letter represents Rosario's own negotiation with the figure of the Virgin of Guadalupe, since she offers her braid to the Virgin in thanks for the opportunity to become an artist rather than a mother:

> I leave my braid here and thank you for believing what I do is important. Though no one else in my family, no other woman, neither friend nor relative, no one I know, not even the heroine in the *telenovelas*, no woman wants to live alone. I do.[47]

---

44 Ibid., p. 55
45 Fitts, 'Sandra Cisneros' Modern Malinche', p. 13.
46 Cisneros, 'Little Miracles, Kept Promises', p. 127.
47 Cisneros, 'Woman Hollering Creek', p. 127.

The letter Rosario writes tells of the challenges of being a modern Chicana, as illustrated by the epithet: 'Mighty Guadalupana Coatlaxopeuh Tonantzin / What little miracle could I pin here? Braid of hair in its/Place and know that I thank you.'[48] The braid of hair reminds us that the image of Rosario (Chayo) De Leon cutting her hair is symbolic of a 'shedding of a stereotypical feminine appearance and behavior', and the braid 'can be seen as representative of Chayo's weaving of cultures'.[49]

Sandra Cisneros offers her book, with its elaborate list of acknowledgments, as a kind of literary ex-voto dedicated to Chicano culture:

> *Gracias a la Divina Providencia que me mandó la muy* powerful and miraculous literary protector … *Virgen de Guadalupe* Tonantzin, *infinitas gracias. Estos cuentitos te los ofrezco a ti, a nuestra gente. A toditos. Mil gracias.* A thousand thanks from *el corazón*.[50]

In most of the stories in *Women Hollering Creek*, Cisneros associates this folk genre with the religious articles and folk healing paraphernalia, particularly in 'Anguiano Religious Articles':

> Because I needed a *Virgen de Guadalupe* … A statue is what I was thinking, or maybe those pretty 3-D pictures, the ones made from strips of cardboard that you look at sideways and you see *el Santo Niño de Atocha*, and you look at it straight and it's *la Virgen*, and you look at it from the other side and it's Saint Lucy with her eyes on a plate or maybe *San Martín Caballero* cutting his Roman cape in half with a sword and giving it to a beggar, only I want to know how he didn't give that beggar all of his cape if he's so saintly, right?[51]

These religious or quasi-religious cultural sites, like other images of U.S. commercial culture, can be purchased by families who could not afford to buy them in other places. They are markers of class and gender, as well as sites for the reproduction of the dominant culture and the production of a resistant ethnic minority culture, which is neither entirely of the U.S. nor of Mexico:

> I was thinking about those framed holy pictures with glitter in the window. But then I saw some *Virgen de Guadalupe* statues with real hair eyelashes. Well, not real hair, but some stiff black stuff like brushes, only I didn't like how *la Virgen* looked with furry eyelashes – *bien* mean, like *los amores de la calle*. That's not right.[52]

Models for womanhood: the Virgin of Guadalupe – Malinche – Llorona

Mexican social myths of gender crystallize with special force in three icons: *Guadalupe*, the virgin mother who has not abandoned us, *Malinche*, the raped mother whom we have abandoned, and *Llorona*, the mother who seeks her lost

---

48 Ibid., p. 127.

49 Jacqueline Doyle, 'Assumption of the Virgin in Recent Chicana Writing', *Women's Studies*, 26/2 (February 1997), pp. 171-201:87.

50 Cisneros, *Woman Hollering Creek*, p. i.

51 Cisneros, 'Anguiano Religious Articles', p. 114.

52 Ibid., p. 115.

children. Sandra Cisneros's work re-evaluates and re-values these three prevalent representations of Mexican womanhood: 'Little Miracles, Kept Promises', 'Never Marry a Mexican' and 'Woman Hollering Creek' consider the passive virgin, the sinful seductress, and the treacherous mother respectfully. As Fitts affirms:

> Rather than merely casting aside these figures, Cisneros searches for a transformation of them that will allow for the past while opening up the future. However, her goal does not seem to be as uncomplicated as merely redeeming these figures as powerful female icons. Instead, she modernizes and adds nuance to their legends and their legacies.[53]

In her essay, 'On Not Being La Malinche', Jean Wyatt considers the two stories 'Never Marry a Mexican' and 'Woman Hollering Creek'. [54] She explains that according to the evidence of Chicana feminist writers, these three 'Mothers haunt the sexual and maternal identities of contemporary Mexican and Chicana women'.

Cisneros makes it clear in 'Little Miracles, Kept Promises' that she considers Mexican icons of femininity to be intimately bound up with individual Chicanas and Mexican women's self-images and self-esteem. So that they can live with them comfortably, there is no way to run away and each women has to 'make her peace with them' in her own way:

> When I learned your real name is Coatlaxopeuh, She Who Has Dominion over Serpents, when I recognized you as Tonantzin, and learned your names are Teteoinnan, Toci, Xochiquetzal, Tlazolteotl, Coatlicue, Chalchiuhtlicue. Coyolxauhqui, Huixtocihuatl, Chicomecoatl, Cihuacoatl, when I could see you as Nuestra Señora de la Soledad, Nuestra Señora de los Remedios, Nuestra Señora del Perpetuo Socorro, Nuestra Señorade San Juan de los Lagos, Our Lady of Lourdes, Our Lady of Mount Carmel, Our Lady of the Rosary, Our Lady of Sorrows, I was ashamed, then, to be my mother's daughter, my grandmother's granddaughter, my ancestors' child.[55]

In 'Bien Pretty' Cisneros also recognizes and acknowledges the prayers of ordinary people addressing the Christian God, the Catholic saints fused with the Aztec goddesses and even the African deities, as a folk discourse worthy of inclusion in a literary text of an emergent minority literature:

> The votive candles are arranged like so. Church-sanctioned powers on one aisle – *San Martín de Porres, Santo Niño de Atocha, el Sagrado Corazón, la Divina Providencia, Nuestra Señora de San Juan de Lagos*. Folk powers on another – *El Gran General Pancho Villa, Ajo Macho/Garlic Macho, la Santísima Muerte*/Blessed Death ... Back to back, so as not to offend. I chose one from the pagan side and a *Virgen de Guadalupe* from the Christian.[56]

---

53 Fitts, 'Sandra Cisneros' Modern Malinche', p. 11.

54 There is an explicit reference to Malinche and also to Cortes in 'Never Marry a Mexican', since Drew looks like Cortes, with his dark beard and white skin, and he used to call Clemencia his *Malimalli*, another name for Malinche. Jean Wyatt, 'On Not Being La Malinche: Border Negotiations of Gender in Sandra Cisneros's "Never Marry a Mexican" and "Woman Hollering Creek"', *Tulsa Studies in Women's Literature* 14/2 (1995), pp. 243-72:243.

55 Cisneros, 'Little Miracles, Kept Promises', p. 128.

56 Cisneros, 'Bien Petty', pp. 158-9.

In her essay 'Guadalupe the Sex Goddess', Cisneros describes her own youthful discomfort with her body, and the reluctance to discuss sex or birth control: 'What a culture of denial. Don't get pregnant! But no one tells you how not to. This is why I was angry for so many years every time I saw Virgin of Guadalupe, my culture's role model for brown women like me. She was damn dangerous, an ideal so lofty and unrealistic it was laughable.'[57] And in 'Little Miracles, Kept Promises' we also hear a strong feminist voice, whose ideology is expressed in several miracles, above all in the last one, where the devote Rosary (Chayo) de Leon has a long monologue with the Virgin of Guadalupe/Tonantzin/Coatlaxopeuh, and in a close voice goes on articulating her worries:

> Thank you for making all those months I held my breath not a child in my belly, but a thyroid problem in my throat. I can't be a mother. Not now. Maybe never. Not for me to choose, like I didn't choose being female. Like I didn't choose being artist – it isn't something you choose. It's something you are, only I can't explain it. I don't want to be a mother. I wouldn't mind being a father. At least a father could still be artist, could love some*thing* instead of some*one*, and no one would call that selfish.[58]

While the Virgin of Guadalupe is considered a saint and also a powerful popular icon, her image is still that of the Virgin who connotes all the negative aspects about women's sexuality that the cult of virginity entails. Doyle refers to her as 'a threshold between human and divine, the living and the dead, and as a mediator between competing cultures',[59] and Jeanette Rodriguez dedicates her book to *Our Lady of Guadalupe*, where she analyzes how the Virgin 'is often experienced as a Marian image to support and encourage passivity in women, and thus is viewed as an instrument of patriarchal oppression and control'.[60] Moreover, feminist critics, such as Anzaldúa, cannot fail to see the power of such an omnipresent female icon. In fact, she sees the figure of the Virgin of Guadalupe as 'a synthesis of the old world and the new, of the religion and culture of the two races of our psyche, the conqueror and conquered'.[61] This is Sandra Cisneros's accomplishment in *Woman Hollering Creek* as well. In this collection of stories, Cisneros deals with a number of Mexican religious and cultural icons, particularly those female archetypes whose images often still define the role of Chicanas.

Conclusion

In short, among all cultural icons, the position of the Virgin of Guadalupe as a cultural mediator is so important and the omnipresence and force of her figure in

---

57 Sandra Cisneros 'Guadalupe the Sex Goddess' in Castillo, *Goddess of the Americas*, pp. 4-51:48.

58 Cisneros, 'Little Miracles, Kept Promises', p. 127.

59 Doyle, 'Assumptions of the Virgin', p. 181.

60 Jeanette Rodriguez, *Our Lady of Guadalupe: Faith and Empowerment Among Mexican-American Women* (Austin, 1994), p. xviii.

61 Anzaldúa, *Borderlands/La Frontera*, p. 63.

the Mexican and Chicano cultures is undisputed, since it provides a link between the Mexican past and the American present.

Through her heroine Chayo in 'Little Miracles, Kept Promises', Cisneros says that she came to her own acceptance of the Virgin through a knowledge of her pre-Colombian past, and most importantly, she affirms: 'My Virgin of Guadalupe is not the mother of God. She is God. She is a face for a god without a face, an *indigena* for a god without ethnicity, a female deity for a god who is genderless.'[62] This understanding of the Virgin, which seems to be the one at which Chicana thinkers eventually arrive, is a clear reflection of their claims for the Virgin as a mediator of not just culture, but also gender, race, and history. However difficult it may be to accept a representation of female power and cultural complexity, and also a symbol of women's passivity and oppression, for Chicanas the Virgin of Guadalupe is an ethnic symbol tied to their Mexican heritage.

Bibliography

Anzaldúa, Gloria, *Borderlands/La Frontera: The New Mestiza* (San Francisco: Aunt Lute Press, 1987).

Bergmann, Emilie L. and Paul Julian Smith, (eds), *¿Entiendes?: Queer Readings, Hispanic Writings* (Durham, North Carolina: Duke University Press, 1995).

Burgin, Victor, *The End of Art Theory: Criticism and Postmodernity* (Atlantic Highlands, NJ: Humanities Press International, Inc. 1986).

Carbonell, Ana María, 'From Llorona to Gritona: Coatlicue in Feminist Tales by Viramontes and Cisneros', *MELUS*, 24/2 (Summer 1999): 53-74.

Castillo, Ana, (ed.), *Goddess of the Americas: Writings on the Virgin of Guadalupe* (New York: Riverhead Books, 1996).

Castillo, Ana, 'Introduction', *Goddess of the Americas: Writings on the Virgin of Guadalupe* (New York: Riverhead Books, 1996): v-xxiv.

Cisneros, Sandra, 'One Holy Night' in *Woman Hollering Creek and Other Stories* (New York: Random House, 1991): 27-35.

Cisneros, Sandra, 'Woman Hollering Creek', *Woman Hollering Creek and Other Stories* (New York: Random House, 1991): 43-56.

Cisneros, Sandra, 'Never Marry a Mexican', *Woman Hollering Creek and Other Stories* (New York: Random House,1991): 68-83.

Cisneros, Sandra, 'Anguiano Religious Articles', *Woman Hollering Creek and Other Stories* (New York: Random House, 1991): 114-15.

Cisneros, Sandra, 'Little Miracles, Kept Promises', *Woman Hollering Creek and Other Stories* (New York: Random House, 1991): 116-29.

Cisneros, Sandra, 'Bien Pretty', *Woman Hollering Creek and Other Stories* (New York: Random House, 1991): 137-65.

Cisneros, Sandra, 'Guadalupe the Sex Goddess' in Ana Castillo, (ed.), *Goddess of the Americas: Writings on the Virgin of Guadalupe* (New York: Riverhead Books, 1996): 4-51.

---

62 Cisneros, 'Little Miracles, Kept Promises', p. 50.

Cisneros, Sandra, 'Notes to a Young(er) Writer', *The American Review,* 15/1 (Spring 1997): 75-87.

Cypess, Sandra Messinger, *La Malinche in Mexican Literature: From History to Myth* (Austin: University of Texas Press, 1991).

Doyle, Jacqueline, 'Assumptions of the Virgin in Recent Chicana Writing', *Women's Studies,* 26/2 (February, 1997): 171-201.

Fitts, Alexandra, 'Sandra Cisneros's Modern Malinche: a Reconsideration of Feminine Archetypes in *Woman Hollering Creek'*, *International Fiction Review* (Jan. 2002): 11-23.

Gaspar de Alba, A., *Chicano Art Inside/Outside the Master's House: Cultural Politics and the CARA Exhibition* (Austin, University of Texas Press, 1998).

Hurtado, Aida, '"Sitios y Lenguas": Chicanas Theorize Feminisms', *Hypatia,* 13/2 (Spring 1998): 134-62.

Moraga, Cherrie, *Loving in the War Years* (Boston: South End Press, 1983).

Mullen, Harryette, 'A Silence Between Us Like a Language: The Untranslatability of Experience in Sandra Cisneros' *Woman Hollering Creek'*, *MELUS,* 21, 2 (Summer 1996): 3-20.

Paz, Octavio, *The Labyrinth of Solitude* (New York: Grove Press, 1961).

Rodriguez, Jeanette, *Our Lady of Guadalupe: Faith and Empowerment among Mexican–American Women* (Austin: University of Texas Press, 1994).

Rodríguez Aranda, Pilar E., 'On the Solitary Fate of Being Mexican, Female, Wicked and Thirty-Three: An Interview with Writer Sandra Cisneros', *The Americas Review,* 18/1 (1990): 65-6.

Todorov, Tzvetan, *The Conquest of America: The Conquest of the Other,* Richard Howard, trans. (New York: Harper and Row, 1985).

Wyatt, Jean, 'On Not Being La Malinche: Border Negotiations of Gender in Sandra Cisneros's "Never Marry a Mexican" and "Woman Hollering Creek"', *Tulsa Studies in Women's Literature,* 14/2 (1995): 243-72.

Yarbro-Bejarano, Yvonne, 'The Lesbian Body in Latina Cultural Production' in Emilie L. Bergmann and Paul Julian Smith, (eds), *¿Entiendes?: Queer Readings, Hispanic Writings* (Durham, North Carolina: Duke University Press, 1995): 181-97.

Chapter 8

Bihishti Zewar:[1]
A Text for Respectable Women?[2]

Raana Bokhari

Introduction

> At the end of the day, no matter what *Bihishti Zewar* or anything else says, I am an Abdullah [servant of Allah]. Everything else, any other rule or description is just an adjective.
>
> (Aishah)

Aishah is a participant in an ethnographic study based on Gujarati Sunni Muslim women in Leicester, examining the concept of public space. Muslim women's activities and movements in 'public space' have been defined and dictated by theology over the centuries. Whilst this is an empirical study, the theology crucial to this research centres around *Bihishti Zewar*, a late nineteenth/early twentieth century text written in Urdu, by Muhammad Ashraf Ali Thanawi (1864 - 1943).[3] *Bihishti Zewar* is a didactic manual,[4] and is considered to be one of the leading texts of reformist Islam: freedom movements in India aimed at raising self-esteem and pride in one's religious identity. Hence *Bihishti Zewar* was a guide for the 'respectable woman' and written initially for well-to-do women from privileged families, who were supporting the reformist agenda.[5] Over time, however, the book was accessed by ordinary working-class women and indeed the text was edited by Thanawi to

---

1 Muhammad Ashraf Ali Thanawi, *Bihishti Zewar, Ashrafi Asli Mudallal wa Mukammal,* 1902, reprint 2002 (Karachi, new edition 2002). Various translations are available, however, I have used my own translation from Urdu to English throughout most of this work, but have cross-referenced with others (Barbara Metcalf, *Perfecting Women: Maulana Ashraf Ali Thanawi's Bihishti Zewar* (Oxford, 1990); Muhammad Masroor Khan Saroha (English translation) *Heavenly Ornaments, Bahishti Zewar,* (Karachi, 1991) and Muhammad Mahomedy (trans. and commentary) *Heavenly Ornaments, Bahishti Zewar, A Classical Manual of Islamic Sacred Law* (Karachi, 1999).

2 The term 'respectable' is Barbara Metcalf's. See Metcalf, *Perfecting Women*, p. 3.

3 Muhammad Ashraf Ali Thanawi, in his introduction to *Bihishti Zewar* (Karachi 1902), dates the publication of the first part of the book as 1902-1903.

4 Virginia Hooker, 'History: East, South and Southeast Asia' in Suad Joseph, (ed.), *Encyclopaedia of Women and Islamic Cultures* (Leiden-Boston, 2003), vol. 1, pp. 350-57:353.

5 Metcalf, *Perfecting Women*, p. 3.

include new categories of people, namely men and Muslims outside India.[6] The term 'respectable' is perhaps used by Metcalf in the sense that Thanawi believed Islamic knowledge to empower a woman with morals and upright behaviour; therefore whilst Islam already made a woman respectable, she might not be aware of this unless she was aware of its teachings.

Thanawi was an Indian reformist scholar who trained at the Sunni school of Deoband, some ninety miles northeast of Delhi. At the height of the British Raj in India, he saw it as his duty to produce a theological compendium for women, explaining their role in life and the need for them to be religiously educated.

> My heart had been sick with worry for quite some time in watching the destruction of the women of India, and had been consumed by the worry of finding a cure. The main reason for this worry was that this destruction was not just confined to their religion, but had also affected their worldly life. Many of the effects had passed on to their children: in fact even their husbands were affected. From the speed at which this destruction was taking place, it was evident that unless there was some reform, this disease would become incurable. Therefore my worry to find a cure increased. By God guiding me, and through my experience, logic and education, I found that because women were unfamiliar with the knowledge and sciences of religion, their beliefs, their deeds, their dealings with people, their manners and their social life were all falling into ruin ... I therefore proposed writing a book specifically for women, written in simple language, compiling all the important laws together, and omitting those laws which were just relevant to men. It would be sufficient enough to be a guide for daily life, without having to consult other books.[7]

Therefore real accurate knowledge was essential for an ordered society.[8] *Bihishti Zewar*, often translated as 'Heavenly Ornaments' is considered to be one of the most influential scriptural reforms.

The 'heavenly ornaments' are not women, but metaphorically the virtues and traits that will 'earn them (men and women) the pearls and bracelets of heaven'.[9] Thanawi quotes verse 22:23 of the Qur'an which states: 'God will admit those who believe and work righteous deeds, to gardens beneath which rivers flow: they shall be adorned there with bracelets of gold and pearls, and their garments there will be of silk', as being the raison d'etre of his title.[10] The treasures that await in heaven

---

6   Raana Bokhari, *Places and Perspectives: Gujarati Muslim Women in Leicester,* in Wanda Krause, Jeremy Henzell-Thomas and Anas al-Shaikh Ali, (eds), *Citizenship, Security and Democracy: Muslim Communities and Activism in the West* (London, forthcoming). *Bihishti Zewar* is also now compulsory reading for members of the Tablighi Jamaat (an offshoot of the Deobandi school) in the UK, see Metcalf, *Perfecting Women*, p. 5.

7   This is my translation of Ashraf Ali Thanawi's reason for writing the book, found in his Introduction, *Bihishti Zewar,* pp. 21-3. This Urdu copy is titled *Ashrafi Asli* which means 'Ashraf's Original', by the publishers in order to validate its authenticity. There are abridged versions available, but the publishers claim that theirs is the only complete Urdu version of the original text. My translation here may be cross-referenced with Metcalf, *Perfecting Women*, pp. 47-9.

8   Metcalf, *Perfecting Women*, p. 3.

9   Ibid., p. 12.

10   Thanawi, *Bihishti Zewar*, p. 23.

would be immeasurable – hence this book is often a gift given to brides at their wedding.[11]

Although in the first instance the book was written for Muslim women in India, today it is taught as the seminal textbook in those *madrassahs* (schools of religious learning) for girls throughout England run by the Gujarati community. Two questions concern this paper. First, for a Gujarati Muslim community that is very traditional and austere in its practice of Islam (for example most of the women in this study prefer to wear black overcoats and face veils), how far is *Bihishti Zewar* used to define, inform and shape their use of public space, in twenty-first century Britain? Secondly, how does the text allow the women to carry their spirituality into the public domain?

These two questions are explored through textual analysis and empirical fieldwork via interviews. Indeed, as most of the Gujarati women in Leicester whom I have met, do go out of their homes regularly, their opinion on how that is sanctioned by *Bihishti Zewar* is important. The inside/outside and public/private themes give us particular insight into gender relations and politico-cultural change, often mirroring how 'sacred' a community believes itself to be, by reference to the extent of seclusion and control of its women.[12] The conclusion of this chapter points toward the importance and relevance of a sacred secondary source text, both in terms of authority and time-space applicability. Whilst Islamic secondary sacred texts are still used in the Western context, their applicability is often questioned and their use is often reconfigured.

Methodology

This research is qualitative and is shaped by: data collated 'systematically and rigorously'[13] via ethnographic observations and participation conducted between 2004 and 2006; local history archives; and thirty in-depth semi-structured interviews and conversations with Gujarati women in Leicester. Participants in this research reflect a cross-section of ages (from eighteen to seventy), and different socio-economic backgrounds (seamstresses, lawyers, teachers, and full-time mothers). Most conversations and interviews were conducted in English and/or Urdu/Gujarati. The majority of the younger women were born in England, but others migrated either from Gujarat in India, from Baruch, Kutchch and Surat, or from East Africa, from Malawi, Zimbabwe, Kenya, and South Africa. Throughout, the women give their definitions of 'public space' and spirituality.

This is a study of women's lived experiences, using their voices – the voices of a minority religious group – to define themselves and their own notions of space, spirituality and texts. This is not a ventriloqual agenda, but one that recognizes that good ethnography ought to present precisely the views and voices of those researched. In many ways, this reflects Shrikala Warrier's opinion that the studies

---

11 Metcalf, *Perfecting Women,* p. 3.
12 Hooker, 'History: East, South and Southeast Asia', p. 352.
13 Jennifer Mason, *Qualitative Researching* (London, 1996), p. 5.

of Asian communities in Britain has historically been from a male perspective, with women not being accessed directly and often portrayed as subordinate:

> Given the assumption that South Asian women are – and always have been – a muted group, a "social problem" perspective has almost always been adopted in analyses of their behaviour. This pathologizing tendency is particularly striking whenever the new roles and strategies devised by such women have led them to either challenge, or to re-negotiate traditional conventions. This account, by focusing on women as *active participants* in the migration-settlement process, seeks to restore women to their proper place at the centre of family life.[14]

This is an interesting objective of research on Muslim South Asian women. While this chapter also aims to voice the opinions of Gujarati Muslim women, this is done by deconstructing the use of a religious text written in the colonial period that has informed the life of Gujarati women for over a century; a text that reflects the genre of its time as theology for women, but not by women. Gail Minault comments that the newly emerging Muslim identity of the time when *Bihishti Zewar* was written sought to define women's identities and roles, and often women complied, and at other times they asserted their own identities.[15]

This chapter is not concerned with how women acted in resisting the colonial empire; instead it is concerned with how *Bihishti Zewar*, as a text from that period, addressed women. The interesting twist in the tale is how a hundred years on, Muslim women who settled in England, the heartland of the former empire, use that same text. Therefore understanding context is just as important as understanding text.

Leicester's Gujarati Muslim women

Overseas theological ideologies have heavily influenced and shaped current Muslim communities settled in Britain. One of these communities is the Gujarati Sunni[16]

---

14 Shrikala Warrier, 'Gujarati Prajapatis in London: Family Roles and Sociability Networks', in Roger Ballard, (ed.), *Desh Pardesh: the South Asian Presence in Britain* (London, 1994), pp. 191-212:191.

15 Gail Minault, 'South Asia: Mid-18th to early 20th Century', in Joseph, *Encyclopaedia of Women and Islamic Cultures*, vol. 1, pp. 176-85:178.

16 *Sunni* in Islamic theology refers to a person who follows the *Sunnah*, that is the second primary source of *Shariah* which embodies the life of the Prophet Muhammad (the first primary source is the Qur'an, the divinely revealed sacred text.) Suffice to say here that the ideal Muslim way of life is that of the Prophet's, therefore, emulation of this is the aim of every Muslim. This can only be achieved by referring to records of the Prophet's life, which in turn are found in the corpus of *Hadith* literature, compilations of his actions and sayings. The *hadith* literature embodies the *Sunnah,* the precedent (Muhammad Zubayr Siddiqi, *Hadith Literature: Its Origin, Development and Special Features* (Cambridge, 1993)).

In reality Gujarati Muslim women who follow this theological course ought to be simply referred to as 'Muslim'. However, the term *Sunni* is in opposition to the minority *Shia* community who follow the Prophetic example as transmitted in his familial heirs, with their own sources of *hadiths*. Over time, the study and scrutiny of the two primary sources led to scholars and jurists establishing detailed rules and procedures of both categorizing the community in Leicester, which began settlement from 1951 onwards, coming largely from East Africa.[17] Michael Twaddle[18] records that the Africanization policies in Uganda and Kenya led to most settled Asians fleeing largely to Britain by virtue of being from Commonwealth lands. This was not without problems as cities such as Leicester displayed their initial hostility towards prospective migrants, with the City Corporation placing its infamous advertisement in the *Ugandan Argus*, warning Ugandan Asians, 'do not come to Leicester'.[19] Valerie Marett's work traces the migration of Hindu and Muslim South Asians into Leicester.[20] By 1981, Leicester had 10 percent of the UK South Asian immigration from East Africa.[21] As far as current demographics are concerned, the 2001 Census indicates that out of the total population of just under 280,000 44.7 percent are Christian, 14.74 percent Hindu, 11.03 percent Muslim, and 4.2 percent are Sikh.[22] At 30,885 Leicester's Muslim

---

laws, but also scrutinizing their 'minutest detail for their essential meaning' (David Waines, *An Introduction to Islam* (Cambridge, 1995) p. 64). This scientific jurisprudential activity spanning several centuries is collectively known as *fiqh*, covering the theory and philosophy of law as well as imposing a system of methodology and juridical logic (Wael Hallaq, 'Consideration of the Function and Practice of Sunni Legal Theory', *Journal of the American Oriental Society*, 104:4 (1984): 679-689). Several schools of law (*madhahib*) developed in this pursuit, in different regions of the growing Muslim world, and at slightly different times. One of these schools, followed mostly in the present day Indian subcontinent, Turkey and parts of Iraq is the Hanafi school, named after its founding father Imam Abu Hanifah (died 767 CE). The Gujaratis who I refer to then are Hanafi *Sunnis*. However, a further subdivision in legal and theological practices has resulted amongst the schools of law, again which are largely regional, and also theological. Some are very Sufi and mystically orientated, hence following largely esoteric interpretations of sources, and others are jurisprudentially orientated, hence favouring exoteric laws. The Deobandi school in India falls into the latter category, although many of its scholars had Sufi roots. For the purposes of this chapter, the women of this study are from the Sunni tradition, from the Hanafi school of law, with specific teachings emerging from Deoband. They will, however, be simply referred to as 'Gujarati women in Leicester'.

17 For a detailed analysis see Bokhari, *Places and Perspectives*.

18 Michael Twaddle, (ed.), *Expulsion of a Minority: Essays on Ugandan Asians* (London, 1975); Twaddle, 'East African Asians Through a Hundred Years', in Colin Clarke, Ceri Peach and Steven Vertovec, (eds), *South Asians Overseas: Migration and Identity* (Cambridge, 1990), pp.149-63; Michael Twaddle, 'The Development of Communalism among East African Asians', in Crispin Bates, (ed.), *Community, Empire and Migration: South Asians in Diaspora* (Basingstoke, 2001), pp. 109-22.

19 Richard Bonney, *Understanding and Celebrating Religious Diversity in Leicester's Places of Worship Since 1970* (Leicester, 2003), p. 14.

20 Valerie Marett, *Immigrants Settling in the City* (London, 1989).

21 Ahmed Andrews, 'Muslim Women in a Western European Society: Gujarati Muslim Women in Leicester', in J. Fulton and P. Gee, (eds), *Religion in Contemporary Europe* (Lewiston, 1994), pp. 78-92.

22 www.about-leicester/demographic. Accessed August 2005. Leicester prides itself in its diversity. It appears to be 'ahead of the rest of the UK and Europe in developing a policy to make diversity, as manifested in the place of religious buildings for all faiths, central to all relevant planning deliberations' (Bonney, *Understanding and Celebrating Religious Diversity*, p. v.). It has settled Jewish, Sikh, Hindu, Christian and Muslim communities. It was the first place to debate during a court case which version of the Qur'an witnesses ought to swear on

community is the tenth largest in England and Wales[23] and the majority of Muslims are Gujarati.

Essentially, the Muslim Gujaratis are self-sufficient. Their community structures could operate without much interaction with others outside their community.[24] The majority of Gujarati Muslims live in the densely populated Highfields area of Leicester, and some in the more affluent wards of Evington, Knighton and Oadby. Politics and political participation shape the development and infrastructure of communities and yet all four Muslim councillors are male.[25]

Culturally, Gujarati Muslims in Leicester are a mix of both British and Indian culture. Theologically, they follow the traditionalist Deobandi madrassah of learning, which not only favours a traditional curriculum, but also seeks to emulate that globally: the Deobandi madrassah has outposts in Africa, and indeed in the UK.

Bihishti Zewar

The work is encyclopaedic and is divided into ten parts, concerned largely with religious and family law and the chapters cover standard ritual laws on prayer, ablutions, fasting, pilgrimage, alms-giving, marriage, divorce the Hereafter, and also hobbies, games, manners, and women's desires.[26] Its language is quite emotive, yet at the same time

> Thanawi brings Urdu prose into its own using colloquial Urdu, rather than the Begamati Urdu of his family, to make his work accessible. Thanawi avoids ecstatic poetry, relying heavily on legal ritualised principles. He uses irony … for literary effect, for example when

---

– English, or Arabic (ibid., p. 4.). Ravat records 14 faiths being present in Leicester (Riaz Ravat, *Embracing the Present, Planning the Future: Social Action by the Faith Communities of Leicester* (Bury St Edmunds, 2004), p. 6), and with 76% of its population having named religious adherence in the 2001 Census (in Bonney, *Understanding and Celebrating Religious Diversity* p. 10.), practically all faith groups are involved in social projects (ibid., p. 17.). Furthermore, Leicester is the first city in the UK that will probably have an ethnic minority *majority*, as currently, 50% of its primary school intake is from ethnic minority communities (ibid., p. 11.).

23 Ibid., p. 33.

24 Bokhari, *Places and Perspectives*.

25 www.leicester.gov.uk/councillors. Accessed August 2005.

26 A detailed breakdown of the book is as follows:
   Part 1. Beliefs, sins and purification via ablutions.
   Part 2. The five daily prayers, optional prayers, and method of performing the prayers.
   Part 3. Fasting, paying poor due (*zakat*), and pilgrimage.
   Part 4. Marriage, divorce and death, veiling, seclusion.
   Part 5. Gifts, loans, contracts, mortgages.
   Part 6. Hobbies, games, childbirth, marriage ceremonies, and other celebrations.
   Part 7. Manners: eating, drinking, talking, pride, miserliness, spiritual guide.
   Part 8. Reward and punishment.
   Part 9. Day of Judgement, hell and heaven.
   Part 10. Faith, the soul, desires, women.
   Part 11. Fear of God, good acts, advice (an addition).

referring to local customs which he often condemns, he uses the term *shariah* (divine law), indicating his disapproval that the Indian Muslims have replaced the authentic *shariah* with their own *shariah*.[27]

Although claiming that men and women are equal in seeking knowledge, Thanawi also claims in Part 10 that women are associated with the lower soul, the *nafs*.[28] 'In women, men see the lack of control they most fear in themselves',[29] hence an obsession with trying to control women.[30] However, Thanawi sees women's practice of wasteful pastimes as both a source and symbol of the Muslim community's decline.[31] Thanawi spends a lot of time addressing women and analysing their past times, and traits. For example, he often alludes to the shortcomings of women.[32] In Part 10, he lists that they talk too much, they take too long getting ready for a journey into town, they interrupt each other, have no sense of urgency and are in the habit of leaving pins and needles lying around.[33] Whilst appearing to be very critical and sexist, the text must be understood in its historical and cultural context. Thanawi was writing at the same time as Victorian England held its own stereotypical views of women, yet, ironically, Thanawi makes it clear that 'there can never be a *prima facie* case that women are morally inferior to men'.[34]

Unlike many other patriarchal texts, the *Bihishti Zewar* challenged cultural traditions within the home, and defined the role of the *ulama* (religious scholars) as distinct from the state. Thanawi did not envisage reform as state led, but as self-reform, policed individually. In aiming the text at women and equipping them in their usually private roles with a depth of Islamic knowledge, which up to then had largely been the privilege of men in the public domain, the text aims to enlighten women and allow them equal rights to education. However, at the same time, it cleverly extends the authority of men into the private sphere in areas where previously men had not dictated to women.

Let us take a few examples of the representation of women and the public domain. The text does not specifically define 'public space' perhaps because there was no call for it, as Indian Muslim society at that time was clearly demarcated. For instance, the market and work place was male dominated, the home was the place where the women folk were free to move, and men were excluded.[35] For our purposes, to elicit Thanawi's comments and construction of the public sphere, we have to probe those sections of his text where he refers to women's covering and veils, outdoor pursuits and celebrations. Thanawi, like other traditional scholars, believed that women

---

27 Bokhari, *Places and Perspectives*.

28 Metcalf, *Perfecting Women*, p. 318.

29 Ibid., p. 14.

30 Bokhari, *Places and Perspectives*, and see also Metcalf, *Perfecting Women*, pp. 318-27.

31 Minault, 'South Asia: Mid-18th to Early 20th Century', p. 179.

32 Metcalf, *Perfecting Women*, p. 14.

33 Ibid., pp. 338-42.

34 Ibid., p. 8.

35 Bokhari, *Places and Perspectives*.

should be removed from the public sphere, including mosques.[36] Whilst quoting a prophetic tradition, he argues that if it is not considered good for women to go out for their prayers, then it cannot be good for them to go out for other reasons.[37]

Thanawi urges women, in Part 6, to be careful in dropping everything in order to go out visiting friends, because the sins of pride in wanting to show off garments, putting financial pressure on the husband to cover all expenses, and envy and greed in seeing what friends have, could be involved.[38] Indeed, Thanawi claims that even going to weddings is not a good practice, and visits to parents' homes are sanctioned, but only once or twice a year. These are the limited legitimate reasons for women entering the public domain.[39] That is, women are urged, amongst other things, to only go out of the home when absolutely necessary, and then to cover themselves completely (including the hands, feet and face) in the company of men who are not from the immediate family.[40] In order to understand the context in which *Bihishti Zewar* was written, let us look historically at late nineteenth century India.

British India: reform movements and the Deoband school

At the time that *Bihishti Zewar* was being written, India was under British rule. The British Raj faced great opposition during the 1857 Mutiny, and at the forefront of the anti-colonial movement was the Deobandi School in U.P, which was set up to resist the British Raj. Opposition to the British rule had been gathering momentum for quite some time and whilst the empire was at its height in the late nineteenth century, India was beginning cultural opposition and Muslim scholars in the north of India were beginning to resist. For example, Sayyid Ahmad Khan (1817-1898) founded the Aligarh University, where Islam was combined with a social identity that was to harness European sciences and arts.[41] But, for Ahmed Khan, women 'were symbols of his community's decline'.[42] On the other hand, some Indians were searching for a more authentic Indian identity by emphasizing religious observances and attacking customary rituals. Two key figures in this movement, Muhammad Qasim Nanautwi (1833-1877) and Rashid Ahmad Gangohi (1829-1905), were instrumental in founding the Deoband School of learning.[43]

---

36 Metcalf, *Perfecting Women,* p. 7.

37 Ibid., p. 206.

38 Ibid., pp. 108-10.

39 Thanawi is not alone in this 'control' of women's movements. The greatly revered Sufi scholar al-Ghazali (d. 1111CE) commented that a respectable woman should stay home engaged in domestic chores and devotions, but if she had to go out of the home, then it should be with the permission of her husband and not to crowded market places (Barbara Andaya, 'Malay World: 18th to Early 20th Century', in Joseph, *Encyclopedia of Women and Islamic Cultures,* vol. 1, pp. 135-42:138.

40 Saroha, *Heavenly Ornaments,* part 4, p. 342.

41 Barbara Metcalf, *Islamic Revival in British India: Deoband 1860-1900* (Oxford, 1982), p. 11.

42 Minault, 'South Asia: Mid-18th to Early 20th Century', p. 197.

43 Metcalf, *Islamic Revival in British India,* p. 76.

It is not clear how much a role Nanautwi and Gongohi played in the 1857 Mutiny,[44] although Deobandis believe that they actively fought.[45] Metcalf and Metcalf point out that Deobandi literature pre-1920 insisted that the scholars had been apolitical, but post-1920 presented the founders as freedom fighters who took a firm political stance after the First World War, supporting Gandhi in opposition to British rule.[46] It could be argued that the Deobandi School was political from its inception, as resistance to the Raj was the impetus for its establishment.[47] Despite the differences in scholarly opinions, it is agreed that in the aftermath of 1857, the founding scholars escaped to their home villages away from the heavy presence of the British in Delhi, and concentrated on developing educational institutions so that Muslims could be empowered through their own tradition.[48] Their initial quietist work came to fruition in Deoband, a small town where all the founders had links and found spiritual inspiration, which meant that Deoband had been divinely decreed in 1866.[49] Deoband was Islamicized, that is consecrated, as a new religious space by the founding fathers relating dreams that they had, where the Prophet himself urged them to build a school of religious learning. Thus the small town became a place blessed by the Prophet himself, this in turn authenticating the seminary.[50]

The teaching at the seminary involved traditional learning of Qur'an, *hadith*, *shariah* and the *fiqh* of Abu Hanifa, the emphasis being on developing a reformist and empowering Islam, in opposition to the imperial rule, '… showing that their standard of correct belief and practice defined them as a group not only separate from but morally superior to the British'.[51] This mother school's teachings were spread to other schools set up to follow the same curriculum and teachings.[52] In time, Deobandi teaching came to be known as 'Indian Islam' with students from Peshawar, Bengal, and Madras.[53]

Ashraf Ali Thanawi

The Deobandis were not only scholars of the Hanafi fiqh, but also Sufis. Ashraf Ali Thanawi was one of the most influential Indian Sufis[54] and Thanawi was a second generation student and scholar of Deoband. In his thirties, he retired to his small home town of Thana Bhawan, in U.P, northern India. There, he wrote prolifically,

---

44 Ibid., p. 82.
45 Moulana Diyar-Rahman Faruqi, *The Ulama of Deoband: Their Majestic Past* (South Africa, 1999), p. 39.
46 Barbara Metcalf and Thomas Metcalf, *A Concise History of India* (Cambridge, 2002), p. 7.
47 Bokhari, *Places and Perspectives,* forthcoming.
48 Metcalf, *Islamic Revival in British India,* p. 85.
49 Faruqi, *The Ulama of Deoband*, p. 46.
50 Bokhari, *Places and Perspectives.*
51 Metcalf, *Islamic Revival in British India*, p. 153.
52 Ibid., p. 125.
53 Ibid., p. 136.
54 Francis Robinson, *Varieties of South Asian Islam* (Coventry, 1988), p. 5.

and was famous for the spiritual guidance that he offered. As a reformer, Thanawi was facing the challenges of Muslim political dominance having been replaced by British rule, which encouraged the development and strengthening of religious identity. The new ensuing social dislocation, together with emerging cultural values led to the Deobandis, and Thanawi in particular, responding with a call to renew one's identity. And for the first time in Indian Muslim history, it aimed its mainstream Islamic teaching at women.[55]

Thanawi did this because women up to then had not been seen as the guardians of tradition and knowledge; that was left to the men in the public domain. The text is an example of the cultural transformations that were taking place on the Indian landscape in the modern world. At the beginning of the text, Thanawi advocates that men and women, being the same in intellectual ability, need education in order to become good moral citizens. Society was seen as degenerate and in need of reform, which could only be done by reforming the individual.[56] For some critics, the text is interesting because not only does it instruct women to take individual responsibility for learning, but also because it does not point to any physiological, spiritual, emotional or intellectual differences between men and women.[57] However, this new responsibility to learn was in the context of separate gender roles, that is, men were still the authority in the home: 'Women were meant to be socially subordinate to men and adhere to the shariat standards of seclusion, when possible, inside the home.'[58] Thanawi's aim then, was to rescue the Shariah, the law, embodied in the Qur'an and Sunnah and local scholarly opinions from cultural superstitions, and to allow women direct access to these sources so that social order would prevail. This could only be done by reforming the private lives of women.

The impact of *Bihishti Zewar* cannot be under-estimated. In 2001, the Deobandi seminary had over 3000 students enrolled, and many outpost colleges.[59] Today the text is still taught in madrassahs to Muslims of Indian descent the world over and the Gujaratis in Leicester are no exception. Its impact is now far-reaching due to several English translations available, allowing migrant Muslims and their settled western born children to access the source. Whatever assumptions Thanawi makes about women ought to be understood in the Indian context at the turn of the last century. However, the interesting tension is how the Gujarati community in Leicester uses *Bihishti Zewar* a hundred years after it was written, ironically in the heartland of the former colonial master, Britain. For Metcalf, such a manual was in fact 'at the heart of socio-political change'.[60] However, whether Thanawi could himself have predicted that the changes made by his text would not just be limited to the lives of Muslims in India but indeed globally, is difficult to tell.

---

55 Metcalf, *Perfecting Women,* p. 7.
56 Bokhari, *Places and Perspectives.*
57 Metcalf, *Perfecting Women,* p. vii.
58 Ibid., p. 9.
59 Metcalf, *Islamic Revival,* 2002 (1982), p. xii.
60 Ibid., p. 5.

Leicester's Gujarati women and *Bihishti Zewar*

Within this community, practices of veiling in the form of black outer garments that also cover the hands, feet, and face are usual. It appears that the women from this traditional austere community are silent and removed from the public. But on closer examination, that could not be further from the truth. All the women I interviewed received religious instruction, whether at home or in a madrassah, and all moved in public spaces outside the home to varying degrees. Some had very strong formulated views about *Bihishti Zewar*, whereas others had not given the matter much thought, by either not questioning the text, or conversely not using it much.

The majority of women commented on the text being a compendium of ritual laws and used it as a reference text, useful for its legal and jurisprudential rulings and as a resource for the ritual practice of Islam, not a source for spirituality. Salima, 30, is a young mother of four, born and brought up in Blackburn, but living in Leicester since her marriage almost 11 years ago. She went to madrassah until the age of 11:

> I use *Bihishti Zewar* as a reference point, even to this day. But it's usually for practical *fiqh* issues, like, will dental treatment break my fast. But when I was taught in madrassahs, I was taught parts of the book, and made to memorize it. I always liked the book, but I don't get a great sense of spirituality from it – it's not like that. It's for day to day life … For spiritual stuff, I use other books …

Salima's experience of the text is very similar to Anisha's, 29, born and bred in Leicester. She also went to madrassah until 11, then went on to a further madrassah for girls, where she then taught. She now works as a librarian, and had also recently married. Anisha stated:

> Before I would use it for everything. Then at 18, I started searching my faith for myself, so I turned to other sources too. But I know chunks out of *Bihishti Zewar* by heart which always stay with me, even the bits that I don't use – you know, I know what the religious rules are for purifying a well if an animal falls into it – now I'd need that if I were a farmer in India, but not here!

Whilst the majority of women interviewed showed a good working knowledge of *Bihishti Zewar,* and often used the text, Aishah was unusual in her criticism of it. Aishah, 32, was born in Zimbabwe and then migrated to England at 18, moving to Leicester at 19 on her marriage. She went to madrassah in Zimbabwe until 11. In England, she worked as the PA to the Director General of a reputable Muslim research institute, before moving into a career in teaching Arabic in a Muslim faith school and to women. She commented:

> Gujaratis haven't always been religious. I'm proud of being Muslim and was educated in Islam, but did not necessarily practise.

Three generations earlier her family had moved to Africa, worked very hard, instilling good values of hospitality, honesty, and reliability in their children. Zimbabwe was a very mixed society, and her father was employed by a Jewish man. Eventually, a new conscious religious identity began to emerge in Zimbabwe. Aishah's mother started to veil after the age of 40, but her father would protest, calling her an 'old lady'.

Aishah lived a life where she accessed different cultures and books. Her fondest memories were of her father's library, which had books on Islam as well as other faiths. On asking her what a religious life was, she expressed that she felt 'religious' reading George Eliot:

> Eliot makes me think about religion more than organized religion; she has very self-effacing curbing characters.

Yet as far as *Bihishti Zewar* was concerned, she was adamant that:

> We shouldn't be using it. I feel really disconnected from it. I pick it up, and it just doesn't grip me. A lot of what we read is tied to time and place, even commentaries on the Qur'an, so the parables [Thanawi] uses are apt for India, but not here. I remember the only interesting bits I found as a nine year old reading it were the spiritual parts, about Last Days.

In many ways, then, whilst she advocated abandoning the text as a teaching tool, she probably is a minority in finding spirituality in its pages, something that Thanawi hoped he could offer the readers.

However, Aishah offers a contrasted reading to Hawwa, 36, a migrant at the age of 6 from Malawi, also from the teaching profession as a head teacher of a local Muslim girls' school. She described the text as a manual of *fiqh*, but also commented that rather than being critical of the text, it had to be appreciated in its context:

> Circumstances have changed now. There is a lot of *jahilliyah* [ignorance of religion]. If that is addressed, then women can move freely in public spaces.

Hawwa explains, as a traditionally trained scholar, and heralding from a family of Islamic scholars, that *Bihishti Zewar* had to be understood as a text written in India over a hundred years ago, and that whilst it was a guidebook, it was not the basis of Islamic knowledge. The book was taught to her, and according to the school syllabus, it was also taught to the younger girls in her school. Older girls, training to be scholars, then progressed onto specific Arabic texts. *Bihishti Zewar*, however, was not easily dispensable.

Religious texts are being deconstructed and in a Western context. Some of the women in this chapter were reluctant to challenge Thanawi's work, whereas others did openly. The challenges were not made to the ritual laws, but to the moral advice to women in cultivating a domestic role and withdrawing from public life. For Aishah:

> of course you don't have to stay indoors. You see we forget that when Thanawi was writing, the homes were buzzing with life, and women weren't isolated. But in England, you'd be cut off if you stayed home. I think if we look at the Qur'an and Sunnah, it doesn't follow what he says – we should take our personalities out of matters when writing about what we can or can't do, we should follow the sources correctly.

This ties in with her definition of public space:

> Public space is everywhere, except the upstairs of my home – even my ground floor is public because I open it up to people. I want to. Space is not tangible for me … it's about the personal relations that you have, and about attitude. I don't think the categories are clear.

Salima challenges Thanawi's views on women and public space, but not the text generally:

> I rebelled against religion for many years … But I didn't blame the book … I still use it … I might get clarification, but I won't question it.

But when asked for her response to the passages on women's restricted movements (at weddings or visiting parents) she responded:

> You see, I would challenge those bits – on the bits about your religion, I think he's very good, but on women, he's derogatory. He says you can only visit your parents once or twice a year, but Maulana Mohammed (a local Indian scholar in Leicester) says you can go to your parents every week, without permission, it's your right. I find that some parts of the *Bihishti Zewar* are not following the Sunnah. Things have to be applicable in your environment. Like, it's normal to hold hands with your husband in England when you're out and about, but not in India.
> So I leave bits out …
> You can't live according to the Indian subculture 100 years ago.
> Even at weddings, we aren't totally segregated. I have my veil on, but we're not in separate rooms always – it's not possible here …

Salima therefore displays incongruence with the lifestyle of Muslim women in the UK, who go about their daily chores, take children to and from school, go shopping; and the demands to limit their movements made by Thanawi. However, this was not done in the name of 'modern progress', but as a way of returning to authentic sources:

> But I can't imagine that when the Prophet's companions travelled, he didn't encourage them to adapt the existing culture.

For Salima, going out of the home to carry out her daily chores is nothing short of a form of worship.

Whilst for the majority of women Bihishti Zewar is a reference work, it is not a text that informs or shapes their spirituality. The important underlying theme to this chapter is women's defining 'public space' and what informs those definitions. On being asked, 'what informs your spirituality and how you are to interact with people in the public sphere?' Salima responded:

> Partly the *Bihishti Zewar*, but not really. It's more oral information, and culture – I couldn't give you precise references for that … it's really a mixture of what's acceptable now, things change according to where you live … we can access more information now … Now you know that you can question things …

For Aishah, many sources shaped her, but;

> *Bihishti Zewar* does not shape your identity. I don't teach it. I draw inspiration from a load of books – books actually by the same author I found out later, but which look at character traits, and the Sufi path. My Tunisian Arabic teacher has really shaped my identity.

Public space for Salima was '… the minute I step outside my front door' whereas for Anisha it 'depends on the gathering for me. Anywhere where there are men who are not my close relations, that is public space.' The same was true for Hawwa, Farida (27, housewife) and Rashida (35, lawyer). Public space dictated full covering of the body, hair and face. However, in defining public space as such, all women were mirroring Thanawi's definition. Yet they reconfigured space by taking ownership of it. The public sphere was no longer a male dominated space, but one where these women moved with authenticity – that is, whilst they challenged secondary sources, they legitimized their claim to the space by referring to primary texts, and by complying with strict laws of covering. As Anisha admitted:

> We weren't taught those bits [of *Bihishti Zewar* referring to staying indoors] thank God, because my teacher was a female scholar, so I think she felt they were outdated and so left them out. Culturally his rulings are irrelevant … I'm not being modern, I'm following the Prophet's hadiths and guidance which allowed women freedom of movement. May be those sections were relevant in India …

Whilst Rashida worked effectively as a lawyer, she veiled her face, felt fully justified in being present in the public arena, and was now comfortable with her Muslim identity, which as a teenager growing up in London, was often difficult. However, her use of Bihishti Zewar was minimal.

Maryam, 32, was the only respondent who believed that Thanawi was right, even in a British context, in urging women to stay home:

> I think really that a woman should stay home and make it peaceful. Look at me, I work from home, childminding. It suits me, and my husband.

Maryam voiced her opinion that in venturing out of the home, problems could creep into the domestic space. However if it were acceptable by a husband, then a women could go out to work or study. If it would cause problems, then she ought to 'use some wisdom' and stay home.

Whilst this research focused on women, some male scholars were also interviewed. One such Muslim scholar studied in the *Darul-Ulum* (madrassah for boys) in Bury, Lancashire, and in Egypt, and is the Imam of a local mosque. Interestingly, he stated about *Bihiishti Zewar:*

> I don't favour the use of such texts, because they aren't relevant here. I run a private madrassah, and this book is not taught there. Only the young women study it, and this is for the sections on women's personal hygiene and purification laws etc. I don't consider myself a Deobandi. I have no connection there, I've never been. We have graduates from the western hemisphere like myself who might have been taught by Deobandi scholars, our seminaries might have an affiliation with Deoband, but we have moved on. We are not

Deobandi, we are not in India. The Deobandi school is the most influential in India, but we live in a different environment.

When asked about women's movements in the public space, he responded:

> You can't say women can't go out. They go to work, they study – if they are upholding their Islamic values, why should they not. We need youngsters out and about in society … As far as dress is concerned, men and women both should uphold Islamic values, not just women … Women need to cover their hair, but not face in my opinion.

Whilst the scholar was not invalidating the text, he was giving it a time-space context, like Hawwa and Aishah. What he and Aisha however seemed to be pointing at was a need for contemporary texts in the western context, in the absence of which the *Bihishti Zewar* was still being used. However, secondary sources were open to criticism whereas primary sources were not challenged in the same way.

Conclusion

To conclude, *Bihishti Zewar* is no doubt a very influential text, which to this day is taught in homes and schools. Its impact varies depending on the communities that access it, yet whilst being taught in the UK, it appears that the emphasis has changed dramatically from Maulana Thanawi's original vision. His text was written to make respectable women knowledgeable in their faith. What appears to have happened is that its ritual chapters are emphasized, as opposed to the cultural requirements, which shape a woman's identity. Ironically then, whilst Thanawi rejected certain Indian cultural practices as ignorant and in need of 'Islamic' reform, a hundred years on his own conclusions and alternative modes of behaviour seem to be considered 'culturally Indian' and out of place in modern day Leicester. Women in Leicester are opting for their version of what the *shariah* expects of them, not Thanawi's version. As Salima stated:

> *Bihishti Zewar* has not had a big influence in my life. It's in our homes because of tradition. I guess if it wasn't this book, then it would have been another.

This raises significant questions, not just about how gender relations are being constructed in the Leicester community, but also about how religious texts are being used in new settings. As many of the participants stated, they access several texts to inform their theology and spirituality. Mary Layoun[61] states Islamic literature is modern literature, informed by traditional Islamic cultures from centuries: this is true of Bihishti Zewar. It is a religious text, which is also 'modern' as it reflects its own 'Indian' cultural traits. Its continued use by the community collectively is a statement of self-identity. However, the women in this research are engaged in

---

61 Mary Layoun, 'Literary Studies', in Joseph, *Encyclopaedia of Women and Islamic Cultures*, vol.1, pp. 383-8:383.

a process of hermeneutical deconstruction,[62] whereby the community (both men and women) insists on using the text, but certain individuals are dispensing with it in its entirety and others are selecting sections of it. Spirituality and public space is then being redefined and former definitions being reconfigured, by the women themselves.

Bibliography

Andaya, Barbara, 'Malay World: 18th to Early 20th Century', in Suad Joseph, (ed.), *Encyclopaedia of Women and Islamic Cultures* (Leiden-Boston: Brill, 2003): vol. 1, pp. 135-142.

Andrews, Ahmed, 'Muslim Women in a Western European Society: Gujarati Muslim Women in Leicester', in John Fulton and Peter Gee, (eds), *Religion in Contemporary Europe* (Lewiston: Edwin Mellen Press, 1994): 78-92.

Ballard, Roger, (ed.), *Desh Pardesh: the South Asian Presence in Britain* (London: Hurst and Co., 1994).

Bokhari, Raana, 'Places and Perspectives: Gujarati Muslim Women in Leicester', in Wanda Krause, Jeremy Henzell-Thomas and Anas al-Shaikh Ali. (eds), *Citizenship, Security and Democracy: Muslim Communities and Activism in the West* (London: Legacy, forthcoming).

Bonney, Richard, *Understanding and Celebrating Religious Diversity in Leicester's Places of Worship since 1970* (Leicester: University of Leicester, 2003).

Clarke, Colin, Ceri Peach, and Steven Vertovec (eds), *South Asians Overseas: Migration and Identity* (Cambridge: Cambridge University Press, 1990).

Faruqi, Moulana Diyar-Rahman, *The Ulama of Deoband: Their Majestic Past* (South Africa: Madrasah Arabia Islamia, 1999).

Fulton, John and Peter Gee, (eds), *Religion in Contemporary Europe* (Lewiston: Edwin Mellor Press, 1994).

Hallaq, Wael, 'Consideration of the Function and Practice of Sunni Legal Theory', *Journal of the American Oriental Society*, 104:4 (1984): 679-89.

Hooker, Virginia, 'History: East, South and Southeast Asia' in Suad Joseph, (ed.), *Encyclopaedia of Women and Islamic Cultures* (Leiden-Boston: Brill, 2003): vol. 1: 350-57.

Joseph, Suad, (ed.), *Encyclopaedia of Women and Islamic Cultures* (Leiden-Boston: Brill, 2003).

Layoun, Mary, 'Literary Studies', in Suad Joseph, (ed.), *Encyclopaedia of Women and Islamic Cultures* (Leiden-Boston: Brill, 2003): vol.1: 383-8.

Mahomedy, Molana Muhammad, trans. *Heavenly Ornaments: Bahishti Zewar, A Classical Manual of Islamic Sacred Law* (Karachi: Zam Zam Publishers, 1999).

Marett, Valerie, *Immigrants Settling in the City* (London: Leicester University Press, 1989).

Mason, Jennifer, *Qualitative Researching* (London: Sage Publications, 1996).

---

62 Katherine Young, 'Religious Studies', in Joseph, *Encyclopaedia of Women and Islamic Cultures*, vol.1, pp. 423-27:425.

Metcalf, Barbara, *Islamic Revival in British India: Deoband 1860-1900* (Oxford: Oxford University Press, 2002, [1982]).

Metcalf, Barbara, (trans. and commentary), *Perfecting Women: Maulana Ashraf Ali Thanawi's Bihishti Zewar* (Oxford: Oxford University Press, 1990).

Metcalf, Barbara, and Metcalf, Thomas, *A Concise History of India* (Cambridge: Cambridge University Press, 2002).

Minault, Gail, 'South Asia: Mid-18th to early 20th Century', in Suad Joseph, (ed.), *Encyclopaedia of Women and Islamic Cultures* (Leiden-Boston: Brill, 2003): vol. 1: 176-85.

Ravat, Riaz, *Embracing the Present, Planning the Future: Social Action by the Faith Communities of Leicester* (Bury St Edmunds: Leicester Faiths Regeneration Project, 2004).

Robinson, Francis, *Varieties of South Asian Islam*, Research Paper no. 7 (Coventry: University of Warwick, 1988).

Saroha, Muhammad Masroor Khan, trans. *Heavenly Ornaments, Bahishti Zewar* (Karachi: Darul Ishaat, 1991).

Siddiqi, Muhammad Zubayr, *Hadith Literature: Its Origin, Development and Special Features* (Cambridge: Cambridge University Press, 1993).

Thanawi, Muhammad Ashraf Ali, *Bihishti Zewar, Ashrafi Asli Mudallal wa Mukammal*, second edition, (Karachi: Darul-Ishaat, 1902) (reprinted 1981, second revised edition 2002).

Twaddle, Michael, (ed.), *Expulsion of a Minority: Essays on Ugandan Asians* (London: Athlone Press, 1975).

Twaddle, Michael, (ed.), 'East African Asians through a Hundred Years', in Colin Clarke, Ceri Peach, and Steven Vertovec, (eds), *South Asians Overseas: Migration and Identity* (Cambridge: Cambridge University Press, 1990): 149-63.

Twaddle, Michael, 'The Development of Communalism among East African Asians', in Crispin Bates, (ed.), *Community, Empire and Migration: South Asians in Diaspora* (Basingstoke: Palgrave, 2001): 109-22.

Waines, David, *An Introduction to Islam* (Cambridge: Cambridge University Press, 1995).

Warrier, Shrikala, 'Gujarati Prajapatis in London: family roles and sociability networks', in Roger Ballard, (ed.), *Desh Pardesh: the South Asian Presence in Britain* (London: Hurst and Co., 1994): 191-212.

Young, Katherine, 'Religious Studies', in Suad Joseph (ed.), *Encyclopaedia of Women and Islamic Cultures* (Leiden: Brill, 2003): vol.1: 423-7.

Internet Sources

www.about-leicester/demographic. Accessed August 2005.
www.leicester.gov.uk/councillors. Accessed August 2005.

Chapter 9

Forming Community in the Third Wave: Literary Texts and Women's Spiritualities

Dawn Llewellyn

And when you are so sort of spiritually bereft […] reading opens up so many possibilities that you hadn't realised that were there […] for developing yourself spiritually and knowing there are other people out there like you.

(Louise, Goddess Feminist)

Introduction

A key feature of third wave feminism is finding ways that enable 'woman', as a fragmented subject in process, to be the grounding for feminist politics, often looking for inclusive motifs where individual differences are connecting and forming community. However, this third wave feminist search has been in some measure myopic. While feminist theologians have tried to unpack the relationship between the splintering of 'woman', 'women's experiences' and the possibility of 'solidarity'[1] a fleeting glance at recent publications reveals that women's religious or spiritual experiences are generally absent from third wave feminist discussions.[2] These publications have made a vital contribution to third wave discussions, and are widely referenced across feminist third wave writings. However, while including sociological and cultural analysis, the experiences of religious and spiritual women appear only briefly.[3] This 'religious-blindness' may be an accidental oversight, but as

---

1   See Margaret D. Kamitsuka, *Feminist Theology and the Challenge of Difference* (Oxford, 2007) for a recent critical overview of approaches to these issues.

2   There are a number of publications asserting the arrival of the third wave: Barbara Findlen, (ed.), *Listen Up: Voices from the Next Feminist Generation* (Emeryville, [1995] 2001); Rebecca Walker, (ed.), *To Be Real: Telling the Truth and Changing the Face of Feminism* (New York, 1995); Leslie Heywood and Jennifer Drake, (eds), *Third Wave Agenda: Being Feminist, Doing Feminism* (Minneapolis and London, [1997] 2004); Jacquelyn N. Zita, (ed.), *Third Wave Feminisms* spec. issue of *Hypatia: A Journal of Feminist Philosophy*, Vol. 12, No. 3 Summer 1997; Jennifer Baumgardner and Amy Richards, *ManifestA: Young Women, Feminism and the Future* (New York, 2000); Rory Dicker and Alison Piepmeier, (eds), *Catching a Wave: Reclaiming Feminism for the 21ˢᵗ Century* (Boston, 2003); Stacy Gillis, Gillian Howie and Rebeca Munford, (eds), *Third Wave Feminism: A Critical Exploration* (Basingstoke, 2007) and Jo Reger, (ed.), *Different Wavelengths: Studies of the Contemporary Women's Movement* (London and New York, 2005).

3   See Sonja D. Curry-Johnson 'Weaving an Identity Tapestry' in Findlen, *Listen Up*, pp. 51-58; Robin M. Neidorf, 'Two Jews, Three Opinions' in Findlen, *Listen Up*, pp. 59-66

a result the third wave is missing motifs that are not only crucial to many women's lives but neglects instances where women's individual experiences in religious and spiritual settings are connecting and becoming community outside usual religious settings.

Drawing on interviews with women from a range of (self-identified) spiritual and religious positions, this chapter considers how literary texts[4] and women's spiritualities form communities within third wave feminism. It begins with the rise of the third wave as presented by authors who identify explicitly with this stage of feminism, providing some background for the motifs of individuality and community running through third wave writings. This chapter then turns to participants' reflections on their readings of literary texts,[5] in the context of their religious and spiritual practices, suggesting that from these personal encounters with literature three textual images of community emerge: intimate, outward and imagined. These communities suggest a site woven with individual experiences and commonality, and are thus emblematic of third wave feminist discourses. However, not all participants identified themselves as feminist, thus allowing women with no feminist attachment to contribute to feminist discourses, increasing the opportunity to find places where expressions of contemporary feminism reside.

Participants expressed varying attachments to a range of religious and spiritual communities: denominational churches,[6] ritual groups, Quaker meetings, a Druid Grove, a feminist coven, Julian Meetings, an inter-faith group, L'arche, the emerging church, Pagan groups and a Sea of Faith discussion group. These are intrinsic to participants' faith outlooks and yet, as Louise's comment at the beginning of this chapter implies, literature is also a resource for community in women's religious and spiritual lives. This chapter explores how literature becomes community in women's spiritualities, and brings this into the context of third wave feminism.

---

and Bhargavi C. Mandava 'Ghosts and Goddesses' in Findlen, *Listen Up,* pp. 89-100; Susan Muaddi Darraj 'Third World, Third Wave Feminism(s): The Evolution of Arab American Feminism', in Dicker and Piepmeier, *Catching a Wave,* pp. 188-205.

4   Literature (texts not traditionally considered Christian sacred scripture) has been a vital source for feminist theology and spiritualities see Carol Christ, 'Feminist Studies in Religion and Literature: A Methodological Reflection' in *Journal of American Academy of Religion* (1976), 44/2: 317-325; Carol Christ, *Diving Deep and Surfacing: Women Writers on a Spiritual Quest,* (Boston, 1995 [3rd Ed.]); Cynthia Eller, *Living in the Lap of the Goddess: The Feminist Spirituality Movement in the States* (Boston, 1993), pp. 10-11; Katie Cannon, *Black Womanist Ethics, (*Atlanta, 1988), Heather Walton, *Literature, Theology and Feminism* (Manchester, 2007) and Walton's chapter in this volume.

Separating scripture from literature was purposive in terms of my fieldwork. By encouraging participants to reflect on the texts they considered spiritually important, the relationships between the Bible and other texts emerged within the findings, rather than being inherent in the research design.

5   In this respect, this chapter concentrates on the reading experiences of participants, rather than offering a textual analysis and commentary on literature mentioned in the interviews.

6   Participants belong to Catholic, Methodist, Anglican, Evangelicalical, Baptist, Quaker and Christadelphian churches.

From second to third wave, from difference to diversity

Feminism has arguably entered a third wave[7] and accompanying its arrival is a range of feminist discourses that question the identity, unity and collectivity of categories such as 'woman' and 'feminist' – terms co-dependent with the chronological developments of secular and religious women's and feminist movements. Feminist history is usually presented as progressing through three distinct phases. The first wave peaked in the late nineteenth century with suffragist campaigns and the second wave arrived in the late 1960s with the onset of the Women's Liberation Movement. This was followed in the late 1980s by a third stage usually associated with the academic discourses of poststucturalism and postmodernism, and also with a 'young/er' generation of feminist awareness, activism, backlash and popular cultural analysis.

Traditional views of womanhood, abundant prior to the second wave, tended to assume that all women are constituted as women on account of specific biological characteristics. Second wave feminists and religious feminists questioned this vision, divorcing biology from gender to identify that 'while being female may require certain anatomical features, being a woman is something different, dependent on identification with the feminine gender (the social traits, activities and roles that make up femininity)'.[8] For the second wave, 'woman' was the common denominator and the founding principle from which to do and think feminist strategies that could challenge and overcome patriarchy and its sexist manifestations in the public and private arenas. 'Woman', as a class distinct from men was unified through a privileged identity category with patriarchy as a common point to rally against. However, underlying this agenda was an assumed universal female identity. Epistemologically dependent upon the experience of white, middle-class women, and in a gesture that echoed the hierarchical structures of patriarchy, feminism had in effect silenced diversity by excluding women outside of white, middle-class hegemony.

The most pointed and fruitful criticism of second wave feminism, voiced by women of colour, highlighted how 'woman' has been shaped by race, class, and heterosexual privileges, as bell hooks explains:

> ... this simplistic definition of women's liberation is a dismissal of peace, and class as factors that, in conjunction with sexism, determine the extent to which an individual will

---

7   I say 'arguably' to avoid announcing the demise of earlier waves when the third wave is still surfacing, and its boundaries and origins are contested. Although waves conveniently describe the history of feminisms, they disguise co-existence and have provoked intergenerational conflict and disconnection between different feminist cohorts. See Findlen, *Listen Up;* Heywood and Drake, *Third Wave Agenda;* Dicker and Piepmeier, *Catching a Wave;* Zita, *Third Wave Feminisms;* Astrid Henry, *Not My Mother's Sister: Generational Conflict and Third Wave Feminism* (Indiana University Press, Bloomington, 2004); Gillis, Howie and Munford, *Third Wave Feminism;* Reger, *Different Wavelengths;* Kristen Aune and Louise Livesy, 'Reclaiming the F-Word and Recovering Dialogue: Younger Feminists, Older Feminists and (Mis)communication' (Unpublished article, 2007).

8   Alison Stone, 'On the Genealogy of Women: A Defence of Anti-Essentialism' in Gillis, Howie and Munford, *Third Wave Feminism,* pp. 16-29:18.

be discriminated against, exploited, or oppressed. Bourgeois white women interested in women's rights issues have been satisfied with simple definitions for obvious reasons. Rhetorically placing themselves in the same social category as oppressed women, they were not anxious to call attention to race and class privilege.[9]

The work of women of colour, womanist, *mujerista*, lesbian, Asian, and other self-named theories and theologies are recognized by Heywood and Drake as the 'definitional moment' of third wave feminism.[10] The appraisal of second wave feminism demanded '"new subjectivity"' in what was up to that point, white, middle-class, first world feminisms'.[11] The second wave insistence *on* (gendered) difference was being (rightly) usurped by a third wave challenge *of* differences and the critique from diversity. This critique provoked a realization that 'woman' was a fragile category and the capacity of 'woman' to 'bear the weight of all contents and meanings ascribed to it' was called into question.[12] 'Woman' has imploded, and third wave feminisms emerge from anti-essentialist voices dissenting from and responding to this singular category.

Being individual, being community

With the third wave feminism's insistence on gendered differences and 'the multiplicity of every person's possible identifications'[13] as the basis for feminist thinking and activism, comes a growing directory of complex and fluid identities. This fragmentation may have encouraged and approved of the pursuit and practice of local feminisms,[14] but it seems to have made it difficult – some might say impossible and unwelcome – for 'woman/women' to be the grounding for a united class. Third wave feminism attempts to release this tension by acknowledging the diversity and individually located difference of 'woman', without essentializing or universalizing her, but maintaining the possibility of the category woman/women as the basis for a political movement. Being individual whilst being community draws on motifs where subjective experiences overlap and meet, finding some commonality from which a community across differences can flourish.

There has been a call for new subjectivities within third wave feminism and the focus on differences has been translated in practice into an emphasis on individuality and the personal 'I' rather than a collective 'we'.[15] As Heywood and Drake note,

---

9   bell hooks, *Feminist Theory: From Margin to Centre* (Boston, 1984), p. 18.

10   Heywood and Drake, *Third Wave Agenda*, p. 8.

11   Catherine Orr, 'Charting the Currents of the Third Wave', *Hypatia,* 12/3 (Summer 1997), pp. 29-45:37.

12   Gillis, Howie, and Munford, 'Introduction', *Third Wave Feminism*, pp. xxi-xxxiv: xxi.

13   Julia Kristeva, 'Women's Time', in Toril Moi, (ed.), *The Kristeva Reader* (Oxford, 1986), pp. 187-213: 210.

14   Naomi Zack, *Inclusive Feminism: A Third Wave Theory of Women's Commonality* (Maryland, 2005), p. 3.

15   Henry discusses the individuality of third wave feminism in more detail. Henry, *Not My Mother's Sister,* pp. 40-45.

despite knowing its dangers 'the ideology of individualism is still a motivating force in many third wave lives'[16] which overshadows notions of sisterhood and solidarity that were central to previous feminisms. Drawing on the profits gained by the renovation of the second wave, third wave feminists are emphasizing the uniqueness and particularity of gendered identities. For instance, Baumgardner and Richards articulate the multiple possibilities of being 'women':

> middle-class white women, rich black lesbians, and working-class straight Asian women, an organic intertwining with movements for racial and economic equality, as well as gay rights, is inherent in the feminist mandate [...] In reality, feminism wants you to be whoever you are – but with a political consciousness. And vice-versa: you want to be a feminist because you want to be exactly who you are.[17]

Here, 'women' carries different combinations of identity. The repetition of 'you' at the end of this paragraph is heavy, stressing that women's *personal* not collective franchise is enabled via feminism in the third wave.

Third wave feminist voices have a penchant for defining feminism in their own terms, a proclivity encapsulated in Rebecca Walker's statement: 'I *am* the Third Wave.'[18] In this sentence, Walker does not draw on a notion of collectivity or community, but relies on an emphatic use of the first person to underscore her experiences of feminism. This emphasis on individuality runs through anthologies heralding the third wave. Walker's *To Be Real*, Findlen's *Listen Up* and Natasha Walter's *On the Move*[19] are edited volumes containing autobiographical essays from self-identified young feminists. As a testament to this, the editors are careful to state the diversity of positions and experiences included in their collections. For instance, Walker notes 'the group you will read here is an eclectic gathering of folks';[20] Findlen opens with a list of the different identities claimed by her contributors, 'Chicana single mother; Asian bisexual; punk; politically astute, active woman; middle-class black woman; young mother; slacker;'[21] and Walter comments that her authors 'don't spring from any one background, one class, one political persuasion or one ethnic group.'[22]

These anthologies employ 'I' to embody the fragmentation of the feminist subject in process and to shatter the notion of a monolithic feminism.[23] As Walker writes, feminists of the third wave are 'seeking to create identities that accommodate

---

16 Heywood and Drake, *Third Wave Agenda,* p. 11.

17 Baumgardner and Richards, *ManifestA,* p. 56-7.

18 Cited in Astrid Henry, 'Solitary Sisterhood: Individualism Meets Collectivity in Feminism's Third Wave' in Reger, *Different Wavelengths,* pp. 81-98:83.

19 Walker's and Findlen's collections come from an American context, while Walter's is based in Britain. See Walker, *To Be Real*; Findlen, *Listen Up*; and Natasha Walter, *On the Move: Feminism for a New Generation* (London, 1999).

20 Walker, *To Be Real,* p. xxxvi.

21 Findlen, *Listen Up,* p. xvi.

22 Walter, *On the Move,* p. 2.

23 See Lynne Pearce's analysis of the use of the personal pronoun in feminist discourses in *The Rhetorics of Feminism: Readings In Contemporary Cultural Theory and the Popular Press* (London and New York, 2004).

ambiguity and our multiple positionalities: including more than excluding, exploring more than defining, searching more than arriving'.[24] Despite the highly personal reflections upon the authors' particularized definitions and experiences, authors and editors position these compilations as belonging historically and theoretically to the feminist movement.

Bridging 'being individual, being community' begins by finding places where, as Deborah Siegel eloquently observes, individual voices 'coalesce in the space between differences'.[25] This evokes locations where subjective experiences brush alongside each other to form, even if briefly or momentarily, connections and points of contact. The third wave implements a language that speaks of 'linking across our many differences';[26] of 'shared purpose ... beyond our personal spheres'[27] of collectivity and community, while realizing the specific historical contexts from which feminists speak and the different sets of challenges faced with each historical location. In *ManifestA,* Baumgardner and Richards appeal to Sarah Hoagland's notion of 'autokeonony' or 'self in community' and demand its inclusion in their third wave agenda.[28] Autokeonony is the place of the 'individual in community'[29] echoing Richards's call that *ManifestA* and the third wave feminism it presents, is part 'of a big, visible, passionate movement'.[30] The third wave emphasis on individuality tries not to preclude common ground, but contradictory and subjective experiences nestle within, and remain the basis for community.

Women's individual experiences with literary texts are the basis for communities that supportively take part in their spiritual and religious lives. All participants (except one) began their religious or spiritual life within a Christian context, but owing to a perceived dissatisfaction are seeking to supplement or replace this with other types of community. For participants, a significant part of this search has taken a textual form, as community is sought through the subjective experiences of reading literary texts. The women participating in this research are emphasizing the specificity of their experiences while searching for ways in which these experiences register with others, connecting particular readings of their individual collections of texts.

Intimate, outward and imagined communities

Within this research, there are glimpses of how women's subjective experiences of reading literary texts within their spiritual and religious lives become community in the third wave. While reading has not always been and is not always an unspoken act, it is usually taken as a silent and often solitary affair. But this is only one side of the reading story. Reading is an activity encased in social networks and so is potentially a

---

24 Walker, *To Be Real,* p. xxxiii.

25 Deborah Siegel, 'The Legacy of the Personal: Generating Theory in Feminism's Third Wave' *Hypatia,* Vol 12, No 2 (Summer 1997), pp. 46-74:58.

26 Heywood and Drake, *Third Wave Agenda,* p. 11.

27 Baumgardner and Richards, *ManifestA,* p. 125.

28 Ibid., p. 219.

29 Ibid.

30 Ibid., p. xxviii.

fruitful place to find the building blocks, and expressions of community for women's spiritualities in the third wave. Various signs within the interview narratives suggest that reading does not just begin and end with the picking up and closing of a book, but extends the reading experience from the contexts in which a reader first meets a text, to the social implications once the page turning has ended.

The agreement between participants on the significance of literary texts as a source for spirituality, and specifically the suggestion that texts are ways of accessing community, reflects their membership of an 'interpretative community'. According to Stanley Fish, an interpretative community is comprised of 'those who share interpretive strategies' that 'exist prior to the act of reading'.[31] Interpretative communities are extensions of a community's shared theoretical perspectives, bringing the reader and the text into the social sphere: 'it is interpretive communities, rather than the text or the reader that produce meanings'.[32] For Fish, the text is deposed as the source of meaning production, and is replaced by a set of discourses moving through a given community at any one time.[33] To some extent, this project places participants into community, binding participants collectively as 'women who consider literature to be important to their spiritual/religious lives.' As Fish might argue, as women readers located within their religious and spiritual worlds, who consider reading and spirituality to be integral to their lives, they are forming communities bound by their interpretative strategies.

The notion of an 'interpretative community' considers agreements inside, and disagreements between interpretative communities. This leaves little space to consider deviating reading strategies that may exist within an interpretive community or the agency of the reader in relationship to her interpretive community. Literary theorist Lynne Pearce tests the stability of a feminist interpretative community by asking five groups of feminist readers to respond to three texts, with reference to their political and national identities.[34] Pearce's tight textual focus is a control from which she explores the interpretive strategies at play amongst participants, providing a common starting point that allows for comparison and contrast. Rather than uncovering only shared interpretations, Pearce's participants' responses were often in tension, leading her to remark that an interpretive community 'does not represent a set of fixed, and shared, values with which the reader mindlessly agrees. Rather, it should be thought of as its own site of struggle, a group whose position is constantly being renegotiated and legitimized by its members even while its consensus is publicly held.'[35] Pearce acknowledges that a literary community may share interpretative strategies, but simultaneously frees the reader from passivity and from being swallowed by her interpretative community. Reading processes are individual, but sit with a wider, connected body of reading strategies.

---

31 Stanley Fish, *Is there a Text in this Class?* (London, 1980), p. 170-1.

32 Fish, *Is there a Text in this Class?* p. 14.

33 Membership of one interpretative community does not disqualify membership of another.

34 See Lynne Pearce, *Feminism and the Politics of Reading* (Aldershot, 1997), p. 260.

35 Ibid., p. 212.

Pearce initiates a more radical understanding of interpretative communities, but like Fish, she situates an interpretative community around a specific (textual) event. Fish's work focuses on what interpretive communities bring to a single text, while Pearce provided her participants with set reading materials. This research ventures further. It invites a degree of textual chaos and imbues participants with a more prominent degree of agency by asking women in this study to self-select the texts to reflect on; naming the literature they felt influenced their religious or spiritual selves. Subsequently, interviewees offered discrete and exclusive collections of texts, with titles and authors rarely overlapping. Therefore, tropes of community that surface within the interviews do not rely on a singular text, but are being formed when participants' *experiences* of their individual readings of disparate literatures meet and find common ground.

While departing from a singular textual event, the material text (and its effects) is paramount. For the women in this study, the text channels their subjective reading experiences from an initial encounter between reader and text, outward to community. The remaining section of this chapter traces the text as it moves figuratively and literally through three different forms of textual community. First, an intimate community is formed through the close relationship between reader and text. Second, community is found tangibly in the recommendation and discussion of a text, mechanisms which place the text directly into broader networks to create newer community links. Finally, textual encounters also build 'imagined communities'[36] that stretch beyond the immediate, venturing into the symbolic.[37] Where the reading of different literary texts within women's spiritual and religious lives evokes experiences that contact and connect with each other, a third wave community occurs as distinctive voices converge in moments of proximity.

The text as a 'textual other'

Within participants' narratives, the text emanates as the focus of the intimate, outward and imagined relationships leading to community. Interviewees use language associated with relationships to portray the religious or spiritual significance of their literary encounters, with the text featuring as the 'other', or more specifically as Pearce connotes, the 'textual other' with which readers engage.[38] Textual others are the range of textual and contextual factors such as the subjective experience of the text, the author function or certain textual devices such as a character or a narrative theme.[39] It is the point of contact that allows Pearce to figure the reading process as an implicated relationship; an emotional, affective, effective and I would add, spiritual or religious liaison.

The strength of the textual other is its fluidity, encapsulating the fluctuating reasons why readers visualize their connection with a text as interpersonal. Within

---

36 Benedict Anderson, *Imagined Communities* (London, 1991), pp. 6-7.

37 This is not to suggest a linear reading process that begins with an intimate connection and broadens neatly outwards; communities can co-exist.

38 Pearce, *Feminism and the Politics of Reading,* pp. 17-20.

39 Ibid., p. 17.

the interviews, participants often describe the textual others that have contributed to marking the text as spiritually significant. For instance, Sophia is a participant in her early thirties and has 'transitioned out' of her Baptist history because 'things in church started not to fit with me anymore'. She draws on *The Namesake* by Jhumpa Lahiri, singling out the main character's life experiences 'of being inside and outside' American and Indian cultures as one she also shares generally, and in church. This parallel with her own life is the textual other driving the significance of *The Namesake*. Another interviewee, Eleanor, is a member of a Pagan group, serves in her parish church and volunteers at her local cathedral. She reflects that the important texts, her 'landmarks' are those Eleanor 'reads' as helping her balance and connect her Pagan and Christian identity. The textual other can be an isolated phrase of prose or a line of poetry that stops her feeling 'alone' in her spiritual search. While for Helen, a committed Anglican, it is the painful context of deep personal grief that manifested as the textual other, during a time when reading short stories and poems became a strategy for finding some relief from nursing her terminally ill son.

Although there are a range of textual others that bring the reader and text into a relationship, the text bears the most weight when participants begin to place their subjective reading experiences into wider communal networks. When forming intimate, outward and imagined communities, the material text emanates as the dominant 'other'; the text that is literally held, read and handed on to others and placed on a bookshelf.

An intimate community: 'It's friendship really' (Jane, Quaker)

An intimate community is the closest connection formed by participants' individual engagement with a text; and is poignantly expressed by participants as friendship. The search for close connection and personal attachment is often what encourages participants to turn to reading as part of their spiritual lives. For instance, Eleanor says she reads, 'To find a friend, [...] so I'm not alone'. Often in response to a perceived lack of religious or spiritual community, participants are reading in order to help fill this gap. When asked how she regards her selected texts, Jane, a Quaker and a feminist in her forties, warmly described the books that have significantly inspired her as her 'friends'. For Jane, her key texts include 'mind/body/spirit' writings, poetry by Wordsworth, Muir and the Romantics, plus fiction by George Eliot and Somerset Maugham. She connects these texts to her spirituality by describing how they evoked feelings of affirmation, a deepening in her self-understanding that helped her 'find my own identity'. While these are complicated claims, Jane summarises her encounter with her texts as close connection: 'you're having a relationship, a conversation with somebody'. The metaphor of friendship is sincere and one spoken of to denote the special significance a literary piece has had upon spiritual or religious lives.

Like the forming of friendship, an intimate community is forged by nurturing familiar, cherished alliances. Lizzie uses the term 'female spirituality' about her spiritual searching which she describes as 'a whole mis-match and mix-match rather of traditions and ideas that I've got through experiences and from books'. She refers to *Women Who Run With The Wolves* by Clarissa Pinkoles Estes as having been 'her constant companion', carrying a copy, keeping it close in her handbag long after she had completed her first reading. Lizzie's edition is lovingly well worn, a testament to the many times she has revisited its pages and, like an old friend, spent many times in its company. It is a central text as Pinkoles' stories help Lizzie 'develop her spiritual self' and awakened her to nurturing this aspect of her life.

Maggie, a member of an ecumenical church and inter-faith group, describes how Michèle Roberts' *The Wild Girl* and *The Women's Room* by Marilyn French 'feel like friends'. Maggie explains that like other (non-textual) friendships, these books have been supportive, nourishing and strengthening. While Jane, Lizzie and Maggie are able to pinpoint particular themes, characters and devices within the text that engaged them, these elements are parts of the whole encompassed between the outer leaves of their named texts.

An intimate community is a way of being individual and being community. Community is experienced in the intimate friendship between these readers and text(ual others). It is individual because participants do not seem to share textual others; participants' collections of significant texts were unique to their spiritual and religious development and context. It is community not only because these are shared experiences within the interview narratives, but because textual friendship occurs in the one-to-one relationship between reader and text.

Reading outwards: recommending and discussing

Perhaps the most recognizable way in which individual textual encounters become community occurs when readers discuss their reading experiences and recommend a text. Participants remain within the intimate community, but via recommending and discussing their reading experiences they permeate further. In the interview, a text's spiritual or religious significance was often marked by the amount of passionate discussion it provoked and the extent to which readers felt compelled to pass on the experience by inviting others to delve into the pages and be involved in a particular reading encounter.[40]

Salient spaces in which discussion and recommending collide are in book group meetings, communities deliberately organized to enable book-talk. According to Jenny Hartley, whose research documents the growing popularity of book groups in the UK, the most common reason for setting up these societies is to arrange an outlet for review. Lone readers desiring the opportunity to share their thoughts and feelings seek out other bookworms, and a key factor to a group's success and longevity depends on fulfilling this need. Fostering a collective that reads together (in whichever way the group manages their reading lists and reactions) and the subsequent conversations are often perceived as the most rewarding, and challenging aspects of membership and the most important by-product of forming a book community.[41]

---

40 Rather than being two separate processes, a heartfelt recommendation is often accompanied by an enthusiastic and detailed description of the texts, and vice versa. The complement of description and recommendation are parts of the reading process and its extension into a wider social sphere.

41 See Jenny Hartley, *Reading Groups* (Oxford, 2001).

Belonging to a reading group was common among participants, with eleven respondents regularly attending women-only book gatherings. Although this suggests that book fellowship was important to just over a quarter of participants, it did not feature heavily as a theme in the interviews. Texts that were significant in terms of participants' spirituality arose from many other sources, and the threads of discussion and recommendation materializing outside of a pre-fabricated meeting were more central to participants' religious lives. This is not to dismiss the importance of book groups, but to indicate that the titles designated key texts by participants were generally not literary works read as part of a book group. While the context in which readers come across their selected texts informs the reading process and contributes to the significance of a text for a reader's spiritual life, I suspect the way book groups manage their material and present reading lists to their members precludes these texts from making it into participants' special collections.[42]

Hartley explicitly links conversation as the medium through which reading groups are 'about reading in the community'.[43] Hartley seems to position discussion at the end of the reading experience, as a signifier of completeness that adds a further layer to the reading experience or as Richard Ohmann has argued, 'Reading a book becomes meaningful when, after completion, it is shared with others.'[44] However, participants in this project turn this around. Instead, discussing a particular literary work is part of the reading experience rather than signifying the closure of the reading process; the reading experiences continue in the process of passing on the text to others and discussion tends to illustrate a book's importance, rather being the cause or origin of meaningfulness. In this respect, the community emerging from this research does not follow the book group blueprint. For participants, discussion and recommendation are vehicles continuing the reading process and are the means through which readers place their subjective reading experiences alongside other individual textual encounters. Being community in the third wave surfaces from the array of individual texts, built by the collective mechanisms of discussion and recommendation.

Written works perceived to have certain spiritual and religious significance were accompanied by an acute urgency to share the reading experience vocally. Laura, 29, is Christian and a member of an emerging church. She states: 'I probably sit outside the established Church but alongside it. So I have a relationship with "The Church" [...] but I think there are lots of issues within the institution [...] so my faith has probably taken me outside of that.' She lists one of her 'top five' as Douglas Copeland's *Hey Nostradamus!* For Laura, its significance for her faith lies in her analysis that the novel's fundamental themes are hope, redemption and belief. Laura's reasons for including *Hey Nostradamus!* are theologically sophisticated, and

---

42 Perhaps this is because the slightly contrived and regimented reading of a book group, coupled with on-going discussion reduces the efficacy of the personal reading encounter. It may be that texts that are 'met' and 'selected' individually by participants provoke a stronger sense of ownership over the text proffering more meaningful interactions.

43 Ibid., p. 138.

44 Hajda, cited in Richard Ohmann, 'The Shaping of a Canon: US Fiction, 1960-65', *Critical Inquiry*, 10/1 (1983), pp. 199-223:201.

are ideas that she has formulated and refined since her initial reading of Copeland's work. In contrast to these later considerations, her immediate reaction was more visceral. When asked why the text is important, her first response was to describe the situation in which the reading occurred, rather than elaborating on the particular features of the story. Her first thought is not to unravel any theological meaning, but to share her experience. She tells of her excited attempt to take the reading process out of a personal alliance and into a more public place:

> … I just wanted to find somebody who'd read it and talk to them about it […] I just remember going round to people going 'have you read any Douglas Copeland, have you read *Hey Nostradamus!?* I really need to find somebody to talk to about this book!

Laura's impassioned search to 'find somebody to talk to' is a quest to remain with the reading experience after the book has been closed. This can be fulfilled by turning outward and trying to prolong her reading by placing it into a social space outside of the initial intimate community between Laura and *Hey Nostradamus!* albeit with at least one other person who has hopefully read the same book! Finding someone to share her reading maintains the reading process, tying her subjective experience to another.

For participants, recommending a treasured text by physically passing it on or through a verbal suggestion is one way of inserting it into a more open forum. For instance, Karen's[45] enthusiasm for one of her key texts (*The Last Hours of Ancient Sunshine* by Thom Hartmann) is unabashed and she unapologetically tells of her attempts to advertise the book:

> I made a slip of paper putting down the ISBN number, the author, basically what the book is about and, well, 'read this book' and I would hand this out to people!

Karen's committed endorsement stems from a reading that had such bearing she felt compelled to take direct action. However, while passing out slips of paper endorses the material text, it is also an extension of Karen's reading experience, taking this particular reading event into a more extensive social place. Karen admits to being 'deeply' affected by the book, a belief which fuels her commitment to recommending it:

> So when I come across a book that can change the world and can really deeply, deeply affect how people perceive things I want to spread it around.

This intensity of this 'deep effect' with the desire to 'spread it around' is suggestive, including the reading, the effect, and the recommendation as part of the reading process. Not only is Karen intent on forwarding Hartman's work, but also the impact of reading this book.

Nicola describes herself as a Christian Feminist, and notes that this causes some tension between church and her politics. She presents a gentler but still emotive

---

45 Karen does belong to a particular religious community. She acknowledges her Quaker roots, but states 'somehow that isn't broad enough.'

approach to situating a text in community. For Nicola, a recommendation involves gifting the physical text, her impression of the text and a giving of part of herself:

> [...] when you recommend a book to somebody it's almost like saying this, within the pages of the this book, I have experienced something pretty powerful [...] It's like here's a bit of me that's been so profoundly moved and I want you to have this book [...]

Nicola's comments hint at the third wave dovetail of individuality and community. Her personal experiences are the basis and impetus for making a recommendation and therefore a connection with another. Nicola's experiences of the text and the reading encounter are wrapped in recommending the text to others.

The highly personal engagement that occurs when a reading touches upon a reader's religious or spiritual life means that this kind of personal recommendation is often stronger than a favourable mention or critical review, and seems closer to becoming a compulsion to read a particular text. This deep conviction verges on imposition, and supposes that another reader will have a similar reaction to the text.[46] Yet there is a tension between this expectation and the consistent assertions in interviews that the text is open and reading an activity that depends upon 'your own interpretation', sounding like the third wave asserting of the importance of individual experiences. Or put another way, the implicated relationship with possible textual others is recognized as personal for each reader, but the possibility of some shared experiences is open. Participants did not expect their experiences to be replicated exactly and were often attuned to the specific historical and cultural position of their and others' readings but remained hopeful that any (religious or spiritual) benefit they felt might resonate with another.

Textually imagined communities

Intimacy, discussion and recommendation are tangible motifs for tracing the extension of the reading process into community. However, the textual community harboured through individual readings also goes beyond the physical, locating significant texts conceptually into the social. To a certain extent, all communities exist notionally, or as Benedict Anderson notably suggests, as 'imagined communities'.[47] This term captures the feeling that we belong to something, even if it is indeterminable: 'in the minds of each lives the image of their communion.'[48] Anderson acknowledges that reading works as a tool to form imagined communities, as it is a device that builds 'the deep horizontal comradeship'[49] that connects people to those within proximate networks of family, friends, neighbours and so forth, but also to 'others' one does not see and cannot know.

Imagined communities come into view within participants' reflections on their spiritual or religious readings. For example, Scarlet states she is a 'lesbian/feminist/

---

46 It also implies that the text, message and effects are stable.
47 Anderson , *Imagined Communities*, pp. 6-7.
48 Ibid., p. 6.
49 Ibid., p. 7.

quaker/pagan' in a way that recalls the third wave insistence on multiple, fluid identities. Although the daughter of Quaker parents, she eschews traditional religion but has woven together different aspects of her spiritual life: 'I can still pick out the threads [...] I can say this bit's ... Quaker, this bit's empowerment stuff.' She keeps her five 'sacred texts' on a separate shelf in her study.[50] This is both practical (Scarlet likes to know where these books are, so she can access them conveniently and quickly) and commemorative (they are stored away discretely from her other texts to signify their special status). She is clear that her textual encounters with these books place her within a very specific type of hypothetical (but not unreal) community:

> [...] those books there give me a sense of wider community [...] I actually don't know ... very many people who would have that same lot of books [...] so I feel like this represents a community [...] who, I could sit down and have a conversation with, any of the people who've written them, or any of the people who appear in them.

Scarlet's claim resonates with third wave individuality. Her collection is an assembly of works that not many other readers (anywhere) would share and her set of texts is used to mark her divergence from others. However, Scarlet is not isolated. She is part of community, accessed through her readings, comprised of authors and characters who share in her experience of the text, albeit in different ways. There is a sense that reading forges virtual or symbolic partnerships with authors, characters in the texts, other texts and other readers. Unlike the implicated relationship with a specific book, or the direct act of discussion and recommending, the imagined community exists beyond immediate associations. Scarlet imagines herself to be part of an individualized textual community. It is unlikely that anyone else would offer the exact texts as being influential and part of her spiritual library, but there is an envisaged connection with other possible readers even in other places and other times, whose existence may be unverifiable and unknown, but are within community.

Conclusion

This chapter brings women's spiritualities to an expression of third wave feminism. It proposes that reading, as an implicated engagement with a text(ual other), is a process where 'being individual, being community' is possible. By demonstrating that within the spiritual lives of women readers, individual reading experiences connect and become communities, this paper suggests a motif through which women's fluid subjectivities find common ground. As the women in this study name literature as a vital source to their spirituality, individuality is represented by the unique collections

---

50 Her books are: *The Lesbian Reader* (edited by Gina Covina and Laurel Galana); Celeste West's *The Lesbian Love Advisor* and *Lesbian Polyfidelity: A Pleasure Guide for the Woman Whose Heart Is Open to Multiple Concurrent Sexualoves or How to Keep Non-Monogamy Safe, Sane; Positive Magic: Ancient Metaphysical Techniques for Modern Lives* by Marion Weinstein and Vicki Noble's *Mother Peace: A Way to the Goddess Through Myth, Art and Tarot*.

of texts participants name as significant to their spiritual or faith lives. Community occurs as the text and its affecting experiences are extended beyond the page turning of a book, to becoming intimate relationships of friendship, outward communities through recommending and discussing, and symbolic 'imagined communities'.

Situating these textual communities, founded through women's reading experiences and women's spiritualities, in third wave feminism aspires to prise a wider opening for increased discourse between recent articulations of feminism and women's spiritualities. Although some feminist thought has reconstructed theology to think through the fragmentation of 'woman', the third wave has tended not to look to women's religiosity. The third wave advocates and searches for places where 'being individual, being community' is feasible, and women's spiritualities contain places where the third wave, and in particular the interlocking themes of individuality and community are ascending.

As reading (literature) is one of the most important sources for women's spiritualities, 'being individual, being community' takes a textual form. The textual communities emerging from readers' subjective experiences supplement, replace or reside together with church, faith and spiritual groups to which these women belong – supplying support. The existence of these multiple communities to which participants belong is a testament to the fluidity of third wave spiritual positionings, and a site where the subjective experiences in women's spiritual lives reside side by side, connecting to form community.

Acknowledgement

With thanks to Katharine Moody, Deborah F. Sawyer and Marta Trezebiatowska, and in particular Sarah Gibson.

Bibliography

Anderson, Benedict, *Imagined Communities* (London: Verso [1983] 1991).

Aune, Kristen and Louise Livesy, 'Reclaiming the F-Word and Recovering Dialogue: Younger Feminists, Older Feminists and (Mis)communication' (Unpublished article, 2007).

Baumgardner, Jennifer and Amy Richards, *ManifestA: Young Women, Feminism and the Future* (New York: Farrar, Strause and Giroux, 2000).

Cannon, Katie, *Black Womanist Ethics* (Atlanta: Scholars Press, 1988).

Christ, Carol, 'Feminist Studies in Religion and Literature: A Methodological Reflection', *Journal of American Academy of Religion* 44/2 (1976): 317-25.

Christ, Carol, *Diving Deep and Surfacing: Women Writers on Spiritual Quest* (Boston: Beacon Press, 1995 [3rd Ed.]).

Curry-Johnson, Sonja D., 'Weaving an Identity Tapestry' Barbara Findlen, (ed.), *Listen Up: Voices from the Next Feminist Generation* (Emeryville: Seal Press [1995] 2001):51-8.

Dicker, Rory and Alison Piepmeier, *Catching a Wave: Reclaiming Feminism for the 21st Century* (Boston: Northeastern University Press, 2003).

Eller, Cynthia, *Living in the Lap of the Goddess: The Feminist Spirituality Movement in the States* (Boston: Beacon Press, 1993).

Findlen, Barbara, (ed.), *Listen Up: Voices from the Next Feminist Generation,* (Emeryville: Seal Press [1995] 2001).

Fish, Stanley *Is there a Text in this Class?* (Harvard University Press: London, 1980).

Gillis, Stacy, Gillian Howie and Rebeca Munford, (eds), *Third Wave Feminism: A Critical Exploration* (Basingstoke: Palgrave, [2004] 2007).

Hartley, Jenny, *Reading Groups* (Oxford: Oxford University Press, 2001).

Henry, Astrid, 'Solitary Sisterhood: Individualism Meets Collectivity in Feminism's Third Wave' in Jo Reger, (ed.), *Different Wavelengths: Studies of the Contemporary Women's Movement* (London and New York: Routledge, 2005): 81-96.

Henry, Astrid, *Not My Mother's Sister: Generational Conflict and Third Wave Feminism* (Indiana University Press, Bloomington, 2004).

Heywood, Leslie, and Jennifer Drake, *Third Wave Agenda: Being Feminist, Doing Feminism*, (Minneapolis and London: University of Minnesota Press, [1997] 2004).

hooks, bell, *Feminist Theory: From Margin to Centre* (Boston: South End Press, 1984).

Kamitsuka, Margaret D., *Feminist Theology and the Challenge of Difference* (Oxford: Oxford University Press, 2007).

Kristeva, Julia, 'Women's Time', in Toril Moi, (ed.), *The Kristeva Reader* (Oxford: Blackwell): 187-213.

Mandava, Bhargavi C., 'Ghosts and Goddesses' in Barbara Findlen, (ed.), *Listen Up: Voices from the Next Feminist Generation* (Emeryville: Seal Press [1995] 2001): 89-100.

Moi, Toril, (ed.), *The Kristeva Reader* (Oxford: Blackwell, 1986).

Muaddi Darraj, Susan, 'Third World, Third Wave Feminism(s): The Evolution of Arab American Feminism' in Rory Dicker and Alison Piepmeier, (eds), *Catching a Wave: Reclaiming Feminism for the 21st Century* (Boston: Northeastern University Press, 2003): 188-205.

Neidorf, Robin M., 'Two Jews, Three Opinions' in Barbara Findlen, (ed.), *Listen Up: Voices from the Next Feminist Generation* (Emeryville: Seal Press [1995] 2001): 59-66.

Ohmann, Richard, 'The Shaping of a Canon: US Fiction, 1960-65' *Critical Inquiry*, 10/1 (1983): 199-223.

Orr, Catherine, 'Charting the Currents of the Third Wave', *Hypatia,* 12/3 (Summer 1997): 29-45.

Pearce, Lynne, *Feminism and the Politics of Reading* (Aldershot: Ashgate, 1997).

Pearce, Lynne, *The Rhetorics of Feminism: Readings In Contemporary Cultural Theory and the Popular Press* (London and New York: Routledge, 2004).

Reger, Jo, (ed.), *Different Wavelengths: Studies of the Contemporary Women's Movement* (London and New York: Routledge, 2005).

Siegel, Deborah, 'The Legacy of the Personal: Generating Theory in Feminism's Third Wave' *Hypatia,* 12/2 (Summer 1997): 46-74.

Stone, Alison, 'On the Genealogy of Women: A Defence of Anti-Essentialism' in Stacy Gillis, Gillian Howie and Rebeca Munford, (eds), *Third Wave Feminism: A Critical Exploration* (Basingstoke: Palgrave, [2004] 2007): 16-29.

Walker, Rebecca, (ed.), *To Be Real: Telling the Truth and Changing the Face of Feminism* (Anchor Books: New York, 1995).

Walter, Natasha, *On the Move: Feminism for a New Generation* (London: Virago, 1999).

Walton, Heather, *Literature, Theology and Feminism* (Manchester: Manchester University Press, 2007).

Zack, Naomi, *Inclusive Feminism: A Third Wave Theory of Women's Commonality* (Maryland: Rowman and Littlefield Publishers, 2005).

Zita, Jacquelyn N.,(ed.), *Third Wave Feminisms*, spec. issue of *Hypatia: A Journal of Feminist Philosophy*, 12/3, (Summer 1997).

PART IV
Accessing the Spiritual

Part IV

Accessing the Spiritual

Deborah F. Sawyer

The concluding part to *Reading Spiritualities* opens even wider the horizons our project has been attempting to articulate so far. Here we demonstrate the infinite possibilities for 'accessing the spiritual' by offering four different studies from the diverse worlds of architectural studies, film, internet studies, art and literature. Although the media differ, all these contributors engage with theological tools to express and interpret their subjects. The three parts of the volume presented so far have been largely concerned with texts as they are conventionally conceived, that is as written pieces of literature. However, these chapters recognize that as the concept of sacred text is not static, so the means to convey it can take myriad forms. Although the media that are utilized in this section are clearly diverse, as a group they serve to illustrate the differing sites in which the sacred is constructed and represented. The authors of these chapters each engage subtly with their particular medium, producing four discrete 'readings' of their 'texts', however these harmonize through their sensitive and creative approaches.

In the first chapter Ozayr Saloojee presents Solomon's Temple as a textual metaphor, working from an Islamic standpoint, tracing the narrative thread of this conceptualized building through the Abrahamic traditions of Judaism, Christianity and Islam. At the heart of the chapter lies the link between text and architecture, understanding the text of the Qur'an as a generative influence on Islamic art. In this chapter Saloojee attempts to locate the spiritual impetus and expression within architectural processes that allow for the material realization of the sacred.

In the next chapter we move away from what is, perhaps, a more familiar traditional religious milieu to contemporary Neopagan web-sites. This is not as abrupt a switch of subject as it might seem since both Saloojee and Maria Bittarello focus on the constructed visual as a means of experiencing and expressing the sacred. In contextualizing the form of the phenomenon of web based religious texts, Bittarello uses the analogy of medieval texts, namely the Book of Kells where she discovers striking resemblances in presentation. The intricate combination of images, text and commentary found on these web sites has much in common with the layout of medieval manuscripts. The distinctiveness of religious texts situated on the web lies not so much in their visual format, as in their universal accessibility. Furthermore, and uniquely, their 'mythopoeic modalities', that is, their interactive nature (a phenomenon discussed by Moody in Chapter 6), enables them to be re-created, visually and textually, by those who access them.

Continuing with relationships between visual and written forms, Graham Holderness's chapter examines the similarities and differences between the

Christologies found in Franco Zeffirelli's film for television, *Jesus of Nazareth*, and Anthony Burgess's novel *Man of Nazareth*, both produced in the early 1970s. He notes surprising differences in the presentations of this sacred text, namely, the person of Jesus. Whereas one might expect the unbelieving Burgess to shy away from the supernatural and the traditional Catholic, and Zeffirelli to heighten it, Holderness discovers the reverse. In examining these two contemporary Christological portraits, Holderness discovers in them reconfigurations of theological discourse both in terms of their creation and their reception.

This focus on the incarnation of the Christ figure serves as a point of continuity with our final chapter. David Jasper's study of the relationship between the sacred and the profane, actualized in the image of Jesus' cadaver, the ultimate image of the vulnerability of the incarnate word, provides the central subject for this chapter. Jasper's work is notable for discovering reconfigurations of theological discourse in diverse cultural sites, and this piece is no exception. His chapter opens with a reference to Heather Walton, who is another contributor to this volume and a reviewer of his work. In her review, Walton utilized vivacious images from Michèle Roberts's *Impossible Saints*, to bring to the fore a kind of mimetic feminist re-imagining of Jasper's 'lonely desert landscape' depicted in his book *The Sacred Desert*. As well as neatly bringing our volume full circle with reference to Roberts, whose interview forms the opening chapter, Jasper's work encapsulates all that we have been attempting to portray throughout.

Setting Holbein's painting of the *Dead Christ* as the focal point, or more accurately, as the text for his chapter, and through interweaving the reflections of theologians and writers down the centuries, including contemporary novelists concerned with the sacred, Jasper demonstrates how the icon of the crucified Christ, in its most profane and desolate form, allows Christianity to truly demonstrate the heart of its gospel. This chapter expresses how one pictorial representation can embody the richness of two centuries of religious tradition, and with Jasper's creative use of a range of interpretive tools these rich pickings are carefully arrayed before us.

These final chapters open up vistas that have not always been traditional loci for theological or spiritual reflection. They encourage us to look at familiar religious sites with new eyes and encounter new ways of identifying and encountering the sacred.

Chapter 10

Solomon's Narrative:
Architecture, Text and the Sacred

Ozayr Saloojee

Introduction

History is not a work of philosophy, it is a painting; it is necessary to combine narration with the representation of the subject, that is, it is necessary simultaneously to design and to paint; it is necessary to give to men the language and the sentiments of their times, not to regard the past in the light of our own opinion.

Francois René de-Chateaubriand[1]

The biblical description of the Temple of Solomon in Jerusalem has generated many diverse architectural speculations throughout our history. According to tradition, the Temple followed the designs of God and can therefore be interpreted as the archetypal work of architecture – a work that revealed a true order beyond the whimsical tastes of man and any temporal expressions of political power.[2]

The narrative of this research, as noted in the title of this text, is a story shared by the three great Abrahamic traditions of Judaism, Christianity and Islam and its representation is a metaphor that shifts and transforms through the timelines of these faiths. The narrative in this case is just that – a narrative. This is a caveat to preface this work: this exploration is framed with the premise that the narratives of the *T'nakh*, the New Testament and the *Qur'aan* are narratives and do not focus on a critical historiography of these texts. Because, in the end, in addition to being rich and contested historical documents, these are remarkable stories that are rich in imagery and metaphor.

What exactly is this narrative? It is first an attempt to define a series of lenses to *see* and *know* architecture and to trace a trajectory through the Abrahamic faiths in order to posit a strategy (or series of strategies) by which we might understand, critique, interrogate and propose ideas of sacred space in modern contexts. The primary goal is to allow for the extraction of new meanings, drawn out of history, tradition and narrative in the contemporary expression of Islamic architecture.

---

1   Cited in Ferenc M. Szasz, 'The Many Meanings of History, Part II' in Ferene M. Szasz, *The History Teacher* (Long Beach, Ca., 1974) vol.8., no.1. pp. 54-63:56.

2   Alberto Perez-Gomez, 'Juan Battista Villalpando's Divine Model in Architectural Theory', in Alberto Perez Gomez and Stephen Parcel, (eds), *Chora Three: Intervals in the Philosophy of Architecture* (Montreal, 1999), pp. 125-56:126.

In the Islamic religious tradition, Solomon was the builder prophet, with control over the wind, the elements, the *Djinn* and the animals, all of which were active participants in his building enterprise. As the builder prophet, Solomon seemed, years ago when this course of research was about to inform graduate research in architecture, to be a suitably appropriate muse. The Jewish, Christian and Islamic manifestations of Solomon and the Temple he would build became the origin of this investigation. Jerusalem became the background context for this research, with the Temple of Solomon serving as a metaphor for the Divine in these faiths.

Judaism

In the Jewish spiritual tradition, David begins the preparations for the Temple, after moving the Ark of the Covenant into the city renamed 'ir David (The City of David), but his son Solomon ultimately builds and completes it. In 1 Chronicles 22:5-10, we read:[3]

> … David said, "My son Solomon is young and inexperienced, and the house to be built for the LORD should be of great magnificence and fame and splendor in the sight of all the nations. Therefore I will make preparations for it." So David made extensive preparations before his death. Then he called his son Solomon and charged him to build a house for the LORD, the God of Israel. David said to Solomon, " My son, I had it in my heart to build a house for the Name of the LORD my God. But this word of the LORD came to be: "You have shed much blood and fought many wars. You are not to build a house for my Name, because you have shed much blood on the earth in my sight. But you will have a son who will be a man of peace and rest, and I will give him rest from all his enemies on every side. His name will be Solomon and I will grant Israel peace and quiet during his reign. He is the one who will build a house for my Name and he will be my son, and I will be his Father. And I will establish the throne of his kingdom over Israel forever.

The building of the temple is first prefaced by war, then adultery (David sleeps with Bathsheba, the wife of his general, Uriah), then murder, plague, atonement, and in the end, a massive civil infrastructure reconstruction project. During the siege of Rabbah (near Amman in present day Jordan), David notices Bathsheba. David is struck by her beauty, sends for her and beds her. Attempting to hide this indiscretion, he orders Uriah to the frontline of the battle, where he is, as intended, struck down and killed. David is rebuked by the prophet Nathan and as a consequence of this, his first son with Bathsheba dies shortly after birth.

In response to David's indiscretions and the planned murder of Uriah, and the numbering of the people, Yahweh offers David a choice between three consequences: three years of famine, three months of being at the mercy of his enemies, or three days of plague. He chooses the plague and 70,000 of his people die. The T'nakh texts claim that Yahweh was distraught at this loss of life and orders the Angel responsible to cease the punishment. David sees the angel, standing with arms outstretched at the threshing floor of a man named Araunah. David purchases the land from Araunah and together they build an altar to honour Yahweh. The plague of Jerusalem is averted

---

3   All biblical references are from New International Version (Grand Rapids, 1984).

and the site of the Temple is thus prepared. Solomon is born to David and Bathsheba sometime later.

While the temple is described in both Kings and Chronicles, the clearest description is in 1 Kings:5. We are told that the exterior dimensions of the temple are 60 cubits long, 20 wide and 30 high. The Temple was made of stone quarried from the hills around Jerusalem. The interior was panelled and detailed with carved cedar and inlaid with gold, such that no individual stone could be seen from the inside. The floor was covered with cypress boards. The walls were adorned with rich carvings of cherubim, 'each ten cubits high … The wing of one cherub touched one wall while the wing of another touched the other, and their wings touched each other in the middle of the room'.[4] Biblical accounts also place the altar of Isaac's intended sacrifice at this same side. The *Akeda* (literally, 'binding', for Isaac's limbs were bound like an animal) by Abraham became the floor of Araunah and then the seat of the Temple.

Jewish scholars have noted that the bond between that of Israel and the spiritual mission of its people is a supreme religious ideal, that is, it is *not* a right justifiable by birth, but one that has been determined by God. The emphasis on the land of Israel as a unique gift of God is explicit in the text of Genesis. The location of God's dwelling place on earth has been determined in the first book of Moses.

Prior to Solomon there is the *Even Shetiyah*, the Foundation Stone. Talmudic tradition asserts that the *Even Shetiyah* is the navel of the world and is the root *and* seed from which it has grown. The Kabbalist text, the *Zohar*, observes that:

> When the Holy One, blessed be He, was about to create the world, He detached one precious stone from underneath His throne of glory and plunged it into the abyss; one end of it remained fastened therein, while the other end stood out above. Out of the latter the world started, spreading itself to the right and left and into all directions.[5]

The *Even Shetiyah* marks the place from which Jewish prayer travels to the abode of Heaven and is given physical and corporeal presence when Solomon builds the Temple for Yahweh. As biblical accounts locate the *Akeda* at this site, so rabbinical texts also claim that this is where Jacob rested his head, and from where he dreamt of the ladder reaching heaven. An extract from the *Midrash Tanchuma* notes:

> The land of Israel is the middle of the earth. Jerusalem is the middle of Israel. The Temple is the middle of Jerusalem. The Holy of Holies is the middle of the Temple. The Holy Ark is the middle of the Holy of Holies. And the Stone of Foundation is in front of the Holy of Holies.[6]

Yahweh, the *Shechinah* (the Divine Presence) is the centre of this expanding circle, and moves outward from the earth to the Ark, to the Holy of Holies and defines the edges of the Temple of Solomon, the sacred site of God's essence. This is the

---

4   1 Kings 6:23-28.

5   Jewish Heritage Online Magazine, Volume 10.7. July 2007,

http://www.jhom.com/topics/stones/foundation.html

6   Joan Comay, *The Temple of Jerusalem* (New York, 1975), pp. 49-50.

ultimate geographic determiner. The Divine Temple, for the Jewish faith, is fixed in place, anchored in site.

Christianity

> The Eternal Being, who knows everything and who created the whole universe, became not only a man but (before that) a baby, and before that a foetus inside a Woman's body. If you want to get the hang of it, think how you would like to become a slug or a crab. The result of this was that you now had one man who really was what all men were intended to be: one man in whom the created life, derived from his Mother, allowed itself to be completely and perfectly turned into the begotten life. The natural human creature in Him was taken up fully into the divine Son. Thus in one instance humanity had, so to speak, arrived: had passed into the life of Christ.
>
> C.S. Lewis[7]

With the New Testament and the advent of the Christian religious tradition, the emphasis on site/geography of the Solomnic metaphor shifts. Mary and Jesus directly illustrate how this metaphor shifts from the site-oriented significance of the Judaic tradition into the Christian emphasis on the body. Of the synoptic texts, Luke is the one that directly links Mary to the Temple. Mary's Annunciation is paralleled and prefaced with the story of Zecheriah and Elizabeth and of the miraculous birth of John the Baptist. Mary's Annunciation is the moment that the temple metaphor – the house for the Divine – transforms from site to body.

Luke's portrayal of Mary is the one that comes to dominate traditional and contemporary understandings of the Virgin, although later Gnostic texts, such as the *Protoevangelium of James* add increasingly rich narrative depictions to Mary's life.[8] In the Gospel of Luke, Mary is shy, innocent, young, and, after her annunciation by Gabriel, becomes the Mother of God: sincere, devout, the Queen of Heaven. She is *Mary Magnificat* and *Magna Mater*. Parallels are drawn between her and Eve, as both were born without the stain of original sin. Mary becomes, through God's grace upon her, the chosen womb for His incarnation upon the earth. She becomes the Temple, the Ark of the Covenant and the Holy of Holies; a vessel that housed, carried and surrounded the presence of God. She is the *Shechina*, remade. Mary is the Temple made flesh.

The Lukan Gospel also details the life of Jesus including his presentation at the Temple and his teaching there. Jesus is tempted by Satan who attempts to provoke him to throw himself down from the Temple heights and trust in God to save him. Jesus drives the moneylenders out of the Temple, claiming angrily to them that they have turned 'my Father's house into a den of robbers' (Luke 19:45). He heals the sick and the lame at the Temple, and continues to teach there upon his return to Jerusalem. Christ prophesies his betrayal, death, resurrection and the destruction of the Temple at a number of instances in the synoptic texts. In the Gospel of John

---

7   www.philosophyforlife.com/mc27.htm [Accessed June 2007].

8   The *Protoevangelium of James* (also known as the Gospel of James) is an apocryphal text believed to have been written in the mid second century, around 150 CE. http://www. earlychristianwritings.com/text/infancyjames-mrjames.html. [Accessed June 2007].

2:19-22, following his cleansing of the Temple, he is asked by what miracle can he prove his so-called authority and he says:

> 'Destroy this temple and I will raise it up again in three days.' The Jews replied, 'It has taken forty-six years to build this temple, and you are going to raise it in three days?' But the temple he spoke of was his body. After he was raised from the dead, his disciples recalled what he had said.

This statement is brought in evidence against him at his trial before Caiaphas (Matthew 26:59-61, and Mark 14:55-9) and the people echo, 'We heard him say, "I will destroy this man-made temple, and in three days, I will build another, not made by man."' Jesus' physical connection to the Temple begins well before his birth, and continues throughout his later life. As Mary is the beginning of the Christian Solomnic Metaphor, Jesus is at the end. John notes in 1:14 that, 'The word became flesh and lived among us.' In Matthew 12:6, Jesus exclaims, 'I tell you that one greater than the Temple is here!' Subsequently in Matthew 12:40 we read that:

> For as Jonah was three days and three nights in the belly of a huge fish, so the Son of Man will be three days and three nights in the heart of the earth. The men of Nineveh will stand up at the judgment with this generation and condemn it; for they repented at the teaching of Jonah, and now one greater than Jonah is here. The Queen of the South will rise at the judgment of this generation and condemn it; for she came from the ends of the earth to listen to Solomon's wisdom, and now one greater than Solomon is here.

After Mary, Christ becomes the Temple and the metaphor is made corporeal and is not constrained to place or site. The Word became flesh and made his dwelling among us.

Islam

> If, then, the universe is the effect of some act; that act itself, the effect of a Being, and of a need, a thought, a knowledge, and a power which belongs to that Being, it is then only by an act that you can rejoin the grand design, and undertake the imitation of that which has made all things. And that is to put oneself in the most natural way in the very place of the God. Now, of all acts the most complete is that of construction.
>
> Paul Valéry[9]

We have observed the shifting of the Temple metaphor as it begins in Judaism, is re-defined in Christianity and is further transformed in the Islamic understanding. David moves the Ark into 'ir David and thus consolidates his reign, but anchors the earthly abode of the *Shechinah* in place. The Christian (Catholic) tradition adopts the Temple-Body metaphor, which sacralizes the human as the dwelling of the Divine. The Islamic understanding of the metaphor is predicated upon the notion that the Qur'aan, as the revealed Book of God, is the inheritor and completion of Judaism

---

9   Cited in William Alexander McClung, 'The Matter of Metaphor: Literary Myths of Construction', *The Journal of the Society of Architectural Historians*, 40/4 (1981), pp. 270-88:280.

and Christianity.[10] The Islamic tradition does not proceed directly from the Christian (as Christianity does from Judaism, incorporating the five books of the Pentateuch as part of the Old Testament), but rests in the central messages of the text of the Qur'aan, and redefines the notion of the Temple as understood in Judaism and Christianity.

The Qur'aan, the central text of the Islamic faith, is the axiomatic reality of Islam. It is the book in which the Divine message of God is contained, unaltered and original. It is the Divine acting upon human language, compared to the collections of rabbinic or gospel human writers of Judaism or Christianity. For the Christian tradition, John 1:14 states, 'In the beginning was the Word, and the Word was with God, and Word was God ... The Word became flesh and made His dwelling among us.' In a way, the Islamic understanding of the Solomnic metaphor is a return to origins.

For the Islamic tradition, the *Logos* is the Qur'aan. Seyyed Hossein Nasr writes in his text, *Ideals and Realities of Islam,* that 'The efficacy of canonical prayers, litanies, invocations, etc, is contained not only in the content but also in the very sounds and reverberations of the sacred religion.' The first word revealed to Islam's prophet Muhammad by the Archangel Gabriel was *iqr,* which means 'read'.

> The text of the Qur'aan reveals human language crushed by the power of the Divine Word ... The Qur'aan displays human language with all the weakness inherent in it becoming suddenly the recipient of the Divine Word and displaying its frailty before a power that is infinitely greater than man can imagine.[11]

The text, for the Islamic tradition *becomes* the Temple. The language of the Qur'aan lies at the heart of the understanding of the Solomnic narrative in the Islamic tradition and the lexicographic and semantic structure of the way that language is used is critical. The science of exegesis in the Islamic tradition observes the use of both the explicit and interpretive phrasing in the text of the Qur'aan. This combination of the explicit and the interpretive, combined with the rich etymology of Arabic and Arabic vocabulary, allows this text to be understood as formative, generative, and transformative.

> Rather, the Qur'aan is like Christ for the Christians, who is himself the word of God brought into the world through the Virgin Mary. She, therefore, plays a role analogous to that of the soul of the Prophet; both are pure, immaculate, and virginal before the Divine Word.[12]

---

10 It is important to underscore here that the Islamic tradition sees itself as the inheritor of the previous traditions of Judaism and Christianity, and emphasizes the honour accorded to past prophets and Divine revelation. We can read in the Qur'aan (4:163) that: 'Indeed, We have revealed to you [O Muhammad], as We revealed to Noah and the prophets after him. And We revealed to Abraham, Ishmael, Isaac, Jacob, the Descendents (the 12 tribes of Israel, descended from Jacob), Jesus, Job, Jonah, Aaron and Solomon, and to David We gave the book [of Psalms] ...'

11 Seyyed Hossein Nasr, *Ideals and Realities of Islam* (London, 1994), p. 47.

12 Seyyed Hossein Nasr, *Islamic Art and Spirituality* (New York, 1987), p. 4.

The Qur'aan is the fountainhead for Arabic literary structure. It informs poetry, the spoken language of communication, artistic enterprise. In short, it is the core of the Islamic worldview. The science of lexicology, which establishes the meanings and etymology of words, is seminal to understanding Qur'aanic language. Arabic is a layered language. Sentences and Qur'aanic verses may have probabilistic or definitive contexts and words themselves can offer, through their unique etymologies and root structures, many levels of complex meaning.

There is no distinction in Islam between the sacred and the secular, between church and state and the mosque, as the sacred architecture of Islam, is the heart of the community, and the apex of the architectural tradition in Islam. The term *mosque* is derived from the Arabic *masjid* (pl. *masajid*), which means literally 'place of prostration' and is derived from the same root word as *sujjud*, or 'prostration'. *Sujjud* is the highest level of prayer, the worshipper with forehead to the ground, physically elevating heart over brain, and soul over intellect.

The central tenet of Islam is the Divine Unity of God, expressed in the *shahada*, the testament of faith, as '*La ilaha, ill-allah*', 'There is no God, but God', and is encapsulated as a totality of existence by the text of the Qur'aan.

The fundamental goal of Islam is the contemplation of God (*dhikr*) through a fulfillment of '*ubudiyyah*'.[13] The sacred architecture of the mosque is the material fulfilment of a place of worship, and the spiritual realization of connecting the mosque back to nature (the entirety of which God has decreed as being created as a place of prayer) and ultimately, to the Divine. Seyyed Hossein Nasr notes that,

> Islamic art is the result of the manifestation of the Unity upon the plane of multiplicity. It reflects in a blinding manner the Unity of the Divine Principle, the dependence of all multiplicity upon the One, the ephemerality of the world and the positive qualities of cosmic existence or creation about which God asserts in the Qur'aan, 'Our Lord! Thou createst not this in vain' (3:191). This art makes manifest, in the physical order directly perceivable by the senses, the archetypal realities and acts, therefore, as a ladder for the journey of the soul from the visible and audible to the Invisible which is also Silence transcending all sound.[14]

Through the recitation of the Qur'aanic verses in prayer, one is connected to the sacred nature of God's decree and also returned to an inner reality and beginning known as *al-fitrah* (the initial disposition of the human to God). The ritual motions of the Islamic prayer emphasize this spiritual connection. Regardless of geographic location, prayer is oriented towards the *Ka'ba* (located in Makkah) the foundation of which was laid by the Archangel Gabriel.

---

13 *Ubudiyyah* is a complex and difficult term to translate into English. The most commonly used English equivalent is 'worship'. The term *ubudiyyah*, however is not to be understood as purely objective and when using the word 'worship', it is imperative to understand it within the entirety of the Islamic religious and spiritual system. It is worship in terms of *Tawhid* (the One-ness of God), Cosmology, Law, and *al-akhlaq* (character). A verse in the Qur'aan observes that 'And I have not created Djinn and Man except that they should worship Me' [*Wa ma khalaqta al-jinn wal ins illa liy'abudun*]. Qur'aan 51:56. All Qur'aanic references are from *The Qur'aan*, Saheed International, (ed. and revised), (Jeddah, Saudi Arabia, 1997).

14 Nasr, *Islamic Art and Spirituality*, p. 7.

The body postures from *qayyam* [standing] to *ruku'a* [bowing] to *sujud* [prostration] progressively establish the spatial orientations and ultimately the place. During the *qayyam* the lateral plane of the body defines the parallel of the boundary wall that is behind the *qibla* wall that is in front. As the torso descends into the ruku'a and is held up by arms bracing the knees, a plane is defined that locates the man, the mihrab, and the Ka'ba. Finally the body reaches the state of sujud, as the forehead, hands, knees and feet define a heptagonal piece of the earth. As praise to 'Lord the High' is uttered three times, the upright axis between man, the enlivened earth, and God – the one whose throne encompasses the cosmos – is finally established. At that time, as the individual musalla [prayer carpet/area] becomes the global mosque, the man for a brief moment has connected to the Divine. For an instant, all materiality has disappeared. But as he raises his head, and as he returns to the world of shapes and forms he finds himself sitting in the center of the Cordoba Mosque , or in the courtyard of Sultan Hassan, or perhaps under the dome of the Süleymaniye.[15]

Components of Islamic architecture stem from the Divine Oneness of God, articulated by the text of the Qur'aan, and are enlivened through prayer and it is through prayer that the connection to the Divine is established. Islamic tradition holds that Muhammad was given the gift of prayer by God, and after his night journey to the heavens, leads all the assembled prophets of history in prayer. It is at this point too, that Muhammad is instructed to change the orientation of prayer towards Makkah, away from Jerusalem.

Etymologically in Arabic, the word 'Throne' and 'Floor' or 'Ground' are part of the same root structure. Semantically then, the floor of the mosque (where the believer places his forehead in *sujjud*) and the throne of God are connected *in* and *through* prayer.

The Qur'aanic story of Solomon provides a wealth of information about the creation of architecture, the most telling of which is the entrance of Sheba before Solomon and his court. The architectural splendour implied in the descriptions of Qur'aan 27:43-4 makes the Queen aware of, and commits her to, the Divine Unity of God. While there have been many different interpretations of this verse, these variations must be understood as approaching a 'meaning' that is comprised of infinitely diverse, but not opposing, interpretations.

The *tafsir* [exegetical text] *Tafhim al Qur'an*, notes that Solomon tells Sheba that the Temple Floor was a 'glossy floor of glass' (27:44). The *tafsir* by Muhammad Faruki Azzam Malik notes that it is a floor 'trained smooth with glass', whereas the text used for this writing notes that the floor was transparent, and water flowed underneath. In Ibn 'Arabi's text *Fusus al Hikam*, the Queen of Sheba uncovers her legs as she walks over what she believes to be a pool of water. Solomon tells her that '… this is a palace, paved with crystal'.[16] The central message of the story is the same, yet the possible descriptions are many. This *polysemy* is what Paul Ricoeur

---

15 Syed Gulzar Haider, 'Islam, Cosmology, and Architecture', in M.B. Sevcenko, *Theories and Principles of Design in the Architecture of Islamic Societies* (Cambridge, 1988), pp. 73-85:78-9.

16 Muhyi-D-Din Ibn, 'Arabi. *Fusus al-Hikam*, trans. Titus Burckhardt and Angela Culme-Seymour (Gloucestershire, 1975), p. 91.

posits as the generative nature of successful metaphor; the understanding of the text is not fixed, and subsequently, neither is the Temple that this text describes.

The infinite discourse that Ricoeur speaks of as a temporal event occurs with each recitation of the Qur'aan, and with each recitation of the Story of Solomon, the possible interpretation of the above verse changes. This changing mental imagery of the floor and palace can be noted by what Paul Ricoeur notes as 'a being pertaining to language'.[17] The language of the Qur'aan is, to use Ricoeur's terms, quasi-scientific and quasi-ordinary, particularly in relation to the *muhkamat* (the explicit commands of God) – where clarification is for the practices and actions of everyday life – and for the elimination of polysemy with regard to absolute realities (The Divine Unity of God, Muhammad as the final prophet).

This metaphor, this Temple of the mind, is contingent upon the language of the Qur'aan – one that in a *mutashabihat* (probabilistic) language provides for a multitude of interpretations and architectural possibilities. These possibilities lie in the recitation of the verses that initiate a discourse with the Divine.

> The revelation of the Qur'aan was auditory before becoming crystallized in a written text. The Prophet first heard the term iqra' and only later recited the first revealed verses on the basis of their audition. The whole experience of the Qur'aan for Muslims remains to this day first of all an auditory experience and is only later associated with reading in the ordinary sense of the word. There is an ever-present, orally heard, and memorized Qur'aan in addition to the written version of the Sacred Text, an auditory reality which touches the deepest chords in the souls of the faithful, even if they are unable to read Arabic. [18]

The later chronological stories of the Qur'aan, both the historic and eschatological, provide an alternate context for Solomon. The Temple that resulted from the Covenant with Abraham is not the Temple understood by the Qur'aan. The Temple of the Qur'aan transcends placement or location, as demonstrated by Sheba's spiritual transformation. The architecture of the Temple becomes a metaphor of Qur'aanic revelation.

Some Implications

> Architecture in the 'revealed' history acquires an essential moral dimension and cannot be treated free of the intentions underlying it. The architectural achievements of David and Solomon as well as those of Pharoah and nations of Aad and Thamud are recognized but placed on the opposite sides of the moral divide. While the former are in submission (Islam, tasleem) towards God, the latter are in denial (kufr) and thus in rebellion against God. On one hand the architectural magnificence is a 'sign' of God and their rule a domain

---

17 Paul Ricoeur, 'The Metaphorical Process as Cognition, Imagination, and Feeling', in Sheldon Sacks, (ed.), *On Metaphor* (Chicago, 1981), pp. 141-58:145.

18 Seyyed Hossein Nasr, 'Oral Transmission and the Book in Islamic Education: The Spoken and Written Word', in George Atiyeh, (ed.), *The Book in the Islamic World: The Written Word and Communication in the Middle East* (Albany, 1995), pp. 57-70:57.

of justice. On the other hand the arrogant disbelief of Pharoanic Egypt, Aad and Thamud pollutes their achievements and earns the heavenly wrath and destruction.[19]

The Qur'aan is not prescriptive about art or architecture, but of the possibility of their 'inner' qualities (*batin*) and their *haqai'iq* (*realities*). It is through these that the Qur'aan reveals the principal realities of the cosmos.[20]

One of the central challenges in Islamic art and architecture has been the tendency of academic scholarship to be written from a detached, exterior perspective. The texts of art historians and academics such as Oleg Grabar, Sheila Blair and Jonathan Bloom, Richard Ettinghausen and J.M Rogers have contributed to a largely archeological, geographical, stylistic and socio-political exploration of Islamic Architecture.[21] A more 'interiorized' study of Islamic architecture is needed in order to explore the balance, inherent to Islam, between the scientific and the poetic. The Solomnic metaphor is dependent on an interpretation of the text that is not geographic, formal or stylistic or socio-political (although it certainly may have these consequences). This interpretation honours the revelatory characteristic of the narrative by making its source primary. This is not to say, however, that the work provided by this scholarship is not valuable. On the contrary, the wealth of information that these scholars have provided is extraordinarily useful and necessary. Nor does this mean that the alternate 'interior' scholarship suggested here is universally appropriate.

The challenge for orientalists and traditionalists is precisely what the Solomnic metaphor attests to as the primary focus for the Judaic, Christian, and Islamic religious worlds. The Qur'aan, is *not* a prescriptive architectural text, and does not advocate a regionalist or historicist architecture to 'solve' problems of context or identity. The challenge for contemporary Islamic architecture is to overcome an excessive and overly historicized and romanticized reading and interpretation of cultural contexts. This approach to architecture results in a culture that cannot situate itself in a new environment and does not allow for the multiplicity that the Qur'aan suggests in a way to a kind of reverse orientalism, whereby Islamic architecture has no dynamic, immediate context, but looks broadly, as things did 'back home'. In a way, to echo the architectural scholar Kenneth Frampton, Islamic architecture needs to identify its own critical regionalism, particularly in Europe and the West. As

---

19 Syed Gulzar Haider, 'Islamic Architecture and Cities' in *Great Civilizations*, UNESCO, Vol. V, forthcoming.

20 Seyyed Hossein Nasr, *Islamic Art and Spirituality* (Albany, 1987).

21 See Oleg Grabar, (with Reneta Holod, James Knustad and William Trusdale), *The City in the Desert* (Harvard, 1978); *The Formation of Islamic Art* (New Haven and London, 1987); *The Mediation of Ornament* (Princeton, 1992) and *The Shape of the Holy: Early Islamic Jerusalem* (Princeton, 1996). Sheila Blair and Jonathan Bloom, *The Art and Architecture of Islam 1250-1800* (New Haven and London, 1994); Richard Ettinghausen, *Islamic Art and Archeology: Collected Papers* (New York, 1984) and *Islamic Art and Architecture 650-1250* (New Haven and London: 2002); J.M Rogers, *Islamic Art and Design: 1500-1700* (London, 1983). For a more comprehensive elaboration of this point, including an expanded list of scholars and texts of this dual aspect of scholarship, please see Syed Gulzar Haider's introduction to the second edition of *The Sense of Unity: The Sufi Tradition in Persian Architecture* in Nader Ardalan and Laleh Bakhtiar (Chicago, 2000), pp. xix-xxvii.

Seyyed Hossein Nasr notes in *Islamic Art and Spirituality*, 'Islamic art is the result of the manifestation of Unity upon the plane of multiplicity.'[22]

The power and eloquence of Islamic architecture, as evidenced in the Solomnic Metaphor, is its potential for transformation, what Ricoeur has noted as 'the power of metaphor ... to break out through previous categorization and to establish new logical boundaries on the ruins of the preceding ones'.[23] Islamic architecture, if it is to be inspired by the Qur'aan, cannot be a fixed entity situated only in historical discourse or an interiorized, self-glorifying and sadly self-referential argument. To resort to this is to deny the transformative nature of the Qur'aan.

The power of this metaphor for Islamic Architecture is that it is *generative* through the axiomatic reality of the Islamic faith itself – the Qur'aan. As Ricoeur observed, 'What a reader receives is not just the sense of the word, but through its sense, its reference, that is, the experience it brings to language. And in the last analysis, the world and temporality it unfolds in the space of this experience.'[24] Umberto Eco famously has observed that 'translation is the art of failure'.[25] We can posit that he is referring to the linguistic process when he makes this particular remark and not to the nature of translation between 'text' and 'architecture'. Here, however, we can respond in the disputative, and argue instead that the translation and (re)presentation of the sacred – from word to form – can be richly, uniquely and vibrantly polysemic in nature, yet still retain a sense of the Origin, or the Divine or the Sacred.

> This path in its length is unlike the existing distances that people cover by feet according to their strength and weakness: it is rather a spiritual path that is tread by hearts which cover it with thought according to the faith and insight of the seeker. Its origin is a heavenly light (*nur samawaî*) and a divine look (*nazar Illahi*) which descend on the heart of the servant who uses it to see the reality of both worlds.[26]

What is striking is the extent to which the traditions of Judaism, Christianity, and Islam have interpreted a common narrative character, and the extent to which this has coalesced in the Islamic tradition. The Solomnic metaphor in the Islamic faith exists due to the Qur'aanic text. This metaphor is dependent in a unique way on a space for prayer and a place of orientation. In a way, we can see the convergent path of this Solomnic metaphor in the Islamic tradition; it incorporates a site specifically as an orientation device (The *Ka'ba*), the Body becomes a magnifying lens through

---

22 Nasr, *Islamic Art and Spirituality*, p. 7.

23 Paul Ricoeur, 'Word, Polysemy, Metaphor: Creativity in Language' in Mario Valdes, (ed.), *A Ricoeur Reader: Reflection and Imagination* (Toronto, 1991), pp.65-85:85. The Islamic scholar and community leader Hamza Yusuf Hanson once remarked in a lecture that 'To continually glorify and return to the exploits of the past is to be full or satiated on a meal that someone else has eaten.' (Extract from speech given by Hamza Yusuf at Rihla Spiritual Retreat, Toronto, Canada, 1996).

24 Don Ihde, 'Text and the New Hermeneutics', in Don Wood, (ed.), *On Paul Ricoeur: Narrative and Interpretation* (London, 1991), pp. 124-39:130.

25 http://thinkexist.com/quotation/translation_is_the_art_of_failure/226242. html[Accessed June 2007].

26 Mustafa Abu-Sway, 'The Development in al-Ghazali's Epistemology, *Intellectual Discourse*, Vol.2/2 (1994), pp. 167-76:174.

the physical acts of prayer, and the recitation of the text of the Divine completes the connection to the Divine. That we can generate a contemporary Islamic architectural expression from the nature of this text and for it to be enlivened in the numerous experiential ways each time a worshipper comes to prayer, is a powerful form of being for the contemporary present. The connection with the Divine is achieved through man and woman's recitation of the text of the Qur'aan, and for an instant in prayer, establishes a link to realms of angelic ephemerality.

> Then, however, when in his cave refuge,
> immediately the recognizable one: the angel trod,
> upright, the honorable and fiery luminous:
> then cast he all claims aside and implored
>
> to be allowed to remain the merchant
> confused within by his journeys, which he was;
> he had never read—and now even
> such a word too much for a wise man.
>
> The angel, however, lordly, revealed and revealed
> to him what stood written upon his leaf,
> and gave not way and wanted again: *Read.*
>
> Then he read: such that the angel bowed.
> And was already one who *had* read
> and could and obeyed and fulfilled.
> (Rilke)[27]

Bibliography

Abu-Sway, Mustafa, 'The Development in al-Ghazali's Epistemology', *Intellectual Discourse*, Vol.2/2 (1994): 167-76.

Ardalan, Nader and Laleh Bakhtiar, *The Sense of Unity: The Sufi Tradition in Persian Architecture* (Chicago: Abjad Book Designers and Builders, 2000).

Atiyeh, George (ed.), *The Book in the Islamic World: The Written Word and Communication in the Middle East* (Albany: State University of New York Press, 1995).

The Bible, New International Version (Grand Rapids: Zondervan Publishing House, 1984).

Blair, Sheila and Jonathan Bloom, *The Art and Architecture of Islam 1250-1800* (New Haven and London: Yale University Press, 1994).

Cohn, Stephen, trans. *New Poems: A Bilingual Edition* (Boston: Northwestern University Press, 1998).

Comay, Joan, *The Temple of Jerusalem* (New York: Holt, Rhinehart and Winston, 1975).

---

27 Rainer Maria Rilke, 'Mohammed's Summoning', *New Poems: A Bilingual Edition* trans. Stephen Cohn (Boston, 1988), p. 280.

Ettinghausen, Richard, *Islamic Art and Archeology: Collected Papers* (New York: Metropolitan Museum, 1984).

Ettinghausen, Richard, *Islamic Art and Architecture 650-1250* (New Haven and London: Yale University Press, 2002).

Grabar, Oleg, with Reneta Holod, James Knustad and William Trusdale, *The City in the Desert* (Harvard: Harvard University Press, 1978).

Grabar, Oleg, *The Formation of Islamic Art* (New Haven and London: Yale University Press 1987).

Grabar, Oleg, *The Mediation of Ornament* (Princeton: Princeton University Press, 1992).

Grabar, Oleg, *The Shape of the Holy*: *Early Islamic Jerusalem* (Princeton: Princeton University Press,1996).

Haider, Syed Gulzar, 'Islam, Cosmology, and Architecture', in M.B. Sevcenko, *Theories and Principles of Design in the Architecture of Islamic Societies* (Cambridge: Aga Khan Program for Islamic Architecture, 1988): 73-85.

Haider, Syed Gulzar, 'Islamic Architecture and Cities' in *Great Civilizations* (UNESCO, Vol. V, forthcoming).

Haider Syed Gulzar, 'Introduction' in Nader Ardalan and Laleh Bakhtiar, *The Sense of Unity: The Sufi Tradition in Persian Architecture* (Chicago: ABC International Group, [Second Edition] 2000): xix-xxvii.

Haider, Syed Gulzar, *Great Civilizations* (UNESCO, Vol. V, forthcoming).

Ibn 'Arabi, Muhyi-D-Din, *Fusus al-Hikam*, trans. Titus Burckhardt and Angela Culme-Seymour (Gloucestershire: Beshara Publications, 1975).

Ihde, Don, 'Text and the New Hermeneutics', in Don Wood (ed.), *On Paul Ricoeur: Narrative and Interpretation* (London: Routledge, 1991): 125-39.

McClung, William Alexander, 'The Matter of Metaphor: Literary Myths of Construction', *The Journal of the Society of Architectural Historians*, vol. 40/4 (1981): 270-88.

Nasr, Seyyed Hossein, *Islamic Art and Spirituality* (Albany: State University of New York Press, 1987).

Nasr, Seyyed Hossein, *Ideals and Realities of Islam* (London: Aquarian, 1994).

Nasr, Seyyed Hossein, 'Oral Transmission and the Book in Islamic Education: The Spoken and Written Word', in George Atiyeh, (ed.), *The Book in the Islamic World: The Written Word and Communication in the Middle East* (Albany: State University of New York Press, 1995): 57-70.

Perez-Gomez, Alberto, 'Juan Battista Villalpando's Divine Model in Architectural Theory', in Alberto Perez-Gomez and Stephen Parcel, (eds), *Chora Three: Intervals in the Philosophy of Architecture* (Montreal: Queen's University Press 1999): 125-56.

Perez-Gomez, Alberto, and Stephen Parcel, (eds), *Chora Three: Intervals in the Philosophy of Architecture* (Montreal: Queen's University Press 1999).

The Qur'aan (edited and revised), (Jeddah, Saheeh International, 1997).

Ricoeur, Paul 'The Metaphorical Process as Cognition, Imagination, and Feeling', in Sheldon Sacks, (ed.), *On Metaphor* (Chicago: University of Chicago Press, 1981): 141-58.

Ricoeur, Paul, 'Word, Polysemy, Metaphor: Creativity in Language' in Mario Valdes, (ed.), *A Ricoeur Reader: Reflection and Imagination* (Toronto: University of Toronto Press, 1991): 65-85.

Rilke, Rainer Maria, 'Mohammed's Summoning', in Stephen Cohn, trans. *New Poems: A Bilingual Edition* (Boston: Northwestern University Press, 1998).

Rogers, J.M., *Islamic Art and Design: 1500-1700* (London: British Museum Publications, 1983).

Sacks, Sheldon, (ed.), *On Metaphor* (Chicago: University of Chicago Press, 1981).

Sevcenko, M.B., *Theories and Principles of Design in the Architecture of Islamic Societies* (Cambridge: Aga Khan Program for Islamic Architecture, 1988).

Szasz, Ferenc, M, 'The Many Meanings of History, Part II', *The History Teacher,* vol. 8 (Long Beach: California State University, 1974): 54-63.

Valdes, Mario, (ed.), *A Ricoeur Reader: Reflection and Imagination* (Toronto: University of Toronto Press, 1991).

Wood, Don, (ed.), *On Paul Ricoeur: Narrative and Interpretation* (London: Routledge, 1991).

Internet Sources

http://www.earlychristianwritings.com/text/infancyjames-mrjames.html. Accessed June 2007.

www.philosophyforlife.com/mc27.htm. Accessed June 2007.

http://www.jhom.com/topics/stones/foundation.html. Accessed June 2007.

http://thinkexist.com/quotation/translation_is_the_art_of_failure/226242.html. Accessed June 2007.

Chapter 11

Reading Texts, Watching Texts: Mythopoesis on Neopagan Websites

Maria Beatrice Bittarello

Introduction

This chapter examines the ambiguous relationship between text and image on a computer screen, and how such relationships are shaped, and shape, the mythopoeic expressions that characterize Neopaganism on the Web. Studying Neopagan religious texts on Internet websites also involves reconsidering the relationship between textuality and religion in the digital age. Neopagans, who do not have sacred texts in the sense given to the expression by other religions, use as religious texts a number of different works, which often include popular culture products and literature from genres such as fantasy and science. Thus, Neopagan websites forcefully re-propose a number of key questions, such as: What is a religious text? Who controls such texts, and to what purpose? Who is excluded from the production of the texts? Are purely textual rituals on a screen still rituals? How are they challenging current theories about ritual and embodiment? In other words, Neopagan religious texts on the Web pose problems of authority and tradition, and impose a re-inscription of ritual and a re-evaluation of terms such as virtuality and reality, play and performance.

I refer to several of the issues mentioned above in the course of the chapter, and will focus on the interplay between text and image on the Web and how precisely such interplay becomes the vehicle for Neopagan mythopoesis. This chapter will examine some representative examples of Neopagan websites devoted to gods and goddesses from the Greek, Roman and Celtic religions, showing how the layout and content of such websites present certain common features. Neopagan sites usually host examples of 'sacred texts' such as ancient hymns, rituals, ancient texts narrating myths, and/or links to texts and images of the gods/goddesses together with new texts, which often rework ancient materials.

The first part of the paper, after a short introduction on Neopaganism and Neopaganism on the Web, will show how there are substantial differences between the way religious texts are presented on the Web and the way they are presented on paper. Such differences are both formal (for example, the length of the text, the use of quotes and the presentation of images with texts) and functional (what role are such web texts/images playing?). Therefore, web-texts are perceived in a different way from texts written on more traditional materials such as paper. The key question is whether the combination of text and image reinforce the importance of visual representation or does the ambiguous relation between written word (printed or on screen) and image remain unresolved? Is the religious message conveyed by images and written words differently perceived depending on the writing material? The importance of such questions becomes clear if we compare, for example, religious texts written on stone, to myths represented and glossed on Greek vases or temples, to Egyptian bas-reliefs, which used images and hieroglyphs, and to web pages (combining texts and images), which express the religious ideas of a New Religious Movement such as Neopaganism. In each case the medium is far from neutral; it shapes the message in a peculiar way, involving claims to authority and stability, while expressing a range of power relations.[1]

The second part further explores some of the issues raised by the presence of religious texts on the Web. In the first place, the paper points out how publishing a sacred text on a web page, making it available to every surfer, is itself an act that opens up the text to both fruition (even consumption) and original re-creation (mythopoesis). Here lies the main difference from medieval codices such as the famous *Book of Kells*,[2] which combined text, image and commentary on the text on a single page, as web pages do. The question is then whether the combination of text and image reinforce the importance of visual representation or vice versa. This is not an idle question, since the authors of web pages live in a society where the combination of images and written texts (and spoken words and music) has been used in advertising commercials for so many more years. The influence of popular culture on Neopagan imaginary should not be undervalued.

Secondly, I will examine the issue of how a web page or website can be conceived of as space, which is made 'sacred' by Neopagans. A spatial conception of the Internet is openly expressed on many websites dedicated to a particular god or goddess from in or out of the classical tradition, websites that call themselves a 'virtual temple' or a 'virtual shrine'; moreover, the Web is used as a space for specific religious practices, such as virtual pilgrimages or cyber-rituals and rites.

Neopaganism on the Web

What is Neopaganism? And, is Neopaganism on the Web somewhat peculiar? Scholars and Pagans use the terms 'modern' or 'contemporary' Paganism as well as Neopaganism or Neo-Paganism (the hyphenated American spelling) to indicate a diverse religious movement. Neopaganism is:

> a general and inclusive category for a range of specific traditions, all of which may in varying degrees be described as *nature religions* in the sense that they involve a

---

1   The study of writing materials is an important element in a discipline such as the history of archives, which shows that different choices have not only practical consequences, but a deep symbolic value. Different cultures have chosen to use different writing materials to preserve their memory and such choices reveal the values that each culture deems important and how specific cultures decide to represent themselves.

2   Written around 800 CE.

reorientation towards, and a resacralization of, both external nature and our own physical embodiment.[3]

Among the traditions that recognize themselves as Neopagans or Pagans are (Neo) Druids, (Neo) Shamans, Wiccans, Odinists (also called Heathenists or Asatrù), Hellenic, Roman and Celtic Reconstructionists. Such complex phenomenon is characterized by the absence of normative sacred texts and a hierarchy that controls authoritative sources and by a stress on personal research and choice.

Pagans have been one of the first religious groups to use the Web, and, as Christopher Helland has documented, their online presence has been quite remarkable since the 1980s.[4] Not only are there Pagan portals such as *WitchVox*, which lists websites, resources and commercial materials, but there are also other Pagan resources available, usually produced by individuals or small groups. Some websites publish online ancient texts, as well as new prayers, hymns, rituals, and essays on Neopagan religions.

Sacred space online?

Neopagan websites do not look too different, at first sight, from the page of a book, since a few of them may consist of one page, which contains texts and pictures. However, with the growing diffusion of free and easy to use web editing software, which does not require the knowledge of the languages that form the hidden code of a web page (for instance, HTML), most websites appear to be formed by a variable number of pages (from three or four to hundreds) connected by hypertext links. The key difference between a book and a website is that the various pages of the website can be read in whatever order the reader decides; it is the reader who chooses what parts of the website, and in what order, s/he will explore by jumping from one hypertext to the next. Exploring and jumping suggest a movement in space – an element that is important to underline, since several commentators have begun to point out that a spatial conception seems to inform the way scholars and the media refer to the Internet. Since this is not the focus of this chapter, it will suffice saying that studies conducted since the end of the 1990s have highlighted how the Internet is purposefully presented, and thus perceived by users, as a space where several different activities can take place.[5] Neopagans seem to have adopted such a view, as confirmed by the existence of virtual temples and virtual pilgrimages – the web space

---

3   Joanne Pearson, Richard H. Roberts and Geoffrey Samuel, 'Introduction', in Joanne Pearson, Richard H. Roberts, and Geoffrey Samuel, (eds), *Nature Religion Today: Paganism in the Modern World* (Edinburgh, 1998), pp. 1-12:1.

4   Christopher Helland, 'Popular Religion and the World Wide Web: A Match Made in (Cyber) Heaven', in Lorne L. Dawson and Douglas E. Cowan, (eds), *Religion online: Finding Faith on the Internet* (New York-London, 2004), pp. 23-35. For an overview on Internet Pagan cultures see Douglas E. Cowan, *Cyberhenge: Modern Pagans on the Internet* (London and New York, 2005).

5   For examples of this, see Nick Bingham, 'Unthinkable complexity? Cyberspace otherwise', in Mike Crang, Phil Crang and Jon May, (eds), *Virtual Geographies: Bodies, Space & Relations* (London-New York, 1999), pp. 244-60, and Elaine Graham, '"Nietzsche

is made 'sacred' and thus becomes an alternative plane where religious activities can be performed.

As we shall see, a digital space can be made 'sacred' by *writing* on a web page the words pronounced and describing actions performed offline. For example, there are formal dedications to the chosen god or goddess, or to the whole pantheon: 'this space is dedicated to' or 'sacred to' or 'this is the virtual temple/ temenos/ shrine / altar of …' These dedications set apart that particular page or website from the rest of the digital space. Neopagan web pages usually host an ancient or modern image of the deity, and very often a short quote from ancient sacred texts, or longer texts such as prayers, hymns, and myths referring to that specific god or goddess. Sometimes, the bottom of the page includes the formula 'for (name of the god/goddess)'. Some websites offer a virtual space in which prayers can be posted and ritual acts such as libations can be performed virtually by using interactive ritual tools to fill in a form with written words saying that the surfer/devotee is offering a libation.[6] As casting a circle makes space sacred in the physical world, specific ritual written words are used to make the web space sacred. As O'Leary[7] has suggested, for cyber-rituals taking place in online environments, the written word becomes the means through which the religious action is performed.

What is interesting is that 'reading' religious texts like formulae, prayers, hymns or even the forms recording a libation on the Web is intrinsically different from reading the same words in a book. On the Web, such texts are 'public' (as opposed to the traditionally private act of reading a book),[8] potentially open to all those who have Internet access, and certainly open to replication and modification since they can be cut and pasted from one website to another.

Sacred texts, religious texts and images in Neopaganism

Since Neopagans do not have normative sacred texts – nothing comparable to the Bible or the Qur'an – answering the question of what a religious text is for Neopagans is not easy. While Neopagans write and circulate hymns, rituals, poems and reformulations of myths, they do not claim them, in general, to be writings inspired by divine beings. Neopagan religious literature often includes work that it is often inspired not only by original texts from the Greek, Roman, Celtic (e.g. the

---

gets a modem": Transhumanism and the Technological Sublime' *Literature & Theology*, 16/1 (2001): 65-80.

6   See, for example, the *Thiasos Lusios* website http://www.winterscapes.com/ thiasoslusios/.

7   Stephen D. O'Leary, 'Cyberspace as Sacred Space: Communicating Religion on Computer Networks', *Journal of the American Academy of Religion*, 64/4 (1996): pp. 781-807.

8   Reading as a private act is a relatively new practice. In the ancient world, until the age of Ambrose, reading silently was somewhat unusual.

Mabinogi), or Norse religions,[9] but by works of genre literature such as fantasy and, to a lesser degree, science fiction books,[10] as well as scholarly works.[11]

An example of what can become a sacred text in Neopaganism is found in two interesting websites, *Sacred Texts* and *The Theoi Project*. *Sacred Texts* lists diverse texts such as Leland's *Aradia*,[12] Gardner's *Book of Shadows* (or at least one of its many variants),[13] and excerpts from popular novels as Neopagan sacred texts.[14] *The Theoi Project* is a remarkably accurate resource on Greek mythology, which has been conceived and realized outside the academic realm by Aaron Atsma. It offers well-organized and free information about gods, goddesses and heroes of Greek and Roman mythology, as well as excerpts from ancient texts.[15]

Such websites are important resources for Neopagans, who, as pointed out above, draw on ancient and modern, popular and scholarly works to construct their religious imagery. I have already stressed that Neopagans do not have normative sacred texts. However, the prayers, hymns, interactive ritual devices, and narrations of (or allusions to) ancient myths from Atlantis to Diana's deeds found on Neopagan websites are examples of religious texts, which in one way or another make reference to, or retell myths, which are re-created and given new meaning. In other words,

---

9   See for example Prudence Jones, 'The European Native tradition', in Joanne Pearson, Richard H. Roberts and Geoffrey Samuel, (eds), *Nature Religion today. Paganism in the modern World* (Edinburgh, 1998), pp. 77-88.

10 See Graham Harvey, 'Fantasy in the Study of Religions: Paganism as Observed and Enhanced by Terry Pratchett', *Diskus* 6 (2000)

http://web.uni-marburg.de/religionswissenschaft/journal/diskus/harvey_2.html.

11 See Linda Jencson, 'Neopaganism and the Great Mother Goddess: Anthropology as Midwife to a New Religion', *Anthropology Today* 5/2 (1989), pp. 2-4, and Prudence Jones and Nigel Pennick, *A History of Pagan Europe* (London and New York, 1995).

12 Charles Godfrey Leland, *Aradia or, The Gospel of the Witches* (London, 1899). The author of this literary work claimed to have collected the ancient oral traditions of Italian witches: http://www.sacred-texts.com/pag/aradia/index.htm.

13 The story of Gardner's *Book of Shadows* is one of the most interesting examples of how contemporary Pagan sacred texts have been (and are) compiled and how they are still far from being normative. Gardner never published the *Book of Shadows* that he completed in the early 1960s, but it was transmitted from coven to coven (each Wiccan coven has its own). Nonetheless, a *Book of Shadows* has been compiled and posted on the Internet by Aidan Kelly, an American academic, poet and Pagan practitioner, based on Gardner's manuscripts. Since British Wicca is an initiatory religion, this text does not include all that Gardner wrote. Further, at some point Gardner was strongly influenced by Doreen Valiente, who apparently re-wrote Gardner's original text (see Ronald Hutton, *The Triumph of the Moon: A History of Modern Pagan Witchcraft* (Oxford, 1999)). Also, Pagan practitioners who follow Wiccan tradition(s) today tend to compile their own *Book of Shadows*. The *Book of Shadows* on the *Sacred Texts* website is Kelly's compilation http://www.sacred-texts.com/pag/gbos/index.htm.

14 http://www.sacred-texts.com/pag/index.htm. Texts can be downloaded for free, though there is a CD available. Also, the website hosts a number of links to online bookselling websites.

15 Currently, the website is publishing translations of ancient texts, which include some works that are difficult to find even in specialized libraries.

Neopagan web-pages are examples not only of the selective borrowing of materials from other cultural contexts, but of mythopoeic recreation – mythopoesis literally means 'creation/crafting of myths'.

The issue here is that the term 'myth' is currently used in at least three different ways. One conception is rooted in the distinction between myth and philosophy, where myth is understood as a 'false story'. According to such a view, as Pamela Sue Anderson synthesizes: 'Whereas myths comprise stories about embodiment, birth and death, passion and desire, philosophy claims to be dispassionate discourse whereby pure reason takes control of disorder and rejects impure experience.'[16] A second conception is found in studies on ancient myths, which are interpreted as stories founding reality. 'Since Eve ate of the forbidden fruit ...' human beings have to live a dangerous, insecure life on earth, and finally die. Such stories have a somewhat special value and do not give – or are not interested in giving – what we would consider rational explanations. Finally, a third conception is found in modern conceptions of myth that, in spite of several key differences, have all originated from reflections on ancient myths and consider myth to be a source of guidance, of inspiration, as a shared knowledge, and conveying hidden meaning.

On Neopagan websites we find both the second and third conceptions. In other words, we have a re-telling and re-visualizing of ancient myths, where stories are written and represented again in a creative way and used as a source of inspiration in order to re-organize meaning.

Layouts and meaning

This section analyses some of the differences between readers'/viewers' perceptions of religious texts and images published on the web and those written on paper by examining the layout and features of some Neopagan web pages. The differences between web-texts and texts on other materials are formal, for instance the length of the texts, the use of quotes, the use of special alphabetical characters, and the inclusion of images, pictures and paintings. There are also functional differences, as the presentation changes the role played by the religious text considerably. As web-documents are characterized for by non-linearity (you can visit a website in the order you wish, and ignore certain pages), recent studies have proposed to consider it as a specific genre. Furthermore, digital genres are hyper-textual as they can be linked to one another and contain sounds, images and movies, thus acting not only as text but also as medium.[17]

There are some Neopagan websites that are exclusively textual, but use alphabetical signs as graphics, and websites combining texts and images. The use of words as graphics is typical of contemporary popular culture, for instance in graffiti art forms and advertising. An example of such use of graphics is a Hellenic

---

16 Pamela S. Anderson, 'Myth and feminist philosophy', in Kevin Schibrack, (ed.), *Thinking Through Myths: Philosophical Perspectives* (London and New York, 2002), pp. 101-22:101.

17 Inger Askehave and Anne Ellerup Nielsen, 'Digital Genres: a challenge to traditional genre theory', *Information Technology & People*, 18/2 (2005). pp. 120-41.

Reconstructionist website, *Devotion: A Simple Shrine to the Gods of the Greeks*, which is connected to the largest American Hellenic Reconstructionist association, Hellenion. The association honours the gods and goddesses of the ancient Greek pantheon; its members aim at recreating Greek religion today, based on ancient materials, which are, nonetheless, given new meaning. The author of *Devotion,* a woman who calls herself Hearthstone, does not use images at all, but rather uses an alphabet that mimics the ancient Greek alphabet.[18] Here signs become images, as in a page written by a calligrapher. Another Reconstructionist website, affiliated to Hellenion, *The Hellenion Proto-Demos tes Hagnes Persephones*, also uses very few images, apart from a Greek motif and a symbolic logo that separates sections of text. In the title square it also uses as decoration the Greek greeting, *Chairete,* written in the Greek alphabet.[19]

Most Neopagan websites, however, combine text and images, even if some pages on a website may end up being purely textual. There are two additional factors influencing the format and design of Neopagan websites. The first is that they are often set up using free hosting services; therefore they have to accept banners and other forms of advertising on their pages and have a limited amount of web space. The second is that pages using only (or mostly) texts are easier to download than pages containing several images (especially pictures). It is worth remembering that publishing web-pages that are easy to download also means making the content available to those surfers who do have the most recent software (or hardware). In other words, using mainly text and a few well-chosen and simple images demonstrates both the ability of the webmaster and his/her attempt to make the content available to the widest possible audience.[20] This is coherent with the democratic and inclusive slant of most on- and off-line Paganisms.

Re-elaborating the past: creative mythopoesis

Neopagans publish both ancient and new religious texts on their websites. The ancient texts hosted on Neopagan websites share some key features. The first is that the ancient religious texts presented are usually translated from texts that are already in the public domain and can be downloaded from websites that make texts available for free on the Web (such as *Project Gutenberg, Perseus* or *The Theoi Project*). The second feature is that texts are usually short, or divided between several pages and often include extracts from longer texts. The third feature is that web-texts are often annotated, that is, surfers are given some explanations about the language used in the text (for example, the names of the gods are translated). In several cases short quotes from ancient texts are used as an epigraph to a page. For instance, the website *Ave Diana,* 'the Virtual temple and home to the goddess Diana',[21] includes a few

---

18 http://www.geocities.com/hellenicdevotions/gaia.html.

19 http://persephones.250free.com/.

20 Such considerations are also valid with regard to the use of PHP, ASP pages, CSS and JavaScript. All browsers can read HTML, but only recent and more expensive browsers can read PHP, ASP, CSS, or JavaScript.

21 http://www.avediana.net/pages/1/page1.html.

translated verses of *Carmen Saeculare* by the Latin poet Horace. Often new and ancient texts coexist on the same page, or can be found on different sections of a website.[22]

However, the websites' authors do not just select ready-made ancient or modern religious texts and images, but create new texts and images, usually by re-elaborating old materials. I have chosen as examples three websites: *The Bibliotheca Arcana*, *The Hymnodia Project*, and *A Virtual Temple Honoring Hermes*. The first two can be categorized as freely available resource centres – as well as centres of mythopoeic recreation – while the third is a self-styled virtual temple. *The Bibliotheca Arcana*, which collects ancient and new texts pertaining to Hellenic Reconstructionism (though there are links to websites set up by other traditions), is an important, rich resource for new religious texts, which comprise both hymns and newly created rituals.[23] Another example is *The Hymnodia Project,* which is hosted on a section of the official website of the Hellenic Reconstructionist group Hellenion. *The Hymnodia Project* aims at creating a collection of original hymns and rituals, which are sent to the website by various authors. This is a very interesting example of the creation and sharing of new religious texts online, particularly because the intention does not seem to be to establish a 'canon'. On the contrary, the collection appears to be open-ended and is constantly growing.[24]

On *A Virtual Temple Honoring Hermes*, a website that declares to be a virtual temple to the Greek god Hermes, we can find an image closely inspired by an ancient statue of Hermes.[25] A prayer is published next to the god's head and has been written by the Unitarian Universalist priest Christa Landon:

Hermes,
Dancer across boundaries,
Guide of Souls,
Teacher of the Mysteries,
Guide those who seek
through the maze of illusion.
Lead us safely through the darkness.

This text is a good example of how Neopagan texts draw upon ancient religions. The author uses Greek titles for Hermes, such as 'Guide of souls' (*Psychopompus*), as Hermes was thought to guide the souls in their journey to the Other World after they had departed from their bodies. He also looked after boundaries: Hermai were located at the borderline between states and at the trivia, and his connection with mysteries is well attested. Even if the author uses ancient epithets for Hermes, the figure of Hermes now acquires new significance since the god is presented as a guide

---

22 For example, on the *Hagnes Persephone* homepage, we find a link to 'something I (Gitana) wrote on prayer in Hellenismos' and another link to 'Some prayers from Classical literature' http://persephones.250free.com/.

23 http://www.cs.utk.edu/~mclennan/BA/.

24 http://www.hellenion.org/Hymnodia.html.

25 The website has been set up a Unitarian Universalist minister, Christa Landon http://paganinstitute.org/T/Hermes.html. The painting represents a statue of Hermes from Turkey (second century BCE).

for seekers, a term often used in the New Age. Text and image are new in the sense that new meaning is constructed by using fragments of original information. Above the picture of Hermes, on the left, there is another image with strong symbolic value: a small logo, representing a temple and a brazier. The logo alludes to the flame of Paganism that is now burning again. The rest of the page consists in a series of texts, both ancient and modern, referring to the god. The author has put online several temples, devoted to different Greek gods and goddesses; she uses the same template – a table with a logo on the left, title page, marbled pale rose background – which is a predefined FrontPage theme. All the websites demonstrate an attempt to create new myths that express new meaning by creatively reworking ancient texts and images.[26]

Sacred texts in complex (virtual) sacred space

Until now, I have examined single web pages that surfers scroll down. Even if there are several differences between such examples and written pages on paper, one could argue that such differences are not particularly important. However, several Neopagan websites are composed of several sections and pages, which are coherently organized and structured in an often complex way. I will examine three examples: first, a virtual shrine to the Greek goddess Athena, second, a website devoted to the Eleusinian mysteries, and third, a website dedicated to Brighid, read as both goddess and Christian saint.

The website, *The Shrine of the Goddess Athena*, has been set up to allow a virtual pilgrimage of 'The Temple of the Goddess Athena'.[27] The homepage is bordered on both sides by Doric columns and on the centre page, a picture of the Athenian Parthenon. The hyper-textual links located below the picture offer the chance to access the altar, open the door, or enter the Museum. However, a specific browser is required to access the altar; if one tries to reach the page by using another browser, a popup message appears and blocks admission.[28] Other links bring the surfer to the naos, the cell where the statue of the goddess was kept. There we find a picture showing a reconstruction of Athena's *agalma* (a cultic statue) by Phidias. Following other links we can access the Museum, where texts on Athena are collected. If we follow all the links, we will end up completing a journey of the online shrine – something that is not infrequent on Neopagan and other religious websites. There are several examples of such phenomenon, which have been called 'virtual pilgrimages'.[29] In such a complex virtual environment we also find prayers to the goddess Athena. The

---

26 Such as the website devoted to Demeter and Persephone http://paganinstitute.org/T/2goddesses.html.

27 http://www.goddess-athena.org/index.

28 The pop up message reads: 'Sorry. Your browser is incompatible with the Altar. You must have the Netscape Communicator 4 or higher' http://www.goddess-athena.org/Temple/index.htm.

29 See Mark W. MacWilliams, 'Virtual Pilgrimages on the Internet', *Religion,* 33/4 (2002):315-335 and Glenn Young, 'Reading and Praying Online. The Continuity of Religion Online and Online Religion in Internet Christianity', in Lorne L. Dawson and Douglas

'prayer to Minerva' – the Latin goddess who corresponds to the Greek Athena – is a hymn by the Neo-Platonist philosopher[30] which appears in a pop up window when surfers reach the statue of the goddess and are metaphorically in the presence of the goddess. The most interesting aspect is the attempt to re-establish the relationship between the ancient religious text,[31] the goddess's cultic image and the ritual act of praying online. Not only is the surfer/devotee supposed to read the prayer, but the short text below the picture of Athena gives a precise description of the actions visitors to the temple should perform, even if virtually. When the surfer is viewing the page showing the naos, the text describes what is (or should) be happening, by using the words of the ancient tourist/pilgrim Pausanias and then giving some choices to the visitor.[32] Approaching the naos, the visitor finds a description of the atmosphere in the room as well as (what are supposed to be) his/her own feelings: 'Walking through the sanctuary, the sound of your feet on the marble floor is all you hear. Burning spices scent the air. As you approach the statue, you notice the beautiful two-level colonnade dividing the interior in two parts: a central area and a perimeter. At the central area is the statue of the Goddess Athena, herself. You are awed by her magnificence'.[33] The experience is presented as involving all the five senses but in this case, the imagination takes the place of the 'real' experience.

On *The Eleusinian Mysteries: Healing and Transformation*, a website devoted to a virtual pilgrimage/guided meditation on the Eleusinian mysteries, images and texts help the visitor to focus on the ritual's stages. This website, hosted on a free space host server (Geocities), features some important features shared by Neopagan websites.[34] Images and text blend as in the miniature pages of a medieval manuscript. The background has a symbolic value, since it shows a field of grain, with ears of corn signifying Demeter's care over the cultivation of cereals. Given the symbolic value that the ear of corn seems to have had at Eleusis, we see how images communicate powerfully by alluding to the authors' ideas. Colours are also used effectively, for instance the reddish colour of the ruins of Eleusis and the golden yellow of the background mix effectively. The authors use ancient and modern sources: the title of the homepage is a quote from the *Pseudo Homeric Hymn to Demeter*, but there is also a long passage by Aleister Crowley, some terms transliterated from the Greek

---

E. Cowan, (eds), *Religion Online: Finding Faith on the Internet* (New York and London: Routledge, 2004), pp. 93-105.

30 The author gives the following as reference in the pop up page hosting the prayer: 'Proclus' Hymn to Athena / Harleian MSS, British Museum / translated by Thomas Taylor http://www.goddess-athena.org/Temple/index.htm.

31 It is worth noting the choice of a late antiquity hymn rather than of other, more ancient texts.

32 The text reads: 'As you approach "the statue of Athena is upright, with a tunic reaching to the feet, and on Her breast the head of Medusa is worked in ivory. She holds a statue of Victory about four cubits high, and in the other hand a spear; at Her feet lies a shield and near the spear is a serpent"(Pausanias 1.24.7). You feel the desire to: know who is the Goddess Athena, visit the rear room, visit the Museum of the Goddess Athena just next door or leave the sanctuary' http://www.goddess-athena.org/Temple/index.htm.

33 http://www.goddess-athena.org/Temple/index.htm.

34 http://www.geocities.com/Athens/Aegean/3193/stations2.htm.

(*mystagogoi, epoptai, Iacchos*) and even one word, *Iasion,* who was Demeter's mythical lover, is written in the ancient Greek alphabet, which not all surfers will be able to read. The website creatively re-imagines the mysteries by combining ancient and modern material and explicitly makes reference to the Roman Catholic practice of the Via Crucis, where images of the Passion of the Christ guide prayers and meditations.[35]

The website, devoted to 'Brighid Goddess and Saint', is the creation of Paul Williment. It is a Neopagan website, as is clear from the author's words: 'This section lists books, compact disks and other resources that have been useful in the drafting of this website and in the preparation of rituals in honour of Brighid.'[36] The website is quite well structured, with several links to photographs taken by the author depicting what he defines a 'pilgrimage of discovery' to places connected to Brighid all over the UK. Even if the website does not claim to be a sacred space, but rather a resource for those interested in Brighid,[37] it hosts several prayers to Brighid. There is a green column on the left of each web-page containing links, the centre of the page hosts the main text (explanations, and other information), while on the right in a smaller size font there are prayers and invocations to Brighid, often in the original language accompanied by an English translation. There is also a banner on top of each page, where several symbolic images are beautifully combined: 'The banner above depicts Brighid against Eilean Bhride in the Hebrides. The scroll honours all those who have preserved Her story throughout the ages. The red hot iron spiral represents the goddess and suggests a crosier as a reminder that St. Bridget was consecrated as a religious using the form of the ordination of a bishop.'[38] Here, fragments of folkloric and high culture traditions combine to create, in texts and images of natural landscapes, Neopagan altars and rituals, and old symbols a new myth, the myth of Brighid as goddess and saint.

Conclusion

The survey of some representative Neopagan websites allows us to re-evaluate the way in which religious texts and images complement each other on the Web. The first conclusion refers to the blending of images and texts on web pages. We have seen how on most Neopagan websites religious texts and religious images are combined; is this practice really new and original? And what significance does it have?

What is new is the way in which such combination is used in order to convey messages. Both texts and images work together in telling a story, and while texts are usually predominant, when we find both, there does not seem to be a subordination of the image to the written word. Rather, they seem to work together which recalls

---

35 See for online examples of the *Via Crucis* practice Young, 'Reading and Praying', pp. 101-104.

36 http://www.brighid.org.uk/resources.html.

37 Willett also invites surfers to send their original work for free publication with full credit for authors on his website. http://www.brighid.org.uk/about.html.

38 http://www.brighid.org.uk/.

the medieval codices, which combined text, image and comments to the texts, upon a single page sacred in the actual, physical space.

Thus, the web page could be considered as a 'sacred artefact' combining visual and textual elements. One formal new aspect is that one has to scroll a page to read it, as in ancient papyri, but there are also functional differences. Websites are intrinsically different from medieval manuscripts, because the latter were symbols of authority, power and wealth and were treasures to be preserved, not shown to the widest possible audience. Web pages, instead, are ephemeral – because of the support, of the frequent re-stylings, and their open text nature – and open to virtually every surfer.

Therefore, we could rather compare web pages to Greek vases, or to tapestries. In contrast to medieval manuscripts, Greek vases and tapestries were made to be shown; short texts painted on vases, and probably weaved on tapestries, helped viewers to identify the characters involved, thus recalling to the mind of the viewer, the oral narration of a specific myth. On both vases and tapestries, however, images were predominant and texts were merely labels – as for instance in the case of the famous Vase François.[39] The comparison between tapestries and web pages is nonetheless suggestive, particularly if we recall Bella Debrida's comments on women weaving stories (myths). She argues for an original connection between women and song (i.e. myth, story), which emerges from expressions that connect the 'telling of a story' to activities traditionally reserved for women, such as weaving ('weaving a story') and spinning ('spinning a yarn').[40] Debrida's point acquires particular significance if we consider that several Neopagan websites have been set up by women, who thus re-appropriate the mythopoeic activity for so long denied them. Setting up a website thus becomes a re-appropriation of agency.[41] The combination of images and texts on web pages is not, as such, completely new; what is new is that Neopagan mythopoesis on the Web is expressed through such combination, or rather blending, of images and texts even more effectively than Christian myths on the pages of medieval manuscripts. The novelty, in most cases, is in the attempt to convey meaning through collaboration between text and image. Texts are not subordinated to images (the text is not simply a label, or an explanation) and images are not subordinated to texts (they are not simply illustrations of a text). Both images and text are integral parts of the message, and the message emerges from a combination of the two.

---

39 Vase François was found in 1884 near Chiusi, Tuscany, by the painter Alexander François. The huge Greek crater (570-60 BCE) is signed by the ceramist Ergotimos and the painter Clitias, and decorated with scenes representing the myths of the heroes Peleus, Achilles, and Theseus, and the return of Ephestos to the Olympus (see Jean, Charbonneaux, Roland Martin and François Villard, *La Grecia arcaica,* 3rd ed. (Milano, 1988), trans. Marcello Lenzini and Libero Sosio. (Or.tit. *Grèce archaïque*. Paris: Gallimard, 1968), pp. 64-9.

40 Bella Debrida, 'Drawing from Mythology in Women's Quest for Selfhood', in Charlene Spretnak, (ed.), *The Politics of Women's Spirituality* (London and New York, 1982), pp. 138-51:139. Debrida gives as further examples Penelope's cloth and the myth of Arachne.

41 See Wendy Griffin, 'The Goddess Net', in Lorne L. Dawson and Douglas E. Cowan, (eds), *Religion Online: Finding Faith on the Internet* (New York and London, 2004), pp. 189-203.

Despite the generally modest level of artistic creativity and aestheticism, Neopagan websites have the merit to revise and to change the traditional Western relationship between text and image, where text (word) opposes image, and one of the two is subordinated to the other. The relationship is more ambiguous than one might assume, and Western culture would probably be more aware of this had writing been considered as art, as it is in other cultures where written signs are pictures.

The ambiguity of the relationship between texts and images on a screen is also highlighted by the presence of commercial banners on religious web-pages. Particularly when the layout has been accurately designed by the webmaster, the balance and harmony of the elements composing the page (texts, pictures, logo) is inevitably altered by the presence of elements upon which the author has no control. The resulting, often dynamic screenshot (several banners contain moving images) ends up being perceived by surfers as an image rather than as a text.

As for the significance of Neopagan websites, we could read the setting up of a website as a creative act and one more form of Neopagan art, analogous to the setting up of an altar. Sabina Magliocco has interpreted ritual as a form of Pagan art.[42] The setting up of a website can be read as an art form; from collecting materials such as logos, old texts and images, the re-shaping and even creating new materials such as new hymns, new images, and finally ordering them on the screen.

I have argued that (as other Neopagan art forms, including rituals), Neopagan websites can be read as mythopoeic expressions. Mythopoesis takes the form of a re-writing of myths so they are re-told in a coherent narrative form, (for example the hymns composed by Hearthstone), by alluding to and re-interpreting a story through text and images (as in the case of the website on the Eleusinian Mysteries), or by creating new and re-worked visual representations of gods and goddesses. Such mythopoeic recreation supports a specific worldview, which can be either slightly conservative, as it is the case of the Shrine of the goddess Athena, or expressing a liberal, inclusive and feminist perspective (Hermes, Eleusinian Mysteries). Although the limited number of websites examined here does not allow general conclusions to be drawn, what is clear is the presence on Neopagan websites of mythopoeic expressions that combine text and images to recreate old myths in a unique, original and sometimes surprising way. Moreover, the development of such combinations and blending of text and image, medium and message, merged with hyper-textual links, appears to be an interesting new element, well worth further analysis.

Bibliography

Anderson, Pamela S., 'Myth and Feminist Philosophy', in Kevin Schibrack, (ed.), *Thinking Through Myths, Philosophical Perspectives* (London and New York: Routledge, 2002): 101-22.

---

42 Sabina Magliocco, *Neo-Pagan Sacred Art and Altars: Making Things Whole* (Jackson, 2001).

Askehave, Inger, and Anne Ellerup Nielsen, 'Digital Genres: A Challenge to Traditional Genre Theory', *Information Technology & People*, 18/2 (2005): 120-41.

Bingham, Nick, 'Unthinkable Complexity? Cyberspace Otherwise', in Mike Crang, Phil Crang and Jon May, (eds), *Virtual Geographies: Bodies, Space & Relations* (London and New York: Routledge 1999): 244-60.

Charbonneaux, Jean, Roland Martin and François Villard, *La Grecia arcaica*, (Milano: Rizzoli, 1988), 3rd ed. trans. Marcello Lenzini and Libero Sosio. (Or.tit. *Grèce archaïque*. Paris: Gallimard, 1968).

Cowan, Douglas E., *Cyberhenge: Modern Pagans on the Internet* (New York and London: Routledge, 2005).

Crang, Mike, Phil Crang and Jon May, (eds), *Virtual Geographies: Bodies, Space and Relations* (London and New York: Routledge, 1999).

Dawson, Lorne, L., and Douglas E. Cowan, (eds), *Religion Online: Finding Faith on the Internet* (New York and London: Routledge, 2004).

Debrida, Bella, 'Drawing from Mythology in Women's Quest for Selfhood' in Charlene Spretnak, (ed.), *The Politics of Women's Spirituality* (London and New York: Doubleday, 1982): 138-51.

Graham, Elaine, '"Nietzsche Gets a Modem": Transhumanism and the Technological Sublime', *Literature & Theology*, 16/1 (2001): 65-80.

Griffin, Wendy, 'The Goddess Net', in Lorne L. Dawson and Douglas E. Cowan, (eds), *Religion Online: Finding Faith on the Internet* (New York and London: Routledge, 2004):189-203.

Harvey, Graham, 'Fantasy in the Study of Religions: Paganism as Observed and Enhanced by Terry Pratchett', *Diskus* 6 (2000). 16 Jul. 2006 http://web.uni-marburg.de/religionswissenschaft/journal/diskus/harvey_2.html.

Helland, Christopher, 'Popular Religion and the World Wide Web: A Match Made in (Cyber) Heaven', in Lorne L. Dawson and Douglas E. Cowan, (eds), *Religion Online: Finding Faith on the Internet* (New York and London: Routledge, 2004): 23-35.

Hutton, Ronald, *The Triumph of the Moon: A History of Modern Pagan Witchcraft* (Oxford: Blackwell, 1999).

Jencson, Linda, 'Neopaganism and the Great Mother Goddess: Anthropology as Midwife to a New Religion', *Anthropology Today*, 5/2 (1989): 2-4.

Jones, Prudence, 'The European Native Tradition', in Joanne Pearson, Richard H. Roberts, and Geoffrey Samuel, (eds), *Nature Religion Today: Paganism in the Modern World* (Edinburgh: Edinburgh University Press, 1998): 77-88.

Jones, Prudence and Nigel Pennick, *A History of Pagan Europe* (London and New York: Routledge, 1995).

Leland, Charles, Godfrey, *Aradia or, The Gospel of the Witches* (London: D.Nutt, 1899).

MacWilliams, Mark W., 'Virtual Pilgrimages on the Internet', *Religion,* 33/4 (2002): 315-35.

Magliocco, Sabina, *Neo-Pagan Sacred Art and Altars. Making Things Whole* (Jackson: University Press of Mississippi, 2001).

O'Leary, Stephen D., 'Cyberspace as Sacred Space: Communicating Religion on Computer Networks', *Journal of the American Academy of Religion*, 64/4 (1996): 781-807. Reprinted in Lorne L. Dawson and Douglas E. Cowan, (eds), *Religion Online. Finding Faith on the Internet* (New York and London: Routledge, 2004): 37-58.

Pearson, Joanne, Richard H. Roberts and Geoffrey Samuel, 'Introduction', in Joanne Pearson, Richard H. Roberts, and Geoffrey Samuel, (eds), *Nature Religion Today: Paganism in the Modern World* (Edinburgh: Edinburgh University Press, 1998): 1-12.

Pearson, Joanne, Richard H. Roberts, and Geoffrey Samuel, (eds), *Nature Religion Today: Paganism in the Modern World* (Edinburgh: Edinburgh University Press, 1998): 1-12.

Schibrack, Kevin, (ed.), *Thinking Through Myths, Philosophical Perspectives* (London and New York: Routledge, 2002).

Spretnak, Charlene, (ed.), *The Politics of Women's Spirituality* (London and New York: Doubleday, 1982).

Young, Glenn, 'Reading and Praying Online. The Continuity of Religion Online and Online Religion in Internet Christianity', in Lorne L. Dawson and Douglas E. Cowan, (eds), *Religion Online: Finding Faith on the Internet* (New York and London: Routledge, 2004): 93-105.

Internet Sources

Ave Diana. 6 Apr.2007 http://www.avediana.net/pages/1/page1.html.

Bibliotheca Arcana. 15 Apr.2007 http://www.cs.utk.edu/~mclennan/BA/.

Brighid Goddess and Saint. 31 Mar.2007 http://www.brighid.org.uk/about.html.

The Eleusinian Mysteries: Healing and Transformation. 31 Mar.2007 http://www. geocities.com/Athens/Aegean/3193/stations2.htm.

Hagne Persephone. 4 Apr.2007 http://persephones.250free.com/.

Devotion. A simple shrine to the Gods of the Greeks: Gaia. 6 Apr.2007 http://www. geocities.com/hellenicdevotions/gaia.html.

A Virtual Temple Honoring Hermes. 4 Apr.2007 http://paganinstitute.org/T/Hermes. html.

Hymnodia Project. 18 Dec.2006 http://www.hellenion.org/Hymnodia.html.

Perseus. 05 Apr.2007 http://www.perseus.tufts.edu/.

Project Gutenberg. 05 Apr.2007 http://www.gutenberg.net/.

Sacred Texts. 05 Apr.2007 http://www.sacred-texts.com/pag/index.htm.

The Shrine of the Goddess Athena. 15 Apr.2007 http://www.goddess-athena.org/ Temple/index.htm.

The Two Goddesses. 4 Apr.2007 http://paganinstitute.org/T/2goddesses.html.

Theoi Project. 31 Mar.2007 http://www.theoi.com/.

Thiasos Lusios. 18 Dec.2006 http://www.winterscapes.com/thiasoslusios/.

Chapter 12

Word and Image: Burgess, Zeffirelli, and Jesus the Man of Nazareth

Graham Holderness

The genre of film is radically different from the Gospel genre. The latter, as well we know, is the medium of the written word, clear, elementary, the word of faith, born and transmitted through the oral tradition, a holy word which for Christians is inspired and guaranteed by God … *En outré, la parole filmique n'est jamais d'inspiration divine, quelle soit approuvée et louangée par les autorités ecclésiastiques ou non.* [Furthermore the filmic word is never divinely inspired or guaranteed, regardless of how approved or praised it might be by ecclesiastical authorities].[1]

The distinction offered here by Lloyd Baugh encapsulates the confrontation of disciplines that occurs when academic theology and film studies attempt to converge. Here, a Jesuit academic invokes what seems to me a simplistic understanding of the Gospels, traditional in religious studies, but highly controversial anywhere else; and a reductive definition of film, derived uncritically from the secular discipline of film criticism and theory. It is possible, in my view, to accept the Gospels as the word of faith, but also to regard them, even in the process of their original composition, as sophisticated literary texts, and as writings that certainly cannot be accessed independently of the vast project of literary interpretation, adaptation and appropriation that has been going on in and around them for over two millennia. Conversely the medium of film is no more immune than any other art form to divine inspiration. Notwithstanding its technological dimensions and context of popular entertainment, film also has 'the potential' as David Jasper says of literature 'to reconfigure theological discourse'.[2]

This chapter focuses on Franco Zeffirelli's TV film *Jesus of Nazareth* (1977) and its tortuous relationship with Anthony Burgess's novel *Man of Nazareth* (1979), in the light of Baugh's distinction. The relationship between any Jesus-film and the literary and other texts on which it is predicated is always much more complex than film-makers care to admit. Directors will claim that their primary source is the

---

1 Lloyd Baugh, *Imaging Jesus in Film: Sources and Influences, Limits and Possibilities* (Saskatchewan, 2007), p. 5. This Canadian lecture alternates between English and French (p. 34, n. 9).

2 David Jasper, *The Sacred Desert: Religion, Literature, Art and Culture* (Oxford, 2004), p. 5.

Gospels,[3] but even these foundational sources exist of course in multiple and contested versions, and in a tangled relationship with non-canonical apocryphal narratives.[4] The Gospels are silent on many aspects of Jesus' human existence in which the agent of historical or biographical reconstruction will naturally be interested.[5] Centuries of narrative interpolation and redaction overlay the Gospel texts; and centuries of traditional appropriation have elaborated on the Gospel narratives, producing stories and images that in popular culture have become inseparable from the Gospels themselves.[6] Two millennia of scriptural exegesis and interpretation, produced by innumerable different Christian sects, interpose between the contemporary artist and the texts on which his or her art is based.[7]

Zeffirelli commissioned Burgess to write a screenplay for his planned TV film, which was later developed by Zeffirelli and the Italian screenwriter Suso Cecchi d'Amico. Burgess's script was preceded by a draft of the novel that was later published as *Man of Nazareth*.[8] The novel and the film are so radically different that most people assume little of Burgess's script survived the making of the film, and certainly Burgess in his autobiography implied that this was the case. To complicate the issue further, the film's producer Vincenzo Labella commissioned a

---

3   For instance Mel Gibson claimed this for *The Passion of the Christ*, a film based more immediately on a nineteenth century text, *The Dolorous Passion of Our Lord Jesus Christ*, and incorporating traditional non-scriptural elements such as the Stations of the Cross. See Mel Gibson, 'Foreword', in Ken Duncan and Philippe Antonello, *The Passion: Photography from the Movie 'The Passion of the Christ'* (USA, 2004); and Graham Holderness, '"Animated Icons": Narrative and Liturgy in *The Passion of the Christ'*, *Literature and Theology,* 19:4 (2005), pp. 384-401.

4   'We have not only competing images of Jesus in the New Testament itself, but also additional images from non-canonical material'. Douglas K. Mikkelson and Amy C. Gregg, *'King of Kings': A Silver Screen Gospel* (Lanham, NY, 2001), p. 6.

5   See Anthony Burgess, *Man of Nazareth* (New York, 1979), p. 79.

6   'In many of the Jesus-films, the source material for the portrait of Jesus is not the canonical gospels but rather the non-canonical, apocryphal gospels or popular-devotional biographies of Jesus'. Lloyd Baugh, *Imaging the Divine: Jesus and Christ-figures in Film* (Kansas City, 1997), p. 4.

7   A more textually purist approach is evident in Pasolini's *Il Vangelo Secondo Matteo*, which makes it something of a *cause celebre* for scholars of the Jesus-film. Richard Walsh in *Reading the Gospels in the Dark: Portrayals of Jesus in Film* (Harrisburg, P.A, 2003) attempts to pair up Jesus-films with specific gospels.

8   Critics sometimes appear unsure about the sequence. For example, Frank Kermode states: 'His new novel is based on the scripts that he wrote for the television production' ('Love and Do as You Please', *New York Review of Books*, 16th August 1979, p. 44); and an anonymous reviewer in *Booklist*: 'Burgess developed this impressive novel from his screenplay' (quoted in Paul Boytinck, *Anthony Burgess: An Annotated Bibliography and Reference Guide* (New York, 1985), p. 82). Boytinck is correct: 'On this novel, first published in France, Burgess based his filmscript for Zeffirelli's *Jesus of Nazareth*' (*Annotated Bibliography,* p. 82). The novel was published first in French translation as *L'Homme de Nazareth*, trans. Georges Belmont and Hortense Chabrier (Paris, 1976), and in Italian as *L'Uomo di Nazareth*, trans. Liana Burgess (Milano, 1978) before publication in English as *Man of Nazareth* (New York, 1979).

'novelization', 'based on the film' and 'from the script', written by the prolific Scots academic theologian and popular communicator William Barclay, and published in 1977. Barclay claimed:

> The book is based on Anthony Burgess's script of the television film of Jesus of Nazareth. The script of the film was in my hands when I wrote it, and there are large areas of the book where I did no more than change the script into narrative form.[9]

This was done however without the knowledge or approval of Burgess, who recalled waking up one Sunday in May 1977 to find Barclay's book topping the best-seller lists, 'It was made out of my own script for the Zeffirelli series, the script being a commodity bought by the production company, its novelization assigned to a novelizing hand not mine'.[10] The result was quite strikingly different from either Burgess's novel or Zeffirelli's film.

I will initially describe the process by which Burgess and Zeffirelli together and separately approached their respective tasks of novelist and director. Then I will explore, through comparative examples, the parallels and dissimilarities between novel, film, and to a lesser extent novelization. The primary aim of this study is to describe the relationship between film and novel as an illuminating model of how in practice the 'life' of Jesus is reproduced as fiction and as film. In addition to mapping this complex process of textual production I will seek to disentangle some of the theological ideas implicit in, and disseminated by, the fertile matrix of these linguistic and audio-visual artefacts.

Burgess explained that his customary method was to draft a novel before producing a scenario, and the draft *Man of Nazareth* was written in the summer of 1975.[11] In his autobiography Burgess, a self-confessed unbeliever[12] committed to collaborating with orthodox Catholics, appears acutely conscious of his own sceptical and independent viewpoint on matters of faith and doctrine. He re-read the Gospels, and distinguished between the synoptic Gospels and the 'highly romantic novella written by St John', the Gospel of choice for orthodox Roman Catholicism, and therefore naturally Zeffirelli's own 'romantic preference'.[13] The Evangelists leave him 'dissatisfied with their telling of the sacred story', as 'They remain fine propagandists but mediocre novelists'.[14]

---

9   William Barclay, *Jesus of Nazareth* (London, 1977), p. 8. The 'novelization' clearly had some official status beyond the producer's commissioning; Lew Grade signed copies and distributed them to cast members. Barclay's theological writing is not without value, but his novelization of the TV film has no literary merit, and often reads like lesson-plans for Sunday school instruction.

10   Anthony Burgess, 'Lord Grade's Will', *Observer Review*, 20 May 1977, p. 28.

11   Anthony Burgess, 'Author's Note', *The Kingdom of the Wicked* (London, 1985), p. 379; Anthony Burgess, *You've Had Your Time: Being the Second Part of the Confessions of Anthony Burgess* (London, 1999), p. 303.

12   Anthony Burgess, 'On Being a Lapsed Catholic', *Triumph*, February 1967, p. 31.

13   Burgess, *You've Had Your Time*, p. 304.

14   Ibid.

Out of this draft novel came a script which Zeffirelli considered 'ludicrous'.[15] Burgess was not at all surprised. He thought it provident that members of the ecclesiastical advisory panel, appointed by the production company Radiotelevisione Italia to advise on the project, had not read the draft novel, which even at that stage contained a married Christ.[16] Burgess admits that he never delivered a 'satisfactory script', and that Suso Cecchi d'Amico also failed to produce what Zeffirelli required. Burgess implies that Zeffirelli then simply re-wrote the script himself. Burgess proposed publishing *Man of Nazareth* in tandem with the broadcasting of the film, but Labella had already pre-empted this by facilitating Barclay's novelization. Zeffirelli also established literary ownership of the project by publishing in 1977 his own 'spiritual diary' of the making of the film, *Il Mio Gesu*.[17]

With some sourness Burgess comments that his book had to be published in French and Italian before being published in English, and then not in Britain but America.[18] Clearly he felt disowned by the very successful Zeffirelli project. He makes very little comment in these reminiscences on the film itself, but the overall impression created here is that, in his perception, very little of his contribution survived into the making of *Jesus of Nazareth*.

Zeffirelli's description of the process by which Burgess produced the script is interestingly different from Burgess's own. Zeffirelli states: 'In only sixteen days he sketched a skeletal story of six acts',[19] a draft script 'profoundly permeated with the tone and meaning of the Gospel narrative', but with dialogue that 'did not fit the Gospel records'. Hence 'a conflict arose between my aim and the historical, theological and mystical reworking of the Gospels that Burgess had prepared'.[20] Burgess wanted to give Jesus 'mere human words'; while Zeffirelli felt that the words attributed to Jesus in the Gospels were definitive and 'irreplaceable'.[21] Burgess's construction of a 'humanly believable' Jesus was destructive of Zeffirelli's own higher Christology: 'Burgess ultimately destroyed the charismatic, mystical stature that for me sustained the character of Christ'. However, Burgess in Zeffirelli's recollection had given him enough to be going on with:

> In those sixteen days of work, carried almost to the limits of human endurance, Burgess dashed off the story of Christ as he remembered it. And so he put an outline at our disposal, a framework that ... embodied all the story lines I as director needed for the film.[22]

---

15 Ibid.

16 Ibid.

17 Franco Zeffirelli, *Il Mio Gesu* (Milan, 1977); *Franco Zeffirelli's Jesus: A Spiritual Diary*, trans. Willis J. Egan (San Francisco, 1984).

18 According to Boytinck the novel was rejected by American and British publishers. See Boytinck, *Annotated Bibliography*, p. 82.

19 Zeffirelli, *A Spiritual Diary*, p. 39.

20 Ibid.

21 Ibid., p. 44.

22 Ibid., p. 43.

Burgess then, according to Zeffirelli 'took leave of us' and was not heard from for two years. Zeffirelli claims that Burgess saw the first print of the film and was 'profoundly moved' and approved it.[23]

Zeffirelli clearly did not object to the structure of Burgess's draft script, or for the most part with the Gospel episodes and incidents he chose to include and exclude. The six-part narrative structure is visible in the novel, evident in the film and closely copied by Barclay in the novelization.[24] Gospel materials common to novel and film include the betrothal of Joseph and Mary, the Annunciation, the birth of Jesus in Bethlehem, Jesus and the Elders, the Baptism and the calling of the disciples. Also present are various miracle cures (of a possessed man, a paralytic, a man born blind, the Centurion's servant, Jairus' daughter and Lazarus) and miraculous interventions (the draught of fishes, the miracle of the loaves and fishes). We hear the Sermon on the Mount, the Paternoster, several of the parables, and we see Peter's confession of faith, the woman taken in adultery and Jesus chasing the money-changers from the Temple. Novel and film both conclude with a full repertory of Passion events, the Last Supper, Gethsemane, the Trial, the Crucifixion and the Resurrection.

Significant Gospel episodes missing from the film, but present in the novel, are represented only by the Temptation in the Wilderness, and the Wedding at Cana; while missing from both are the Transfiguration, and the story of Jesus walking on the waves. The film also preserves some material invented by Burgess that has no precedent in the scriptures, such as Jesus meeting Barabbas, the Rabbi from Nazareth accompanying Mary to Golgotha, and in particular the invented character of Zerah, who plays a major role in the events leading to the crucifixion, and serves to completely reorientate the role of Judas.[25] Thus in terms of content, structure and in terms of their incorporation of biblical and invented material, novel and film remain very close to one another.

However, there is a contrast apparent from the very opening words of the novel. Burgess frames his novel with opening and closing reflections from a narrator, 'Azor

---

23 Ibid., p. 44. See also Franco Zeffirelli, *An Autobiography* (New York, 1986), p.275 and p.277.

24 Barclay's Chapters 1-6 cover virtually the same ground as Burgess's Books 1-6, except that Barclay's Chapter 2 includes the Temptation in the Wilderness which opens Burgess's Book 3. In the 347 minute broadcast version of the film, the chapters or 'scenes' are distributed evenly across the divisions of Burgess' six books, especially the sequence from Book 3 to Book 6. Part Two of the film is shorter, not surprisingly, as most of Burgess's Book 2 is concerned with Jesus' married life. References to the film are to the DVD edition *Jesus of Nazareth*, produced by Vincenzo Labella, directed by Franco Zeffirelli (ITC Entertainment/ Television Italia, 1977; DVD, Granada Ventures Ltd., 2006). This recording represents the 374 minute version initially broadcast in two parts on Palm and Easter Sundays of 1977 by NBC Television. The film is divided into four episodes, each sub-divided into 12 or 13 'chapters'. My references to the film cite episode and chapter of the DVD.

25 Zerah is Burgess's most obvious and isolable contribution to the screenplay. Baugh strangely refers to the Zerah of the film as an 'invention of Zeffirelli'. Although he acknowledges in a note that Zerah is there in Burgess's novel, this seems to be an afterthought, as his whole discussion presupposes that Zeffirelli invented Zerah '*ex novo*' (Baugh's phrase). See Baugh, *Imaging Jesus*, p. 76.

the son of Sadoc'. The narrator is characterized in some detail, and given some degree of obtrusive presence within the text (though for most of the narrative he recedes into invisibility). Azor is a writer and a linguist fluent in many tongues; he has many nicknames; he is learned and of a philosophical inclination; and he takes a sceptical and independent view of the material he is presenting to the reader. In other words he is a semi-transparent proxy for the polyglot, polymathic, pseudonymous, sceptical author Anthony Burgess himself.

The device of a narrator enables Burgess to avoid that 'absolute directness of presentation'[26] characteristic of the Gospels, replicated by the Hollywood Jesus-film, and which Zeffirelli clearly wanted to emulate. Instead the text becomes pervaded by modernist irony and detachment, distance and indirection. Azor sees the practice of crucifixion as evidencing 'a great principle of wrong in the world'[27], which is then extrapolated to a description of the universe as dualistic in nature: 'the world is a twofold creation', a Manichean balance of good and evil, light and darkness.[28] At the end of the novel Azor makes his free-thinking perspective explicit: 'I am no Christian'. He anticipates that 'official' accounts of Jesus will be written, and will acquire the status of enforced orthodoxy.[29] His version makes no claim to be a sacred text, but is rather the kind of 'disinterested' account that could be produced only by a 'non-believer'.[30] Burgess styled himself a 'Manichean', asserting that 'duality is the ultimate reality',[31] and was clearly much more concerned here with promoting his own postmodern point of view on the universe, than attempting a historical reconstruction of early Christianity, or with satisfying the theological requirements of the project.

Zeffirelli stated that one of his objectives was to recreate in film 'the historical Jewish Jesus'.[32] Burgess also conceived of the project very much in historical terms, reading by way of preparation Josephus and other documentary sources, pursuing Jesus as a character 'who grew', in Zeffirelli's words, 'out of the cultural, social and historical background of the Israel of his time'.[33] To this extent Burgess was working within the parameters of the Jesus-novel as defined in Theodore Kiolkowski's term

---

26 Bruce Babington and Peter William Evans, *Biblical Epics: Sacred Narrative in the Hollywood Cinema* (Manchester, 1993), p. 98.

27 Burgess, *Man of Nazareth*, p. 5.

28 Ibid., p. 6. Azor is supposed to be writing in the first century CE before the composition of the Gospels, so he anticipates Manicheism by two centuries.

29 Ibid., p. 354.

30 Ibid., p. 355.

31 Burgess quoted in John Cullinan, 'Interview with Anthony Burgess', *Paris Review*, 56 (1973), reprinted in Geoffrey Aggeler, *Critical Essays on Anthony Burgess* (London, 1986), p. 44. See also Burgess, 'The Manicheans', *Times Literary Supplement*, 3rd March 1966; John J. Stinson, 'The Manichee World of Anthony Burgess', in Harold Bloom, (ed.), *Anthony Burgess: Modern Critical Views* (New York, 1987), pp. 51-62 and Harold Bloom, 'Introduction', *Anthony Burgess: Modern Critical Views*, pp. 4-5.

32 Zeffirelli, *Autobiography*, p. 275.

33 Ibid., p. 274.

'fictionalizing biography'.[34] In fact Burgess used an almost identical phrase when he affirmed that the historical novel 'is at its best when it is a fictionalized biography'.[35] As Martina Ghosh-Schellhorn says, however, *Man of Nazareth* is not a fictionalized biography, but rather a 'parody of the mode of fictionalizing biography through the character of Azor the narrator'. The novel does not take you closer into a more intimate understanding of Jesus in his history, but rather displaces and diverts the object of its representation via scepticism, irony and grotesque comedy. All this stylistic postmodernism, this 'overtly emphasized artificiality', is consistent with Burgess's 'grotesque vision',[36] but incompatible with a positive and affirmative Christian spirituality. What is left of history, biography and faith in a novel which, to quote a negative review, 'behaves throughout as though the secret of revitalization lay solely in lightness or off-handedness – in empty urbanity, breezy colloquialism and the rhetoric of scepticism and comical play'?[37] Did Burgess produce, in short, a postmodern version of the liberal-theological Jesus-novel in the tradition of George Moore, as one reviewer read it: 'the portrait of Jesus as a good and brilliant man for whom the kingdom of heaven could be on earth'?[38] Or did he rather produce, as Gerald Twomey put it, 'a "fifth" gospel': 'Burgess's novel succeeds admirably in depicting Jesus as both true God and true man'?[39]

In order to explore this problem I propose to examine a number of episodes in novel and film where the events derived from the Gospels initially involved some form of supernatural agency. Although both novel and film omit two such incidents, the Transfiguration and Jesus walking on the waves, both novel and film include key kerygmatic events from the life of Jesus such as the Annunciation to Mary; the Baptism; the raising of Lazarus; the Last Supper with the Institution of the Eucharist; and the Crucifixion and Resurrection of Christ.

In the novel both the Annunciation, and its precursor the vision of Zacharias in the Temple, are given a full-dress supernatural treatment. The Archangel Gabriel appears in the concrete solidity of a tangible apparition to both Zacharias and Mary. Burgess does not suspend his ironic and humorous tone for a heavenly revelation: Gabriel is busy curiously cleaning his fingernails, 'as if he had only recently been issued with them';[40] and when he dissolves into air, his fingernails are the last things to disappear.[41] In the Annunciation to Mary, the angel disturbs the family pets, a

---

34 Theodore Kiolkowski, *Fictional Transfigurations of Jesus* (Princeton, N.J., 1972), p. 13.

35 Burgess quoted in Martina Ghosh-Schellhorn, *Anthony Burgess: A Study in Character* (Frankfurt-Am-Main, 1981), p. 156.

36 'The true grotesque vision sees the position of man in the universe as radically incongruous. Given hints and longings of immortality, man must live in an organism that he realizes all too painfully is finite'. Burgess, 'The Manicheans', quoted in Stinson, 'The Manichee World', p. 55.

37 Benjamin de Mott, 'The Gospel According to Burgess', *The New York Times Book Review,* 15th April 1979. p. 20..

38 Anon., *Kirkus Reviews*, 47:4 (15 February 1979), p. 206.

39 Gerald Twomey, 'Life Taken Whole', *America*, 140:23-25 (23 June 1979), p. 517.

40 Burgess, *Man of Nazareth*, p. 15.

41 Ibid., p. 16.

cat and a dog. Gabriel speaks words very close to those of Luke, though cast into a more idiomatic style. He enchants the cat who leans against his ankles, and falls over when the angel disappears.[42]

In these passages Burgess finds a playful and facetious way of bringing the supernatural onto the same level as the natural, and thereby transmitting the full miraculous content of the scriptures in the medium of fictional prose. The formal language characteristic of these exchanges in the Bible is cleverly adapted so that colloquial observations lead easily into the great familiar scriptural utterances. There is humour and irony, but no satire or historical criticism. The comedy does not undermine the spiritual realism: after all, as Elizabeth says, it is possible that God Himself take an amused view of the world: 'May one say that God is a laughing God and dearly loves a jest?'[43]

Burgess's dramatization of the Baptism in the Jordan is, by contrast, entirely dismissive of mystery and supernatural revelation. In the Gospels the Baptism represents a moment of epiphany, in which Jesus is recognized as the Lamb of God, acknowledged as the Son of God by a voice from heaven and marked by the appearance of the Holy Spirit in the form of a dove. In *Man of Nazareth* John recognizes Jesus, but only because he is already well-known to him. Azor the narrator rejects the 'superstitious tales' that have 'obscured' this event, stories involving birds and sudden accessions of light.[44] John is baptising a garrulous old man, who seems to speak the gospel words: 'This is my beloved son ...' John asks him what he said, and it was only 'it didn't take long'.[45] Burgess has removed any basis for perceiving this event as miraculous, as an extraordinary moment of epiphany through recognition, or as a manifest revelation of divine favour.

The raising of Lazarus is by contrast confronted directly as a genuine miracle. There is no doubt whatsoever that Lazarus is dead and decomposing, and that Jesus brings him back to life. Even doubting Thomas differentiates this revival from the earlier awakening of Jairus' daughter: 'I don't think this one here was asleep'.[46] Jesus uses the Johannine words 'I am the Resurrection and the Life', and the incident is the immediate precursor of his entry into Jerusalem. Burgess hedges the miracle with critical and sceptical suggestions. He notes that Lazarus' life was not worth saving, since the rest of it was 'wholly vicious'.[47] Thomas questions Lazarus about what it's like to be dead, but he remembers nothing. 'God ... gives nothing away', comments Thomas.[48] And Judas is inspired by the miracle to rush to carry the 'good news' to his contact in the Sanhedrin, and thus to begin the process of Jesus' betrayal. But all this is in keeping with the Gospel of John, so the miracle is left to stand on record.

Burgess's narration of the Last Supper, with the Institution of the Eucharist also evokes the supernatural. Although the event does not entail any miraculous incident,

---

42 Ibid., pp. 25-6.
43 Ibid., p. 17.
44 Ibid., p. 121.
45 Ibid., p. 122.
46 Ibid., p. 237.
47 Ibid., p. 238.
48 Ibid., p. 237.

in representing the very historical foundation of Christian worship, it is predicated on and expressive of, an unmistakably divine power preparing to enact a sacrifice of redemption. Burgess shirks nothing of the Catholic meaning of the Eucharist, depending heavily on John's Gospel, and giving Jesus speeches that draw directly on the definitions of faith made by the early church councils. He speaks of his own immolation as 'the last of the sacrifices of flesh and blood' and of its salvific nature: 'it will be made to redeem mankind of all its sins'.[49] The sacrifice must not only be remembered but repeated, re-enacted daily in the ritual of the Mass. Jesus insists that the Eucharistic sacrifice will involve the real presence of the divine: 'when the words are spoken, it is also my body, my presence'.[50] Jesus even anticipates the Reformation critique of the Eucharistic real presence, saying that the bread and wine in the future will be interpreted merely as symbols. But they do not constitute 'mere remembrance', but actual presence: 'I must be truly with mankind in these forms'.[51] Frank Kermode comments that this scene 'insists a little more than it had to on the doctrine of the Real Presence'.[52] By using the Johannine version as the master-text, and by invoking the language of Nicaea and Chalcedon, Burgess has welded his fiction so closely to Catholic tradition that the reader has little choice but to accept (or reject) an affirmation of the Eucharistic mystery.

These examples seem to reveal that Burgess was apt to strain at a gnat and swallow a camel. He demystifies the Baptism in the Jordan into a mere brief encounter; and yet narrates as miraculous the Annunciation and the Raising of Lazarus, and uncompromisingly promotes an orthodox Roman Catholic view of the Eucharist. Finally Burgess treats the Crucifixion and Resurrection with the same apparently random mixture of scepticism and faith. Azor discusses 'the legends that have accumulated about this moment' and disposes of them as mere superstitions. The storm was coming anyway; there was no earthquake; the veil of the Temple was rent only by an old priest falling and tearing it. Finally, Azor accounts 'in the light of probability' for the story of Jesus' body transfixed by a spear producing water and blood, by suggesting that these details arose from the corpse's spontaneous phallic erection and involuntary emission of semen.[53]

And yet, despite all this, in the following chapters, the tomb is empty, and Jesus appears as a resurrected man. Claiming to be happy back in the flesh again, and with his mission at an end, he resembles D. H. Lawrence's 'Man Who Died'.[54] But unlike Lawrence's Christ, Burgess's Jesus affirms that he has achieved a conquest of death ('there is no death'), and reassures the disciples that he will be with them always, 'even unto the end of the world'.[55]

---

49 Ibid., p. 281.
50 Ibid., p. 283.
51 Ibid.
52 Kermode, 'Love and Do as You Please', p. 45.
53 Burgess, *Man of Nazareth*, pp. 325-6.
54 D. H. Lawrence, 'Man Who Died', *The Escaped Cock* (Paris: Black Sun Press, 1929).
55 Ibid., p. 352.

Burgess's reasons for accepting the Jesus of Nazareth commission were opportunistic and mercenary.[56] Zeffirelli's were by contrast primarily religious and evangelical. A committed Catholic, he saw himself as literally called to a missionary vocation, to take the good news of Christ to the world through film and television. Although anxious to secure Catholic approval of his work, he conceived of his audience as universal. Hence his Jesus had to be an ecumenical figure who would appeal to everyone, 'acceptable to all denominations'.[57]

Zeffirelli evidently felt under some pressure from his Catholic affiliates to produce a 'low Christology' Jesus who would be virtually indistinguishable from any other common man of his time, but his attempt to 'show the humanity of Christ'[58]might seem to entail showing him as ordinary: 'There were still those who wanted an interpretation other than mine: Christ as the common man, Christ as someone indistinguishable from those around him'.[59]

The producers objected to the way in which Zeffirelli ensured his Jesus would be highly visible and distinctive: 'Those that held this view sniped away at my film for turning Christ into a star and for surrounding him with the famous faces of Hollywood'. Zeffirelli stuck to his guns and was rescued from this particular pressure by Lew Grade.[60] The criticism voiced there became however the basis of a routine castigation of *Jesus of Nazareth* in reviews and academic criticism. Here for example is Lloyd Baugh:

> Zeffirelli's 'unfortunate decision to use "name" actors' is one of the major flaws of the film, and one of the major reasons for the perceived weakness of his Jesus. The character of Jesus ought to stand out morally and dramatically. Zeffirelli's Jesus gets lost 'in the shuffle' of 'guest stars'.[61]

Baugh criticizes the film for its overtly 'self-aware theatricality' and 'virtuoso composition', which 'draw attention to themselves as fiction rather than to the very real mystery of the life, death and Resurrection of Jesus the Christ they are meant to represent'.[62] Zeffirelli was of course trying to do something quite different. He did not read the Gospels as 'lean ... tough text', nor did he make any attempt to drill down to some pure gospel bedrock by clearing away accrued layers of Catholic

---

56 Burgess, *You've Had Your Time*, p. 303

57 Zeffirelli, *Autobiography*, p. 274.

58 Ibid.

59 Ibid.

60 Ibid. p. 284.

61 Baugh, *Imaging the Divine*, p. 78. Baugh draws heavily on prior opinion: here he is quoting from Roy Kinnard and Tim Davis, *Divine Images: A History of Jesus on the Screen* (New York, 1992), p. 189.

62 Baugh, *Imaging the Divine*, p. 79. Wedded to what he calls the 'lean elliptical, challenging, tough text and style of the gospels', Baugh naturally prefers Pasolini's *Il Vangelo Secondo Matteo* as the definitive Jesus-film. Pasolini's film, Baugh says, 'in the minds of most serious critics' is 'still the greatest, the most authentic, the most religious film on Jesus ever made' (Baugh, *Imaging the Divine*, p. 94.) 'Zeffirelli created a very free adaptation of all four Gospels, in the end producing a work more of fiction than Gospel ... Pasolini, inspired by the raw power of Matthew's text, was determined to be utterly faithful to it'(Ibid., p. 95).

tradition. It is true that he brought to the film his own characteristic skills of design and visual composition, influenced by pictorial theatre and renaissance painting. He also, however, engaged with some of the fundamental problems of realising Jesus on film as they were explored in Burgess's novelistic treatment.

I will now compare Zeffirelli's presentation in the film of the same kerygmatic episodes discussed in the novel: the Annunciation, the Baptism, the raising of Lazarus, the Last Supper and the Resurrection. These analyses will show that the filmic text of *Jesus of Nazareth*, often dismissed as if it were a piece of crude televangelism, was in fact produced from a complex matrix of determinants, all present in the Burgess text, including both high and low Christologies, an interest in historical context, and a willingness to use the medium of film to incorporate the language and gesture of Jewish and Christian liturgical language and worship.

Zefferelli said that when approaching the Annunciation scene, he could not conceive it literally. He 'obviously rejected the idea of having an angel with wings and a halo', which is not far off Burgess's version in the novel:

> Instead, God's message comes in the form of a silent beam of light that passes through a high aperture in the little mud-brick room to fall on the face of the young Madonna.[63]

Baugh comments on this scene that Zeffirelli tries 'rather artificially' to create 'a sense of mystery', 'with light and the sound of wind and almost baroque camera angles and movements'.[64] In fact the artifice of the film here could scarcely be more naturalistic. Zeffirelli gives no physical presence to the heavenly messenger, showing only Mary's reaction to what she alone hears and sees. The wind is just wind sighing through a window and the lighting suggests an enhanced natural light rather than a divine illumination. And yet the scene creates an extraordinary atmosphere of spiritual wonder. Mary at first kneels quite naturally, in rapt attention; then clings to the wall in fear; and finally sinks to her knees in a formal and iconographic posture of prayer. You hear no message, only her reply; you see no angel, only the light on her face. The scene is beautiful in its purity of design; Zeffirelli himself rightly described it as 'heart-stopping'.[65] Perhaps the most compelling aspect of this scene is the way in which Zeffirelli has solved the Christological problem of linking human and divine into a single medium, managing to secure both simplicity and transcendence. For Zeffirelli, this is how God comes into the world; this is how the divine irrupts into the everyday. This is Incarnation.

Zeffirelli's Baptism scene[66] again operates in the opposite way from the novel. The Baptism in the novel is demystified, rationalized and presented as a historical event. Zeffirelli renders the Baptism as a supremely transcendent moment of recognition and acknowledgement, but he does this without a voice from heaven or a descending dove. What the viewer sees first of all is the compelling expression

---

63 Zeffirelli, *Autobiography*, p. 280. The Annunciation is Chapter 1.2 of the film. Barclay restores the angel, who speaks like a scoutmaster: 'God has chosen you for a very precious privilege' (Barclay, *Jesus,* p. 11).

64 Baugh, *Imaging the Divine*, p. 75.

65 Zeffirelli, *Autobiography*, p. 380. See also *Spiritual Diary*, pp. 80-81.

66 Chapter 2.1 of the film.

of wonder and fear on the face of John the Baptist (Michael York) as he recognizes Jesus. The two faces in extreme close-up exchange expressions; but all the charge of meaning is on the face of York, as his expression registers the impact Jesus has on him. This moment exactly captures the spirit of St John's Gospel. For instance, as the light reflects onto John's face rather than glowing from the face of Jesus and the words that in scripture come from heaven, here come through John ('I heard a voice saying..')[67] are displaced as they are in the novel, but returned to their true scriptural and sacramental meaning. John looks upwards, and a dove drifts and circles in the air, quoting rather than representing the iconography of the Gospel. As Jesus walks away, John beckons Andrew and Simon to watch and to follow Jesus, and says, 'Behold the Lamb of God … You must follow him now, not me'. These are the words attributed to John the Baptist in the Gospels and carry all the weight of Old Testament prophecy and are employed economically as an indexical sign to denote John's concession of authority to Jesus. But these formal liturgical words are spoken not just as dialogue or narrative, but also in a choric space of worship opened up within the film by the imagery and drama. They connect the text of the film directly into the language and context of daily Catholic worship.

A similar dimension of extra-contextual scriptural commentary appears in Zeffirelli's scene of the raising of Lazarus.[68] The episode is set firmly within the structure of the Passion story. As Jesus and the disciples are heading for Jerusalem, John and James talk of Jesus' mission: 'He said he was to be put to death … and will rise again'. As Jesus approaches the tomb through the bleached white landscape of the cemetery, camera positions alternate between long shots towards the tomb, and medium shots from inside it. From behind, Jesus kneels in prayer; from within the tomb, the Lazarus view, we see him preparing to exercise his power. The disciples stand behind in medium shot, with John positioned centrally. We hear Jesus pray the words of John 11.41. Then from behind him, John the Evangelist is seen in close-up to quote from the Book of Jonah:

> I went down into the countries underneath the earth,
> to the peoples of the past.
> But you lifted my life from the pit.[69]

Jesus raises his arms, outstretched in power but with an echo of the posture of crucifixion, and Lazarus emerges. Jesus quotes John 11.25: 'he that believes in me though he were dead yet shall he live', a familiar echo from Christian services for the burial of the dead.

---

67 'A voice is heard, which I imagine as resounding in John's inmost conscience and becoming the inner voice of the Baptist', Zeffirelli, *Spiritual Diary*, p. 76. Barclay again restores the Gospel reading: 'and then came a voice from heaven'. Before that John 'had a sudden flash of recognition' (Barclay, *Jesus*, p. 24). Chapter 3.6 of the film.

68 Chapter 3.6 of the film.

69 *Jonah*, from *The Jerusalem Bible* (London: Darton, Longman and Todd, 1966), p. 1495, ll. 8-10. *Jonah* is the only book in this edition to have been translated by J. R. R.Tolkien (see *The Letters of J.R.R. Tolkien*, ed. Humphrey Carpenter (London: George Allen and Unwin, 1981), p. 378.

Thus Zeffirelli has woven his materials together so as to emphasize the theological and dogmatic significance of the raising of Lazarus. The awakening of the dead man is both a demonstration of divine power, and a dress rehearsal for Jesus' own resurrection. The film uses the words of John's Gospel to render the theology explicit, and also incorporates a passage from the Hebrew Bible in order to link Jesus back to Old Testament prophecy. The filmic image is thus both historical and future-oriented, as befits an episode of apocalyptic ('Take away the stone!') awakening. Lazarus stands at the mouth of the grave enfolded from head to foot in his white, anonymising shroud, as a type of humanity. We do not see him divested of his cerements, or restored to individuality again. The familiar echo of the burial service links the spectator's own knowledge of loss with historical bereavement, both mediated through the saving power of Christ.[70]

Zeffirelli's portrayal of the Last Supper, although beautifully composed and lit, with the company seated on the floor in the low-ceilinged upper room, is not presented primarily as spectacle at all.[71] The shots that establish the visual design of the scene are few and short. Most of the drama is concentrated on the faces of Jesus and his disciples. The scene is dramatized more as a sacred ritual or liturgy than as a reconstructed historical event, though it is that too, with its detailed rendering of the traditional Passover feast. But the long expository passages of John 13-17, paralleled by Anthony Burgess's lengthy theological excursions on the meaning of the Eucharist, are here cut down to a text that aligns closely with the language of the Mass. Jesus speaks and acts as much like a priest celebrating Mass as a redeemer instituting that same custom of celebration. The apostles sit facing him, not alongside him as in many Da Vinci-inspired Last Suppers, in the position of a congregation. Thus the scene is anachronistic, in that it shows a group of believers performing a liturgy that has yet to be established, and presupposes a sacrifice that has not yet taken place. When Jesus directs them to take the bread, they simultaneously lift bread to their mouths with the absorption of communicants raising the host to their lips. Jesus makes clear that the Passover feast they are historically celebrating is now superseded, and that from now on a new covenant will unite God and humanity.[72] Matthew holds the chalice and the bread together, as in the elevation of the Mass. The emotions of the scene are those of wonder, rapture and distress. The traditional remembrance of exile embodied in the Passover merges with mourning for the loss that all know is imminent, but has not yet come to pass. The luminous eyes of Jesus are by the end filled with tears and the scene cuts straight to the Agony in the Garden.

---

70 Barclay deviates from both novel and film by restoring Gospel details, showing Jesus delaying his journey, promising glorification and weeping over Lazarus' death. When revived, Lazarus is uncovered by the sisters, and his gaze falls on Jesus. 'The incident' Barclay comments, 'was awesome' (Barclay, *Jesus*, p. 72).

71 Chapter 4.2 of the film.

72 Zeffirelli is unashamedly supersessionist: ' The Last Supper ... marked the moment when Jesus superseded the ancient rite and gave his disciples and all humanity the Eucharistic mystery' (Zeffirelli, *Spiritual Diary*, p. 93).

The Crucifixion[73] scene is presented, as it is in *Man of Nazareth*, very much in terms of the human drama. Zeffirelli allows in a muted thunderstorm and some heavy rain, but otherwise no overtly supernatural events. The emotional pitch is of course at its most extreme, but the significance of the event is not to be read in the language of heavenly signs, but on the faces of the participants: the Centurion, Nicodemus, Mary, Mary Magdalene and John. A most powerful contribution is made by showing Nicodemus (Laurence Olivier) speaking the words of Isaiah on the Suffering Servant. Like John's quoting of Jonah at the Raising of Lazarus, this choric note links the Christian sacrifice back to the Old Testament and forward to the Redemption of humanity.[74]

Zeffirelli's handling of the Resurrection presents the most striking contrast between his Jesus and that of Burgess. In *Il Mio Gesu* he describes an unsuccessful attempt to film a resurrection scene that did not seem to work, as it was veering towards the sentimentality of the Hollywood epic. He prepared to film another scene, which was disrupted by the onset of a huge desert storm: 'From that moment on, the Resurrection scene remained an unkept appointment. For me it was an admission of defeat, or a secret lesson, a reminder of the limits of my professional powers of inspiration. It was a surrender …'[75]

Burgess suggested that Zeffirelli planned to end with the *Pietà* and forgo the Resurrection altogether.[76] Zeffirelli records how he realized the film could not be completed without the Resurrection, and had to search through hours of tape to find a test passage that would serve, a scene of the resurrected Jesus talking to the disciples. Clearly this whole episode caused Zeffirelli much anguish: he tried to alter the account of his 'surrender' when the book was already in press, as noted by his editor Tiziano Barbieri, who added a brief postscript to set the record straight.[77]

The similarities and differences between novel and film are not therefore what one would expect from the explicit credentials of novelist and director. The most extreme contrasts do exist, and accord with their respective 'house styles' of unbelief and orthodoxy: we could not imagine Burgess staging a Pieta in a thunderstorm, or Zeffirelli speculating about post-mortal erection. But as my examples show, Burgess was perfectly willing to narrate wholly supernatural events; while Zeffirelli preserves a remarkable restraint in avoiding any such overt and explicit supernatural reference. Burgess's Annunciation and Baptism are kerygmatic and divinely-staged; Zeffirelli's equivalents are modest and naturalistic. Both novelist and director show the raising of Lazarus and the Resurrection of Jesus as historical events. The unbeliever Burgess confronted the Resurrection with the imperturbable confidence of his own Jesus; while the orthodox Catholic Zeffirelli almost missed it out altogether.

---

73 Chapter 4.10 of the film.

74 Dismissed by Baugh as 'utter theatricality' (Baugh, *Imaging the Divine*, p. 78) this moment is a supremely beautiful liturgical composition that takes film beyond the limits of its secular paradigms.

75 Zeffirelli, *Spiritual Diary*, pp. 95-7

76 'Zeffirelli was not quite orthodox in wishing to end the series with a great *Pietà* … he had to be reminded, gently, that the Resurrection was the whole point of the death'. Burgess, *You've Had Your Time*, p. 307.

77 Zeffirelli, *Spiritual Diary*, pp. 115-16.

In terms of high and low Christologies, Zeffirelli resisted external pressure on him to lower the theological horizon, but in the event delivered a Jesus who is both credibly human, and capable of a divine impact on those around him. Burgess played with both high and low Christologies, but again pays due tribute to the necessity of both in a fully incarnational Christian fiction.

The most compelling evidence for a certain imaginative sympathy between novelist and director, co-existing with the more obvious intellectual and artistic antipathies, is the way in which both novel and film incorporate into their language elements of liturgy and ritual which tie their fictions to gospel intertextuality and traditional Catholic worship. I have shown how this feature connects their respective versions of the Last Supper. Zeffirelli was much criticized for the 'utter theatricality' of those moments in the film where characters quote scripture as choric commentary on the action. Here in fact both novel and film are adhering closely to the Gospels, not as spare simple narratives, but as the dense palimpsests of quotation and re-quotation they really are. In the film, after the Massacre of the Innocents, Zeffirelli inserted a holy unscriptural appearance for Simeon, who emerges on the steps of the Temple and quotes words of lamentation from the prophet Jeremiah (31.15). Or at least the historical Simeon is quoting from Jeremiah. The filmic Simeon is quoting from the New Testament that has not yet been written:

> In Rama was there a voice heard, lamentation, and weeping, and great mourning, Rachel weeping for her children, and would not be comforted, because they were not ... (Matthew 2.17-18).

Or rather both are quoting directly from Antony Burgess' *Man of Nazareth*, where the narrator Azor pre-empts the composition of Matthew's Gospel:

> This, they say, was foretold by Jeremiah the prophet. Something about a voice heard in Rama, weeping and great mourning, Rachael weeping for her children. And she would not be comforted, for her children were no more.[78]

Bibliography

Aggeler, Geoffrey, *Critical Essays on Anthony Burgess* (London: G.K. Hall and Co., 1986).

Anon., *Kirkus Reviews*, 47:4 (15 February 1979).

Babington, Bruce and Peter William Evans, *Biblical Epics: Sacred Narrative in the Hollywood Cinema* (Manchester: Manchester University Press, 1993).

Barclay, William, *Jesus of Nazareth* (London: Collins, 1977).

Baugh, Lloyd, *Imaging the Divine: Jesus and Christ-figures in Film* (Kansas City: Sheed and Ward, 1997).

Baugh, Lloyd, *Imaging Jesus in Film: Sources and Influences, Limits and Possibilities* (Saskatchewan: Campion College, 2007).

---

78 Burgess, *Man of Nazareth*, p. 67.

Bloom, Harold (ed.), 'Introduction', *Anthony Burgess: Modern Critical Views* (New York: Chelsea House Publishers, 1987):4-5.

Bloom, Harold (ed.), *Anthony Burgess: Modern Critical Views* (New York: Chelsea House Publishers, 1987).

Boytinck, Paul, *Anthony Burgess: An Annotated Bibliography and Reference Guide* (New York: Garland Publishing, 1985).

Burgess, Anthony, 'The Manicheans', *Times Literary Supplement*, 3 March 1966.

Burgess, Anthony, 'On Being a Lapsed Catholic', *Triumph*, February 1967.

Burgess, Anthony, 'Lord Grade's Will', *Observer Review,* 20 May 1977.

Burgess, Anthony, *L'Homme de Nazareth,* trans. Georges Belmont and Hortense Chabrier, (Paris: Laffont, 1976).

Burgess, Anthony, *L'Uomo di Nazareth,* trans. Liana Burgess (Milano:Editoriale Nuovo, 1978).

Burgess, Anthony, *Man of Nazareth* (New York: McGraw-Hill, 1979).

Burgess, Anthony, 'Author's Note', *The Kingdom of the Wicked* (London: Hutchinson, 1985).

Burgess, Anthony, *You've Had Your Time: Being the Second Part of the Confessions of Anthony Burgess* (London: Heinemann, 1999).

Cullinan, John, 'Interview with Anthony Burgess', *Paris Review*, 56 (1973), reprinted in Geoffrey Aggeler, *Critical Essays on Anthony Burgess* (London: G.K. Hall and Co., 1986): 44.

de Mott, Benjamin, 'The Gospel According to Burgess', *The New York Times Book Review*, 15th April 1979.

Ghosh-Schellhorn, Martina, *Anthony Burgess: A Study in Character* (Frankfurt-Am-Main: Peter Lang, 1981).

Gibson, Mel, *The Passion of the Christ*, (USA: Icon Distribution, 2004).

Gibson, Mel, 'Foreword', in Ken Duncan and Philippe Antonello, *The Passion: Photography from the Movie 'The Passion of the Christ'* (USA: Icon Distribution, 2004).

Holderness, Graham, '"Animated Icons": Narrative and Liturgy in *The Passion of the Christ', Literature and Theology,* 19:4 (2005).

Jasper, David, *The Sacred Desert: Religion, Literature, Art and Culture* (Oxford: Blackwell, 2004).

Kermode, Frank, 'Love and Do as You Please', *New York Review of Books*, 16th August 1979.

Kinnard, Roy and Davis, Tim, *Divine Images: A History of Jesus on the Screen* (New York: Citadel Press, 1992).

Kiolkowski, Theodore, *Fictional Transfigurations of Jesus* (Princeton, N.J.: Princeton University Press, 1972).

Lawrence, D. H., 'Man Who Died', *The Escaped Cock,* (Paris: Black Sun Press, 1929).

Mikkelson, Douglas K. and Gregg, Amy C., *'King of Kings': A Silver Screen Gospel* (Lanham, NY: University Press of America, 2001).

Pasolini, Pier Paolo, *Il Vangelo Secondo Matteo* (Ano Films, 1964).

Stinson, John, J.,'The Manichee World of Anthony Burgess' in Harold Bloom, (ed.), *Anthony Burgess:Modern Critical Views* (New York: Chelsea House Publishers, 1987):51-62.

The Jerusalem Bible (London: Darton, Longman and Todd, 1966).

Tolkien, J. R. R., *The Letters of J.R.R. Tolkien*, ed. Humphrey Carpenter (London: George Allen and Unwin, 1981).

Twomey, Gerald, 'Life Taken Whole', *America*, 140: 23-25 (23 June 1979).

Walsh, Richard, *Reading the Gospels in the Dark: Portrayals of Jesus in Film* (Harrisburg, P.A.: Trinity Press International, 2003).

Zeffirelli, Franco, *Il Mio Gesu* (Milan: Sperling and Kupfur, Editori-Campi and C., 1977).

Zeffirelli, Franco, *Franco Zeffirelli's Jesus: A Spiritual Diary,* trans. Willis J. Egan (San Francisco: Harper and Rowe, 1984).

Zeffirelli, Franco, *An Autobiography* (New York: Weidenfeld and Nicolson, 1986).

Zeffirelli, *Jesus of Nazareth,* (ITC Entertainment/Television Italia, 1977; DVD, Granada Ventures Ltd., 2006).

Chapter 13

Do Not Hide Your Face From Me: The Sacred and Profane Body in Art and Modern Literature

David Jasper

After the publication of my book *The Sacred Desert* in 2004, the 'death of God' theologian Thomas J. J. Altizer wrote to me with the following words:

> I think I detect one crucial potentiality that is here all too partially fulfilled. And that is the body, and the depths of the body itself, depths which are finally "spirit" as well as body, and yet depths evoked only by an absolute desert, and perhaps unreal and invisible apart from that desert. Ultimately I think that this can only be an evocation of the depths of the Body of the Godhead, and if that Body is a Crucified Body, perhaps it can be most real to us through everything that you call forth as an absolute desert, and not simply a sacred desert in the common sense, but a sacred desert that is an absolutely profane desert.

A little later, Heather Walton reviewed the book, and perhaps rightly pointed out the rather 'boy's own' quality of its fascination with the harsh, lonely desert landscape and its crazy people. In the last paragraph of her review she refers to Michèle Roberts's book *Impossible Saints*, saying:

> Roberts has her own version of the legend of Mary of Egypt, the repentant harlot who disappears naked into the desert. In Roberts' story Mary is the former housekeeper of a Catholic priest who keeps an inn named the Oasis on the edges of the desert and is fond of sunbathing wearing nothing but pink nail varnish. Here she seduces her former employer in a shady courtyard of vines and oleanders. She tempts him with delicious lamb kebabs, cold beers and hot sex. I am fully in agreement with Jasper's concluding intuition that theology of the desert and the theology of the oasis are somehow inextricably intertwined and both need the other. However, while he sojourns with the wild beasts among the ruins, I think I'll be lodging at Mary's.[1]

These two comments in their different ways provide the starting point for this essay. For they rightly confuse, at various levels, the sacred and the profane body, they revisit the necessary relationship between body and spirit, they acknowledge the endless ambiguities of being 'in the body', and Altizer, at least, returns us to the

---

1   Heather Walton, 'Review of *The Sacred Desert*', *Literature and Theology*, 19:2 (2005) 190.

Crucified Body that remains at the heart of Christianity, which is also the religion of the incarnate Word.

At the beginning of her essay 'Holbein's Dead Christ', Julia Kristeva quotes at length from Fyodor Dostoevsky's novel *The Idiot* (1868) the description by the character Ippolit of Hans Holbein the Younger's 1522 disturbing painting *The Body of the Dead Christ in the Tomb*.[2] The picture is of a cadaver before rigor mortis has set in, and the narrative emphasizes the utter desolation such a body must have brought to those who had taken it from the Cross: 'And if, [asks Ippolit] on the eve of the crucifixion, the Master could have seen what He would look like when taken from the cross, would he have mounted the cross and died as he did? This question, too, you can't help asking yourself as you look at the picture'.[3]

We see a tortured body that has just passed from life to death by the most ghastly means imaginable, an image so awful that even Jesus himself would have rejected the enormity upon which we are asked to gaze and avoided the cross. Yet we are reminded also of the first revelation to Dame Julian of Norwich, when she sees 'the red blood trickling down from under the crown of thorns, hot, fresh and plentiful'; or Richard Rolle's 'More yet, Sweet Jesu, thy body is like a book written all with red ink; so is thy body all written with red wounds'; or Isaac Watts in the eighteenth century bidding us '*See* from his head, his hands, his feet/ Sorrow and love flow mingled down.'[4] In this terrible contemplation, have Holbein and Dostoevsky hit upon the true horror, that which simply asks too much of us – a true descent into hell wherein the necessary gaze upon Christ's dereliction is our participation in his own God-forsakenness; an impossible looking at the absolutely sacred, the absolutely profane, and indeed a radical reversal of Christian consciousness?

This reversal is quite opposite to the deliberately perverse readings of Christianity offered by Slavoj Žižek in his much-discussed book *The Puppet and the Dwarf*, which are simply a flight from the spiritual.[5] Rather it is a deep return to the spirit, precisely in its very insistence on the body that the Christian tradition itself has rarely if ever been able to tolerate beyond a small company of ragged mystics, poets and idiots, like Prince Myshkin. It is realized in a body that is beyond access but with nothing beyond it. In this lack of a beyond lies the sacramental heart of the insistent 'real presence' of the Eucharist, in which, even from the time of Paul, the followers of Christ took the intolerable flesh into their own bodies. Elaine Pagels emphasizes the insistence by Tertullian, and Justin Martyr, after the gospel narratives, on

---

    2   Julia Kristeva, 'Holbein's Dead Christ', in *Black Sun: Depression and Melancholia*, trans. Leon S. Roudiez (New York, 1989), pp. 105-38.

    3   Ibid., p. 109

    4   Julian of Norwich, *Revelations of Divine Love*, trans. Clifton Wolters (Harmondsworth, 1966), p. 66. Richard Rolle, *Meditations on the Passion*, quoted in Gabriele Finaldi, *The Image of Christ* (London, 2000), p. 148. Isaac Watts, 'Crucifixion to the World by the Cross of Christ', in Donald Davie, (ed.) *The New Oxford Book of Christian Verse* (Oxford, 1981), p. 146.

    5   Slavoj Žižek, *The Puppet and the Dwarf: The Perverse Core of Christianity* (Cambridge, Massachusetts, 2003).

the shocking fact that the Christian 'mystery' invites initiates to eat human flesh – even if only symbolically. Pagans might be repelled by the practice of instructing newcomers to drink wine as human blood, but devout Jews, whose very definition of *kosher* (pure food) requires that it be drained of all blood, would be especially disgusted.[6]

Yet the oblivion of theology has tended to obliterate this scandal, the scandal of the crucified, unwatchable body, the body in hell, that yet we take into ourselves. Against the visual background of Dostoevsky, Holbein and Mattais Grünewald's *Isenheim Altarpiece* (see p. 232) I read the final words of Margaret Miles's recent book *The Word Made Flesh*:

> The religion of the incarnate Word consists of the struggle to 'keep body and soul together'. It is a *project* of comprehending, incorporating, and participating in the 'Body of Christ'. Addressing the deep human longing for integrity of body and soul, Christianity makes the wildly counter-evidential, counter-cultural claim that 'in my flesh shall I see God'. The meaning of that claim can never be definitively articulated, but it forms and informs historical and contemporary Christians who seek to understand it, not only conceptually, but also, and more importantly, *in the life*.[7]

I find myself at once attracted and repelled by this statement, for it contains truth, but yet its claims for the Christianity of the Church and Christendom must be almost wholly untenable. For this struggle, this *project*, involves a being in the depths of the body that is profane beyond belief if salvation is to remain for us in the absolute self-emptying, or *kenosis*, of Christ's body. What then is this struggle for the integrity of body and soul? What does it mean?

'In my flesh I shall see God' (Job 19 26). You can read that statement, which in Hebrew is quite obscure, in at least two ways: 'I shall see God in this flesh of mine.' Or: 'When I see God I shall be clothed in my flesh.' Either way there is anticipated the later Christian insistence on the resurrection of the flesh, the odd perversity of which is beautifully caught by Jorie Graham in her poem *At Luca Signorelli's Resurrection of the Body*:

> See how they hurry
>   to enter
> their bodies,
>   these spirits.
> Is it better, flesh,
>   That they
> Should hurry so?[8]

---

6 Elaine Pagels, *Beyond Belief: The Secret Gospel of Thomas* (London, 2003), p. 19.

7 Margaret R. Miles, *The Word Made Flesh: A History of Christian Thought* (Oxford, 2005), p. 391.

8 Jorie Graham, *Erosion* (Princeton, 1983), p. 74. Luca Signorelli (c.1441/50-1523) was commissioned in 1499 to complete the fresco cycle in Orvieto Cathedral, Italy, which had been begun by Fra. Angelico in 1447. Their subjects are the End of the World, the Coming and Fall of Anti-Christ and the Last Judgement. He was an important influence on Michelangelo.

This fleshly rush to see God, even when evildoers assail and seek to devour the poor flesh, is, perhaps, caught by a much earlier poet, the writer of Psalm 27, as rendered by the New Revised Standard Version:

> Hear, O Lord, when I cry aloud,
> Be gracious to me and answer me!
> 'Come,' my heart says, 'seek his face!'
> Your face, Lord, do I seek.
> Do not hide your face from me.
> (vv.7-9a)

No doubt these words have a cultic origin in Jerusalem, but the problem remains in verse 8: '"Come," my heart says, "seek his face!"' The Hebrew is literally: 'To thee my heart has said, "Seek [plural] my face"', and *The Oxford Bible Commentary* suggests for this, 'From thee my heart conveys the message "Seek my face"': whatever that means![9] In the midst of scholarly confusion over obscure Hebrew, I prefer to have recourse to literary guides, in this case John Updike's novel *Seek My Face* (2002) and the novelist's literary interplay with the Bible.

In Updike's novel, Hope Chafetz, now an old woman is seeking. She recounts her life with an impossible genius – the novel is clearly largely based on the domestic life of the artist Jackson Pollock – and now sees herself, no longer beautiful, but an old, aged woman. She seeks that which is hidden by life – and in the final few pages she re-enters her childhood with her grandfather, who 'saw into her life'. Hope views her aged body, without compromise, almost as something separate from herself, and almost *reads* it as Richard Rolle once *read* Christ's body on the cross:

> The back of her hand is mottled and scarred by sun and age as if once scalded, the more prominent veins making patterns like wiggly letters she can almost read, random little rivers that have stayed in their courses all her life. The swelling of arthritis in a number of joints has caused the top segments of her fingers to deviate from the straight. She marvels that this gnarled crone's hand is hers.[10]

With her grandfather, however, she sees herself as a young child again, regarding him physically, always watching. And it is the game with the coins which she remembers; how he would hide two coins down the side of the chair, so that she had to push her hand down and feel for them, seeing for the first time the markings on a fifty cent piece. Throughout her life she would continue to search for the coins in the chair (her chair that had been his chair) the trace of the forgotten face, although now her body was too stiff to bend down. But more than that:

---

9   C. S. Dodd, 'Psalms', in John Barton and John Muddiman, (eds), *The Oxford Bible Commentary* (Oxford, 2001), p. 375. This suggestion is drawn from J. H. Eaton, *Kingship and the Psalms* (London, 1986), p. 76.

10   John Updike, *Seek My Face* (Harmondsworth, 2002), p. 272.

Hope thinks of exploring between the two big plaid cushions right now, but her back and hip hurt in anticipation of getting down, grunting, on her knees on the oval rag rug, *and she is afraid of finding nothing.*[11] [Emphases added]

These are the last words of the novel. We seek, and are afraid that we might find nothing. Yet the body that we see is at the same time intolerable, subject to decay, damaged, unlovely. We are afraid, even as we utter the words, 'Do not hide your face from me.' At the end of a very different work, Elie Wiesel's *Night* (1958), the young boy recently liberated from Buchenwald sees, for the first time, his own face in a mirror. He needs to see himself, to know who he is:

> I wanted to see myself in the mirror hanging on the opposite wall. I had not seen myself
> since the ghetto.
> From the depths of the mirror, a corpse gazed back at me.
> The look in his eyes, as they stared into mine, has never left me.[12]

Or again, in fiction, we read in the last pages of Joseph Heller's *God Knows* (1984) of the aged King David reflecting upon his dying condition: 'I think of Saul in his wordless gloom and torment every time I came to his chamber to play for him, and I realize as I remember that I never saw a sadder face on a human being until a little while ago, when Abishag the Shunammite held a mirror up for me to see and I looked into mine.'[13]

The seeing, of self and other, and of self as other, is absolutely necessary, yet intolerable. It is to know, and yet not to know, seeing the self as wholly other and alien; and yet still we are afraid of finding nothing. It is like hunting for lost coins, though the finding is as terrible as the fear that there is nothing there. And yet to *see* the broken body takes us back to Dostoevsky's description of Holbein's *Dead Christ*: 'The people surrounding the dead man none of whom is shown in the picture, must have been overwhelmed by a feeling of terrible anguish and dismay on that evening *which had shattered all their hopes and almost all their beliefs in one fell blow.*'[14] We, like these viewers, are always the unseen, haunted because the body that we see is our own – the corpse gazing back at us: and yet there is the insistent – 'in my flesh I shall see God'. With the vitriol of Jacobean tragedy, we ask, 'What thing is in this outward form of man to be beloved?',[15] yet we still stand at the foot of the cross, caught between the two verses of the *Stabat Mater*:

> For his people's sins, in anguish,
> There she saw the victim languish.
> Bleed in torments, bleed and die:
> Saw the Lord's anointed taken;
> Saw her Child in death forsaken;
> Heard his last expiring cry.

---

11 Ibid., p. 276

12 Elie Wiesel, *Night*, trans. Stella Rodway (Harmondsworth, 1981), p. 126.

13 Joseph Heller, *God Knows* (London, 1985), p. 446.

14 Dostoevsky, *The Idiot*, quoted in Kristeva, *Black Sun*, p. 109.

15 From John Webster, *The Duchess of Malfi* (1623).

May his wounds both wound and heal me,
He enkindle, cleanse, anneal me,
Be his Cross my hope and stay.
May he, when the mountains quiver,
From that flame which burns forever
Shield me on the judgement day.[16]

The seeing is at once a wounding and a healing, the ascent also a descent into the deepest hell. It would be an easy transition from here into the familiar sadomasochism of the eroticism of wounds and bondage, and its theological equivalent concerning the wound of knowledge, or even the wound of reason. But between the body as both sacred and profane I am seeking to retrieve another way, a different and darker narrative than the customary defences of the necessary resurrection of the body and 'a Jesus concretely continuous with the earthly leader and friend of the days of the ministry'.[17] The way is, I think, both simpler and yet more complex than that.

Consider the early and continuing Christian obsession with the Song of Songs, that great cry of erotic longing for the beloved which is also an unfulfilled search, another searching for lost coins, perhaps, its eroticism embedded in both a presence and an absence that provokes the power of metaphor. One of the first great Christian commentators on the Song was Origen (c. 185-254 CE) and while my reservations about that great scholar are immense, in the context of the present discussion he remains profoundly important. For if, for Origen, the body and the material world are bestial and a prison house, yet it is still through corporeality that revelation is possible – the light shines *in* the prison house.[18] There is undoubtedly a nasty side to the tradition that begins here. Leaping across the centuries to St. Bernard of Clairvaux (1090-1153) and his unfinished *Sermons on the Song of Songs*, I share with Don Cupitt a suspicion of a particular kind of Christian piety that misunderstands profoundly what is going on here *bodily* – a false escape into soul-talk, as if that can be divorced from this awkward stuff of physical being. Cupitt, in his book *Mysticism after Modernity* (1998) reads Rowan Williams on St. Bernard. Bernard first as he

> ... distinguishes between the successive stages of kissing Christ's feet, his hands, his mouth; and the kiss of the feet, with which we begin, is like the kiss of the sinful woman in the Gospel, the kiss of fear and penitence, as we wait prostrate for the Lord's words of forgiveness.[19]

Then Williams' commentary, and finally Cupitt's one word judgment on it:

> 'Bernard ... compares the union of self and God with the mixing of water into wine ...' Warming to his theme, he speaks of how we should learn 'ever greater openness to the pressure of God's love'. If that is not explicit enough, he continues while expounding

16 Jacopone da Todi (ascribed), 'Stabat Mater Dolorosa' trans. Bishop Mant, Aubrey de Vere, and others. *The English Hymnal* (London, 1933), No. 115, p. 158.

17 Rowan Williams, *Resurrection* (London, 1982), p. 106.

18 Rowan A. Greer, *Introduction to Origen: Selected Works* (Mahwah, NJ, 1979), p. 28.

19 St. Bernard *Sermons on the Song of Songs* (3, §§2-3), quoted in Don Cupitt, *Mysticism after Modernity* (Oxford, 1998), p. 44.

Eckhart: 'having arrived at that nakedness where the naked reality of God can enter, the soul is fertilized into divine life'. Hm.[20]

Bernard advocated what he called a 'carnal love for Christ'. 'Notice,' he said, 'that the love of the heart is, in certain sense, carnal because our hearts are attracted more to the humanity of Christ and the things he did while in the flesh.'[21] He expands this, in his *Sermons on the Song of Songs*, in terms of three kisses, beginning with the verse from Psalm 27:

> My heart rightly says to you, Lord Jesus, 'My face has sought you; your face, Lord do I seek'. In the morning you showed me your mercy. When I lay in the dust to kiss your footprints you forgave my evil life. Later in the day you gave joy to your servant's soul, when, with the kiss of your hand, you gave him grace to live a good life. And now what remains, O Good Lord, except that now in full light, while I am in fervour of spirit, you should admit me to the kiss of our mouth, and grant me the full you of your presence.[22]

The point here is that for Bernard, drawing upon the Song of Songs, there is no false dichotomy between the body and soul in the search for the Lord's face. 'In my flesh I shall see God.' He does not indulge in rather unsavoury *metaphors* about the soul being fertilized into divine life, having entered God's naked reality. But, we might object, do not his *Sermons* still see Christ as the bridegroom of the soul and the Church, a common enough theme in twelfth century mysticism? Indeed, but the point is that this, for him, is not merely a metaphor. Rather, the image takes its reality from the experience of the body and erotic experiences that also contain an element of unknowing, beyond the profane and in spite of the sacred. One of Bernard's favourite texts was II Corinthians 3:18: 'And all of us, with unveiled [unhidden] faces, seeing the glory of the Lord as though reflected in a mirror, are being transformed from one degree of glory to another; for this comes from the Lord, the Spirit' (NRSV). Through Bernard we are not so far from St. Paul to John Donne at his most fleshly in his poem *The Good Morrow* in the enchantment and re-enchantment of the self.[23]

Before we begin to weave back to the awful body of Holbein and Dostoevsky, one further brief excursion into Christian theology is required to further provoke the narrative. St. John of Damascus' (c.655-c.750 CE) *Three Treatises on the Divine Images*, written in the eighth century against the iconoclasts are a passionate defence

---

20 Ibid. p. 44. The quotation from Williams is taken from *The Wound of Knowledge: Christian Spirituality from the New Testament to St. John of the Cross* (London, 1979), pp. 108-15.

21 St. Bernard of Clairvaux, quoted in Miles, *The Word Made Flesh,* p. 150.

22 St. Bernard of Clairvaux, *Selected Works*, trans. G. R. Evans (Mahwah, NJ, 1987), p. 223.

23 John Carey, (ed.), *The Oxford Authors: John Donne (Oxford: Oxford University Press,* 1990), p. 89-90.

> 'I wonder by my troth, what thou, and I
> Did, till we loved? Were we not weaned till then,
> But sucked on country pleasures, childishly?'
> (John Donne, first lines of *The Good Morrow*)

of icons and their veneration. John establishes the centrality of the terms image and icon in the Christian tradition, through, for example Trinitarian relationships – the Son as the image of the Father[24] – to the nature of the relationship between God and the created order within which visual images give clues and intuitions of invisible realities. Attacking the materiality of images is, for John, tantamount to attacking the whole of Christian theology. This is not to deny that, in his words, 'it is impossible to depict God who is incommensurable and uncircumscribable and invisible'.[25] Rather, he says:

> I am emboldened to depict the invisible God, not as invisible, but as he became visible for our sake, by participation in flesh and blood. I do not depict the invisible divinity, but I depict God made visible in flesh. (I:4, p.22)

At this point I presume not so much to diverge from John as to revise his relationship between terms. He concludes: 'For if it is impossible to depict the soul, how much more God, who gives the soul its immateriality' (I:4). Nevertheless, I would wish to say, this immateriality is not separate from but utterly co-inherent[26] in the body's materiality, its mystery and the cloud of unknowing traced in the extremes of erotic longing on the one hand,[27] and utterly unbearable horrors beyond imagining that the body can provoke, on the other. Dostoevsky's Ippolit precisely describes the body only just taken down from the cross: 'still retaining a great deal of warmth and life; rigor mortis had not yet set in, so that there was still a look of suffering on the face of the dead man, as though he were still feeling it.'[28]And this is the face upon which we gaze, which is not hidden from us, and from which even Christ himself might have spared us and not, therefore, mounted the cross.

This looking beyond knowing and beyond toleration and circumscription is an experience that is given commentary in more theological terms by another participant in the iconoclastic debate, slightly later than St. John of Damascus, the patriarch St. Nicephorus (758-828 CE) in his *Libri Tres Antirrhetici*. For Nicephorus, the icon is a memorial of *kenosis* (from the Greek verb κενοω, to empty[29]), used by the Greek Fathers to describe the Incarnation: to incarnate, to empty.[30] The crucial distinction is between inscription and circumscription – in Nicephorus' words, 'A man is inscribed in the image that represents him, but he is not circumscribed by it.'[31] Christ's

---

24 See, Andrew Lowth, 'Introduction to St. John of Damascus', *Three Treatises on the Divine Images* (New York, 2003), p. 10.

25 St. John of Damascus, *Three Treatises*, I:7, p. 23.

26 The term 'co-inherence' is developed by Charles Williams in *The Descent of the Dove: A Short History of the Holy Spirit in the Church* (London, 1939).

27 See further, Jean-Luc Marion, *The Erotic Phenomenon*, trans. Stephen E. Lewis (Chicago, 2007).

28 *The Idiot*, quoted in Kristeva, 'Holbein's Dead Christ', p. 108.

29 Philippians 2:7, 'but emptied himself, taking the form of a slave ...'

30 See Marie-José Baudinet, 'The Face of Christ, the Form of the Church', in Michel Fehrer with Ramona Naddaff and Nadia Tazi, (eds), *Fragments for a History of the Human Body, Part One* (New York, 1989), pp. 148-59.

31 *Antirrhetic II*, in Baudinet, 'The Face of Christ, The Form of the Church', p. 158.

uncircumscribability in the icon, his absence, is the very sign of his resurrection. The icon is not a representation of Christ's face, but rather a physical threshold, 'a blessedly vacant object that respects the uncircumscribability of its object.'

The closest discussion in modern times to Nicephorus' discourse on the icon is found in Jean-Luc Marion's book *God Without Being* (1982), which acknowledges that in the icon the invisible always remains invisible within the visible: 'it is not invisible because it is omitted by the aim … but because it is a matter of rendering visible this invisible as such – the unenvisageable.'[32] I would not wish to pursue Marion's argument to its full extent, with its particular freedom of God from the horizon of being. Rather, it is helpful to link it to Nicephorus' perception of the icon as the most profound understanding of the mystery of the Word made flesh – that is the body in its mysterious spatiality and potential acknowledging inscription of the word, but in that inscription transcending the circumscription, its deepest presence an absence, and a freedom *within* and beyond being. In contradiction to this, Christian theology has too readily tended to pervert the iconic mystery of John 1:14, obsessed instead with the flesh made word[33] – that is the circumscription of the body in the definitions of language – bodies perceived as defining words; male, female, virgin, hero. In Western Christian theology's obsession with the body in all its imperfections, its suspicions of bodily functions and its corseting of acceptable behaviour, the mystery of the Incarnation has been reversed. What needs to be recovered is a genuine and radical hermeneutics of the body, freed from the deathly impositions that have been laid upon it.

So far we have looked, as at an icon, at bodily images of excess within the theology of the Christian tradition: the ravaged body of the crucified Christ, and the eroticism of Bernard of Clairvaux in his *Sermons on the Song of Songs*. They have deliberately reflected the two modes presented in Heather Walton's review of the *The Sacred Desert*. But in each there is a darkness of exile, and beyond each there is an absolute desert, utterly profane and deeply sacred where alone becomes possible the body of the Godhead. But before we touch upon that deepest abyss, let us pause for a moment before another image of the body – that is the famous description of St Antony of Egypt, in the *Life* by St. Athanasius, of the moment when he emerges from his tomb-like prison after nearly twenty years of ascetic struggle:

> This was the first time he appeared from the fortress for those who came out to him. And when they beheld him they were amazed to see that his body had maintained its former condition, neither fat from lack of exercise, not emaciated from fasting and combat with demons, but just as they had known him prior to his withdrawal. The state of his soul was one of purity, for it was not constricted by grief, nor relaxed by pleasure, nor affected by either laughter or dejection. Moreover, when he saw the crowd, he was not annoyed

---

32 Jean-Luc Marion, *God Without Being*, trans. Thomas A. Carlson (Chicago, 1991), p. 17.

33 For a feminist study of this reversal, with particular reference to Victorian literature, see Helena Michie, *The Flesh Made Word: Female Figures and Women's Bodies* (Oxford, 1987).

any more than he was elated at being embraced by so many people. He maintained utter equilibrium, like one guided by reason and steadfast in that which accords with nature.[34]

It is easy to be frustrated by or dismissive of this description. It is in utter contrast to the description of Holbein's *Dead Christ*, the ravaged Christ of the Passion. And so what face of Antony here are we being asked to see? It cannot be an historical, actual portrait, but in our reading it provokes puzzlement, awe and even a little weariness with its good order, and its sense of balance and harmony. Antony's 'equilibrium' is beyond our reach, perhaps even beyond our desires, though we can see the point of showing us the saint as humanity deified. And as a legend it has plausibility, even in its impossibility. As Edith Wyschogrod in *her* version of the life of St. Mary of Egypt has suggested, this is not a life actually to be *lived* – though its excessive demands may be profoundly disruptive, disturbing and even destabilizing.[35] So it is with St. Antony. What Athanasius' legendary account has done is narrativize a life of immense struggle and physical endurance so that in the narrative the deepest conflicts are sequentially resolved in that 'equilibrium' that actually provokes them. The narrative mirrors that of the canonical Gospels (with the exception, perhaps, of Mark, which ends, properly with the empty tomb), that restores for us the face of the Crucified Christ in the calm perfection of the resurrection body, the one whom Mary in the garden was forbidden to touch (John 20:17).

We will come back to Antony and Mary of Egypt before we conclude, but for now I want to redescribe this narrative, moving away from the hagiographic and 'proto-novelistic' sense of forward movement and resolution in lives not to be lived, in Wyschogrod's terms, 'not intended to elicit replication but to inspire a new catena of moral events appropriate to the addressee's life.'[36] Rather, it is to see the end or resolution rendered impossible in the immediate enactment of a life lived over an abyss that makes it iconic – that is a life that is inscribed in an image that represents its intolerable impossibility and in its abjection admits an uncircumscribability, an absence that is the true sign of resurrection, even and only possible in the very depths and the darkest deserts of profanity.

Perhaps the most profound illustration of this in Western art is Mattias Grünewald's staggering *Isenheim Altarpiece* (1512-1516), too often misunderstood and trivialized because the central, folded panel of the crucifixion is reviewed in isolation from the rest of the work. In fact, the whole piece, in ten panels, is over fifty feet in width, and even closed it is nine feet high and sixteen feet wide. I can only scratch the surface of its complexity, built upon various levels and physically in three layers of ten panels, some of which must be hidden in order to see others. St. Antony of Egypt appears more than once, in a nightmare version of his Temptations which is opposite a quiet image of him in conversation with Paul the Hermit walking in a wildly tormented natural world, while on the right of the crucifixion itself Antony appears as the patron saint of the Antonines, the community which ran the lazar-house for whose chapel

---

34 St. Athanasius, *The Life of Antony and the Letter to Marcellinus*, trans. Robert C. Gregg (Mahwah, NJ, 1980), p. 42.

35 Edith Wyschogrod, *Saints and Postmodernism: Revisioning Moral Philosophy* (Chicago, 1990), p. 10.

36 Ibid.

the work was completed, because he was invoked against the curse of 'St. Anthony's fire' or the skin disease of erysipelas. When the wing panels are fully opened we see on the left an Annunciation scene, in the centre an Allegory of the Nativity with, in the sky above the Holy Family, an image of heaven and God the Father, while on the right there is the resurrection, Christ rising gloriously from the tomb.

Thus biblical scenes interplay with vivid scenes from the lives of the saints, but at the very centre of all, and always visible, is the terrible crucifixion itself. Even when the panels are closed we see it. There is no relief, yet it hides all these other scenes, all of which are literally enfolded within the suffering body, and only through the contemplation of it are they accessible; on Christ, indeed, on the very viewer, are inscribed the wounds, an emptying of the body in the deepest suffering that renders all else unreal and invisible apart from itself. Here is the true sacred desert. Grünewald's vision of the crucifixion is, of course, far from simple. On the viewer's left, the Virgin, her eyes closed, is supported by St. John while at their feet a kneeling Magdalen looks up in agony at the face of Christ. On the viewer's right stands John the Baptist, book in hand and elongated right forefinger pointing at the Christ, at the very Word made flesh. We see what he reads. In the bend of his arm are the words from the Gospel (John 3:30): 'He must increase but I must decrease.' At his feet is the Lamb, blood flowing from its wounded heart into the Eucharistic chalice. Thus, the picture is at once teaching about the sacrament, visual Bible study, a practical lesson in salvation for the suffering inmates of the lazar hospital – a reminder that he became like them in order that they might become like him – but above all a stunning vision of bodily agony and horror. For the figure on the cross is central to all in its terrible physicality. Nothing is spared the viewer; from the impaled hands and feet, the gasping mouth and chest, the bloody wounds and the dreadful crown of thorns. A few hours later this same figure would become Holbein's *Dead Christ*. We are in the moment and crevice between death and life, a universal moment, and as Dostoevsky's Ippolit was to remark: 'it is nature itself, and, indeed, any man's corpse would look like that after such suffering.' Yet this deepest moment of human being, when the body is most human because at the edge of human possibility, is also the most radical moment of *kenosis*, of emptying and of incarnation. Nor is this a revisionary act, as Harold Bloom describes *kenosis*, an act of strong poets which takes place in relation to the precursor.[37] It is the moment of *absolute kenosis* and self-emptying, when the divine and the human become absolutely other than God and humankind so that the only deathly cry possible is 'My God, my God, why have you forsaken me?' – another echo from the Psalter (Matthew 27:46, Mark 15:34, Psalm 22:1). Grünewald's Christ, despite the other figures at his feet, is utterly solitary, without narrative relationship to past or future. In human terms this is the moment of absolute *metanoia*, or reversal of consciousness, the descent into hell that alone makes possible all else depicted in the *Isenheim Altarpiece* – Antony's vicious nightmares *and also* the vision of heaven above the Nativity. There is no possible profanity greater than this, for it is the death of God, a descent into hell and a perpetual self-annihilation that alone makes possible the presence of the universal and cosmic Christ. For Grünewald, the resurrected Christ always remains the Christ

---

37 Harold Bloom, *The Anxiety of Influence: A Theory of Poetry* (London, 1973), p. 87.

on the cross that is, in the language of Thomas Altizer, the body of the incarnate God who has totally identified himself with experience.[38] Grünewald's figure is physically disproportionately large beside the other four human figures in his painting, literally and in his suffering he grows and increases while John decreases.

This radical insight into the totality of experience was to have a deep aesthetic impact on Western art in ways that the Church and its theology have chosen to ignore in their attempts to articulate reassuring narratives and their obsession with the past and particular body of Jesus. The beautiful and aged peasant women of Velasquez and Rembrandt, the deeply haunted eyes of Van Gogh's self-portraits are portraits of the human soul that is utterly of and in the body, and are deeply, radically Christian, radically sacred in their tragic inscription which goes no further, like the Desert Fathers and Mothers, and Eastern practitioners of Hesychism who simply repeat the Name as the path to salvation. That is all. They utter the profound truth that the divine presence is never a way to avoid humans taking absolute responsibility for everything here and now on earth.

And so, finally, back to the wisdom of the desert: St. Antony, St. Mary of Egypt and others went beyond the *Imitatio Christi* to a radical *cultura Dei* (the earliest Latin translation of the word *askesis* in the *Life of Antony*) actually instantiating in themselves the totality of the Incarnation: in a sense, in their bodies, extravagantly, they even *became* Christ. Their wild ascetic struggles, however, were not the flight from their humanity, but rather an immense journey into its very depths. As Peter Brown well expressed it:

> The ascetic brought with him into the desert fragile tokens of an enduring humanity that he had to defend tenaciously if he was to survive at all and maintain his humanity. He could not sink like an animal into its alluring immensity.[39]

The stories of the *Historia Monachorum*, the fourth century *Lives of the Desert Fathers*, are full of extraordinary, indeed legendary, physical endurance and pain – the cell of the monk is even referred to as the 'furnace of Babylon' – but seen as a wrestling with God in darkness, just as Jacob wrestled at Penuel and suffered a wounding; yet, the story continues, Jacob returns to his brother Esau, whom he had betrayed, with the words, 'Seeing your face is like seeing the face of God.' (Genesis 33:10).[40]

'Do not hide your face from me.' In the *Apophthegmata Patrum*, or *Sayings of the Fathers*, it is written of Apa Pambo 'that just as Moses had taken on the likeness of the glory of Adam, when his face shone with the glory of the Lord, in the same way, the face of Apa Pambo shone like lightning, and he was like an Emperor seated on a throne'.[41] These desert ascetics did not despise or reject their bodies:

---

38 See, Thomas J. J. Altizer, *The Descent in Hell: A Study of the Radical Reversal of the Christian Consciousness* (Philadelphia, 1970).

39 Peter Brown, *The Body and Society: Men, Women, and Sexual Renunciation in Early Christianity* (New York, 1988), p. 218.

40 See, *The Lives of the Desert Fathers*, trans. Norman Russell (Kalamazoo, 1981).

41 See, *The Wisdom of the Desert Fathers*, from the *Apophthegmata Patrum*, trans. Sister Benedicta Ward SLG (Oxford, 1986).

quite the contrary. Rather, they explored their deepest depths. They sought absolute participation in the Body of the Godhead at its deepest depths of humanity; at a point so far beyond the bearable, in the absolute desert, that its own deepest being met God as truly total absence wherein alone is total presence. In this profane moment there can be no severance of spirit from body, for the body, in all its physicality now is nothing but spirit, always unreal apart from that deep desert. In the *Sayings* we can thus find a radical reversal of imagery in a daring celebration of the sacred found only in the profane body, and yet it is not that either. It is a realization that only in the deepest depths of the body can be found spirit as an abyss that is utter negation and only therefore pure presence. Whose face do we seek? A final story, and a little lighter in tone, if not implication, from the *Sayings*; this one from John the Dwarf and then to conclude with St. Mary of Egypt.

> There was in the city a courtesan who had many lovers. One of the governors approached her saying, promise me you will be good, and I will marry you. She promised this and he took her and brought her to his home. Her lovers, seeing her again, said to one another, let us go to the back of the house and whistle for her. But the woman stopped her ears and withdrew to the inner chamber and shut the door. The old man said that the courtesan is our soul, that her lovers are the passions, that the lord is Christ, that the inner chamber is the eternal dwelling place, those who whistle are evil demons but the soul always takes refuge in the Lord.[42]

You can, of course, take that in many ways! Like so many of these little stories from the desert, they have knowing and a sharp edge and seem to be told with a twinkle in the eye. The allegory works alright, but then again ... is this just another story about Mary of Egypt, and which version? For most of this essay we have been out in the desert with the body crucified and profaned, and, I think, necessarily so, absolutely necessarily: but maybe the governor in the story, whoever he was, had the right idea. Perhaps, with Origen, Bernard of Clairvaux, even St. John of the Cross and not a few others, he learned a bit from the Song of Songs, before he blew out the candle in the inner chamber.

Bibliography

Altizer, Thomas J. J., *The Descent in Hell: A Study of the Radical Reversal of the Christian Consciousness* (Philadelphia: J. B. Lippincott Company, 1970).

St. Athanasius, *The Life of Antony and the Letter to Marcellinus*, trans. Robert C. Gregg (Mahwah, NJ: Paulist Press, 1980).

Barton, John and John Muddiman, (eds), *The Oxford Bible Commentary* (Oxford: Oxford University Press: 2001).

Baudinet, Marie-José, 'The Face of Christ, the Form of the Church', in Michel Fehrer with Ramona Naddaff and Nadia Tazi, (eds), *Fragments for a History of the Human Body, Part One* (New York: Zone Books, 1989): 148-59.

---

42 From, Benedicta Ward SLG, *Harlots of the Desert: A Study of Repentance in Early Monastic Sources* (Kalamazoo, 1987), pp. 33-4.

St. Bernard of Clairvaux, *Selected Works*, trans. G. R. Evans (Mahwah, NJ: Paulist Press 1987).

Bloom, Harold, *The Anxiety of Influence: A Theory of Poetry* (London: Oxford University Press, 1973).

Brown, Peter, *The Body and Society: Men, Women, and Sexual Renunciation in Early Christianity* (New York: Columbia University Press, 1988).

Carey, John, (ed.), *The Oxford Authors: John Donne* (Oxford: Oxford University Press, 1990).

Cupitt, Don, *Mysticism after Modernity* (Oxford: Blackwell, 1998).

da Todi, Jacopone (ascribed), 'Stabat Mater Dolorosa' trans. Bishop Mant, Aubrey de Vere, and others. *The English Hymnal* (London: Oxford University Press, 1933)

Davie, Donald, (ed.), *The New Oxford Book of Christian Verse* (Oxford: Oxford University Press, 1981).

Dodd, C. S., 'Psalms', in John Barton and John Muddiman, (eds), *The Oxford Bible Commentary* (Oxford: Oxford University Press: 2001): 375.

Donne, John, 'The Good Morrow' in John Carey, (ed.), *The Oxford Authors: John Donne* (Oxford: Oxford University Press): 89-90.

Dostoevsky, Fyodor, M., *The Idiot*, trans. David McDuff, (London: Penguin Books, [1868] 2004).

Eaton, J.H., *Kingship and the Psalms* (London: JSOT, 1986).

Fehrer Michel, with Ramona Naddaff and Nadia Tazi, (eds), *Fragments for a History of the Human Body, Part One* (New York: Zone Books, 1989).

Finaldi, Gabriele, *The Image of Christ* (London: National Gallery, 2000).

Graham, Jorie, *Erosion* (Princeton: Princeton University Press, 1983).

Greer, Rowan A., *Introduction to Origen: Selected Works* (Mahwah, NJ: Paulist Press, 1979).

Heller, Joseph, *God Knows* (London: Black Swan, 1985).

Jasper, David, *The Sacred Desert: Religion, Literature, Art, and Culture* (Oxford: Blackwell, 2004).

St. John of Damascus, *Three Treatises*.

Julian of Norwich, *Revelations of Divine Love*, trans. Clifton Wolters (Harmondsworth: Penguin, 1966).

Kristeva, Julia, *Black Sun: Depression and Melancholia*, trans. Leon S. Roudiez (New York: Columbia University Press, 1989).

Kristeva, Julia, 'Holbein's Dead Christ' in *Black Sun: Depression and Melancholia*, trans. Leon S. Roudiez (New York: Columbia University Press, 1989): 105-38.

Lowth, Andrew, 'Introduction to St. John of Damascus', *Three Treatises on the Divine Images* (New York: St. Vladimir's Seminary Press, 2003): 10.

Marion, Jean-Luc, *God Without Being*, trans. Thomas A. Carlson (Chicago: Chicago University Press,1991).

Marion, Jean-Luc, *The Erotic Phenomenon*, trans. Stephen E. Lewis (Chicago: Chicago University Press, 2007).

Michie, Helena, *The Flesh Made Word: Female Figures and Women's Bodies* (Oxford: Oxford University Press, 1987).

Miles, Margaret R., *The Word Made Flesh: A History of Christian Thought* (Oxford: Blackwell Publishing: 2005).

Pagels, Elaine, *Beyond Belief: The Secret Gospel of Thomas* (London: Macmillan, 2003).

Russell, Norman, (trans.), *The Lives of the Desert Fathers*, (Kalamazoo: Cistercia Publications, 1981).

Updike, John, *Seek My Face* (Harmondsworth: Penguin, 2002).

Ward, Benedicta, (trans.), *Apophthegmata Patrum*, (Oxford: SLG Press, 1986).

Ward, Benedicta, *Harlots of the Desert: A Study of Repentance in Early Monastic Sources* (Kalamazoo: Cistercian Publications, 1987).

Walton Heather, 'Review of *The Sacred Desert*', *Literature and Theology*, 19:2 (2005): 190.

Watts, Isaac, 'Crucifixion to the World by the Cross of Christ', in Donald Davie, (ed.), *The New Oxford Book of Christian Verse* (Oxford: Oxford University Press, 1981): 146.

Webster, John, *The Duchess of Malfi* (1623).

Wiesel, Elie, *Night*, trans. Stella Rodway (Harmondsworth: Penguin, 1981).

Williams, Charles, *The Descent of the Dove: A Short History of the Holy Spirit in the Church* (London: Longmans, Green and Co, 1939).

Williams, Rowan, *The Wound of Knowledge: Christian Spirituality from the New Testament to St. John of the Cross* (London: Darton, Longman & Todd, 1979).

Williams, Rowan, *Resurrection* (London: Darton, Longman & Todd, 1982).

Wyschogrod, Edith, *Saints and Postmodernism: Revisioning Moral Philosophy* (Chicago: Chicago University Press, 1990).

Žižek, Slavoj, *The Puppet and the Dwarf: The Perverse Core of Christianity* (Cambridge, Massachusetts, 2003).

Index